MW00804275

Racing the SUNRISE

GLEN M. WILLIFORD

Racing the SUNRISE

Reinforcing America's Pacific Outposts, 1941–1942

NAVAL INSTITUTE PRESS
Annapolis, Maryland

Naval Institute Press
291 Wood Road
Annapolis, MD 21402

This book has been brought to publication with the generous assistance of Edward S. and Joyce I. Miller and Marguerite and Gerry Lenfest.

Library of Congress Cataloging-in-Publication Data
Williford, G. (Glen)
Racing the sunrise : reinforcing America's Pacific outposts, 1941-1942 / Glen M. Williford.
p. cm.
Includes bibliographical references and index.
ISBN 978-1-59114-956-9 (hardcover : alk. paper) 1. World War, 1939-1945—Pacific Area. 2. World War, 1939-1945—United States. 3. United States—Defenses—History—20th century. 4. Pacific Area—Strategic aspects. 5. Military convoys—Pacific Area—History—20th century. 6. Garrisons—Philippines—History—20th century. 7. Garrisons—Hawaii—History—20th century. 8. Military bases, American—Australia—History—20th century. 9. United States. Navy—History—World War, 1939-1945. 10. United States. Marine Corps—History—World War, 1939-1945. I. Title.
D767.W4775 2010
940.54'26—dc22

2010030455

Printed in the United States of America on acid-free paper.

14 13 12 11 10 9 8 7 6 5 4 3 2
First printing

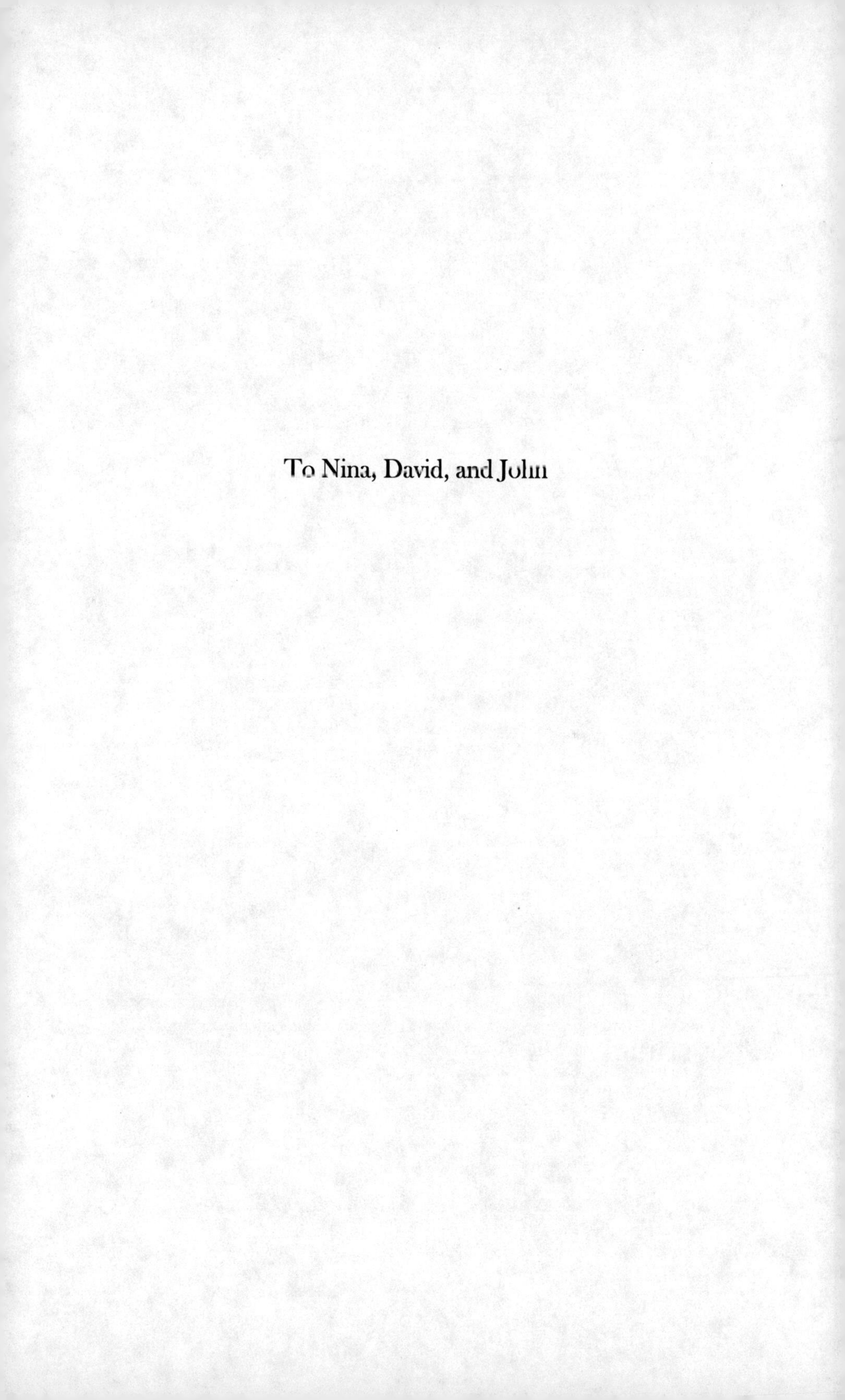

To Nina, David, and John

CONTENTS

MAPS and TABLES

MAPS

TABLES

ACKNOWLEDGMENTS

Many years ago I started developing an interest in the facts behind the Pensacola Convoy and its mission. The lack of information about this journey in the secondary sources available led me to accumulate source documentation for a potential book or article about this subject. However, at the time with a full career and a young family, the project only got as far as a file cabinet of documents and the rough draft of half a dozen chapters. Many years later my friend and occasional research colleague Nelson Lawry urged me to complete the research and finalize the project as a book. I owe him my gratitude for this encouragement; without it I doubt I ever would have pursued the work further. In addition he assisted me with the earliest steps of defining the work's scope and suggested areas in need of additional research. Circumstances prevented him from being involved in the later stages, but the fact remains that there would never have been a book without his initial encouragement.

The pursuit of source documents has involved the active assistance of numerous archivists and librarians. Two research archivists at the National Archives II in College Park, Maryland stand out—Mitch Yockelson with Army records and Barry Zerby with Navy records. They each repeatedly met with me to help better define and locate important documents necessary to my research. Similarly Robert Glass at the National Archives, San Bruno depository, and reference librarian Heidi Myers at the Naval History and Heritage Command in Washington, D.C., admirably assisted my research. Other institutions also promptly responded to inquiries and requests for copies of monographs and records. James Zobel at the MacArthur Memorial, Steven Davenport at the San Francisco Maritime National Park J. Porter Shaw

Library, Peggy Dillard at the George C. Marshall Foundation Archives, and Richard Baker of the Military History Institute at Carlisle Barracks were most helpful.

A number of knowledgeable military history experts supplied critical perspectives and information on matters of Army and Navy organization and weaponry. In particular I wish to thank Alex Holder, Al Grobmeier, and Karl Schmidt for responding to my numerous inquiries and gladly sharing their knowledge. Ricky Stauber contributed with his knowledge of the poison gas situation in the Far East. Tony Feredo helped me struggle through Philippine place names, as well as reading through an early draft of the book to look for consistency and finding a myriad of flaws that had escaped my previous perusals. His assistance was most valuable. Both Tom Kavanagh and Karl Schmidt also read sections of the draft and responded with helpful suggestions.

This being my first major historical work, deep appreciation must be given to the understanding staff of the Naval Institute Press. Author Edward S. Miller, a member of the Naval Institute's board of directors, provided key guidance and encouragement that was most welcomed. His practical advice made this a substantially better work than I would have been able to create on my own. Press Director Richard A. Russell, editorial manager Susan Corrado, and copy editor Jehanne Moharram guided me through the process. All prevented me from making many casual errors and combined to make the effort as painless as possible. I owe all the staff engaged on this book my thanks.

As my project in its final form took some four years to complete, I must surely thank my family for enduring my absence for research trips, for the long phone calls to cooperators, and the odd hours I for some reason used to actually write the text. My wife Nina and sons David and John deserve my sincere appreciation for their patience and support.

In any event, errors of fact and interpretation, which almost inevitably seem to occur, are solely the responsibility of the author.

INTRODUCTION

Just as the bombs and torpedoes were launched by Japanese warplanes at Pearl Harbor on the morning of December 7, 1941 a large convoy of American troops was proceeding westward across the Pacific Ocean. Over 4,500 American soldiers and airmen and tons of equipment destined for the rapidly expanding garrison in the Philippines were quartered on board four Army and Navy transports escorted by the heavy cruiser *Pensacola*. Another 16,000 were to follow the same route within weeks; in fact, quite a few had just departed the docks of San Francisco within the last two days preceding the start of war. The recently approved plan to reinforce Lt. Gen. Douglas MacArthur's Far Eastern command had just achieved its maximum effort when the surprise attack of the enemy interrupted the flow. Ultimately some of the men and much of the matériel of this convoy were sacrificed in a valiant attempt to stop the enemy's advance in the Dutch East Indies. The follow-on reinforcements, much of them initially accumulated for pre-war transfer to the Philippines, were used to bolster the Allied defenses at Hawaii and other key Pacific bases, and ultimately became the nucleus of the first successful offensives against Japan.

America's military strategy for a war with Japan remained surprisingly consistent for many years prior to the start of the Second World War. Generally referred to as the Orange Plan (Orange was the code word for Japan), it envisioned a strong enemy offensive that would conquer and occupy American possessions and outposts in the western Pacific. After a period of mobilization the U.S. Navy would advance major military land forces across the Pacific back to the Philippines. Following a successful fleet action, Japan would be isolated and forced into surrender. American forces in the Philippines (and

Guam) would oppose the inevitable invasion, but ultimately would be defeated and lost long before the return of relieving forces. The local forces would be sacrificed to gain time and inflict casualties on the enemy. Hawaii was to be defended and retained as an important starting point for the offensive phase of the American involvement.

With this plan the reinforcement policy of America's Pacific outposts didn't change much for most of the pre-war years. Even with war beginning in Europe, little in the way of new men or matériel had been sent to Hawaii, the Philippines, the small naval bases at Guam and Samoa, or even smaller bases at Wake and Midway Islands. American military policy emphasized the rearmament and expansion of the mobile fighting services prior to the nation's inevitable involvement in the war. Combined with a foreign policy that materially aided those countries actually fighting the Axis powers, there was little left over in the critical year from June 1940 to June 1941 to have available for the isolated commands in the Pacific—particularly if they were going to ultimately be sacrificed early in the war anyway.

In political terms the Philippines presented a different situation than Hawaii. Even more isolated geographically from the rest of America's military assets, the islands had also been promised their independence and had even begun a significant effort to create their own means of defense under the leadership of military adviser Douglas MacArthur. There were real questions within both the civil and military leadership of the nation about the wisdom of "wasting" precious men and matériel on the defense of a non-strategic, temporary possession. There were also differences between the services. Any successful defense or follow-up relief of a Philippine garrison would require the active participation of the U.S. Navy, and that service was less committed to the archipelago's defense than the Army. Even besides the implications of the mutually adopted Orange Plan the Army had real practical problems in implementing any sort of substantial reinforcement. The War Department blamed the failure to substantially reinforce the islands (at least up till then) on three circumstances: lack of funds, lack of personnel and equipment, and the problematic availability of Navy support.

This situation abruptly changed in mid-1941. Several factors developed mid-year, some of them sudden and others the result of longer-term trends, which made possible a significant change in reinforcement policy. The administration's decision to base the Pacific Fleet at Pearl Harbor occurred in 1940. When the military services realized that this basing would be permanent and not just a temporary assignment, during 1941 adjustments were made to accommodate the fleet's residency. For the Navy, that meant an increased priority in developing advanced seaplane facilities. They needed to establish an effective scouting and support screen to the west of Hawaii. Efforts increased to provide seaplane, landplane, and garrison defense at the island bases of Midway, Wake, Johnston, and Palmyra. The Army, which was charged with the defense of the Navy's facilities at Pearl Harbor, augmented and modernized its air force in the islands as well as attempted to increase the local anti-aircraft and air-warning capabilities.

The reinforcement of the Philippines sprung from different factors. Several key situations came together in July of 1941. The Japanese occupation of French Indochina was viewed by the administration as a serious demonstration of Japan's aggressive policy. An obligation to immediately react and send a warning message to Japan's leadership was pursued by the Roosevelt administration. Economic sanctions were imposed, but increased military pressure by an enlarged, modernized Philippine garrison was also desired. Coincidentally it was perceived that the development of the Philippine army had progressed to the point that calling it to U.S. service and placing it under General MacArthur's command would be a way to openly demonstrate military preparations. Douglas MacArthur turned out to be a persuasive spokesman for the expansion of American military power in the Philippines. His personal efforts to acquire units and equipment for both the American and Philippine armies were successful. Meanwhile in Washington, D.C., Army Chief of Staff Gen. George Marshall and Secretary of War Henry Stimson were beginning to see the fruits of rearmament—just when the demands for reinforcement came there was some relief in supply. Thus for political, military, and personal needs the Philippine policy abruptly changed in July 1941 and the American Army, and to a lesser extent the Navy, saw itself committed to sending relatively large reinforcement contingents to the islands.

This is the story of the efforts in late 1941 and early 1942 to dispatch important military assets to the Philippines and Hawaii (and to a lesser extent the island outposts). Done somewhat at odds to accepted strategic plans, a major effort was mounted. Scarce trained men, equipment, airplanes, and submarines were sent to the Philippines in an attempt to rapidly build up a credible deterrence. The logistical aspects of such a movement presented their own unique set of problems. Carefully organized shipments of units and equipment were escorted in naval convoys across the Pacific to the waiting Far Eastern forces of General MacArthur. Contrary to the conclusions of some early postwar accounts that the Philippines were not supported or were supplied just obsolete munitions, a substantial and to a large degree successful reinforcement program was indeed implemented.

One of the few fortunate circumstances identified by the military at the start of the war was the immediate availability of this pipeline of assets. The process of bringing units and equipment to San Francisco for dispatch to the Far East was already under way. These assets were fortuitously available to enable the rapid reinforcement and replacement of aircraft lost at Pearl Harbor. Forces at sea became the nucleus for the creation of a major new base in Australia—parts were even available to assist the Allied defenses of the Dutch East Indies and mount an attempt (largely unsuccessful) to run the blockade with relief supplies for the beleaguered garrison in the Philippines. In the three months following December 7 the Army and Navy, using techniques and assets largely acquired for the initial Philippine effort, were able to dispatch major task forces to secure the line of communications to Australia and New Zealand.

This is the story of the reinforcement efforts made in the immediate six months prior to the Pearl Harbor attack, and the subsequent use of these troops and equipment for either the defense of the outlying bases or the beginning of the buildup for the subsequent phase of the war.

ABBREVIATIONS

AA	anti-aircraft
AB	air base
ABDA	American-British-Dutch-Australian
ABDAIR	American-British-Dutch-Australian Air Operational Command
AIF	Australian Imperial Force
APL	American President Lines
ASW	anti-submarine warfare
AVG	American Volunteer Group (Flying Tigers)
AW	automatic weapons
CAC	Coast Artillery Corps
CinCAF	Commander in Chief, Asiatic Fleet
CinCPac	Commander in Chief, Pacific Fleet
CinCUS	Commander in Chief, U.S. Fleet
CMH	Center of Military History
CNO	chief of naval operations
CPNAB	Contractors, Pacific Naval Air Bases
CPO	chief petty officer
CWS	Chemical Warfare Service
Fil-Am	the combined Philippine Army and U.S. Army on Luzon
FMF	Fleet Marine Force
GHQ	general headquarters
HQ	headquarters
MAW	Marine Air Wings
NCO	non-commissioned officer
OSP	offshore patrol

PatWing	patrol wing
PBY	Consolidated patrol bomber
PNAB	shortened version of CPNAB (see above)
PS	Philippine Scout(s)
PT	patrol torpedo (boat)
SBD	Douglas scout bomber
Sep	separate (designation of an independent unit not part of a larger organization)
SPMs	self-propelled mounts
SWPA	Southwest Pacific Area
TF	task force
TNT	trinitrotoluene
USAFFE	United States Army Forces in the Far East
USAFIA	United States Army Forces in Australia
USAT	U.S. Army transport
WO	warrant officer
WPD	War Plans Division

CHAPTER ONE

The Situation in the Philippines

The military's internal debate on the nature of Philippine defense had begun almost immediately at the conclusion of the pacification campaign early in the twentieth century. This was an American possession, and as such would require defensive forces to protect its status. While the insurrection had been largely put down by the end of 1902, forces to maintain civil order in case it erupted again were required. The Navy moved the main station of its Asiatic Fleet to Manila, and within a few years began to develop permanent facilities. Fixed fortifications were constructed to protect this base and Manila Harbor from 1904 until 1916. Throughout the 1910s and 1920s the Philippines always had a significant, but not inappropriate, permanent military establishment. However, in the late 1930s the subject took on new significance.

To begin with the Philippines were promised complete independence by the Tydings-McDuffie Act of 1934. In some corners of the military there were strong reservations about increasing or even maintaining defense levels if this possession was going its own way. Why build new, expensive facilities if they were not going to be retained? Plus there were strong demands for the active rearmament and expansion of the American forces as the war winds began to blow in Europe—should not this effort get first priority for men and matériel? As the time approached December 7, 1941 there was also a political aspect. Japanese militarism was increasing, and the fears of their preemptive action to gain new resources and strategic positions were strong. Would increasing force levels in the Philippines encourage or discourage their adventurism? The local commanders within the Philippine Department were continuously striving to improve the fighting capabilities of their command.[1]

Throughout the late 1930s and early 1940s there was a constant stream of requests for additional units and new construction.

A review of the correspondence about the strength of forces in the Philippines in the immediate pre-war period demonstrates a satisfaction, at least in Washington, with the existing situation. In October 1940 a review by Col. Joseph T. McNarney of the War Department staff voiced an opinion that the strength in the Philippines was adequate and should not be reinforced. Requests for increasing the strength of the Philippine Scouts and to bring the regular infantry and coast artillery units in the islands up to authorized levels were routinely turned down. A similar response met requests to fund essential major military construction programs. Finally, with the worsening situation with Japan and a slowly increasing mood in Congress to fund military projects, some of these requests were granted. The secretary of war and Army chief of staff approved in January 1941 a series of actions to: double the strength of the Philippine Scouts, increase the strength of the regular 31st Infantry Regiment by over five hundred men, increase the coast artillery manpower, schedule shipment of additional 155-mm and 75-mm guns, and to include $1.5 million of new construction projects. While these moves indicated a more positive attitude in Washington about Philippine defense, the allocation of scarce weapons and ammunition was still withheld from the islands.

Brig. Gen. Leonard T. Gerow, head of the staff for the War Plans Division in August of 1941, provided an interesting overview and history of Philippine defense allocations. He stated that:

> From 1922 until late 1940 our policy with regard to the Philippines was to maintain existing strength but to undertake no further permanent improvements except as a measure of economy. During that period, several studies were made as to the correct policy for the Philippines. Generally, three courses of action have been discussed:
>
> a. To maintain the status quo.
>
> b. Withdraw our forces from the Philippines and the Far East, and establish our Western Defense Line along the 180th Meridian, or
>
> c. To build up in the Philippine Islands a force of sufficient strength to assure enforcement of our policies, and to protect our interests in the Far East.

Continuing later in the same memo, he opined: "The primary reasons, in the past, for failure to undertake adequate defensive measures for the defense of the Philippine Islands were: lack of funds, lack of personnel and equipment, inability of the Navy to provide adequate support."[2]

In 1941 the basic American war plans were designated the "Rainbow" series. Prior to 1940 war plans were developed for scenarios with individual enemies. For example War Plan Black was for Germany, War Plan Green was for Mexico, and most importantly for this analysis War Plan Orange was for a potential war with Japan. Eventually it was realized that a far more likely scenario involved a war with a variety of allies against a spectrum of enemies. Starting in 1940 the joint war plans committee developed directives for coalition warfare enumerated Rainbow 1 through 5. The plans developed most fully were Rainbow Nos. 1, 3, and 5. Plan No.1 envisioned just western hemisphere defense, Plan No. 3 featured an offensive campaign in the Pacific favored by factions in the Navy, and Plan No. 5 described an active coalition of the United States, the British Empire, and the Dutch deployed simultaneously against the Germans, Italians, and Japanese. The latter plan was the scenario that most resembled the situation that actually occurred in late 1941. The original Rainbow No. 5 plan of 1939–40 had been updated in April of 1940, and again revised in March 1941 based on the American-British staff conversations of January of that year. Published on April 30, 1941, it had several key statements concerning the defense of the Philippines.[3]

The revised plan reiterated again that Germany was the predominant member of the Axis powers, and the Atlantic and European area was considered the decisive theatre. The military strategy in the Far East (with or without the entry of Japan into the war) was to be considered defensive, and specifically it stated that the United States did not intend to add to its current military strength in this area. The Army's role would be to defend the Philippine Coastal Frontier (with naval cooperation), but only with a secondary priority. The only additional forces to be made available were to be such available locally. Presumably this meant the forces of the Philippine Commonwealth and local civilian reserves. Clearly, as of the end of April 1941, both the Army and Navy saw the defense of the Philippines as secondary to higher priority theatres. Rainbow No. 5 was not again officially revised before the war, though as we'll see the actual course taken varied considerably from this strategic document.

In March 1941 the Philippine Department was told that no .50-caliber ammunition was available to send to either active units or the defense reserve; the same message came in April about any 37-mm ammunition. On the last day of April they were explicitly told that the new version of Rainbow No. 5

called for no addition to forces in the islands. In June the wording used was: "[D]o not contemplate reinforcement, but to defend the entrance to the Bay and support the navy by local forces augmented by personnel and facilities as available locally."[4] Despite the (sometimes mixed) messages from Washington, Lt. Gen. George Grunert was consistently firm on his assessment of the dangers in the Far East and on the need to aggressively move ahead on Philippine defenses. On June 12, 1941 he submitted a $52 million estimate for a long shopping list of needs. Chief items required were outlined as:[5]

1. Mobilization of the Philippine Army, $31.8 million
2. New aviation fields, $3.5 million
3. Strategic roads and bridges, $3.1 million
4. Naval installations, $1.3 million
5. War reserves for Philippine Commonwealth, $7.5 million
6. Navy and Commonwealth projects, $5 million

Finally on July 28, 1941 MacArthur was informed that the authorized defense reserves (equipment and stores capable of sustaining a long campaign) were being increased, but no additional forces or equipment would be available for the department's active units. Shortly thereafter a significant strategic change occurred. Suddenly a new policy dictated that the Philippines should be urgently reinforced.

In the pre-war years the logistics of supply for the Philippine garrison had become routine. Each service's transports made a couple of voyages a year from San Francisco to Hawaii and the Far East. Up until 1941 these trips were always made by a single, unescorted transport. However, that changed in the year before the war. Of the four naval voyages performed in 1941, only *Henderson*'s trip in April and May was made as an unescorted, independent sailing. Starting in late January 1941, the Navy saw a significant threat to military seaborne traffic and arranged cruiser escorts for all but one of its western Pacific journeys. Two of these voyages, and a special escorting of a Dutch ship in early 1941, pre-date the major Philippine reinforcement effort. Still, they demonstrate many of the complications in coordinating convoyed traffic and are instructive of the solutions adopted.

In late January 1941 the chief of naval operations directed Adm. James O. Richardson of the United States Fleet (the Pacific Fleet wasn't designated as a command until February 1, 1941) and Adm. Thomas C. Hart of the Asiatic Fleet to provide escort for the transport vessel USS *Chaumont* from

Pearl Harbor to Manila. *Chaumont* was one of the "regular" naval transports making the roundtrip from Pearl to the Orient, stopping at naval bases several times a year. Richardson was more than a little surprised that this trip required escorting, as none of those prior had. Orders required Richardson to provide escort from Pearl Harbor to Guam, and Hart to provide it from Guam to Manila (Guam was administratively managed by the Asiatic Fleet's Sixteenth Naval District). Apparently no reason was stated for the escorting, or at least Richardson remembered none.

However, when Richardson later asked about the situation in Washington, Rear Adm. Royal E. Ingersoll (assistant chief of naval operations) informed him that the decision was based on the presence of German raiders. And in fact, the operational orders for the escorting clearly state the rumored presence of at least three German raiders in the southwestern Pacific.[6] The cruiser escort's duties were specifically outlined as: "Protect transport against interference by German raiders." Attached to the order was a British Admiralty summary description of the supposed three raiders, including tonnage, appearance, and likely markings.

It is true that 1940–41 was the highpoint of German raider activity. German surface ships were still able to productively cruise the sea-lanes, and on January 1, 1941 pocket battleship *Admiral Scheer* was still in the South Atlantic. No German surface warships ever made it into the Pacific during the war. However, Germany also effectively used a number of average-sized merchant vessels as armed auxiliary cruisers for commerce raiding. At the beginning of 1941 six such raiders were at sea: *Kormoran*, *Pinguin*, and *Thor* were in the South Atlantic, *Atlantis* was in the Indian Ocean, *Komet* was crossing the Pacific on her way to the Indian Ocean, and *Orion* was undergoing refit in the Marianas courtesy of her future ally. Thus, while not three but just two ships appear to have been present in the Pacific at the time of the escorting order, there was enough evidence available to justify the assignment. There had not yet been a sinking of an American-flag ship by a raider, Germany still being anxious to avoid conflict with the United States. An American Navy (or Army transport) encounter with a raider would have been a serious political escalation. After this date several more important transports made their way to Manila totally unescorted; what made the voyage of *Chaumont* unique?

Richardson in his biography states that later Admiral Hart told him that *Chaumont* was carrying, in addition to a full load of regular supplies and replacement personnel, a cryptographic device.[7] There are several potential devices this could have been, up to and including the famous "Purple Machine."

It is widely reported that this decryption machine, used for reading the Japanese diplomatic code, arrived in Manila for Navy Station Cast in the spring of 1941—though details of exactly how it was transferred or on what vessel are lacking.[8] In any event the combination of a valid threat and an unusually sensitive cargo could easily explain the sudden and somewhat secretive orders for using cruiser escorts for such a trip.

The actual escorting of *Chaumont* was an interesting choreographed movement of three different consorts. *Chaumont* departed Pearl Harbor on January 23, 1941, with light cruiser *Concord* as escort. Traveling via Midway and Wake, the transport arrived at the Guam naval station on February 1. Here *Concord* returned to Pearl Harbor, and her escorting role was taken over by light cruiser *Marblehead* of the Asiatic Fleet. Leaving Guam on the fifth, the pair arrived (but curiously entered harbor separately) at Manila on February 10. *Chaumont* made her normal run to the China Navy and Marine stations unescorted, and then returned to Manila on the twenty-sixth. For the return voyage, she was escorted by the Pacific Fleet cruiser *Trenton*, departing Manila on March 10, again traveling back through Guam and Wake, arriving at Pearl Harbor on March 23. *Trenton* had made the trip out in order to pick up personnel from the shutdown of the Guam radio-intercept station for reassignment to the Philippines. All three cruisers were of the older *Omaha*-class, but as warships were considered equal to the capabilities of a merchant raider.

The second 1941 escorted sailing occurred hard on the heels of the first. A Pacific Fleet operational order by Adm. Husband E. Kimmel ordered the escorting of yet another Navy transport. This time it was USS *William P. Biddle* headed from Pearl Harbor to Pago Pago in Samoa.[9] *Biddle* was already on her way from San Diego to Pearl Harbor carrying Marine defense battalions. She left California on February 27, and after a two-day layover to deliver the 1st Battalion, she departed on March 9 with just the 7th Battalion left on board. Just like the voyage with *Chaumont*, she received a single light-cruiser escort—USS *Concord* again. In fact, the operational order contained the same wording about German raiders and the same British Admiralty addendum. Also like the orders for *Chaumont*, the ships were not to be darkened, apparently to allow them to be not mistaken for legitimate targets by any potential raider. The cruise occurred without incident. Both ships got under way on the ninth, and arrived in Samoa on March 15. Personnel representing roughly half the strength of the defense battalion, twenty-four officers and 405 enlisted Marines and Navy corpsmen, disembarked on schedule. The ships returned in short order to Hawaii.

The third early 1941 Pacific Ocean escorting took place in late July. In this case the task was combined with a political move aimed at sending a message to the Japanese. The rationale for the escorted voyage was nothing less than the main contingent of personnel destined for the American Volunteer Group (AVG—Flying Tigers). This group of volunteers had been organized the previous winter under the command of Claire Chennault to fight the Japanese in China. While not officially sanctioned by the U.S. government, arrangements were made for the recruitment of aviators and mechanics from active military personnel and for access to modern aircraft types. The administration clearly supported the effort, and actively aided its facilitation—to include help in getting the men and equipment to China.

The first small advance party of technicians (one officer and twenty-nine men) went from San Francisco to Singapore as commercial passengers on the American President Lines' *President Pierce* in July 1941. The second contingent was composed of thirty-seven pilots, eighty-four enlisted technicians, and two female nurses. They were booked passage on the Dutch liner MV *Jagersfontein.* The ship departed San Francisco in mid-July and made a stop in Honolulu.[10] At that point the ship picked up an American naval escort. Task Force 19, under Rear Adm. S. A. Taffinder with heavy cruisers *Northampton* and *Salt Lake City*, was ordered to accompany *Jagersfontein* on her immediate departure on July 16. Unlike the previous movement of U.S. personnel and equipment in U.S.-flag vessels, this situation was less clear. For German raiders, the Netherlands-flag vessel operating under auspices of the government in exile was clearly a legitimate target. For the Japanese, vessels carrying combatants under contract to their Chinese enemies could also be construed a legitimate capture under some interpretations of international law.

The president himself directed the chief of naval operations to ensure the safe arrival of *Jagersfontein* in Singapore (where the men would be transferred by coastal steamer to Rangoon and ultimately make their way to China). An elaborate plan was cast to mislead a potential interception. After leaving Honolulu the merchant ship would begin a direct routing to Manila, but at night, in a darkened condition, she would change course south. Then the American cruisers would join; technically they were ordered to not escort *Jagersfontein*, but rather to accompany her from a distance at a general speed of twelve knots. A new route through southern waters would take the small convoy to the Torres Strait, where the ship would be handed off to a Dutch light cruiser. Peculiar wording was issued to the heavy cruisers—if their consort was intercepted by a foreign war vessel, they would take steps to prevent capture or interference of the American AVG contingent. Force was to be avoided, but authorized if absolutely necessary. Unlike the previous two escorting missions, ships were to remain darkened at night and radio silence observed.[11] The hand-off was made as scheduled, and *Jagersfontein* continued her voyage safely. After safely releasing their charge, Task Force 19 made a planned, but previously unannounced, public visit to Brisbane, Australia.

The Army performed a rather similar shuttle service for its own transports to and from Manila in the immediate pre-war years. With no significant Army deployments in the Pacific besides Hawaii and the Philippines, rarely were any stops made elsewhere. The Army also made extensive use of both the regularly scheduled commercial liners (like the President Lines) calling regularly at Manila and of chartered freighters to get bulk equipment and supplies to the island. The Army's establishment being so much larger than the Navy's meant that more ships made more voyages. Nine Army-operated USAT transport trips were made to Manila in 1940—one arriving every month or two. Through June of 1941 six trips were performed. None of these journeys were escorted. Obviously the Army did not operate its own warships, but it was also insulated from knowledge of the potential threat. It does not appear that the Army ever recognized a potential problem. They never requested naval escort, and never even acted to arm the transports—at least not until late in the year, many months after the Navy began escorting her transports.

In the first half of 1941 most of the trips made can be described as routine in terms of cargo. With 20,000 troops in the Philippines (the usual enlisted period was two years), the normal turnover in enlistments and transfers meant that hundreds of soldiers would arrive and depart on every ship. Until later in 1941, dependents were also routinely living with their servicemen, and were also usually given transport on government ships. Supplies of all types were sent, the Philippines being industrially unable to supply many of the tools of modern warfare. There was one important augmentation to the military strength that did occur in this period: Both Hawaii and the Philippines received important shipments of modern aircraft in the spring of 1941.

In April 1941 Washington approved a transfer of modern aircraft to the Philippines. This addition was long overdue; the existing air strength can only be described as abysmal. Virtually *no* modern aircraft were operated by the Philippine-based 4th Composite Group. A dozen old Martin B-10 bombers (a type first flown in 1932) were the only multi-engine bombers available. Most of the fighters were Boeing P-26As, the first all-metal, monoplane fighter of the Air Corps. Actually, for as weak as it was, the strength of the Air Corps in the Philippines had just recently been reinforced through a curious set of circumstances.

In late 1940 the worsening international situation had led to the cancellation of American export licenses for two separate aircraft orders. First was an order by the government of Thailand for ten fighters and six light bombers from North American Aviation, Inc. Both versions were based on the company's successful AT-6 "Texan" advanced trainer. On October 18, 1940 the U.S. government granted authority for the takeover of the Thai order by the Army Air Corps. The six bomber versions were still in the United States; however, the ten fighters with spare parts had actually shipped when the license was cancelled, and had been unloaded mid-voyage dockside in Manila. The planes, now designated A-27s, were painted in Army Air Corps colors and issued to the 4th Composite Group. Never considered of much value for combat, they were used for training and local transport service.

Of greater value was an order for more modern pursuit planes by Sweden from Republic Aviation Corporation. Some of the order for 120 Swedish versions of the EP-1-06 fighters had already been delivered, but sixty were taken over on October 24 by presidential order. Renamed as P-35A, about fifty-two of these fighters eventually were allocated to the Air Corps in the Philippines. Most (at least forty) were transported from San Francisco on USAT *Etolin* on her voyage in November 1940. Not a bad design in 1938, the aircraft was under-armed, and did not possess pilot protection or self-fueling tanks. It was better than the P-26s, and quite useful for training pilots, but far from competitive with the modern Japanese aircraft it would fight in less than a year. Still, of the aircraft received in the Philippines prior to the summer of 1941, these were just about the only ones that could be considered marginally useful. With USAT *Etolin* and the subsequent voyage of USAT *Washington* were the personnel of the 17th and 20th Pursuit Squadrons to operate these aircraft.

Finally, in April, the Philippines were approved for a shipment of more modern warplanes. Scheduled for transfer were thirty-one Curtiss P-40B fighters and one each C-39 and C-49 cargo planes. These were to be dispatched from San Francisco on the commercial SS *American Manufacturer*, departing San Francisco on April 19, 1941. From Hickam Field on Oahu, eighteen Douglas B-18A Bolo bombers were to be transferred to Clark Field in the Philippines. The bomber ferry route was nowhere near completion, plus this relatively short-ranged medium bomber did not have the fuel endurance to attempt such a crossing. The planes were dismantled and sent from Hawaii on an Army transport (USAT *Washington*). This plane was a medium bomber partially based on Douglas' successful DC-3 transport. They were better than the outmoded B-10, but not much. Even though they arrived just seven months before the outbreak of the war, they were never used for combat missions, but did prove useful as transports and trainers.

Two small, company-sized units arriving in July and early August were the only other positive reinforcements for the Philippine garrison in this early period. USAT *President Taft* departed San Francisco on June 21, 1941, making its normal stop to offload passengers in Honolulu.[12] However, in Honolulu a unit boarded the vessel to be transferred from Hawaii to the Philippines. The 176 men of the 809th Engineer Company (Aviation) would be going to Luzon. Aviation engineer units were very new in the Army. Their sole task was to build airfields, and they were equipped with the heavy graders, rollers, and crawlers to do this job. One of MacArthur's earliest general orders (No. 4 on August 4, 1941) prioritized the construction of new airfields in the islands. An analysis, dated August 15, by Chief of the Air Staff Brig. Gen. Carl Spaatz reported that only Clark Field was suitable for heavy bombardment aircraft. Nichols Field was under construction, and six partially ready pursuit fields were within eighty miles of Manila but were without gasoline or oil, and repair and other service facilities.[13]

The next transport to make the trip was SS *President Coolidge*, another American President Lines ship making her first run to the Orient under Army control. *Coolidge* was a large, fast ship, one of two premium liners built for the company during the 1930s. She was a valuable addition to the Army's fleet and figured heavily in the Philippine reinforcement story over the next six months. Leaving San Francisco on July 15, she arrived after a usual stop at Honolulu in Manila on August 1, 1941. For the Philippine Department she carried 152 filler replacements for various units and 194 men of a unit simply designated the Philippine Air Warning Company. Just as important, with this unit were two SCR-271 aircraft warning radar sets, the first for the defenders.[14]

The Army's plan for aircraft warning radar in the Philippines, for which this was the first contribution of any significance, is of interest. The spring of 1941 saw the first overall plan for a general electronic aircraft warning service for the United States and its overseas departments and bases. Soon five early model sets were authorized for the Philippines, three to be supplied in August

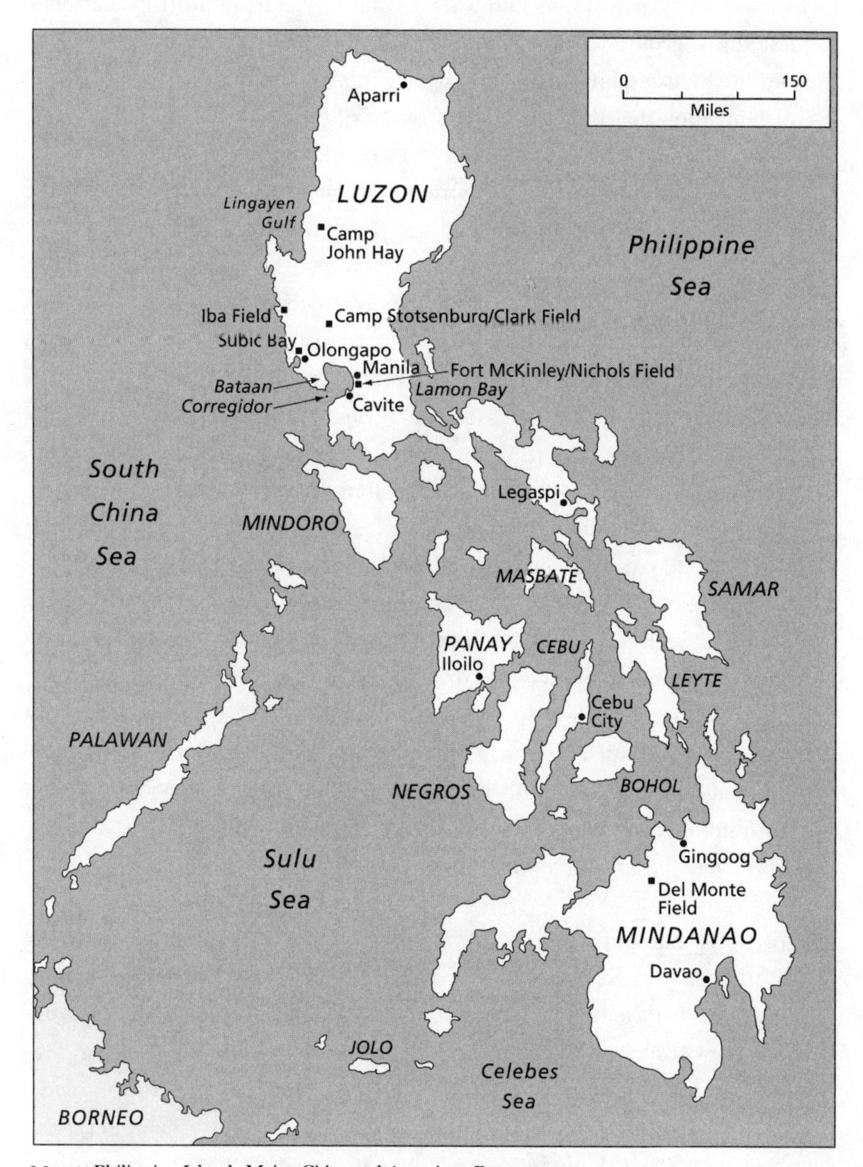

Map 1. Philippine Islands Major Cities and American Bases

1941 and the final two in October. In April $500,000 was allocated to provide these detectors and other related equipment for the Philippine Department, to be used for three stations and an information center. With this plan was requested a special aircraft warning organization. By late summer arrangements were finalized for the unit and its one mobile and two fixed sets.[15] It was this organization that shipped out on *Coolidge*'s July voyage. It was anticipated that seven additional fixed sets would be available in the fall of 1941.

Following the money for equipment, in early June another $430,000 became available for the actual fixed site development. The first three permanent sites were to be set up to generally protect the greater Manila Bay/Clark Field approaches. Two would be placed to cover approaches from the west and north—one at Iba (having the highest priority), and one on Lubang Island (second priority). The third site, and last in priority, was southeast of Manila in southern Luzon at Paracole.[16] These earlier plans were re-packaged in the comprehensive project drawn up by the department in September. This expanded project called for ten long-range detectors and sixteen tracking stations. Despite the apparent availability of funds and approval of plans, the actual construction work at the sites was not undertaken quickly.[17] At the beginning of the war, only the highest priority site at Iba was actually equipped with its radar set and operational. A second site was physically under construction sixty miles west of Aparri, and a third set was in transit to Legaspi. Of course while this was happening, the "old" system was not dismantled. Trained native observers were deployed and connected through the commercial telephone net with the interceptor command at Nielson Field. Far from perfect, for most of the campaign it was the only system that there was to warn of large-scale bomber attacks.

July of 1941 marked a period of intense political confrontation between Japan and the United States. The events and subsequent decisions of that month clearly set the two nations on the path to conflict. Generally relations between the countries were poor throughout the late 1930s. Japanese aggression and occupation of large areas of China had been a concern to a wide range of American economic and political interests. Even the general public clearly sided with the Chinese (at least the nationalist regime of Chiang Kai-shek). When Japan joined the Axis powers by signing the Tripartite Alliance in 1940, its choice of allies for any future conflict were obvious. Japanese strategic direction was decided only after considerable internal debate and at times dissension. The Japanese army had a considerable bias toward a conquest of Siberia, while the Imperial Japanese Navy favored an expansion into Southeast Asia. Here there were even more strategic resources (oil, rubber, tin) and potentially weaker enemies in the form of colonial armies. Obviously the choice of enemy was also influenced by the relative involvement of that particular service—the navy would have a major role in conquering the overseas territories of Southeast Asia, while the army would mostly fight any land campaign in Asia. Even within the political community there were competing philosophies of either directly supporting Germany as an ally in attacking the Soviet Union, or in beginning to establish the Greater East Asian Co-Prosperity Sphere.

An Imperial conference was called by Emperor Hirohito at the Tokyo palace in early July to present and decide upon the immediate future course. The services presented their suggested strategic plans to a closed gathering of admirals, generals, and cabinet officers. At the conference it was decided that an attack on Russia would only be pursued if Germany's victory in the west were certain. The endorsed strategy was to be the pursuit of the Greater East Asian Co-Prosperity Sphere—essentially the navy's favored proposal. Political negotiations, chiefly with the United States, would be continued, but active preparations for a war of conquest were to move ahead. Specifically an immediate advance into French Indochina to gain air and navy bases would be undertaken. Closely following the conference's July 2 conclusion, orders were issued for a full mobilization of the armed forces, for a recall of merchant vessels from the Caribbean and Atlantic waters, and for a general censorship of domestic mail.[18]

France had accepted an armistice and political arrangement with Germany upon its military collapse in June 1940. French Indochina was still aligned with the remaining French government in Vichy. Through several steps the Japanese had pressured the French to allow Japanese forces to occupy northern Indochina and provide basing rights. However, until mid-1941 those same rights had not been allowed in southern Indochina. Such bases were only useful for potential attacks on Malaya, Singapore, and the Dutch East Indies, not for supporting the war or blockade of China. Under pressure from both the Japanese and Germans, the French entered specific negotiations for a new arrangement on July 21. Of course the French were opposed to the occupation, but their position (occupation of half the country by Germany in Europe, and with only a small, poorly equipped military force actually in Indochina) compelled them to reluctantly accept the Japanese requests.

French vice-chief of state François Darlan signed a joint Franco-Japanese defense agreement for Indochina on July 29, 1941 in Vichy.[19] There were three primary elements of the new agreement: a declaration of the continued French sovereignty in Indochina, the agreed rights of both nations to provide the defense of the territory, and a provision that no other agreement would be made with a third party detrimental to Japanese interests. The agreement gave the Japanese rights to a number of airbases, and naval base rights were provided at Saigon and Cam Ranh Bay. The Japanese quickly dispatched prepared troop elements to occupy these locations.

The Roosevelt administration responded to the Japanese move into southern Indochina swiftly and decisively. There had been discussions earlier in the year of applying economic sanctions on the Japanese. Frankly it was about the only step—short of conflict or complete diplomatic break of relations—left in the American bag of tricks. Oddly enough the strongest cabinet members on this approach were not the military members. The hawks were Secretary of State Cordell Hull, Interior Secretary Harold Ickes, and Treasury Secretary Henry Morgenthau. These gentlemen argued for the immediate cessation of trade on all but a few items. Most importantly for Japan's war economy would be the restrictions on high-octane, refined oil products.

Both Adm. Harold R. Stark, chief of naval operations (CNO), and Marshall were opposed to using economic sanctions at this moment. Army Chief of Staff Marshall wanted to delay any break with Japan until the last possible moment—he was worried about the relative preparedness of American forces in the Pacific, particularly the Philippines. Secretary of War Stimson was in complete agreement with like-minded CNO Admiral Stark, who had urged the president on the twentieth to not take the trade embargo route. He thought that the military should not be distracted from the Atlantic crisis, and the division of the fleet between both oceans would tempt the Japanese into an immediate attack.[20] Roosevelt, in his typical fashion, weighed the input of his counselors and modified the embargo to a state somewhat less than "complete." Obviously the administration still hoped (even if pessimistically) that negotiation would forestall or delay open war in the Pacific and give the Japanese some reason to see an opening. He intended that the trade action would not totally shut off all oil; some grades would continue to be offered at 1938 annual amounts.

On July 23, 1941 Japanese envoy Admiral Kichisaburo Nomura requested a presidential meeting that was granted the following day. Roosevelt's proposal to neutralize French Indochina for all nations was not of interest to the

Japanese.[21] Roosevelt did take the opportunity to hint about restrictions on oil trade if a negotiated solution could not be found. On the twenty-fifth Marshall and Stark alerted their tactical commands of the forthcoming economic sanctions, with the wording that while this meant a new, serious level of political confrontation, immediate Japanese hostilities against the United States were not probable. At 8 PM on the twenty-fifth the administration released the press statement containing the embargo executive order. Specifically all Japanese assets in the United States were frozen. The Panama Canal was closed to Japanese shipping. All export trade with Japan was forbidden (except foodstuffs and cotton) unless subsequently authorized by government-issued licenses. It was anticipated that licenses would be available for certain low-grade petroleum products and cotton, and an import license allowed for raw silk. As it turned out slowdowns within the commerce department never permitted any further oil products being authorized, and the intended trade control turned into a de facto total embargo.

The Japanese were somewhat surprised, but not dissuaded from their intended moves by the announcement. One Japanese newspaper called the order a "declaration of economic war."[22] The embargo, particularly the oil, was a serious economic matter. Japan's imports in mid-1941 were heavily sourced on the United States. Even with conservation of carefully accumulated reserves, an embargo with no new sources would mean that even the Japanese navy's battle fleet would have fuel for just two years or less. An embargo of oil would indeed force the Japanese to choose between what they viewed as humiliating submission to the West, or a war of conquest aimed at securing the raw material base the nation required. In fact, the embargo had the impact the Americans hoped for—it was a serious message that forced the Japanese to make a decision. Unfortunately the Americans only managed to drive the Japanese into a corner that they viewed as having only one exit strategy—war. The crisis also influenced American plans for the proactive defense of the Philippine Islands.

In the wake of the crisis yet another significant move was made by the Americans. Also on the twenty-sixth of July, certainly timed to reinforce the message sent by the embargo, a new major command structure was announced for the Army in the Philippine Islands. The reserve forces of the Philippine Commonwealth were being called into service and combined with the U.S. forces to form the United States Army Forces in the Far East (USAFFE). Simultaneously Maj. Gen. Douglas MacArthur was recalled to active duty and named to command this combined force. Now both the organizational structure and command presence were in place to seriously address the defensive needs. While lacking the natural resources of the colonies to the south, the strategic location of the Philippines astride the Japanese communications line to Southeast Asia was apparent to all the protagonists. The proposed calling to service of the Philippine Army had been advocated for some time; in itself the action was not a direct response to the Indochinese crises, but the timing of its announcement certainly was.

The creation of a supreme Army command (at no time before the start of the war did the Manila Army headquarters command naval or Marine units) was not a new concept. Major General Grunert of the Philippine Department had advocated this arrangement at least since January 1941. Washington seemed to approve the idea in concept, but the reality was that the Philippine Commonwealth government was paying for its own army and its shift to direct U.S. command might not be construed correctly. So it was left that the command structure would be created only if a true emergency existed. MacArthur as commander also proved an easy selection. The general had taken leave of active Army service in 1935 to serve as military adviser to the Philippine government. In fact, special congressional legislation had been passed to allow a mission for the commonwealth, and to have it headed by an American officer.[23] The Philippine Commonwealth government, headed by President (and MacArthur's old friend) Manuel Quezon, had specifically approached MacArthur on the position. MacArthur was actively looking for a new position as his temporary job of chief of staff was ending. The new position had great appeal to him—it had much more prestige than the alternative of a corps command or staff position, it was professionally challenging, it was in a country he truly admired and liked, and it was financially rewarding. In addition to his regular major general salary, he negotiated a contract granting him the same compensation as Quezon ($18,000 per year), a $15,000 expense account, and a luxury living suite at the air-conditioned Manila Hotel.[24] Also, in a 1936 ceremony he was designated as field marshal of the Philippines—a rank that didn't even exist in the U.S. Army. By Special Order No. 22 of September 18, 1935, Secretary of War George Dern had detailed Douglas MacArthur to his new duty with the Commonwealth of the Philippines.

Douglas MacArthur came from a family of strong military service: his father Arthur had been a Civil War hero and career Army officer who served in the Philippines in 1898 opposing the insurrection, and even was military governor for the territory. Douglas was born in 1880 at Fort Dodge, Arkansas. He graduated in 1903 from West Point with high honors, and was commissioned in the engineers. His first Army assignment was with the 3rd Engineers in the Philippines, where his duties included surveying part of the Bataan Peninsula. He also met and became friends with a young Filipino nationalist named Manuel Quezon. MacArthur went on to assignments in the United States and Panama, was with the War Department General Staff from 1913 to 1917, and demonstrated heroism and command capability with the 42nd Division on the western front in the First World War. He emerged from that conflict highly decorated and as one of the youngest brigadier generals in the Army. A second tour of duty in the Philippines, this time culminating in command of the department, occurred in the 1920s. In 1930 he was named as Army chief of staff with a temporary rank of four-star general. With the financial resources and time available he had done a credible job in starting the training and organization of the ten reserve divisions that would be the major strength of the Philippine Army. However, by 1941 he was both tiring of the job and looking for other challenges. MacArthur's extensive ego is well known, and even at age sixty-one he still held considerable ambition for himself. In April 1941 he began suggesting that he might be interested in a new Far Eastern command. Failing an immediate response he also suggested he might be a good candidate for the role of U.S. High Commissioner to the Philippines. At one point he even booked his return trip to the United States to go back permanently to San Antonio, Texas.

General Marshall assured MacArthur in June that he was a logical candidate for the USAFFE command, but the timing was not right yet. The crisis over the Japanese occupation of French Indochina changed that. On July 17 Marshall approved a War Plans Division agenda of five items that would establish the Far Eastern command:

1. Call into U.S. service the Commonwealth forces.
2. Extend the command of the Far East to General MacArthur.
3. Obtain $10 million from the president's emergency funds to accelerate training of the Philippine reserve units.
4. Obtain permission to divert the funds from the sugar excise tax for use by the Philippine government for further training and equipping of their forces. (Never approved by Congress.)
5. Dispatch 425 U.S. Army Reserve officers to serve as trainers and advisers to Philippine units.

MacArthur gladly accepted the position on the twenty-sixth, and on the twenty-eighth he became a lieutenant general. On the nineteenth the defense reserve allowance for the Philippines had been increased. On July 31 the Navy announced that Manila Harbor was now actively mined. Clearly serious preparations for war were now, if somewhat belatedly, under way. From the first of August 1941 the question in military circles was when the war would start, not if.

In late July another routine Army transport voyage was made to Manila. Departing San Francisco on July 23, *President Harrison* of the American President Lines made a subsidized commercial voyage to Honolulu, Manila, and Singapore. In addition to a regular allotment of transferring replacement military personnel, one item of the itinerary appears out of the ordinary. An urgent request for small-arms ammunition from the Chinese led to the decision to send a supply from the Philippine stocks to Burma on board *Harrison*. This would be the first, but not the last, case where the American supplies in the Philippines would be temporarily used to fill other urgent Asian demands. *Harrison* started her return from Penang carrying back eight thousand tons of rubber.[25]

The subsequent August sailings carried the usual replacement personnel for the services, and hefty quantities of the routine consumable supplies and goods for the services. No succinct new units or significant new weapon types were included on these voyages—though plans were being intensely scrutinized and implemented to make that happen during September. What is unusual is that the cruiser escorting policy was expanded to include the Army transports for the first time. While the Navy orders for escorting continued to cite German raider activity, one has to wonder if the new level of confrontation with the Japanese starting at the end of July wasn't also responsible for this new policy. The first voyage of the month began when *President Pierce* began her first voyage as an Army Transport Service vessel. On her departure from San Francisco she carried 1,200 men together for Honolulu and Manila. Most were coast artillery personnel (712), but quite a few were for the Corps of Engineers (441). The vessel did call at Shanghai, but then was diverted to Hong Kong. There she embarked a number of Chinese aviation cadets and aircraft mechanic trainees being brought to the United States for training. It was thought that a Shanghai pickup might be contested by (or at least prove to be potentially awkward with) the occupying Japanese administration.[26] Next, USAT *Tasker H. Bliss* left San Francisco on August 9.

She carried 944 replacement personnel for both Hawaii and the onward trip to the Philippines. No special units or unusual quantities of planes or other weapons were on board. She made the entire voyage out and back unescorted, using the usual direct route through the Mariana Islands. It would be the last such voyage.

The next scheduled journey was for one of the Navy's regular runs, this time conducted by USS *Henderson*. Leaving Pearl Harbor on August 22, she traveled via Midway, Wake, and Guam (mostly delivering mail), and upon arrival in the Philippines met units of the Asiatic Fleet at Zamboanga and Tutu Bay to deliver sailors and supplies. *Henderson* went on to Manila and then the China stations. Even though *Henderson* did not have special status (arguably the reason for the earlier escorting of *Chaumont*, *Biddle*, and *Jagersfontein*), and was carrying "routine" supplies and personnel, the Navy assigned her a cruiser escort. USS *St. Louis* accompanied *Henderson* for the voyage to Philippine waters. The usual rationale of the presence of German raiders was given as the reason for the escort. *St. Louis* was ordered to leave her charge once there and proceed directly back home alone. The light cruiser arrived back at Pearl Harbor on September 29. *Henderson* finished her errands in the Far East to catch an escorted return courtesy of heavy cruiser *Astoria*, which had just brought out another small convoy.

While significant quantities of men and equipment were not present on these mid-summer sailings, plans for much more were in the works. Two individuals, not normally the best of friends, combined their actions to personally achieve a significant policy change. Lieutenant General MacArthur used his new position to the utmost. Always the optimist, he touted at every opportunity the capability of the now-combined American and Philippine armies. In particular he was very proud of the progress of training and morale of the new Philippine Army—probably not an unnatural position as he had been directly responsible for its development over the past five years. There is no doubt that he genuinely believed that his forces—if properly equipped, trained, deployed, and supported—could seriously oppose or even dissuade a Japanese invasion. With years dedicated to the Philippines, and a strong affinity for the nation and its people, MacArthur's constitution could not help but bring him to a strategy of successful defense. The published war plans, advocating a retreat to Bataan and most probably an eventual capitulation of forces before any relief, were unacceptable to him. A strong communicator with a message that people wanted to hear, Douglas MacArthur was a persuasive advocate—and he had a definite impact on Washington, D.C.

The other key figure must be identified as Army Chief of Staff George Marshall. Marshall quickly assumed the role of facilitator for reinforcing the Philippines. The rationale for his decision is less apparent than MacArthur's. There were probably several factors influencing his conversion to this position. While he certainly wasn't MacArthur's strongest supporter, he did admire the general's work in the Philippines and his ambitious confidence. Also, Marshall was a supporter of the administration's strategy that America should aid the alliance opposing Germany, Italy, and Japan. Giving the Japanese something to worry about with a strong Philippine defense might mean they would be less likely to start a war against the already embroiled Great Britain. In fact, this was quite similar to Roosevelt's position and support of the buildup. While it may sound convoluted, the logic was that an American buildup in the Far East could be of substantial help to the British and Russians by keeping the Japanese out of the war. And finally General Marshall was anxious to see the rapidly expanding American military forces deployed where they could be influential. For him it was better that American munitions and aircraft be directly arraigned against a potential enemy than being sent as lend-lease to Russia or Great Britain.[27]

In most respects Secretary of War Stimson, who espoused similar positions, supported Marshall. However, not all (or even many) of the general's War Plans Division staff saw the situation in the same light. So, soon after sending repeated messages to the Philippine Department refusing their usual pleas for units and supplies, there was surprise over the rapid change of policy. In fact, the policy change was not reflected in Rainbow and other war plans—it was realized in altered priorities and allocations rather than in printed plans.[28] A month later, on September 19, General Marshall instructed the Joint Army and Navy Board on the change in priority. The board (including its Navy members) concurred that an adequately reinforced defensive force in the Philippines would have a profound strategic effect and be decisive in deterring Japan. At least a portion of the rationale for reinforcing the Philippines was its deterrent effect.[29] Of course we now know that this deterrence did not work, but that doesn't take away from the historical hope that it would.

Within just a couple of weeks—essentially the first two weeks of August—concrete commitments for the progressive reinforcement of the Philippines were under way. There was no overall goal or envisioned end point for the reinforcement. At times the Philippine command issued requests or succinct lists of immediate needs, but in general the perception of requirements constantly changed. Mostly these changed in reaction to "more" being made available, rather than any change in appreciation of Japanese plans or capabilities. On August 7 at the Argentia conference the president approved an increase of air force strength in the Philippines to one group of P-40s and another of B-17s. Air Force commander Maj. Gen. Henry "Hap" Arnold commented that this result was a distinct change of policy that had been previously rejected for being a possibly provocative act.[30] Of course it took time to implement the change of priority; on August 14 the War Plans Division advised that it was doubtful the Philippines could withstand a determined attack with its present means.

CHAPTER TWO

Pacific Fleet Basing and the Problem of Oahu Defense

During the immediate pre-war years the U.S. Fleet was stationed at the major West Coast naval bases. Smaller contingents were organized into the Asiatic Fleet (based in Manila and China), and an Atlantic and Hawaiian detachment. The fleet gathered for its annual exercise known as the "Fleet Problem" on April 2, 1940. For the ensuing year a significant military and political controversy raged about the physical basing of this force. It is also helpful to comprehend that in this time frame, the naval portion of the American military was simultaneously its most modern, best-equipped, and fully mobilized military force. The Army, the Air Force, and even much of the Marine Corps had large deficits of equipment and trained men to address before they could even contemplate undertaking the type of war that was being waged in Europe and Asia. If the United States were able to attract any attention or exert any influence on the behavior of the belligerent parties, it would have to be with its current naval service. Whether and then just how to use this force was at the heart of the emerging debate.

Most of the top administration and Navy Department brass held opinions about what to do with the fleet. There appear to have been three significant options. April and May of 1940 saw the long-anticipated German offensive against its western neighbors—Denmark and Norway, followed in a month by the attacks on Belgium, the Netherlands, and France. The period following the collapse of France in mid-June (and many considered Britain's fall as imminent) was a particularly anxious one. Realistic possibilities of the French or British fleet falling into German hands were postulated. Also, simultaneously, German activity in the Atlantic was increasing—submarine warfare was taking its toll and extending its reach well into oceanic waters, and Axis warships and surface raiders added substantially to the continued destruction of merchantmen. The capabilities of the Germans would inevitably be enhanced by their possession of new bases in western France. As a result the British instituted convoys that consumed a significant portion of their surface navy. In any event the Atlantic was suddenly becoming the focus of much of the U.S. Navy's strategic planners, and the need to substantially increase its force level was apparent. In many of these early discussions the most prominent spokesman for the Atlantic enhancement was Admiral Stark, the chief of naval operations.

The Japanese were also flexing their muscle in the Pacific. The war in China was important politically, but it did not directly impact the United States militarily. However, Japan was getting more aggressive with its extraterritorial moves in Southeast Asia. With the fall of France, Japan soon got basing privileges in French Indochina that had clear implications to the British in Singapore and Malaya, and to the Dutch in the East Indies. A strong, continued presence by the American fleet in the Pacific was thought by many to exert a curbing effect on Japanese adventurism. Figuring out the Japanese thought process and what incentives or threats worked or did not work bedeviled the Americans. It should be mentioned that there were a few that thought too much American force too close to Japan (such as heavily reinforcing the Asiatic Fleet or even just permanently basing the fleet in Hawaii) might have an opposite effect. The Japanese could perceive that they were directly threatened and either move up their plans or even strike preemptively.

And lastly there were real considerations about the ability of the fleet to do any of this. The infrastructure needed for basing a battle fleet was considerable—much money and time had been invested in the dockyards, repair shops, ammunition magazines, aircraft training fields, and fueling depots on the West Coast, and these logistic facilities could not magically appear overnight elsewhere. The interwar years had also not provided the Navy with much in the way of critical auxiliary vessels (such as tankers, depot ships, transports, and tenders) that would be needed if the fleet moved to even a temporary location. The recent expansion of the Navy had created a shortfall in training that could only realistically be addressed at well-equipped American home ports. A vocal quarter urged that for maximum readiness, the fleet would be best served by leaving it where it was and allowing it to improve its training. Not the least of this opinion was the fleet's commander himself—Adm. James Richardson.

At the conclusion of the 1940 exercises, held as they frequently were in Hawaiian waters, President Roosevelt directly ordered the fleet to remain at Pearl Harbor. At the time this was only positioned as temporary, but plans to return to the West Coast were progressively delayed until May 9 when the assignment was made permanent. Richardson vocally opposed this decision, using the rationale of lack of adequate logistic and training facilities (and additionally the impact on morale—most of the officers and CPOs had families back home at their previous home ports). Richardson was an articulate officer of considerable ability, but his strong opinions voiced at the wrong times would ultimately lead to his dismissal from this post. Stark also opposed the retention of the fleet at Hawaii, but he also argued (on June 18, just at the end of French resistance in Europe) an agenda for moving a significant portion of the assets to the Atlantic. Roosevelt's reply reveals the compounding effects of such decisions—he did not look favorably now on moving the ships back eastward, as he did not want to indicate a weakness to the Japanese by such a decision, and embolden them to action. This logic is also tied closely to the administration's thought that German and Italian successes might prompt the Japanese to enter the war at the high tide. Thus once the fleet was at Pearl Harbor, prevailing thought was that it could not be moved without sending the wrong message. In October 1940 Richardson, taking advantage of a trip to Washington, met personally with Roosevelt to present his arguments once more. He was relieved of his post at the end of January. Effective February 1 the Atlantic Patrol Force became the Atlantic Fleet in its own right under command of Adm. Ernest J. King and the Pacific Fleet was simultaneously formed under Adm. Husband Kimmel.

While this maneuvering directly affected the Navy, the Army was not without interest in the decisions. Military doctrine at the time dictated that the Army was responsible for the defense of naval bases, both with conventional land forces (including coast artillery and maneuver forces) and air defense. A major base change would have implications on the deployment of forces. Initially the Army also opposed the Pearl Harbor basing concept; Secretary of War Stimson thought, like Stark, that the action might be too threatening to the Japanese. He probably also realized that the defense capabilities in Hawaii were not adequate and the Army's expansion plans were already stretched beyond comfort. Stark and Stimson, despite their earlier opposition, come across as realists in this situation. The presidential action had been taken and, as mentioned above, once done it was irreversible. Their minds began to gravitate to improving the local defense situation at Pearl Harbor in whatever way they could practically implement.

Toward the end of 1940 Stark became increasingly worried about the fleet's safety at Pearl Harbor. The successful (and well-publicized) British attack by a small batch of carrier-based torpedo planes on the Italian fleet in its base at Taranto in November 1940 surely contributed to the anxiety. Stark ordered Richardson and his district commandant to work closely with the Army on the defense problem. Subsequently a series of strongly worded letters and memos were submitted by the Navy relative to the lack of Army defenses up the chain of command to Navy Secretary Frank Knox. On January 24, 1941 Knox pointed out to his Army counterpart that urgent improvement was needed in the anti-aircraft defenses, in the formation of an advance awareness network (early terminology for radar), and more interceptor fighters.

As one of his final acts, Admiral Richardson elaborated his impression of needs for the fleet based in Hawaii. In a lengthy memo of January 25, he described the most glaring deficiencies affecting the readiness of the fleet as:

> a. the critical inadequacy of A.A. guns available for the defense of Pearl Harbor, necessitating constant manning of ships' A.A. while in port.
> b. The small number and obsolescent condition of land-based aircraft, necessitating constant readiness of striking groups of fleet planes and use of fleet planes for local patrols.
> c. Lack of suitable local defense vessels.
> d. Lack of aircraft detection devices ashore.
>
> It is considered imperative that immediate measures be undertaken to correct the critical deficiencies enumerated above.[1]

Richardson signed off with a note that the memo had been prepared in collaboration with incoming commander Kimmel.

Three of the four needs enumerated were clearly Army responsibilities. Almost immediately Stark pressed his appropriate counterpart (General Marshall, Army chief of staff) and made the offer of Navy help for the transport of reinforcements, even to the use of an aircraft carrier to quickly get more fighter planes to Oahu. The Army was in agreement—if Pearl Harbor was going to be the permanent station of the Pacific Fleet, both Stimson and Marshall knew that immediate steps were required to enhance its defense. Within weeks steps were taken to address some of the most glaring deficiencies.

The most immediate concern was the inadequacy of the interceptor force. While Hawaii was allocated a relatively large and well-equipped conventional infantry force, its air defenses seriously lagged in both quantity and quality. In a general sense this was true for all of the Army: there was a bigger gap to bridge to bring its air component to modern status than for most of its branches. But the situation was even more serious in the Pacific bases—both the Philippines and Hawaii were particularly ill-equipped with trained air units until well into 1941. The needs for purchasing, preparing, and crewing modern aircraft argued for the concentration of resources at stateside bases. Also the direct threat to island bases could only come from aircraft carriers, which were perceived (at least with the mind-set of late 1940) as being very limited in capability. Similar in strength, the two Pacific departments could each muster only a small composite air group of a few short-ranged observation planes, a couple of dozen obsolete medium bombers, and about the same quantity of P-26 fighters dating from the early 1930s. Hawaii did receive twenty P-36As in late1939, at the time the most modern fighter in inventory.

General Marshall wrote a detailed letter dated February 7 to the Hawaiian Department's recently arrived new commander, Lt. Gen. Walter C. Short.[2] In it he indirectly replied to the Navy's request for improved Army defenses and outlined the steps he was preparing to take. He shared with Short some of the frustrations the Army was feeling in getting enough new equipment both for expansion and remediation of deficiencies. Referring to Kimmel's needs, Marshall noted: "What he does not realize is that we are tragically lacking in this matériel throughout the army, and that Hawaii is on a far better basis than any other command in the army. The fullest protection for the Fleet is *the* rather than *a* major consideration for us." Most significant was his statement that he had "arranged yesterday to ship 31 P-36 airplanes by aircraft carrier in ten days from San Diego. This will give you fifty planes of a modern type." He went on to state that arrangements were also being made for shipping fifty P-40B fighters about March 15. This type had just begun production in January, and the planes for the shipment were coming directly off the production line in Buffalo, New York.

The Army acted with urgency in locating and dispatching immediate pursuit reinforcements. The first increment of Curtiss P-36 aircraft was gathered from a variety of existing squadrons and domestic airfields.[3] Sent to San Diego, they were to meet the aircraft carrier *Enterprise* for loading and transport to Hawaiian waters. From close offshore they were to be flown by their

Army pilots directly from the carrier deck to the Army's pursuit field at Wheeler. By the middle of February the shipment was coming together. *Enterprise* left Pearl Harbor on February 7 and loaded the aircraft at North Island Naval Air Station along with a significant detachment of the Marine 1st Defense Battalion. On the fifteenth the small task force was under way again for the Hawaiian Islands. The Army pilots (no doubt with a few anxious moments concerning their training and what must have appeared as a very short runway!) took off safely from the carrier for Wheeler Field. While the P-36s were being absorbed into the fighter command on Oahu, plans did not lag much on the next pursuit shipment. The first combat-worthy model of the P-40 fighter (the P-40B) had begun production delivery in January 1941. An allocation was made from current production, and sent to San Diego for a repeat carrier-delivery attempt. Aircraft carrier USS *Enterprise* again provided ferrying duties, arriving on April 3 to load planes and sailing back to Pearl Harbor.

Airman Allison Ind passed through Hawaii on his ship taking him to the Philippines to become the intelligence officer for the Philippine Department Air Force. Arriving coincidentally just when *Enterprise* delivered her fighters, he described his experience: "Excitement for the Army at the Navy stronghold. A carrier has just come in with a full load of new P-40 types. They fly them right off the deck to the waiting hangars here at Wheeler. The first P-40s they've had. *Hum-m-m!* Wonder what the Philippines really have, if Hawaii is just getting her first 40s?"[4] By the end of April all of the promised planes had arrived and were organized into new fighter squadrons within the department's 14th Pursuit Wing based at Wheeler Field.

The bomber situation in Oahu also received attention, even if not with the same sense of urgency as the fighter problem. Marshall had told Stark that he was looking into providing at least a squadron of Flying Fortress bombers for Oahu. A full allocation of twenty-one B-17D bombers was prepared for transfer from the 19th Bombardment Group in California. The planes were transferred by a groundbreaking over-water flight, arriving on May 14, 1941. Some of these planes (along with eighteen of the B-18s stationed on Oahu) were subsequently transferred to the Philippines before the outbreak of war, but we will get to that situation later. Also in May a squadron of twelve new Douglas A-20A light bombers was shipped by conventional sea transport to the island.

Improvement in Oahu's anti-aircraft capability proved a harder situation to rectify. Production of anti-aircraft guns was at a particularly difficult stage.

The Army's heavy gun was the new 90-mm weapon; while an outstanding piece it was just beginning production. Outside of a few stateside regiments beginning training with the gun, there were none available for even as important a base as Hawaii (much less the Philippines, which also had submitted a request). The previous 3-inch anti-aircraft gun had in the meantime just ended production. While a few gun tubes were awaiting the supply of modernized carriages and sighting equipment, no quantity of "new" guns was available. In his February letter Marshall told Short that he had previously tried to scrounge up twenty 3-inch anti-aircraft guns to meet an urgent Navy request for batteries to protect the Asiatic Fleet's base at Cavite in Luzon. But even after the guns were eventually located, eighteen were handed over to the Marine Corps for the new defense battalions. While these heavy guns could provide some level of protection against high-level formations of enemy bombers, they did not have the rate of fire and quick traverse to allow them utility against low-flying single-engine planes (such as would be expected from a carrier-based attack). For this, heavy machine guns and one of the newer mid-range automatic cannons were needed. For the Army at this time that meant the 37-mm automatic anti-aircraft gun. Unfortunately the 37-mm also was experiencing a major bottleneck in production, and few guns and little ammunition were available. Taking what few guns were available, either from units just starting their training or from a small readiness task force, and sending them to a relatively isolated outpost was not wise.

Short requested 16 more heavy guns, 135 medium guns, 236 .50-caliber guns on anti-aircraft mounts, and 30 sound locators. Manpower was also a concern. At this time the Army's anti-aircraft organization was functionally within the Coast Artillery Corps. In Hawaii the coast defenders served dual responsibilities— not an unusual or unique situation. Many units had both a conventional seacoast defense assignment and an anti-aircraft assignment. Essentially Hawaii didn't have the crew for all its available weapons at the same time, and obviously asking for more guns would just exacerbate the problem. Short requested two more coast artillery regiments and two thousand filler personnel to activate parts of existing units.

Unfortunately for the defense, very few of the identified deficiencies in anti-aircraft matériel were corrected prior to the actual attack. The total anti-aircraft inventory in Hawaii available to the Army at the time of the attack was eighty-six 3-inch guns, twenty 37-mm guns, and 107 .50-caliber guns.[5] Hawaii fared better when it came to manpower. Two new anti-aircraft regiments were activated on Oahu, the 97th and 98th Coast Artillery Regiments

(AA). Drafts of fillers and trainees were sent to the island to fill these units. On multiple shipments in the summer and fall of 1941 the necessary artillerymen were sent. *President Coolidge* sailed on July 15 with 1,006, *President Pierce* brought 712 in August, *President Taft* another 382 later the same month, and more followed even later.[6] The two regiments were activated in July and October. There was still a major shortage of 37-mm and .50-caliber guns, but much of the most critical deficiencies in manpower had been made good.

The third component of the air defense equation was the request for a working air warning system. This meant a command structure, communications facilities (a radio network and operational procedures), and—most critically—radar. Ideally some sort of centralized interceptor command would be formed, tying the air-warning grid to the pursuit squadrons and anti-aircraft batteries. An island base is at a significant disadvantage with the old-style (air observer) type of warning system. When enemy planes are spotted overhead, they are at best just minutes from target with no time remaining to scramble interceptors or man and load anti-aircraft batteries. Only radar could provide the defenders a substantial measure of time to prepare for an attack. However, here again we encounter the same shortage in equipment and trained personnel. Radar was just entering production and usage in the armed forces, and few sets and fewer trained operators were available. Still Marshall and the War Plans Division did what they could to provide this capability for Oahu and specifically Pearl Harbor's defense.

The Hawaiian Department was soon authorized to receive three fixed and six mobile radar sets. Lieutenant General Short is quoted as saying this was "the most important single project in the department."[7] From August of 1940 it had funding to start its air warning service, but still lacked the sets and trained personnel to operate them. The initial equipment, after some delays, was received on June 3, 1941. One enthusiastic comparison noted that the previous sound-locator devices had a practical detection range of 4.5 miles, but the new detectors could reach out more than 120 miles. Even with, at long last, the right equipment and money for construction, problems plagued the radar installation project. An early 1940 survey board had selected three elevated sites (each the summit of a high, extinct volcano) for the best location of fixed sets in the island chain—Kokee on Kauai (4,285 feet), Mount Kaala on Oahu (4,000 feet), and Mount Haleakala on Maui (10,000 feet). These were to get the fixed SCR-271 sets, with six mobile SCR-270 sets at other locations.[8] In early 1941 work began on clearing and developing the sites for the fixed sets. On February 6 the Army asked permission from Secretary of the Interior Harold L. Ickes to begin work on the Maui site, actually on National Park Service property. They encountered institutional bureaucracy in its finest form. The park service would reluctantly grant temporary use of the land, but only upon seeing and approving detailed architectural plans. They would not endure a plan that was not compatible with the natural appearance of the park, or one that might spoil the view.[9] Negotiations dragged on for months. By late November the Maui site was done, Kauai's two-thirds completed, and Oahu's housing facilities just finished. As it turned out, the contentious Maui site was soon abandoned on account of having too much dead space.

On the morning of the attack none of the fixed sites were yet in operation. However, all six of the mobile stations were manned and operational at the "usual" time of 4 to 7 AM. Prevailing thought was that an enemy attack was most likely right at dawn, and with limited manpower the sets could only be operational for this window rather than continuously. Ten men were on station that morning at the new information center near Fort Shafter. At 7 AM five of the stations duly closed, but the one at Opana near Kahuku Point stayed operational on the initiative of its small staff in order to give themselves some additional training time. As chance would have it, they spotted the incoming Japanese first wave. After reporting it to the information center at 7:20, no further action was taken. The Japanese attack was misidentified as the B-17s expected from the mainland at about that same time. Admittedly the personnel at both the station and the information center were new and no one had any experience with this type of situation, but yet again the Japanese had a degree of luck on their side during this first day of the war.

The final elements of the Army's augmentation efforts compose a short shopping list of specific supply items or construction projects. Short asked in mid-February for improvement in his supply of .50-caliber ammunition.[10] With the lack of availability for the 37-mm automatic gun, the .50 was the only antiaircraft gun in the defenses capable of dealing with strafing attacks. The overall American supply was low, but several additional shipments were made to Oahu in the ensuing months. The Hawaiian Department also wanted money and a construction unit to push the building of fighter dispersal fields. In this case the requests seem like one of the easier ones to meet, not requiring any specialized piece of equipment or weapon. Still, the funds made available were insufficient. The 34th Engineer Combat Regiment was activated and stationed at Schofield Barracks in June 1941, and the 804th Engineer Company (Aviation) was expanded to battalion status in July.[11] Both units were under strength, though over one thousand engineer filler replacements arrived later in the fall. Another request for a general service engineer regiment was not actually provided until after the start of the war.

In pre-war 1941 reinforcement of the major combat ground units on Oahu was not considered urgent. The island's mobile defense consisted of an oversized division (the Hawaiian Division) and two Hawaii National Guard regiments. On August 1 the division was ordered to reorganize into two smaller triangular formations—becoming the 24th and 25th Divisions. Curiously it was thought that there was no urgency to complete the proposed expansion of these two divisions due to the presence of the fleet itself—that very presence would reduce the likelihood of any attack and thus lessen the need for ground troop augmentation.

The Navy's buildup on Oahu, besides the obvious basing of the fleet and needs for additional logistical construction to support it, was mostly restricted to enhancing the air component. Most urgent was the need for more patrol bombers. Two separate requirements were at hand: first, a goodly number of planes were needed to directly support the fleet. Squadrons of PBYs (the only modern patrol bomber then available to the service) were required to directly scout for the fleet and provide escort and anti-submarine patrols. In addition to Pearl Harbor, Navy war plans called for two squadrons to operate from outlying bases, initially one at Midway and another to be held at Pearl pending selection or creation of a base due to the fleet's advancement. In addition to the fleet patrol planes, Kimmel had asked for approximately one hundred patrol bombers to be assigned directly to the Fourteenth Naval District. These were intended to fly routine scouting patrols out of Pearl Harbor, plus perform local duties such as harbor entrance patrols and aerial escort for supply runs to the island bases. But like the Army, the Navy's supply of equipment and trained crews could not keep up with the demand. Only a fraction of the patrol planes reached Pearl Harbor prior to December 1941.[12]

Still, some planes were received. For example, Patrol Squadron 21 left San Diego for Pearl Harbor at the end of 1940, and the same base provided Patrol Squadron 14 for Kaneohe Bay on April 15, 1941. At least the planes did not require scarce transport space, as they made the voyage by direct flight. The increase in patrol plane numbers and activity overwhelmed the limited facilities on Pearl Harbor's Ford Island. The construction of a totally new naval seaplane base at Kaneohe Bay was pushed hard in the immediate pre-war months. On July 1, 1941 the Navy split its patrol assets in the Hawaiian Islands into two separate patrol wings—one to be based at Ford Island, the other at Kaneohe Bay (the 2nd and 1st PatWings respectively). However, to achieve centralized control and the best utilization of assets, Rear Adm. Patrick N. L. Bellinger directed the overall utilization of both wings.

One of the critical issues faced by the Navy was the state of training of patrol bomber crews. The rapid expansion of this wing had led to the acceptance of many relatively new pilots, crew members, and ground crew personnel. While they had completed training schools, the new recruits could only absorb the fine points of aircraft operation and servicing with carefully supervised training regimens. The optimal needs for training conflicted with those of active patrolling. Similarly, the physical toll on the aircraft and their engines by daily scouting usage was severe. The result was that just prior to the December attack the Navy's seventy-two PBY patrol bombers were not actively engaged in long-range scouting for any possible enemy approach. The fact was that these resources were both being held in readiness to serve their main purpose—at-sea fleet support—and being intensely trained to the standard that would be expected of them in combat service. In March of 1941 the Army and Navy local Hawaiian air commanders—Rear Admiral Bellinger commanding the patrol squadrons and Maj. Gen. Frederick L. Martin of the Hawaiian Army Air Command—reached a studied agreement about the coordination of long-range aircraft. However, neither service had the resources to implement the plan.

The Marine Corps was also active in relocating some of its forces due to the Navy's Pearl Harbor fleet basing decision. Elements of the Marines' defense battalions were already on a schedule to stage through Oahu, destined eventually for outlying bases. Development of the advance patrol bomber facilities at Wake, Midway, Johnston, and Palmyra benefited from a new sense of urgency. On May 7, 1940 the first defense battalion—the 3rd from Charleston, intended for Midway—arrived at Pearl Harbor on USS *Chaumont*. On February 15, 1941, advance elements of the 1st Defense Battalion were moved to Johnston and Palmyra Islands. The balance of the 1st Battalion arrived on the Navy transport *William P. Biddle* on February 27.[13] The 6th Defense Battalion was intended as a replacement for the 3rd on Midway. They arrived on July 22, 1941, followed by the 4th Battalion (intended for Wake) on several ships arriving in early December. At any given time there could be many hundreds of Marines of the defense battalions on Oahu; over two thousand members of this type of organization were present on December 7.[14] It was never intended that these units have an active role in Hawaiian defense; the Marines were present only as a result of the convenience of Oahu for garrisoning the men prior to their eventual transfer to existing or potentially new island bases.

The Marines had a long-term commitment to operating their own squadrons of aircraft in direct support of their mission. While mostly of just token size during much of the pre-war period, the Marine Corps air strength was rapidly expanding in 1940–41. In mid-1941 the service reorganized its units into separate East Coast and West Coast Marine Air Wings (MAW). While the 2nd MAW headquarters stayed at San Diego, most of its actual air squadrons were gradually formed and deployed either to Oahu or to the outlying Navy air stations. On January 11, 1941 aircraft carrier *Enterprise* brought out Marine Air Group 21 from San Diego to the newly established naval air station at Ewa, Oahu. The primary unit of this group was light bomber squadron VMB-2. Just before the war, part of Marine fighter squadron VMF-211 was delivered directly to Wake and part of another (VMSB-231) was caught in transit to Midway when the war began, while a third (VMF-221) waited for pickup by carrier in San Diego. Two squadrons and the remaining parts of the Wake and Midway contingents were all at Ewa and virtually destroyed during the December 7 Japanese attack.

The reinforcements sent to Hawaii in early 1941 seem barely enough to meet the critical role of the base as the new home of the Pacific Fleet. Altogether the Army was able to send about one hundred relatively modern planes, a handful of additional anti-aircraft guns and ammunition, a few radar sets, and a couple thousand of the most urgent personnel needs. The Navy already had the fleet present, of course (and periodically received new ships as they were being commissioned and readied), but besides sending a couple of additional patrol bomber squadrons did not otherwise reinforce Hawaii. Virtually all the Marine Corps units sent to Oahu in the year preceding the outbreak of war were just there prior to staging to advance bases farther beyond the Hawaiian Islands. However, despite the limited reinforcement, the military forces present in Hawaii were actually drawn down by transfers to theatres of higher priority.

President Roosevelt signed the Lend-Lease Act on March 11, 1941, starting a chain of events that would soon prompt a major diversion of strength from the Pacific to the Atlantic theatre. Until this time the Atlantic Fleet's major force had been in the Caribbean, but now CNO Admiral Stark ordered the creation of a new support force based in Norfolk. Both military secretaries advocated a transfer of additional ships to the Atlantic. While Roosevelt eventually supported this move, careful thought was given to Cordell Hull's concern about Japan's interpretation of the weakening of Pacific strength. On May 13 Roosevelt finally approved a significant transfer of ships. In anticipation, Stark had asked Kimmel on April 19 to ready aircraft carrier *Yorktown* and a destroyer squadron for immediate transfer. Next, three battleships (a division consisting of *Idaho, Mississippi*, and *New Mexico*), four light cruisers, and thirteen destroyers were organized to move via the Panama Canal to the Atlantic in late May. These actions in the spring of 1941 caused almost 25 percent of the Pacific Fleet's combat strength to be sent to an entirely different theatre.

Ironically it appears that the move wasn't really helpful to the Atlantic Fleet. The Germans' most significant surface threat, the battleship *Bismarck*, was on the bottom of the ocean by the first of June. American battleships and cruisers could be of little use combating German submarines. Admiral King was apparently thankful for the new ships, but admitted in his biography that what was needed was more and smaller surface escorts.[15] Even more surface ship transfers were discussed in Washington in June 1941, but the summer crisis in Japanese relations prevented any action on this last proposal. However, other transfers in Pacific waters were accomplished by making further drafts against the Hawaiian assets. In support of the decision by the Army (and fully supported by the president) to actively reinforce the Philippines, the Navy selected certain units and matériel to also send to the islands. Major surface units were not involved, but much of the modern submarine strength was sent from Hawaii to the Philippines in the last half of 1941.

CHAPTER THREE

Initial Reinforcements–September 1941

Army Chief of Staff Gen. George C. Marshall was personally involved in many of the Philippine reinforcement issues. The chief presided over the decisions of the War Plans Division and represented the Army at joint service issues and at the Joint Board.

Born the same year (1880) as Douglas MacArthur, George Catlett Marshall was a 1901 graduate of the Virginia Military Institute. Commissioned as a second lieutenant in the infantry in 1902, like MacArthur his first major assignment was in the Philippines, with the 30th Infantry Regiment. His second tour of duty in the Philippines was from 1913 to 1916, where he wound up as an aide to the department commander. In the First World War he went to Europe with the 1st Division and also exercised a logistics role with the First Army. After an assignment in China, he returned in 1927 to the Army War College as a lieutenant colonel. In 1938 he headed the War Plans Division, did a brief tour in 1939 to Brazil, and was named on September 1, 1939 as a major general (with the position's temporary rank of four-star general) as Army chief of staff. Marshall was adept at maneuvering in Washington's political environment. He provided a strong, even direction to the service through the entire war period, and made even greater contributions to the reconstruction of Europe after the war. While not particularly fond of Douglas MacArthur, Marshall did recognize the strengths of that individual and at times even acted as a buffer between him and the other services, and the administration. His grasp of the overall needs of the Army permitted him to exercise good judgment on balancing men and matériel needs from all quarters.

One of the consistent demands from the Philippines in the pre-war years was for significant augmentation of its anti-aircraft capability. Only a single anti-aircraft regiment had been assigned to the Philippines—the 60th Coast Artillery Regiment (AA). Its collection of fixed and mobile 3-inch guns and .50-caliber machine guns were all deployed around the fixed harbor defenses on the fortified islands of Manila Bay. There were no Army guns for coverage of the naval base at Cavite or for the other Army posts and airfields, much less for Manila itself. As one of the earliest steps of the new reinforcement policy, this deficiency was addressed. On July 31, 1941 the War Department approved plans for sending an entire National Guard anti-aircraft regiment.

On August 14 the anti-aircraft regiment was listed as one of the four additional items needed to allow a successful defense of the Philippines.[1] Selected for transfer was the 200th Coast Artillery Regiment (AA) at Fort Bliss, Texas. In its anti-aircraft form, the unit was organized on July 1, 1940, and inducted into federal service on January 6, 1941. Most of its personnel were drawn from New Mexico; for a state with a very small population, this single unit represented a considerable part of its military contribution. The regiment was organized into two battalions, each with four batteries. One battery was for searchlights, three of heavy anti-aircraft guns (twelve of these guns total), one of .50-caliber guns, and three of new 37-mm automatic anti-aircraft guns (twenty-four guns of this type total). Col. Charles G. Sage received orders to prepare to move his unit on August 17. Just five days later, on the twenty-second, the 1st Battalion boarded rail cars for the journey to San Francisco. The balance of the regiment followed on the thirty-first. Total strength was seventy-seven officers and 1,732 enlisted men. In terms of manpower it was the largest single unit received by the Philippines prior to the start of war.

One of the continuing questions on the reinforcement effort was the combat readiness of the units selected. Some authors have suggested that the units sent to the Philippines were poorly trained and equipped with obsolete equipment. Perhaps that opinion formed because many were National Guard units, some of which later had problems reaching the proficiency level of regular units. Certainly in the available Army correspondence there is no evidence that any criteria besides the relative readiness (in terms of training, troop strength, and completeness of equipment) were considered. The War Plans Division regularly assigned units that were from a relatively short list of "ready," without regard to Army status (regular or National Guard) or home station, and usually not with regard to type of equipment. In several cases the units traded out older model weapons for more modern ones. In other situations changes were made so the armament would be consistent with what was already present or supportable in the Philippines. This was the case with the 200th, which did not take the newly adopted 90-mm M1 anti-aircraft gun it had recently acquired. These were traded out for the still-standard 3-inch anti-aircraft guns. The rationale provided was that the 90-mm was still experiencing production problems, particularly with ammunition and fire-control fixtures.

Certainly in the eyes of the members of the National Guard units, there was no feeling of being Army second-class citizens. In fact, repeatedly the memoirs of the members point with pride to the fact that their particular unit was specifically selected for the Philippines because of its outstanding performance record. A member of a Texas National Guard field artillery battalion wrote after the 1941 maneuvers: "The army had plans for starting some sort of a new combat group, and the highest scoring field artillery battalion out of the two armies was to receive overseas assignment."[2] A soldier in the 200th Coast Artillery described the situation as follows: "Army officials . . . had officially named the 200th the best anti-aircraft regiment (regular or otherwise) now available to the United States Armed Forces; therefore, they had been selected for an overseas assignment of great importance."[3] The men of the two National Guard tank battalions sent made similar statements. However, there is no evidence that the Army specifically chose units based solely on their maneuver performances. All soldiers are proud of their units, and those who also survived the hardship of four years as POWs were naturally convinced that their particular unit was the Army's "best." Still, it is clear that Army staff selected some of the most prepared, best-trained units it could under the circumstances, and it is not a surprise that these same units did very well in training and maneuver circumstances.

Shipping constraints led to the division and separate shipment of the two anti-aircraft battalions. The 1st Battalion was selected to ship over on USAT *Hugh L. Scott*, while the 2nd Battalion and the rest of the regiment went slightly later on USAT *President Coolidge.* Perhaps realizing the inconsistency of providing escort to their own transports to Manila but not the same for Army vessels, the Navy finally addressed the need for a uniform policy. Initially the Navy hoped (on August 18) that escorts would not be needed for either *Hugh L. Scott* or *President Coolidge*—that routing through the Gilbert Islands and then to the Torres Straits would be sufficient protection. Thought was given to having the Asiatic Fleet provide escort for the last thousand miles if such was considered necessary. Within five days the Navy had a change of heart; they offered to provide a cruiser escort from Hawaii to the Philippines.

With this escort (and perhaps some sense of urgency about the cargo's delivery) the direct course through the Mariana Islands was reinstated. The Navy assigned light cruiser *Phoenix* to this duty, with the temporary designation of Task Force 14.

Hugh L. Scott arrived in Honolulu on September 2—but for just enough time to let off passengers, refuel, and quickly load some new special passengers, leaving again later that same evening. The new arrivals were one officer and 174 enlisted men of the 14th Bomb Squadron's ground echelon that was even then crossing the Pacific on the inaugural flight of the Pacific ferry route. On the fourth light cruiser USS *Phoenix* took up station one thousand yards off the starboard quarter, and the two were soon under way. The experience as an Army passenger on one of these journeys must have at the time seemed surreal. Most of the written accounts by surviving POWs after the war (and there are many) spend several pages explaining their experiences on the ship going to Manila. For many of the young men this was their first exposure to international travel; while there are individual differences, the highlights have much in common. After initial excitement and adventure in locating their "bunk," the trip settled into a routine. Some pulled daily watch duty, but most just watched the endless sea, the oddly colored flying fish, and sought refuge in card games of every sort. The swells off San Francisco were notorious; many encountered (either as observer or victim) their first real case of seasickness. While the stay of *Hugh L. Scott* in Honolulu was just measured in hours, a few lucky fellows got shore leave. The reputation of Waikiki Beach and the hotels adjacent (and not too much farther the restaurants, bars, and brothels) was irresistible. Most of the published accounts recall vividly just how those few hours were spent, down to the details of what was eaten in which restaurant. Everyone was glad to see the verdant green of land upon entering the San Bernardino Strait. Even more impressive was the first glimpse of the fortress of Corregidor—where some of the replacement fillers were destined. And then Pier 7 in Manila and the adjacent Manila Hotel, Army and Navy Club, and Dewey Boulevard assaulted the senses. Humidity, tropical weather, strange clothing, a diverse population—all added to the new perceptions.[4]

Before continuing the story with the voyage of *President Coolidge*, the next increment of Philippine reinforcement needs to be described. The same July 31, 1941 letter from the War Plans Division to General MacArthur (apparently an update for him of the status of reinforcement efforts—note it was sent just days after his recall to active service) also promised that a light tank company

Table 1. September 1941 Shipments to the Philippines[5]

Convoy/Ships/Speed/Escort/Dates/Route	Units and Major Cargo Items
Task Force 14 USAT *Hugh L. Scott* 17 knots Escort: USS *Phoenix* Depart SF 8/28/41 Arrive Manila 9/16/41 Direct route through Marianas	1st Battalion, 200th Coast Artillery 14th Bomb Squadron (H) ground echelon (from Hawaii) Replacement and filler personnel Total about 1,100 officers and men
Task Force 17 USAT *President Coolidge* USS *Guadalupe* 17 knots Escort: USS *Astoria* Depart SF 9/08/41 Arrive 9/26/41 Direct route through Marianas	200th Coast Artillery (AA) (–1st Battalion) 194th Tank Battalion (two companies) (includes 54 M3 tanks) 17th Ordnance Company Total about 2,000 officers and men (including 223 fillers) Six PT boats
SS *American Press* Unescorted Depart SF 9/08/41 Arrive 9/29/41 Direct route through Marianas	50 P-40Es 67 vehicles
SS *Yaka* Unescorted Depart SF 9/17/41 Arrive Manila about 10/16/41 Direct route through Marianas	25 T-12 75-mm self-propelled half-track mounts 2 seacoast 12-in gun tubes 97 vehicles Ammunition, grenades, tank parts, 3,096 empty gasoline drums, lumber, rope, airplane engines, blankets, tents, roofing paper, raincoats, subsistence, refrigerated food Dropped 36 quartermaster vehicles in Hawaii on 9/25/41

would be sent on the first available transport. It appears that Washington was trying to address the deficiencies that existed due to new or recently proven tactical innovations—improved defense against airplanes (the new anti-aircraft regiment along with the previously sent air-warning company) and now against tanks. No American tanks of any sort existed in the islands; in fact, the only armored vehicles present were a handful of White M3 scout cars with the 26th Cavalry Regiment. The only anti-tank guns were a total of just nine M3 37-mm guns with only enough ammunition for short periods of training. The Japanese had employed tanks widely in the Chinese theatre and it was reasonable to think they would be used in any attempted landing.

In retrospect the Army, in particular the War Plans Division, was doing exactly the right thing. The highest priority it gave to Philippine reinforcements was for addressing the two newest kings of the battlefield. Improvements for the infantry arm or even artillery were not as immediately fulfilled. Rather the two weapon systems emerging as decisive military inventions in the new European war were aircraft and tanks. The units and weapons sent in the first few months of Philippine reinforcement included useful quantities of strategic bombers (B-17s), defensive interceptors (P-40s), modern anti-aircraft units and guns (the 200th Coast Artillery with its 3-inch and 37-mm guns), and technically advanced radar sets. Offensive units of tanks (two National Guard battalions using the best light tank then made by the United States—the M3) and anti-tank 75-mm self-propelled mounts were also rushed to MacArthur. For a country not yet experiencing the effect of these weapon systems firsthand, and under great pressure to produce and distribute them wisely to its own forces and foreign allies, the decisions made were technically correct.

The request for a tank unit had originated with the Philippine Department. They went so far as to say that if a battalion (usually four companies totaling about seventy-two tanks) was not available, they would settle for the equipment and activate the unit from Filipino troops. The light M3 tank, later popularly known as the Stuart, was in quantity production at the time. While there were heavy demands for American tanks both for the expansion of the armored force and in lend-lease requests, it was thought safe to offer a company of fifteen to seventeen tanks. Soon the allocation jumped dramatically from one company of seventeen tanks to two battalions and over one hundred tanks.

The first unit slated for transfer was the 194th Tank Battalion. This was a National Guard unit pulling men from several states. The 194th was a General Headquarters independent tank battalion, tracing its lineage to the companies that had been organized in California, Minnesota, Missouri, and Washington. However, "D" Company was never formed, and in 1941 "B" Company was lost to an Alaskan assignment. The 194th had been notified of a change in its permanent duty assignment on August 14, and quickly moved to San Francisco. The battalion had trained on the older M2A2 light tank, but would receive M3s stripped from a newly forming armored division. Even though only two companies of men were along, the battalion received the tanks and other vehicles for the phantom "B" Company.[6] Peculiarly, orders had come down that the men and their tanks must be loaded on the same ship. Apparently someone in Washington thought there might be a chance that the contents of this ship alone might have to go into combat, and wanted the men with their tanks together. The configuration of *President Coolidge* would allow the loading of the tanks only if nineteen of them had their turrets temporarily removed, and that was done.[7]

Another small unit moving with the 194th was the 17th Ordnance Company. This was a unit specifically trained in tank maintenance, and was meant to support both tank battalions being sent to the Philippines. Organizationally they could be incorporated into a small provisional tank group with the two battalions—which is exactly what happened when war started. As otherwise there were no tanks in the Philippines and thus no other expertise to exploit, their inclusion was a godsend to the tankers. Even with the problem encountered prior to sailing, getting the turrets off the tanks, they quickly took over and made it happen smoothly.

USAT *President Coolidge* was making her second round-trip to Manila on behalf of the Army Transportation Service. The backlog of men and equipment scheduled to go to the Philippines was now considerable, and there was no problem in filling this large ship's passenger quarters and equipment holds. Some help was provided in finding room for personnel by the War Department's decision in late July to stop allowing passage of dependent spouses and children on Army transports. Still, the movement of the major units in early September 1941 required three vessels. In addition to the transports, more equipment had to move separately on the commercial freighter SS *American Press. President Coolidge* departed the San Francisco Port of Embarkation about 9 PM on September 8, 1941. The usual half-day stop in Honolulu and a relatively good speed combined with good weather allowed her to arrive in Manila eighteen days later, on September 26, just ten days after *Scott.* The operational order of September 11 created as escort Task Force 17; the rationale for escorting remained the same—the alleged presence of German raiders in the Pacific. In fact, postwar records reveal that *no* German raiders operated in the Pacific after March 1941. For the first time the Navy allocated a heavy rather than light cruiser for the escort duty.[8] No specific rationale for this change is given, but perhaps it was due to the fact that for the first time two important ships, rather than one, were to be escorted.

The Navy took the opportunity with this schedule to include the journey of USS *Guadalupe* to Manila. Tanker journeys carrying fuel to the Asiatic Fleet were not unusual, but on this occasion the oiler was also carrying six U.S. Navy PT boats and crew. These belonged to Motor Torpedo Boat Squadron 3, commanded by Lt. (jg) John D. Bulkeley. The tanker had loaded the six boats at berth no. 12 of the Brooklyn Naval Yard on August 16. The following day she completed loading and storing the twenty-four torpedoes and warheads needed as armament for the boats. A long voyage started three days later that would take her through the Panama Canal to Wilmington, California for gasoline and bunker oil, and then eventually to Pearl Harbor on September 9. There gasoline was discharged and a crane alongside removed the torpedoes for charging and overhaul; she was ready to travel again on September 12.

Astoria and *Guadalupe* left Pearl Harbor on September 13, managing 17.5–18 knots. After meeting up with *President Coolidge* at sea, the uneventful voyage to Manila ended on September 26. A postwar published history of *Astoria* contains an officer's recollection of the trip: "The tanker had Buckley's [*sic*] PT boats mounted on deck. The transports were loaded with troops, tanks, and other military equipment. We stood wartime condition watches on the way out and back. I remember the tanks clanking down the piers night and day. . . . [O]n the way back the *Henderson* evacuated all the dependents from the Philippines and Guam."[9] *Guadalupe* discharged fuel over the next couple of days and then she departed Manila Bay for the long voyage back east. Light cruiser *Phoenix*, which had recently escorted *Hugh L. Scott* to the islands, met *Guadalupe* east of San Bernardino Strait and provided escort as far as Pearl Harbor. *Astoria* returned to Pearl Harbor escorting *Henderson*. The pattern was coming into place that a returning cruiser would escort for the trip back the transport from one or two voyages previous. The returning pair left Manila on October 12 and got back to Pearl Harbor October 30.

The men of the 200th Coast Artillery on board *President Coolidge* disembarked on the twenty-sixth as soon as the ship berthed. They were met by an appropriate greeting party and then whisked that same day to their new home at Camp Stotsenburg. This camp was immediately adjacent to Clark Field, one of the sites in urgent need of anti-aircraft protection. Likewise the 194th and 17th went by bus also to Camp Stotsenburg. That is, except for a detail to supervise the proper unloading and reassembly of the tanks and half-tracks of these units over the next few days.

A U.S. Maritime Commission chartered freighter left San Francisco the same day as *President Coolidge*, but did not join the escorted convoy. SS *American Press* was a slower freighter, and not compatible for convoying with the faster *Coolidge* and *Guadalupe*. Still, proceeding directly with good progress, she arrived in Manila on September 29. On board were many vehicles for the units just delivered. Most importantly, *American Press* carried fifty new P-40E fighters. The struggle to secure a quantity of these planes for the Philippines is illustrative of the difficulties of supply facing the Army in the immediate pre-war days.

Since the decision to actively defend the Philippines had been made, Marshall and the planners sought to modernize the fighter defenses. The problem was that there were competitive demands for the just one type in production for American rearmament and foreign lend-lease. The first P-40 pursuits had been produced in 1940, and by mid-year 1941 about 100–150 fighters per month were coming off the production line at the plant in Buffalo, New York. Altogether 2,246 planes of this type were made in 1941, though with the majority being exported, the U.S. inventory at year end was something just over seven hundred. In late summer Roosevelt insisted that Russia be supplied fighters as quickly as America could provide them. In his own words, Marshall told Arnold that he was unalterably opposed to the release of fighter planes until there were established units of this type in the Philippine Islands. Marshall and the Army in fact had four demands pulling on the same small supply of fighters—the Philippines, an urgent need for training of frontline U.S.-based units, a supply held in readiness for basing in Brazil, and needs for the Chinese volunteer group. The batch of fifty new P-40Es (the first of this type was just delivered on August 29) included with *American Press* represented a real juggling effort of the supply situation—and was indicative of the new, increased priority for the islands' defenders.

On July 30 a staff memo revealed that besides the situation with tanks, the Army for some time had discussed the need to provide the overseas departments with more capability for anti-tank warfare. It was realized that any invasion would probably see a superior number of tanks deployed against the defending forces. Coincidentally the Army had been developing an interim self-propelled anti-tank weapon. Stemming from a meeting with the ordnance department in June, a successful matching of the M3 half-track with the standard 75-mm field gun had been developed. The Autocar Company produced an evaluation quantity of thirty-six mounts, designated as the T-12 gun motor carriage, in August and September 1941. Inquiries found that twenty-five additional units could be added by September 1, and 125 by the end of the month. The War Plans Division ordered that fifty more be fabricated without delay and sent to the Philippines—the first twenty-five on a freighter scheduled for September 16, the balance to follow. No special anti-tank ammunition was available, but there were over 600,000 general rounds of the necessary size in the islands already. Besides, the main secondary role of the gun would be beach defense, and high explosive rounds were just fine for that.[10]

As mentioned above, just one day later (July 31), MacArthur was advised that these mounts were in line for shipment. The transport schedule that best fit the availability of the new mounts was SS *Yaka.* This commercial vessel, with a contract for a heavy military cargo, departed San Francisco for Honolulu and Manila on September 17. The guidelines of this date allowed her to sail unescorted, and by the direct route west from Honolulu. A month later that would not have been the situation. The 75-mm self-propelled mounts were sent with spare parts, but they were not accompanied by any organized unit. Even individual drivers, gunners, or other crew members were not sent to the Philippines; all along these were thought of as simply artillery pieces for the Far Eastern forces to use as they would. *If* they were to be organized into succinct units, then that would be done with MacArthur's Filipino troops and not specifically designated American soldiers. SS *Yaka* began her return departure from Iloilo on November 2, and ultimately reached the United States without interference.

The availability of 37-mm anti-tank guns and ammunition is discussed in these same documents. In early 1941 the tables of equipment called for eighteen such guns per infantry regiment. The assistant chief of staff observed that as the Philippines were scheduled for independence in 1946, it was questionable that any military equipment in the hands of U.S. forces would ever be returned. It would be turned over to the Philippine government, probably even without compensation. As the guns were badly needed for training with other active units, it was considered unwise to supply the Philippines any of them. Obviously this concern was virtually ignored in the latter half of 1941, but the attitude expressed does help explain why the rearmament gap was so wide.[11] In any event before the war the Philippine Department only received a grand total of nine of the new 37-mm anti-tank guns. Though the guns were used mostly for training, matters were made even worse by an almost total lack of ammunition even for this small a number of cannon. In April 1941 the department requested 50,000 rounds of armor-piercing ammunition, along with as many of the guns it was deficient as possible. None could be shipped. Finally it was recommended that 24,000 37-mm anti-tank rounds be dispatched. This would be enough to supply one thousand rounds each for the prospective fifteen light tanks and the nine anti-tank guns already there.

By far the largest unit reinforcement discussed prior to the outbreak of the war was for an entire infantry division. Apparently this idea originated solely with the Army in Washington; no separate Philippine correspondence requesting this type of unit has come to light. Brigadier General Gerow of the War Department staff expressed in a mid-August memo that reasonable success in defending the Philippines would require reinforcements of a composite air wing, a new anti-aircraft regiment, additional harbor defense troops, and an infantry division. On behalf of the staff he recommended to Marshall that, pending clarification of the National Guard status overseas and the availability of shipping, a National Guard infantry division be dispatched. Gerow ventured to state that the 41st Infantry Division, home stationed at Camp Lewis, Washington, was finishing its training, essentially completely equipped, and available in September to send abroad.[12]

However, the shipping requirements for this division and the similarly timed anti-aircraft regiment were a daunting obstacle. Together these two units represented something like 20,000 men and 150,000 ship tons of space (for the units, their equipment, initial supplies, and ninety days' worth of maintenance supplies). Immediately the Army's transportation chief chimed in with an innovative scheme to find the necessary shipping. The Navy was just taking possession of three very large troop transports, former private liners. If the Army could secure the necessary priority for their use for two round-trip journeys to the Philippines, and add the large *President Coolidge* for the second trip, the movement could be made. Col. Charles P. Gross, chief of transportation on Marshall's staff, proposed that USS *Wakefield*, USS *Mount Vernon*, and USS *West Point* could be ready as soon as September 5 to begin such a voyage. After a quick return (all three of these ships could manage over twenty-one knots) the same three plus *President Coolidge* could make a second trip starting on October 12. Each of these ships was capable of carrying over three thousand men with their personal equipment, thus seven loads would translate to the 20,000-man capacity required. However, even then additional Navy or Maritime Commission charters would be required for another 36,000 ship tons of freight belonging to the units. One factor in their favor was that the division in question was temporarily at San Luis Obispo, California, as the result of recent maneuvers. It would not have to make much of a move, and could be quartered relatively close and thus not overwhelm the facilities in San Francisco Bay.

Marshall approved Gerow's Philippine reinforcement memo on August 15, though the reference to the dispatch of an entire division had been deleted. For just about the first and only time in this saga, Gen. Douglas MacArthur vetoed an offer of substantial reinforcement. Apparently at this time he was more in need of matériel than troops, and had a strong preference for using the available shipping for this rather than a division. He is quoted as saying: "Equipment and supply of existing forces are the prime essential. . . . I am confident if these steps are taken with sufficient speed that no further major reinforcement will be necessary for accomplishment of defense mission."[13] It is not clear if MacArthur was aware of the special availability of the newly commissioned naval transports for this movement, and that these ships were not otherwise available for "routine" Pacific traffic. Perhaps he assumed that receiving an entire division would totally interrupt his schedule of specialized forces and supplies otherwise already slated for transport. Admittedly Marshall hadn't put the suggestion in the most positive way: "This involves heavy demand on shipping in view of tremendous obligations in Atlantic. It also involves serious convoy problem with jeopardy to naval craft passing mandate bases. It further involves future heavy tonnage requirements for supply to Philippines and probability of this being rendered impracticable."[14] MacArthur was by this time (with the mobilizing Philippine Army) not short of manpower, though he could have used more trained soldiers, and better equipment for those he already had.

In an interesting historical turn, several of the Navy ships lined up as potential transporters of this unit did in fact take an Allied infantry division to fight the Japanese in the Far East. Within two weeks of MacArthur's refusal of the offer, Roosevelt received a note from Winston Churchill. The British wished to reinforce the Middle East with two regular British divisions (about 40,000 men) but did not have the shipping available. The prime minister asked the president to lend ships to accomplish this from early October to February. Churchill thought the early movement of this force could help dissuade Turkey from entering the war and also sustain Russia's continued resistance. Roosevelt quickly and positively endorsed this request, and set Maritime Commissioner Vice Adm. Emory S. Land to finding the shipping required. The newly acquired Navy liners, just previously earmarked for the Pacific division movement, were perfect.[15]

On September 26 a Navy operational memo outlined a plan to use the six new naval transports to implement the administration's scheme. Two naval task groups were formed as Task Force 14 to serve with the Naval Transport Service. Politically this was a most interesting initiative. The United States was still a non-belligerent in the war. Despite our actions of supplying lend-lease and positioning troops in Iceland and the new Atlantic and Caribbean bases obtained from the British, the direct transport of British soldiers on American naval vessels, escorted by American warships, was a new step. It was another example where the American administration was aiding the anti-Axis nations just short of armed conflict. Still, the domestic mood, at least in Congress, was touchy. The offer and ultimate usage of American ships for this transfer was conducted in serious secrecy. It received no publicity at the time, and even after the war the journey has received only the briefest historical reporting. President Roosevelt was trying to obtain a congressional modification to the Neutrality Act at the same time this offer was floated. He thought that the loss of an American transport in British waters would negatively affect congressional opinion. It was found best for the British to first send their troops to Halifax, so the American ships could avoid European waters and only be required for the long journey around Africa. These changes were posted on October 20, with a new sailing date targeted for November 3.[16]

The American task force was to journey to Halifax to pick up the 20,800 officers and men of a British division bound for the Middle East. Most of these were organic to the 18th Division, plus some other minor anti-tank and anti-aircraft units. The Americans were basically carrying just the troops and their personal baggage; most of the heavy equipment was sailing on British freighters. The convoy was now scheduled to leave Halifax on November 9, and touch at Trinidad and Cape Town. Escort was provided by an American task force. Accommodations reflected the unusual legal status of the events. For example, the British enlisted troops were to be fed by the Americans but the expense charged to lend-lease. On the other hand, the British officers could not so qualify, and were to be charged $1.50 per day for meals plus a monthly charge for laundry and mess facilities. All troops were carried as supernumeraries.

The six transports were sent to Halifax and loaded on November 8 and 9. The three big liners each took on essentially an entire infantry brigade, of over five thousand men each. *West Point* also had a small 100-man American field service company destined to operate a logistical center in Persia. Convoy WS-12X departed Halifax on November 10, with the small carrier USS

Ranger, heavy cruisers USS *Quincy* and USS *Vincennes*, oiler USS *Cimmaron*, and eight destroyers as escort. The carrier and two destroyers returned after a short stop at Trinidad. The convoy arrived on December 9 at Cape Town, just after news had reached them of the disastrous attack of December 7. Very quickly the British decided that the ships should go as reinforcements to Singapore rather than the Middle East, and the Americans agreed to the new routing. The majority of the convoy was thus re-routed to Bombay and three weeks later USS *Wakefield* and USS *West Point*, along with three smaller British transports, were sent on to Singapore. The troops and equipment were unloaded quickly, though not fast enough to prevent *Wakefield* from taking a bomb during an aerial attack on December 30. Five men were killed, but the structural damage was limited and didn't prevent the American ships from departing later that same day. On their way out they embarked hundreds of evacuees.

Also, though USS *Wakefield* was lightly damaged in Singapore, all six of the important transports eventually made it back to the United States. Some of them, though, had been unavailable for the movement of American personnel for something like eight months. The movement, in fact, casts an interesting parallel to the story of the *Pensacola* convoy soon to be related. While the British were fortunate to have a large, fully equipped force at sea at a critical turn of events, it ultimately did them little good. The British defense of Singapore collapsed on February 8, 1942. The 18th Division, after a most fortuitous arrival from a very complex shipping situation, went almost directly into Japanese prisoner of war camps.

CHAPTER FOUR

Philippine Reinforcements—October 1941

To base significant numbers of heavy bombers in the Philippines, three critical elements were needed. First, the B-17s themselves were transferred by flying across the Pacific on the newly opened ferry route. Second, the ground elements of this group moved by conventional Army sealift. Third, since the need for runways and airbases had rapidly grown beyond the capability of the aviation engineer company shipped from Hawaii during the summer, an entire specialized aviation engineer battalion was sent with the task of working exclusively on air base development. Together these elements would hopefully provide the islands with the new offensive capabilities (and thus deterrence value) Washington hoped for.

Specialized Army Corps of Engineers units for aviation facilities were quite new. Intended for the construction of airfields, they were expected to be combat rather than just service units. The basic aviation engineer unit was organized as a battalion—about the right size to build a single airfield in a reasonable amount of time. At full strength the battalion would have a headquarters and three companies. Heavy equipment (such as bulldozers, graders, and rollers) was to be fully authorized for the anticipated tasks. Battalions were initially given unit numbers in the "800s." Six such battalions were formed during the summer of 1941 and some quickly dispatched to overseas departments like Alaska, Hawaii, and Panama. The 803rd Engineer Aviation Battalion (Sep) was activated on July 7, 1941 at Westover Field, Massachusetts.[1] It was formed with a headquarters, headquarters' company, and just two of its line companies—"A" and "B." After a few months of training, orders were received on September 12 for special overseas movement. It had most of its heavy engineering equipment, but lacked something like 70 percent of the required trucks and other motor transport—these were to be issued to the unit as soon as was practical. Movement began quickly: the heavy equipment moved out by train on September 18, the men from Westover departed three days later. The total strength at departure was a little less than planned—464 enlisted men, including attached medical personnel.

Establishment of a full bombardment group in the Philippines demanded infrastructure far beyond just the immediate planes and crews. Until 1941 the total air-strength of the department rested in the 4th Composite Group. This was a mixed unit containing bomber, fighter, and observation aircraft for a station that could not justify separate groups dedicated to just one mission type. The 150 or so total aircraft of the department were supported by a slim but appropriate service organization. Also at Nichols Field the department had an air depot that could assemble aircraft shipped in by boat and perform certain other heavy maintenance repairs beyond the capabilities of the air units themselves. When expansion of the air forces came, it was of course necessary to also expand the supporting administrative and maintenance units. The only source of trained, skilled mechanics and service personnel for the Air Force units was to transfer existing stateside units and equipment intact. The establishment of a full bombardment group of heavy B-17 bombers thus required supplying the group's personnel, and the service base units normally associated with such a unit. Meanwhile, in the Philippines on September 26, the old group was replaced by the newly created 24th Pursuit Group. The 28th Bombardment Squadron remained at Clark to be integrated into the new bombardment group being transferred from the mainland.[2]

The new bomber formation was the 19th Bombardment Group. The main flight of B-17s and flight crews began their journey from California on October 16, but before that the ground elements of the 19th Group were sent by Army transport to their new home in the Philippines. After the usual stay at San Francisco's Fort McDowell on Angel Island, the units boarded their transports for the journey west in early October 1941. Altogether almost 1,800 airmen were relocated.

Additionally at this time over three hundred filler personnel for a variety of Philippine-based units required immediate transportation. The movement of this relatively large allotment of troops and men—over 2,100 men—required the Army and Navy to carefully select and schedule their limited resources. Veteran Army Transport Service troopships *Willard A. Holbrook* and *Tasker H. Bliss* would carry the personnel, and Army freighter *Liberty* would carry some of the heavy equipment. Even this lineup did not prove adequate, and much of the motor transport of the units followed later in two chartered freighters. In addition to the aviation engineer battalion and bomber group ground echelon, other important items were included. The bombers would need bombs, of course. Over 1,500 tons of bombs of various sizes were ordered shipped to the Benicia Arsenal to be held for the convoy. Finally the Philippine Army was to receive the complete equipment of an anti-aircraft regiment (less the twelve heavy 3-inch anti-aircraft guns slated for shipment later), and this equipment was waiting in San Francisco for this convoy. Extra space in the three ships was used for the long list of supplies requisitioned by the U.S. and Philippine armies and available at the port of embarkation. Also in the mid-October shipments the next five 75-mm self propelled mounts were sent. The particular ship used for these has not been identified, but the large-sized hatches on *Liberty* could well have proved useful once again.

Even before the shipment of the 200th Coast Artillery, discussions occurred between Manila and Washington about the wisdom of dispatching anti-aircraft units to the Far East. MacArthur originally proposed that just the equipment be sent, and that units could be formed from Filipino troops to man these guns. However, the urgent need to provide protection to the newly expanding air force in the department put that idea away—only trained, ready anti-aircraft men could be effective in the limited time available. Still, as follow-on to the dispatch of the 200th, the idea of providing the complete equipment for a semi-mobile anti-aircraft regiment was kept alive. On the convoy of early October were scheduled most of the organizational equipment for an anti-aircraft regiment. The only things missing were the 3-inch anti-aircraft guns and searchlights. Soon, these too were found. Commercial freighter *Coast Shipper* brought out the twelve required searchlight trucks in October. While only 501 3-inch mobile anti-aircraft guns were in the U.S. inventory in early 1941 (and production was being curtailed in favor of the new 90-mm gun), twelve were located from various units in time to be shipped on *American Packer*, along with six more 37-mm automatic guns, for arrival on November 18. By the end of November the full "kit" necessary to form a third anti-aircraft regiment in the islands was complete, just minus any trained personnel. The matériel was duly stored in Manila at the Philippine Department's ordnance storage depot in Fort Santiago.

The Twelfth Naval District addressed the need for cruiser escort. Routing instructions were prepared for the ships, and assignments made for a naval communications liaison unit to accompany each. The two large transports received a unit of one officer, four signalmen, and four radiomen; the

Table 2. October 1941 Shipments to the Philippines[3]

Convoy/Ships/Speed/Escort/Dates/Route (Data where available)	**Units and Major Cargo Items**
Task Force 11, convoy no. 2001 USAT *Tasker H. Bliss* USAT *Willard A. Holbrook* 16 knots Escort: USS *Chester* Depart SF 10/04/41 Arrive Manila 10/23/41 Direct route through Marianas	803rd Engineer Battalion (Avn) (–Company C) 19th Bomb Group HQ and HQ Squadron 30th, 93rd Bomb Squadron (H) 7th Matériel Squadron, Company C 33rd QM Regiment (Truck) 2nd Platoon, Company C 809th QM Regiment (LM) 440th, 680th, 701st, 724th Ordnance Company (B) 3rd Dct, 3rd Chemical Company 126th Base Hospital Vehicles, medical supplies, subsistence, refrigerated subsistence, troop property, mine equipment, post exchange goods, small arms, clothing, general military stores and supplies Total of 2,594 officers and men (including 333 fillers)
Task Force 18 USAT *Liberty* 10 knots Escort: USS *Portland* Depart SF 10/04/41 Arrived Manila 11/11/41 Southern route through Torres Strait	3,500 500-lb bombs Signal Corps equipment, small arms, ammunition, CWS supplies, subsistence, clothing, troop property, household goods, mine equipment, trucks, and trailers
MV *Perida* 16 knots, unescorted Depart SF 9/25/41 Due Manila about 11/21/41	43 trucks and prime movers, numerous trailers 1,750 fiber locker trunks 1,781 cartons shoes
MV *Pennant* 16 knots, unescorted Due Manila about 10/19/41	186 vehicles 1,146 packages clothing, rubber boots, shoes, lockers, 12,074 rolls roofing paper, 800 boxes gas masks, structural steel, steel rails

Table 2. October 1941 Shipments to the Philippines[3] (*Continued*)

Convoy/Ships/Speed/Escort/Dates/Route (Data where available)	Units and Major Cargo Items
SS *Admiral Cole* 9.5 knots, unescorted Depart SF 10/4/41 Due Manila 11/21/41	Engineer equipment: 10-ton tandem trailer, implements, grader, tractors, carry-alls, shovels, road-mixer. Troop property, trucks.
SS *Coast Shipper* Unescorted Depart SF 10/6/41 Arrive Manila 11/16/41	Mixers and trucks for engineers 12 searchlight trucks General military stores and supplies
MV *American Packer* 14 knots, unescorted Depart SF 10/19/41 Arrive Manila 11/18/41 Direct route through Marianas	26 airplanes (25 P-40Es) 20 T-12 75-mm self-propelled half-track mounts 12 3-in AA guns, 4 37-mm AA guns, 20 60-mm mortars Wire, canned salmon, hay, gas masks, machinery, horseshoes, trucks and other vehicles, barbed wire, ammunition, inert bombs, machine guns, airplane engines, engineer heavy equipment, 1,899 rolls roofing paper
SS *Chant* Unescorted Depart SF 10/23/41 Due Manila 11/11/41	46 trucks for Manila Baggage, industrial gas Also carrying trucks and training airplanes for China to Rangoon

smaller *Liberty* received two signalmen and two radiomen. Cruiser escort was designated. Task Force 11 would consist of heavy cruiser *Chester* under Capt. Thomas M. Shock. The Navy's new convoy designation system would begin with this sailing: this transit would be known as Convoy No. 2001. An operational order provided the necessary routing, radio codes, and orders for darkening ships at night. Estimated departure from Honolulu was October 9. *Chester* was to return directly to Oahu at eighteen knots within four days of arrival. As in the previous Pacific escort missions, reference to German raider presence was again used as the rationale for the assignment of a warship. The two transports departed San Francisco as planned; in Hawaii a short shore leave was granted. With only replacement personnel to disembark, the ships were quickly ready to resume their journey.[4] They rendezvoused with *Chester* and arrived at Manila at 9 PM on the twenty-third. Several accounts by passengers comment about the impact of the escort and darkened-ship condition. As the country was not at war the proximity of a heavy warship and the security of a blacked-out ship added to the anxiety about the trip.

It was obvious to the Navy that the relative slow speed of *Liberty* argued against her inclusion in the convoy. That would greatly delay the other ships at a time when military transport capacity was a very real issue. An entirely separate escorted convoy was organized, though not with the Navy's pleasure. Task Force 18 consisted of just the lone freighter and heavy cruiser *Portland.* No convoy number was assigned. Timed to depart with *Bliss* and *Holbrook*, *Liberty* as a slower vessel (eleven versus seventeen knots) quickly fell behind. She arrived off the Honolulu entrance buoy on the twelfth at 2:30 PM. Leaving again the next day, she met up with heavy cruiser USS *Portland* as planned for the journey. Three days out the sailing orders were changed by *Portland*, and the small convoy of two ships changed to a southern routing to Manila rather than the more direct route via Guam that *Chester* and the two transports had embarked upon just a few days before. Going through Port Moresby and then Torres Strait (November 2), an average of about eight to ten knots was maintained. The combination of increased distance and slow speed delayed *Liberty*'s arrival until November 11. This was nineteen days after the arrival of the *Chester* convoy. The reason for the change in routing is not revealed in the surviving correspondence. Without embarked troops, *Liberty* might have been considered a less valuable vessel to protect; yet if that were true she wouldn't have been given a cruiser escort in the first place.

Unloading of *Bliss* and *Holbrook* progressed well. Within a week of arrival, they were prepared to begin the return voyage. Despite the original operational order to return within four days of arrival, *Chester* was still in Manila. Orders from the Asiatic Fleet were issued for her to escort her charges for a return trip. After meeting up with the convoy thirty miles beyond the San Bernardino light on October 31, the ships followed the great circle route back to Honolulu at seventeen knots. *Portland* refueled at Tarakan and Borneo, called briefly at Manila, and started her return trip alone, arriving back at Pearl Harbor on November 26. *Liberty* arrived in Manila on November 11—the voyage was calculated by the master at a total of 7,208 miles, and took twenty-eight days and two hours at an average of 10.8 knots. After unloading her cargo, *Liberty* was given new assignments to assist the Far Eastern command and participate in the strategic materials program. She was lost after the first of the year and never made it back home.

Upon arrival in Manila the 803rd Engineer Battalion moved immediately to Clark Field and an awaiting tent camp. Within a couple of weeks the companies of the unit were split up to work on several new fields simultaneously. The unit's headquarters company stayed at Clark to work on the long sod runways of this bomber post. Company "A" moved to Camp O'Donnell where a second bomber base was under construction. Company "B" went to Del Carmen for work on a fighter strip there. On the first of December the "old" independent 809th Engineer Aviation Company was incorporated into the 803rd, simply by designating it as the missing "C" Company.[5] The 19th Bombardment Group personnel and service units went to Clark also, where they soon met up with the planes they were to operate.

The Japanese espionage organization in the Philippines tried to keep tabs on the men, units, and equipment arriving in Manila. The Pearl Harbor Investigation report published a number of both the inquiries from Tokyo and responses from Japanese agents at their consulate in Manila.[6] One of the items reported consistently was the arrival of American military personnel. Generally within a day or two of arrival the Japanese relayed the name of the transport, its escort, and an estimate of the troop strength or manifest. For example, on August 4 supposedly six hundred American soldiers arrived in *Coolidge*. Actually there were only 153 soldiers on board, all fillers for other organizations or services already in the islands. On September 19 agents stated that USS *St. Louis* arrived with three other vessels and unloaded explosives (red flags were displayed). More revealing was a report on October 21 that an air base was under construction in central Mindanao due to the expectation of heavy bombers. On October 24 the arrival of USAT *Tasker H. Bliss* (reported by the Japanese under the old name of *President Cleveland*) with 2,500 soldiers was detailed, escorted by cruiser USS *Chester*.

Sometimes the reports were substantially in error. An analysis of air strength in November reported twenty-nine large bombers (not too far off) but also a fantastic total of 324 scout planes, 317 fighters, 302 pursuit planes, and 49 training planes plus over another 250 planes in reserve. Except for the bombers, that is probably four to five times what was actually present at this time. Other messages correctly identified the arrival of tanks, and even three companies' worth of self-propelled artillery was accurately reported. When MV *American Leader* docked on December 4 and began unloading its deck-stored cylindrical underground fuel tanks, the reporter identified them as boilers. Obviously someone was carefully observing or talking to someone else who had seen these firsthand. A few questions did come from Tokyo, like the status of camouflage of aircraft, and more urgently a request to identify the route the large bombers took to the Philippines (a request that went unanswered). Starting in July the reports consistently identified efforts by America to strengthen its Philippine defenses. The American reinforcement was well known to the Japanese, though most of the specifics were not.

In the fall of 1941 a new wrinkle began to affect the return routing of Army transports. In the First World War, the American experience of obtaining non-domestic quantities of critical strategic materials for war production had not been good. Throughout the 1920s and 1930s both the Army and Navy undertook studies designed to identify materials and quantities necessary for a future crisis. Attempts were made to secure funding from Congress for stockpiling strategic materials in advance, but as usual in this time frame, money was scarce—none was forthcoming. On June 7, 1939 Congress finally passed the Strategic War Materials Act, which authorized the joint Army-Navy munitions board to make a definitive list. Funds to secure materials did not become available until the summer of 1940. The lists of just what materials were considered "strategic" varied over time, but in 1940 the munitions board included:[7]

> Strategic Materials (necessary for national defense but not produced in sufficient quantity in the United States): antimony, chromium, manganese, Manila fiber, mercury, mica, nickel, crystalline quartz, quinine, rubber, silk, tin, tungsten.
>
> Critical Materials (similar need, but not as acutely short): aluminum, asbestos, cork, graphite, hides, iodine, kapok, opium, optical glass, phenol, platinum, tanning materials, toluol, vanadium, wood.

A number of these materials were heavily sourced from the Far East. While commercial ships generally carried such items to the United States, it was recognized that additional efforts would be needed if a useful reserve were to be built up. Hence was born the idea that military freighters carrying reinforcement supplies to the Philippines could usefully return with a backhaul of strategic materials. While the personnel transports of the services usually returned with at least a partial load of servicemen with expired enlistments (and their household goods), the freighters were almost always near empty. Of course it would take some organization to set up a return manifest, and also with the exception of Manila fiber none of these commodities were usually available in the Philippines. Additional time for another voyage leg and loading would be required. This was an added burden to the already overstretched military transport system, but the trade-off was still considered worthwhile.

In very little time the voyages began. USAT *Meigs* was diverted from Manila to Singapore and Penang to get a full load of rubber. She departed for Los Angeles, scheduled to arrive on April 15, 1941. Close on her heels both *Ludington* and *Irvin L. Hunt* were scheduled to make similar journeys. In fact *Hunt* was originally scheduled for just Honolulu, not Manila, but changes were made for the journey across the Pacific to load rubber. The arrangements for these early trips were for the Army Transport Service to bill the Reconstruction Corporation (more accurately its subsidiary, the Rubber Reserve Company) for the cost of the shipping. The United States Lines was hired to act as shore agent in Singapore, Batavia, Penang, and Los Angeles. The net funds received by the Army were, in turn, spent on commercial shipments of Army cargo from San Francisco. *Meigs*, *Ludington*, and *Hunt* made their pickups as scheduled. The first two carried just rubber, but *Irvin L. Hunt* was ordered to collect 625 measurement tons of charcoal in Surabaya for use in Chemical Warfare Service filters and gas masks.[8] Additionally, on her next voyage for the Army, USAT *Republic* loaded 15,000 bales of hemp in Manila about April 24, and a similar cargo was loaded on USAT *Washington* in late May. During the summer USAT *Liberty* made a trip after a Manila stop to pick up more rubber and charcoal, while *President Taft* was able to pick up hemp and charcoal in the Philippines.

The outbreak of war did not immediately cease the interest in backhauling strategic cargo from the Far East. In fact, if anything, the immediate urgency of the war and subsequent military production led to a frantic effort to get as much as possible out of Malaya and the Dutch East Indies. All through December 1941 and into January and early February 1942 efforts were made by the Maritime Commission's Emergency Shipping Division to extract strategic materials. As late as February 3, 1942 commission representatives were sent to Batavia and Brisbane to act as liaison for ships returning from the American-British-Dutch-Australian (ABDA) command area. Of particular interest was the space available in the return of *President Coolidge*, *Mariposa*,

Mauna Loa, *Paul Gregg*, *Portmar*, *Meigs*, and *Mormacsun.* Unfortunately several of these were lost in Australian waters before ever returning to the United States.

To supplement the convoyed transports, the month of October saw an increase in the Army's usage of chartered commercial freighters to carry equipment to the Philippines. Six vessels left San Francisco between October 4 and 23 for Manila Harbor. The first to sail was SS *Admiral Cole.* An older, slow ship of the Admiral Oriental Line, she had already been working the freight service to Manila. The Army chartered space for a variety of cargo. The Coastwise Line freighter *Coastal Shipper* departed San Francisco on October 6 with a small amount of space chartered to the Army. Included for equipping an anti-aircraft regiment were twelve searchlight trucks. Apparently the balance of her cargo was filled out for commercial firms. Both MV *Perida* and MV *Pennant* were contracted by the Army to deliver a mixed load of cargo to Manila.

A very valuable cargo was dispatched on the American Pioneer Line freighter *American Packer*. This ship was a fine, new C-1 type freighter, one of five recently completed ships of the type and sister to *American Press* and *American Leader* that are mentioned in the Philippine supply story. Besides a short trip for trials, this was the vessel's first commercial journey. She carried no troops or units but did have some very important military cargo. She took the direct route through the Mariana Islands to Manila, arriving thirty days later on November 18. The cargo carried was generally divided between that for the 19th Bomb Group, 803rd Engineer Battalion, and other Far Eastern Army departments. For the Air Force were, as usual, a number of service vehicles for the ground and air units of the newly arrived bombardment group, along with sixteen spare B-17 engines. Importantly for the Air Force, there were twenty-six airplanes (unassembled). Most of these were brand-new P-40Es, and destined for assembly at the Nichols Field depot prior to being issued to one of the anticipated new fighter squadrons. Quantities of spare parts, wheels, propellers, and service trucks for the depot were also on board. These would be the last airplanes received in the Philippines prior to the Japanese attack.

Finally the Philippine ordnance department was sent some important items. The final twenty T-12, 75-mm anti-tank self-propelled mounts (SPMs) were loaded on MV *American Packer*. This completed the promised fifty such mounts for MacArthur's forces. For the anti-aircraft regiment, equipment were twelve 3-inch anti-aircraft guns (just a month earlier it was thought these wouldn't be available until December!), and four 37-mm automatic guns. Twenty crated 60-mm mortars and seventy-eight machine guns were included. When considering the overall manifest list, particularly the inclusion of the twenty-six aircraft, twenty 75-mm SPMs, and the large quantity of modern anti-aircraft guns, it is a little puzzling as to why the ship was not escorted, or alternately ordered to await the next convoy. Certainly she fits the Navy's criteria, issued just five days prior, of carrying "critical supplies." Perhaps because she was already scheduled, or as a fast ship capable of fourteen knots her voyage was exempted from the escorting order.

It appears that the self-propelled mounts were not immediately employed. They were not a "unit" that required housing, mess facilities, and administrative support. One first-person report mentions a trip to the Manila docks in early December to pick up a newly delivered 75-mm SPM. Probably all fifty mounts were temporarily stored in a warehouse of the ordnance depot prior to being organized into functional units. In any event they were eventually distributed to three new independent Philippine Scout battalions, each having four four-gun batteries (with apparently two mounts as spares). As provisional units they were not given specific designations, just referred to as the 1st, 2nd, or 3rd SPM Battalions. They were each commanded by an American lieutenant colonel. Personnel were scraped up from wherever possible, though mostly coming from the scout units in the Philippine Division. That division was the source of the required fifty trained drivers. One of the practical problems was the lack of experience their commanders and troops had in their tactical employment. One account even states that the people using them didn't even understand artillery![9]

The use of two heavy cruisers for escorting duty in early October finally forced the Navy and Army to come to grips with the needs of Pacific convoys. As we have seen, the Navy's concerns with military cargo ships stemmed from an appreciation of, if not an actual encounter with, German surface raiders. Starting in early 1941 the Navy had assigned an escort from Hawaii to Manila and back for its service's own transports. In all cases this was a single cruiser, thought to be enough to handle any individual raider. Only later in the year did the Navy concede that the Army's freight and troop shipments might need the same sort of protection. Starting with the voyage of USAT *Hugh L. Scott* on August 28, the Navy assigned cruiser escorts for the movement of troop ships. This was followed by the sailing of September 8, and then finally the dual escorting by *Chester* and *Portland* on October 4. Note that these were all troop transfers; freighters (either Army-owned or commercial charters) were usually not escorted but proceeded on their own. Only with USAT *Liberty* on October 4 was a freighter given escort privileges.

Back on August 23, while discussing in correspondence the upcoming voyage of *Hugh L. Scott*, the Navy had set out guidelines for inter-service cooperation. It requested that the Twelfth Naval District receive information about all Army trans-Pacific ship movements. In turn the Navy would provide routing instructions to the ships and information about escorting. This made sense as San Francisco would likely be the source of most Army shipments, and that naval district had the size and resources to coordinate such movements. For return trips, the Sixteenth Naval District (Manila) would serve as the coordinating agency. In early October General Marshall himself made an effort to improve Army communications with the Navy. He issued specific instructions to the quartermaster general and the ports to constantly advise the Navy of the movements of all Army transports and commercial vessels carrying significant amounts of Army supplies.[10] This attention came about as the result of a conference between Rear Admiral Ingersoll (assistant chief of naval operations) and Lt. Col. Frank S. Ross (supply assistant to the Army chief of staff).

On the fourteenth of October the Navy declared that all troop transports and any freighters carrying critical supplies be escorted between Hawaii and Manila. The Navy would also supply all routing or course recommendations and the procedure for radio frequencies and silence. Airplanes, tanks, and field artillery were defined as critical supplies. Also in mid-October Pacific Fleet commander Admiral Kimmel weighed in with some critique of the situation. At this time he had four 10,000-ton cruisers on detached duty of escorting just five Army ships, one of which (*Liberty*) could do just ten knots. The average duration of this duty was well over one month. He complained that he didn't have enough ships, and that this type of scheduling was uneconomical of fuel, a waste of training time, and produced a dispersion of ships that might be dangerous if a true emergency arose. A better alternative might be a system of convoys where the participating ships could be grouped according to speed.[11]

From these comments rose a concrete proposal for a convoy system. Convoys would be organized by speed (slow: ten knots or less, medium: twelve to fourteen knots, fast: sixteen knots or more), and provided escort by the Pacific Fleet the entire distance from Hawaii to Manila with stops at Guam if necessary. They could be organized about every twelve days. The Asiatic Fleet would provide escorts for other stops in Asia. The Twelfth Naval District would still control the formation of convoys, even if the convoy wouldn't form until it got to Hawaiian waters and met its cruiser there. The next upcoming voyage (*Hugh L. Scott* and *President Coolidge*) would be the first of this new system. Also for the first time, the term "Pacific Escort Force" was used to describe the functioning escort organization.

The final organizational steps occurred in November. On the first of the month the commander in chief, Pacific Fleet, (CinCPac) designated the Pacific Escort Force as Task Force 15. It was under the command of the Pacific Base Force, which was headed by Rear Adm. William L. Calhoun. The unit was designed to be a transient command (like most task forces), but generally would have four cruisers assigned, each for about a forty-eight-day duration. In fact, on this date cruisers *Chester* and *Portland* were on escorting assignments, and *Louisville* and *Boise* were alerted to prepare for such service in early November. A further explanation of the organization designated that the selected cruisers were to be assigned in rotation, one each from Cruiser Divisions Four, Five, Six, and Nine. The fleet confidential letter outlining task force responsibilities was clear in tasking this unit "to escort trans-pacific shipping in order to protect trans-pacific shipping against possible attack."[12]

CHAPTER FIVE

The Naval and Marine Reinforcements

The U.S. Navy's primary augmentation for the defense of the Philippines was a significant increase in the Asiatic Fleet's submarine force. In early 1939 six older coastal boats, *S-36*, *S-37*, *S-38*, *S-39*, *S-40*, and *S-41* arrived in Manila. These were serviced by Navy submarine tender USS *Canopus* and rescue ship USS *Pigeon.* This squadron was an integral part of the Asiatic Fleet, intended for patrolling and protecting the Philippine coastline. In October 1939 Admiral Stark, the chief of naval operations, personally approved the first real improvement to this sub force. Submarine Division 14 (under the command of Capt. John Wilkes), with the first seven *"P"*–class boats, was ordered to Manila from Pearl Harbor and San Diego. Subsequently *Porpoise*, *Pike*, *Tarpon*, *Perch*, *Pickerel*, and *Permit* made the voyage.[1] USS *Shark* developed severe engine problems that delayed her a year, but she eventually joined her six sisters. These seven new boats and the six older ones formed Submarine Squadrons 5 and 13 respectively, all under Wilkes' command.

Overall command of the Navy's small Asiatic Fleet was vested in Rear Adm. Thomas C. Hart. Born in 1877, and thus sixty-four when the war started, Hart was near the end of a long naval career. From the Naval Academy he had worked his way up the service's professional ladder with assignments both at sea and in administration. Much of his expertise was with submarines: he commanded a division during the First World War, had supervised the Torpedo Station in Newport, and had been posted to the Navy's General Board where he played a significant role in designing undersea craft. In 1939 he was looking for his final assignment prior to retirement, hoping it would be the command of the U.S. Fleet, but he was given the Asiatic Fleet instead. While an important post for diplomatic purposes, this fleet was by far the smallest in terms of ships and men. He moved to Manila in mid-1939. Despite his age, Hart worked hard at increasing the capabilities of his command. He sought and received carefully thought-out reinforcements, secured and reorganized his command positions, and was able to withdraw most of his assets in China to the Philippines before the start of the war.

Hart and MacArthur did not hit it off. Hart's conservative nature and reserved personality were the polar opposite of MacArthur's optimistic and at times arrogant presence. Neither seems to have taken the other into confidence over war plans, and their personal interactions appear to have been few during the months immediately preceding the war. Apparently MacArthur also held resentment of Hart's technically superior rank. One biography characterizes the Army-Navy relations and communications as "glaring examples of poor coordination, inter-service rivalry, and pigheaded antagonisms."[2] A number of rather nasty conflicts occurred between the two commanders; in some cases the curt letter exchanges (usually instigated by MacArthur) had to be ameliorated by Marshall in Washington before the Navy became too incensed. It is probably fortunate that the defensive plans for the archipelago depended relatively little on the active cooperation of the two services. At the staff level the administration of the Sixteenth Naval District and the Marine Corps contingent cooperated and served well with their Army counterparts.

A significant number of the newest and best Navy submarines were eventually brought to Manila. American fleet submarines had progressively evolved since the 1930 London Naval Treaty. Diesel-powered boats of about 1,500 tons, these vessels were specifically designed to operate for long periods away from their bases in the wide expanses of the Pacific Ocean. Several related designs were produced by class; there were differences in propulsion and armament between these groups, but in general their operational capabilities were similar. American submarines were generally of excellent design, well sized for their mission but still relatively quick to maneuver and dive. Overall the submarine service of the United States performed its duty outstandingly in the war.

In November 1940 Admiral Hart requested submarine reinforcements for the Asiatic Fleet. Apparently Admiral Richardson of the Pacific Fleet (organizationally Hart's counterpart, not his supervisor) opposed transfer of naval strength to Asia, believing that such forces would be lost in the early days of the war.[3] However, Stark in Washington *did* approve Hart's request. Submarine Division 17 (under the command of Cdr. Willis Percifield) with *Seadragon*, *Searaven*, *Sealion*, and *Seawolf* started for Manila by the end of 1940.

On their voyage the long-delayed USS *Shark* joined them. To help handle the new boats the Asiatic Fleet acquired a new commercial vessel, SS *Fred Morris*. She was to be converted into a full-fledged submarine tender at the Cavite yard. Renamed as USS *Otus*, her conversion had not been completed when the war began. She managed to avoid the Japanese air attacks of the first few days of the war, and left Mariveles on December 10 for southern waters.

The publication of the revised Rainbow No. 3 plan in early 1941 was for the most part just a general updating of the Navy's basic plan for war with Japan. One new element was, however, introduced. For the first time in Navy planning, it called for an extensive deployment of submarines based in the Philippines. Other reinforcements anticipated by this plan included mine-sweepers and a squadron of small observation floatplanes. PT boats were also considered, though only after the type had been successfully perfected in the United States. The stated strategic direction is instructive:

> The employment of submarines as proposed is considered suitable and highly desirable. The Navy has responsibilities to the Army, but, under the concept of RAINBOW No. 3, it has greater responsibilities to the British and Dutch, because holding the Malay Barrier would have a profound effect on the outcome of the war. In regard to the shift of base, it is considered essential that aircraft, submarines, and destroyer tenders be moved from the Manila Bay area prior to the commencement of hostilities, if possible, as they will be the only vessels at once available in Malaysia which carry ammunition replacements and material supplies.[4]

Even more submarines were made available later in 1941 to fulfill the strategic requirement. Additionally there are comments recorded in the various Joint Board meetings where the Navy addressed its reinforcement of the Asiatic Fleet in response to the Army's augmentation of MacArthur. It is important to note that there was no "joint" plan between the services to reinforce the Philippines. Rather, in the face of the heavy Army commitment (supported by the administration), the Navy tried to find a way to incrementally add to the strength of the Asiatic Fleet without creating a major dispersion of force. Besides, this addition would aid in its mission to substantially cooperate with British and Dutch forces. Naval strength, unlike Army forces, is usually mobile and thus ships were able to leave the Philippines for an adjacent operating theatre if needed. Additionally the increase in defensive airpower of the Army Air Force on Luzon helped reassure the Navy of the safety of its assets deployed there.

Planning began for an even larger reinforcement of the Asiatic Fleet submarine force in August 1941. By October 21 orders were given to send Submarine Squadron 2 from the Pacific Fleet to the Asiatic Fleet. This unit consisted of twelve of the most modern new fleet boats and the large submarine tender USS *Holland.* Capt. Walter E. Doyle, who was slated to replace Captain Wilkes as commander of Asiatic Fleet submarines, commanded the squadron. There were two divisions in the squadron, holding together twelve *Salmon*–class boats: *Salmon*, *Seal*, *Skipjack*, *Snapper*, *Stingray*, *Sturgeon*, *Sargo*, *Saury*, *Spearfish*, *Sculpin*, *Sailfish*, and *Swordfish*. Eight of the subs arrived between November 8 and 10; the other four, with tender USS *Holland*, came into Manila Bay later in the month. The urgency to transfer these subs was such that they were authorized to move without the naval dockyard overhaul already scheduled. On the first of December, with the new arrivals, the Asiatic Fleet subs were reorganized. Six divisions (each of from four to seven submarines) were formed, all as part of Submarine Squadron 20 under Doyle.

The Navy's commitment of this submarine force should not be minimized. This was *the* largest submarine concentration in the U.S. Navy. Of the Navy's modern fleet submarines, there were now (at the time of Pearl Harbor) twenty-three with the Asiatic Fleet and just twelve with the Pacific Fleet. The Atlantic Fleet had only older submarines for training, and some ancient coastal subs deployed to Panama. Thus almost two-thirds of the Navy's modern subs were committed to Manila. It is also interesting to compare the acquisition cost of some of this military hardware. Of course, there is a lot more to military strength than just what weapons cost; for example, the manpower commitment (and the financial burden of supporting them) of the Army was much greater than that of the Navy in this theatre. Still, the twenty-three modern subs represented $63 million in scarce pre-war military expense (roughly $3 million per submarine). The vaunted B-17 force in the Philippines represented about $10.5 million ($301,000 apiece) and the P-40 air fleet only $4.8 million (eighty-one airplanes at about $60,000 each).

Hart was excited about the reinforcements for the submarine force. With the increase in strength and type of boat he intended to change from passive defense of the Philippine Islands to offensive capabilities. He stated: "When the war comes, these boats are going to be of great value to us. They will be able to hit the enemy hard."[5] In fact, for the first time ever, both the Army and Navy possessed in the Philippine Islands strategic, long-range weapons. Prior to this the forces had been largely constrained to the defense of the islands and its immediate perimeter. But fleet submarines and B-17 bombers could reach out hundreds, even thousands of miles. Americans now possessed forces that could reach Japanese bases. Certainly they could seriously interfere with any supply route to Japanese conquests in the south. Thus Washington had managed to create a force that the Japanese had to think twice about. It was a potential deterrent, but also assured that the Philippines would need to be neutralized by the enemy at the start of any conflict.

There was no naval counterpart to MacArthur, Marshall, and Stimson vigorously pushing for reinforcement of the Far East. The Navy seemed much more content with existing joint war plans—which meant the relatively early loss or abandonment of the Philippines until a return was possible many months or years later. Indeed the Asiatic Fleet had been pushed to develop cooperative plans with the naval forces of the British and Dutch, and actually had the defense of the Malay barrier as a higher priority to the defense of the Philippines.

One of MacArthur's favored schemes for the eventual defense of the islands was the creation of a Philippine navy largely based on motor torpedo boats. It is not clear where this Army man received his introduction to this relatively new form of naval warfare, but it is obvious that he became somewhat infatuated with the concept as early as 1935. MacArthur thought that a fleet of numerous small, heavily armed, high-speed torpedo boats could successfully challenge Japanese landing attempts. They could be used effectively in the many channels and straits that separated the nation's central islands, and also offered a relatively inexpensive investment that could be managed with a minimal infrastructure. The service was never envisioned as a separate branch, but a specialized "corps" not unlike the proposed Philippine Air Corps. The most frequent term used for it was the "Offshore Patrol." No one on his staff in the Philippines, at least in the immediate pre-war years, seems closely identified with this proposal. The plan appears to be of genuine MacArthur origin. However, once he had proposed it, he quickly found someone else to work out the details. In this case MacArthur's naval adviser on the Philippine Army staff—Lt. Sid L. Huff, USN (Ret.)—became the focal point.

In early 1937, on a visit to Washington, D.C., General MacArthur asked for assistance in the project from the secretary of the Navy. The Navy's Bureau of Construction and Repair was requested to come up with a design for these boats (there were otherwise no U.S. Navy designs then, or any such vessels yet in American service). The work was to be funded by a payment of three thousand dollars from the Philippine government. The requirements as presented by Huff were for a relatively large boat (sixty to seventy feet) of high speed (forty-five knots) and long range (seven hundred nautical miles). However, the Navy's experts had to report that the criteria were too optimistic. No American engines at that time could deliver the horsepower needed, and the required range would entail too much fuel-carrying weight on this small displacement. The best Navy design showed forty knots, 250 nautical miles range, and forty tons displacement, with two torpedo tubes.

MacArthur wished to proceed to constructing prototypes, though ultimately he desired production at either local Filipino boat yards or at the Cavite Navy Yard. An initial funding of $35,000 for two boats was forthcoming, but the Navy responded by quoting $237,300 for the pair to be built at the Norfolk Navy Yard. Suspicious that the Navy was using the Philippine order for its own (profitable) learning experience, MacArthur turned to foreign sources. In April 1938 a contract was placed with the British naval construction firm of Thornycroft & Company Ltd. for the boats—a larger one sixty-five feet in length, and a smaller version of fifty-five feet. The unit cost was $70,000 each. The British had considerable experience with this type of vessel, and both boats proved successful. The smaller ship (*Abras* or *Q I*) was finished in January of 1939, while the larger vessel (*Luzon* or *Q III*) was shipped in April. The British engines managed to produce a speed of over forty knots in both ships, little *Abras* hitting 46.5 on trials.[6]

The Philippine government moved ahead with plans to place the smaller torpedo boat design into quantity production in Manila. A construction facility was erected on Engineer Island in the Pasig River. The engines proved to be beyond Filipino industrial capacity, and had to be imported, along with the armament and other special parts. Thornycroft even went so far as to send a technical expert to Manila in 1940 to supervise the company's obligations within the license agreement. Ten new boats were laid down in the yard in the fall of 1941 for an expected delivery in March 1942.

In one of General MacArthur's periodic status letters written to Marshall, he dwells rather splendidly on his personal efforts to create this force. He even claims responsibility for the Navy's own dispatch of a squadron of PT boats for the island's defense. He thought the presence of an American squadron would prove a real impetus to the Philippine army's similar efforts. A special training school for the Offshore Patrol (OSP) was organized at Muelle del Coco near Manila in January 1941, and good progress made with the two completed boats available as training vessels. By March 1941 the first boat to be built in the Philippines (*Agusan* or *Q-113*) was ready to join the little fleet. It was the only one of the domestically produced boats to be completed; the others were destroyed on the stocks at the start of the war. As war approached the three completed vessels were organized into the 1st Offshore Patrol Squadron under Filipino Capt. Alberto Navarrete.

While MacArthur may have exaggerated his role in getting U.S. Navy PT boats to the Philippines, there is no debate that a squadron was dispatched in the late summer of 1941. Rear Admiral Ingersoll informed the Joint Board on August 6, 1941 that a reinforcement of the Asiatic Fleet by this type of vessel was under way. After decades of neglect, the Navy was finally getting serious about the design and deployment of PT boats. Initially it was thought that such boats, inherently short-ranged in nature, would only be needed at the final steps of a Pacific campaign, and thus they were of lesser priority than other types of ships for design and production. Three squadrons, each of twelve boats, were in the process of forming—the first was at Pearl Harbor, the second destined for the Panama Canal, and the third earmarked for Philippine service.

Admiral Hart was informed that he would soon receive reinforcements of twelve modern submarines, a sub tender, and six PT boats in early September. Apparently this decision was made in Washington; these forces were not specifically requested by Hart himself. Half of the PT squadron, the first six boats, were loaded onto the deck of Navy tanker USS *Guadalupe* at the Brooklyn Navy Yard in mid-August. Designated part of Motor Torpedo Boat Squadron 3, the crews accompanying the boats were under the command of Lt. (jg) John D. Bulkeley. Eleven officers and sixty-eight men were with PT Boats *31*, *32*, *33*, *34*, *35*, and *41* when *Guadalupe* set sail on August 19. The boats sent were the "standard" type developed by the Navy, and differed considerably from the Philippine type under construction. Among other differences they were more heavily armed with four 21-inch torpedo tubes and four .50-caliber machine guns. *Guadalupe* moved unescorted through the Panama Canal to San Pedro, where she took on fuel as part of her normal cargo. Joining escorting cruiser USS *Astoria* with transport *President Coolidge* she arrived finally in Manila Bay on September 26. Quickly unloaded the next day, and without a dedicated tender and little in developed tactical doctrine, Bulkeley quickly began to hone his group into combat readiness based out of the Cavite Navy Yard. Fortunately the boats were shipped with nine spare engines, but there was little else in the way of spare parts. *Guadalupe*, after transferring her fuel cargo, didn't linger long, joining return cruiser escort *Phoenix* for the voyage.

These six boats were just half a normal squadron of twelve; the second contingent was actually in transit when war broke out. In a move reminiscent of the first, tanker USS *Chenango* loaded six PT boats as deck cargo in New York and departed on September 4, 1941. Stopping to load oil at Baytown, Texas, she moved through the canal to San Pedro's refineries for gasoline cargo and arrived at Pearl Harbor on October 8. However, as she was not selected to make the ongoing journey, the PT boats were unloaded and *Chenango* departed back for the mainland on the eleventh of the month. Almost two months passed before Pearl Harbor saw the arrival of the next ship selected for the transport mission—tanker USS *Ramapo.* This oiler arrived at Pearl Harbor on the fifth of December, and began almost immediately to load the six awaiting PT boats. This task was only partially completed on the morning of the seventh when the Japanese attack interrupted both the loading and ultimately the delivery to their next station.

The Navy did not neglect the opportunity to reinforce the Philippines with additional patrol bombers (PBYs). Since late 1939 PBYs had been based at a newly constructed seaplane base at Sangley Point, adjacent to the Cavite Navy Yard. The fourteen planes were used with buoys and tended by USS *Langley.* Patrol Squadron 21 flew its planes to the Philippines via Midway, Wake, and Guam. A second squadron (VP-46) flew out in June 1940, delivered its planes, and returned taking VP-21's planes with it for overhaul on the mainland. This was done and the planes were re-sent to the Philippines in December 1940. These twenty-eight planes in two squadrons formed the bulk of naval aviation in the islands at the start of the war. There was a small squadron of short-ranged utility aircraft looked after by the tender USS *Heron*, and whatever floatplanes were assigned to the Asiatic Fleet's cruisers. The fleet's patrol bombers were all PBY-4s; while only powered by two engines the planes had a remarkably good patrol range. However, they somewhat lacked in the capability of self-defense. These early planes had little armor and no self-sealing fuel tanks; they were vulnerable both on the water and in the air if caught by enemy fighters.

Shortly before the war the two PBY squadrons were renumbered, becoming VP-101 and VP-102 of the newly established Patrol Wing (PatWing) 10.

The new patrol wing was commanded by Capt. Frank D. Wagner. Besides *Langley* were small tenders USS *Childs* and USS *William B. Preston*. These were also conversions, being made from old 4-piper destroyers. They had some of their machinery removed to allow storage of aviation fuel tanks. They were basically to be mobile base units—to supply fuel, limited armament, and crew quarters to planes that might operate opportunistically from remote anchorages. Also, a second major base was started for the patrol planes at Olongapo in Subic Bay. This was to be the home of VP-102, while VP-101 stayed at Sangley Point. The Navy long anticipated that its patrol bombers might have to operate in waters beyond the Philippines. In 1941 exercises were accomplished with the planes patrolling off French Indochina, China, and the Dutch East Indies.

The employment of airplanes for long-range scouting was at the root of one of the more visible spats between Hart and MacArthur. In October 1941 Admiral Hart attempted to better organize his patrol bomber assets for offshore patrolling. He was well aware that the Army was now operating long-range B-17s in some numbers in the islands, and equally aware that General MacArthur was much more interested in the land warfare aspects of his command. In Hart's mind it was wasteful that the two forces did not closely coordinate their assets to make sure the most critical aspects of scouting took place. The chief of the Asiatic Fleet in frustration proposed that the Navy take over full control of air search for the American forces in the Philippines. While not arguing against the logic of coordinating efforts, predictably General MacArthur blew up over what he saw was an attempt by the Navy to abscond with some of his forces.

The general aired his views in what Hart called a "perfectly rotten" letter. MacArthur found the proposal entirely objectionable—particularly putting some of the air force under an inferior command (militarily speaking). MacArthur was not attempting to abuse naval professionalism, but rather point out that the major command responsible for the majority of the defense of the islands should retain control of this element. Also typically, MacArthur did not attempt to work out the disagreement locally with Hart (whom he rarely saw or conversed with). His letter to Washington wound up as Marshall's problem. The chief of staff did his usual defense of the general, backing his position but prodding him to work out an agreement with the Navy to the satisfaction of all parties.[7] While there may have been some operational level discussions, it does not appear that a workable plan to integrate Army and Navy scouting was ever created prior to the war's inception.

In the face of growing Japanese belligerence, President Roosevelt personally intervened to create naval demonstrations in the Pacific. At a presidential conference on February 4, 1941, the matter of some visible action came up. Secretary of State Cordell Hull proposed sending ships to visit Far Eastern ports to get Japanese attention. A plan was cast to have ships depart unannounced, but once arrived they were to have maximum exposure. The president delighted in thinking that having ships "pop up" here and there would have the desired effect on the Japanese. Four cruisers—*Chicago*, *Portland*, *Brooklyn*, and *Savannah*, an oiler, and the 3rd Destroyer Squadron were selected to make the cruise, all under the command of Rear Adm. John H. Newton. The force departed Pearl Harbor on March 1. After a short stopover in Samoa, they reached Sydney on March 19. After a week the task force moved north to a repeat of festivities at Brisbane. Coming back, detachments visited Auckland and Fiji. There is no evidence that the cruise had any effect at all on Japanese intentions. In reality sending ships thousands of miles across the ocean to "friendly" ports was not all that earth-shattering an accomplishment.

The Navy was heavily involved in the protection of the trans-Pacific shipment of men and matériel. Two different stratagems helped address the possibility of enemy attacks on transports. First, the Navy could provide escort for the ships. The ranges involved meant that only big cruisers could provide this (heavy cruisers or the larger light cruisers of the *Brooklyn*-class); the armament of these types of ships could handle most encounters with the typical enemy auxiliary-cruiser type raider of 1941. The other solution was with routing. Sending ships (escorted or not) through a southern course via the British Gilbert and Fiji Islands and then through Torres Strait and the Dutch East Indies could avoid transiting Japanese-controlled territory. While routing didn't directly prevent German or Japanese interference, it lessened the chances and provided more safe havens once war or enemy action was initiated. The Navy used both active escorting and routing as reasonable reactions to the situation. When that situation significantly worsened in November, the two alternatives were combined, starting with the *Pensacola* convoy.[8]

One of the practical problems with escorting was the lack of available vessels. Particularly after the transfers on April 1941 to the Atlantic, the number of suitable cruisers available to the Pacific Fleet was limited. The Navy was finding that heavy cruisers were very valuable in screening carrier task forces, and with the usual training and exercises there weren't enough to go around. An escorting trip (particularly if along the southern route) could take four to five weeks in each direction, and with time to unload and refuel in

Manila, an individual cruiser detached for this duty could be absent from the fleet for up to three months. On November 25 the chief of naval operations directed that all trans-Pacific traffic be routed through the Torres Strait. This applied to military transports and all other American-flag commercial voyages.

One final group of naval vessels arrived in Manila Harbor just before the war started, though they were not intended, strictly speaking, as reinforcements. For many years the U.S. Navy had maintained a station ship and a small flotilla of shallow-draft river gunboats in China. In mid-1941 the American naval forces in China were organized as the Yangtze Patrol, commanded by Rear Adm. William A. Glassford Jr. The command consisted of two large gunboats as station ships (USS *Asheville* and USS *Tulsa*), two larger river gunboats also in Shanghai (USS *Luzon* and USS *Oahu*), two smaller gunboats "upriver" (USS *Tutuila* and USS *Wake*), and USS *Mindanao* at Hong Kong. Admiral Hart exercised a measured withdrawal of the China units during 1941. *Tulsa* and *Asheville* left in May and July respectively for Manila. Small *Wake* was left in Shanghai with a skeleton naval reserve crew to act as a radio station for the remaining consul function. The crew was surprised on the morning of December 8 and had to surrender the ship. Three gunboats made a harrowing escape trip to Manila. *Oahu* and *Luzon* received orders to depart Shanghai and did so on November 28; they arrived in Manila on December 5, after which the Yangtze Patrol was dissolved. *Mindanao* also got away from Hong Kong, but *Tutuila* was isolated upriver in Chungking and was turned over to the Nationalist Chinese as a lend-lease contribution in February 1942. In Manila the boats were contributed to the inshore patrol for Manila Bay.

The Navy in the Philippines also had a nominal force of Marines available. There was an independent battalion-strength unit, the 1st Separate Marine Battalion, quartered at Cavite. One of its chief functions was to provide land and air defense for the district's facilities. It manned twelve 3-inch antiaircraft guns and two machine-gun batteries. To improve the efficiency of these guns, a small detachment of radar with technical operators was sent to Manila in October 1941. Arriving in mid-November was WO John T. Brainard and a few Army-trained technicians. Most importantly, they had two radar sets for controlling guns or searchlights, and a single, mobile long-range set. Initially the thirty-six-man unit was attached to the battalion's communication section. Eventually they were sent one hundred miles south of Cavite to provide air warning coverage from that direction. Put under command of the Air Force's 5th Interceptor Command, the unit eventually found itself on Bataan, separated from the Marine battalion. With the early loss of much of the Army's radar equipment, the unit's importance increased. At the end of the Bataan campaign the remaining equipment was either smashed or set on fire and destroyed.[9]

One of the final reinforcements reaching the Philippines came from an unexpected source. Americans had posted a permanent military presence in China since the Boxer Rebellion in 1902. Since early 1938 the force had been entirely of Marines. They were organized into two contingents—the main body in southern China at Shanghai, and a smaller force in north China at Tientsin and with the embassy delegation at Peking. The garrison at that time was composed of the 4th Marine Regiment, commanded by Col. Samuel L. Howard. The contingents were supplied by the regular visits of the same Navy transports that plied the Manila route.

The increasingly aggressive behavior of the Japanese in China convinced Hart that it was time to pull the Marine garrison out.[10] On August 28, 1941 Hart asked Washington for permission to remove the men from China, but was told that the time was not right politically. In fact, for a considerable period of time the policy had been to reduce the strength of the contingent—done by simply not replacing personnel who transferred out when their terms of enlistment expired. Thus the 4th Marines in late 1941was only a two-battalion regiment, and even these were significantly under strength. In fact by December 1 the total strength of all the China Marine units was under one thousand men. The main body of about 770 officers and men, including Colonel Howard, was at its longtime barracks in Shanghai. At Tientsin were fifty-five men of the north China Marines. A small detachment of twenty-one operated a sort of supply depot near Chinwangtao. Finally, actually at the American embassy compound in Peking were the legation Marines—about 165 men under Col. William W. Ashurst. The regiment had no attached artillery or heavy vehicles, but was armed with machine guns, mortars, and an allocation of trucks. The men were mostly long-term, professional soldiers relatively well trained and disciplined.

On November 10, 1941 orders finally came to remove the Marines to Olongapo in Subic Bay. As there was no scheduled arrival of one of the Navy's transports until early January (that would have been *Chaumont* in the *Pensacola* convoy), the Navy scrambled to find alternate ships. None of the Army transports were available—they had their own tight schedule to bring out the men and matériel stacking up in San Francisco. However, two American President Lines (APL) transports on commercial runs in the Far East could be accessed for the proposed movement of the Marines. Both *President Madison* and *President Harrison* were "available." Both ships were technically owned by the Maritime Commission. They had been acquired in the summer of 1941 and allocated to the U.S. Navy. However, both ships were part of the Naval Reserve Fleet; their masters and over half the officers were members of the naval reserve. The Navy constructed new agreements for the use of the ships on November 11. Both masters were given clear orders by the Navy to participate in the revised agenda to remove the Marines, and both complied completely.[11]

President Madison's schedule was just slightly ahead of that for *President Harrison.* Now intended as one of the ships to extract the Marines, she needed to have modifications made to her accommodations—additional latrines, showers, and living space in some of the holds to accommodate the extra four hundred passengers she was about to pick up. In Shanghai she took on 396 Marine Corps passengers. The Navy as usual did not supply surface escorting for China-bound vessels, but in an unusual move allocated the fleet submarines *Perch* and *Permit* to accompany *Madison* on the return trip to Olongapo. She disembarked the Marines in Subic Bay on December 1. *President Harrison* took the other half of the Shanghai Marines. *Harrison*'s master was Orel A. Pierson, one of APL's best and most experienced captains, who was only taking this voyage as a substitute for a captain who had quit. Upon arrival in Manila the Navy ordered *Harrison* immediately to Hong Kong. Strangely she was carrying no passengers or freight for the Philippines. The Navy agreed to pay APL $95 per officer and $26.40 per enlisted man for transport, equivalent to first-class and third-class transit respectively. She arrived in Shanghai on November 23. The Marines embarked at 8 AM on November 27. *President Harrison* left on the afternoon tide and soon met her own pair of shadowing submarines—USS *Searaven* and *Seawolf.* Her contingent of 375 Marines also disembarked at Olongapo and she moved to Manila.

In Manila on December 4 the captains were given new orders: *President Madison* was to resume her around-the-world itinerary while *President Harrison* was ordered by the Navy to make the final journey to Tsingtao to pick up the north China marines and their 1,400 tons of supplies and equipment—it would be the ship's last American voyage. On the way north she noted many Japanese ships and planes about, but none interfered directly. She arrived off the mouth of the Yangtze on the morning of the eighth, picking up the news on radio of the war's start. Master Pierson crafted plans to scuttle the ship by running her aground off Tsingtao. The engine room put on speed and the venerable liner was run up on the rocks of Shaweishan Island. Unfortunately three men were lost when their lifeboat capsized on launch. The captain and crew made it ashore, but were soon captured by a Japanese search party. The ship was seriously damaged, but not destroyed. The Japanese proudly announced her capture, and she appeared in numerous propaganda photos. Later in the war she was repaired and put back into service by the Japanese. Sailing as *Kachidoki Maru* she was sunk by an American submarine. A total of 204 stranded Marines and attached naval personnel had to surrender to overwhelming Japanese forces in north China on December 8.

CHAPTER SIX

Philippine Reinforcements—November 1941

By the middle of October the schedule of units for the next shipment to the Philippines was becoming firm. Enough units and their matériel would be available to justify a shipment on or about the first of November. As both *President Coolidge* and *Hugh L. Scott* would be ready from their last turnaround, the makeup of a "fast" convoy was possible. The key units ready to go were the second of the two National Guard tank battalions earmarked for the islands, the ground echelon of an entire light bomber group, and the lead ground elements of two additional fighter squadrons. Altogether this journey would carry over 2,700 officers and men constituting these units. As usual additional equipment would have to be sent by separate freighter journeys. This convoy would be the largest in terms of fresh units and men to reach the Philippines before the outbreak of war.

The 192nd Tank Battalion was selected to be the armored unit for transfer. Like the 194th preceding it, the unit was one of the four pre-war federalized National Guard independent battalions. Army staff found that the 192nd had been inducted into federal service two months earlier than the 191st (at Fort Meade) or 193rd (Fort Benning), and thus was a little further along in its training and outfitting. In addition to the ex–National Guard units, only a single regular Army independent tank battalion existed, and it was not yet considered combat-ready. Thus the 192nd received a secret radiogram on September 9, 1941 to prepare for an overseas deployment. Without qualms the selection memorandum stated that if a battalion was to go to the Philippines and likely see combat within six months, the 192nd Tank Battalion was the preferred unit.[1] Also authorized for formation and simultaneous move-

Table 3. November 1941 Shipments to the Philippines[2]

Convoy/Ships/Speed/Escort/Dates/Route	Units and Major Cargo Items
USAT *President Coolidge* USAT *Hugh L. Scott* 16 knots Escort: USS *Louisville* Depart SF 10/27/41(*Scott*) and 11/01/41 (*Coolidge*) Depart Honolulu 11/06/41 Arrive Manila 11/20/41 Direct route through Marianas, stopped at Guam for water	192nd Tank Battalion (including 55 M3 light tanks) 27th Bomb Group HQ and HQ Squadron 16th, 17th, 91st Bomb Squadron (L) 48th Matériel Squadron Decon Det 2nd Chem Company Serv (Avn) 1st Chemical Platoon, 2nd Chemical Company Serv (Avn) 454th Ordnance Company (Avn) 5th AB Group HQ and HQ Squadron Decon Det 4th Chem Company Serv (Avn) Det 2nd QM Company Sup (Avn) Det 1st Platoon, Company A, 91st QM BN (LM) 2nd and 3rd Platoons, 693rd Ordnance Company, Avn (Pur) 21st, 34th Pursuit Squadron (of 35th Group) Total 2,739 officers and men Small arms, wire, trucks and other vehicles, subsistence, hay, oil, mail, medical supplies, toilet tissue, gas masks, baggage, seven 18-inch searchlights, airplane wheels and parts, five PT-boat spare engines, 6,790 coils barbed wire, 1,144 boxes .50-caliber ammunition, incandescent light bulbs
SS *President Grant* SS *Cape Fairweather* SS *John Lykes* MV *Dona Nati* MV *American Leader* Escort: USS *Boise* Depart SF 11/09/41 Depart Honolulu 11/18/41 Arrive Manila 12/04/41	23 trucks and miscellaneous trailers Small number of replacement personnel Underground fuel tanks for Nichols Field Miscellaneous military stores and supplies

ment was a small armored group headquarters, not to exceed five officers and ten enlisted men.

At the time of its transfer the unit was actually near Camp Polk, Louisiana, where it had just completed its role in maneuvers. The companies started west by train on October 21, followed by the battalion headquarters. After only a three-day stay in San Francisco the men boarded *Hugh L. Scott.* The usual routine of ship life followed, this time including the complete chipping and repainting of the vessel by the tank troops. Upon arrival in Manila on November 20 the tank battalion men were greeted by their sister unit, including a welcome Thanksgiving dinner.

There were some organizational differences between the 192nd and 194th, at least in what was sent to the Philippines. The 194th, arriving a month earlier, had been sent with just two of its companies. The 192nd had all four of its assigned companies. This accounts for the relative difference of personnel strength (588 vs. 410). Shortly after arrival in the Philippines the obvious step was taken to assign "D" Company of the 192nd to the 194th (designated as its "B" Company) so both would have three tank companies. Apparently this had been planned all along. When shipped over, each battalion took with them the necessary tanks to complete three organic companies—each had fifty-one tanks needed to create three companies of seventeen tanks each. For the tankers the fighting vehicles were brand new. They had turned in the M2A2 tanks used at the maneuvers, and received the newer, improved M3 tank. The tanks were loaded on *Hugh L. Scott* with the men that would use them.

Almost immediately after arrival the two tank battalions were tactically combined. On November 21, the day after arrival, the Provisional Tank Group was created under the command of Col. James R. N. Weaver. It consisted of the small headquarters unit just arrived on *Scott*, the 192nd Tank Battalion (under Maj. Theodore Wickard), and the 194th Tank Battalion (under Maj. Ernest B. Miller). A week later (November 29) the 17th Ordnance Company (under Lt. Col. Richard C. Kadel) was also incorporated in the unit.

Unlike the constantly changing list of requested ground units, the plan for air units remained fairly constant through the latter part of the reinforcement effort. Once heavy bombers were released for use in the islands, the War Department stayed consistent in its goals of an ultimate air force. The planned buildup was to these levels:[3]

- 165 heavy bombers (four groups)
- 52 dive bombers (one group)
- 240 fighters (four groups)
- 19 observation planes (one squadron)

The next unit transferred was the entire three-squadron dive-bomber group, in air force terminology called a bombardment group (light).

Thus the second, and largest, organization selected for this convoy was the 27th Bombardment Group (Light) and its attendant service units. The bomb group headquarters was accompanied by all three of its organizational squadrons—the 16th, 17th, and 91st Bombardment Squadrons (L). The group had been functioning for some time, and most recently had participated in the General Headquarters' maneuvers in the summer of 1941. The group was equipped with Army A-24 "Banshee" dive-bombers. These were Army versions of the Navy's "Dauntless" SBD dive-bombers, without the niceties of arrestor hooks and other purely aircraft carrier equipment. However, the airplanes themselves did not accompany the group; rather, all fifty-two planes were on board the slow Army transport USAT *Meigs*, which attempted to closely follow, but never reached, the group's personnel. With the group was the usual list of small, specialized Army Air Force service units. Initially the units and men went to Nichols Field, but apparently after the planes arrived they were to be based at a new field being constructed at San Marcelino.[4]

Hugh L. Scott, loaded almost exclusively for the Philippine delivery, departed San Francisco on October 27. There was a quick turnaround for workhorse *President Coolidge*—she had arrived back in San Francisco just on the twenty-third but was loaded and ready to leave again nine days later on November 1. After meeting heavy cruiser USS *Louisville* off Hawaii they traveled by the direct route to Guam, where fresh water was taken on—just a stop of twelve hours with no liberty. Arrival in Manila was made on November 20. Several good accounts of the journey by the airmen were published postwar, including that of Capt. Ed Dyess, commanding the 21st Pursuit Squadron. At the time, the unit was very aware of the mounting U.S.–Japanese tensions; they were impatient with the slightest delay, and concerned that hostilities would begin before their arrival. They had no doubt that Manila would be the enemy's first target. At Nichols Field they found preparations for war proceeding at a furious pace.[5] Like the 27th Group, there was concern over the lack of planes accompanying the unit, but there were some extra fighters already in the Philippines, and a load of twenty-five P-40s arrived in Manila just five days after the men disembarked.

The 48th Matériel Squadron moved from maneuvers at Barksdale, Louisiana, to their home station at the Savannah Army Air Base just in time to transfer west. Trains left on October 22. They went through the usual medical checks at Fort Mason, San Francisco on the twenty-eighth prior to spending a few days at Fort McDowell on Angel Island. A few "unfortunates" had to be separated due to medical conditions. The journey over in *President Coolidge* was remembered as particularly luxurious. Officers and senior enlisted men had their own cabins. Meals (and choices!) were served with just four men at a table and an attending waiter. Even for the enlisted men a sense of worry, at least about security, was evident. The story was told about how some sensitive items were broken into, and a steward of German ancestry was questioned hard about the circumstances. Likewise, a close encounter with a foreign merchantman, which turned out to be an Allied Norwegian-registry ship, caused some excitement. Everyone seemed to know or sense that the situation was close to boiling over and hostile action was possible at any moment.[6]

Not much time was wasted on quickly unloading the vessels, hurrying their units off to the appropriate quarters or camps, and preparing the ships for the return voyage. The days when the escort would shuttle back the previous convoy were over; the turnover was soon fast enough that *Louisville* could escort her two valuable charges back to Hawaii. The Asiatic Fleet also began using the Navy's new convoy nomenclature, this returning convoy being designated No. 6001. On this trip *President Coolidge* brought back service dependents that had been ordered home by the Army. For freight she helped with the strategic cargo effort in loading almost 14,000 tons of rubber and hemp. As an additional precaution, even though escorted, the ships were directed by the CNO's office to take the southern course home through the Torres Strait and Rennell Islands. As a result of the increase in distance, the three ships were still far from home when war broke out on December 7.

Ammunition supply for automatic weapons was a major concern in the days preceding and following the start of the war. The standard American rifle cartridge was the .30-caliber Model 1906 round. It was used in all the most commonly used rifles and light machine guns in the islands. The Philippine Department's projected requirement for .30-caliber ammunition, prior to the rapid expansion of American and Filipino forces in late 1941, was usually stated at about 100 million rounds.[7] In July of 1940 the inventory reported was 58 million rounds, which while deficient from perceived requirements was still a significant stockpile. In September of 1940 the War Department approved the dispatch of an additional 25 million rounds. However, shipment was not immediately made, and eventually it was decided to supply half (12.5 million) in March 1941, and keep the balance in abeyance depending on the military and production situation. The larger .50-caliber round was in even shorter supply. This round was used in a heavy infantry ground-support machine gun, in the most common light anti-aircraft weapon, and was widely used on airplanes. The production of .50-caliber ammunition seriously lagged behind needs prior to the start of the war. On the first of January 1940 there were less than 1 million rounds (917,000) in the Philippines. It was simply impossible to fully rectify this deficit; the ammunition just did not exist anywhere in American inventory.

Throughout 1941 incremental installments to both these sizes of ammunition stocks were made. During that year almost every major voyage that originated from San Francisco saw at least some quantity of small-arms ammunition included. For example *Yaka* in September brought three thousand boxes, *Holbrook* and *Bliss* brought more in October, *American Packer* in early November brought three hundred boxes, and *Scott* and *Coolidge* later in the month delivered a quantity of .50-caliber armor-piercing rounds. On November 1 it was reported that 80 million rounds of .30-caliber and 3.8 million rounds of .50-caliber ammunition were in stock to cover both the American and Philippine components of USAFFE.[8]

One more successful convoy made it through prior to the Pearl Harbor attack. In early November the Navy was notified that the American President Lines' *President Grant* would be leaving San Francisco for her trip to Manila on November 9. Routing plans were finalized on the seventeenth to reflect the new policy of batching merchant ships for the voyage west. More than any other voyage, this trip reflects the new policy of protecting the ships themselves, rather than just providing escort based on the importance of the cargo. It appears that three of the ships on the journey carried no significant military cargo whatsoever, but were still ordered to sail in an escorted convoy. The ships were all capable of fourteen to fifteen knots, thus meeting the criteria of a medium-speed convoy.

In addition to *President Grant*, four other commercial merchantmen were given routing orders to join this convoy, even though they were not chartered by the Army or, with one exception, even carrying any Army cargo. MV *American Leader* was a new commercial freighter of the Maritime Commission's American Pioneer Line. She carried a deck load of large fuel tanks intended for Nichols Field to be part of the underground aviation fuel storage at that airbase. SS *John Lykes* and SS *Cape Fairweather* were both commercial freighters bound just for Manila. Finally, the Philippine-registry MV *Doña Nati* of the De La Rama Steamship Co. was along. She departed San Francisco on November 2, but like the others had stopped at Honolulu awaiting the formation of a suitable convoy. Orders were to pursue a generally direct route west, bypass close (but not stop at) Guam, and then approach Manila Bay via the San Bernardino Strait. This was to be the final convoy to go the "direct" route. Already independently sailing ships were plodding along the southern routing, and the return of the *Louisville* convoy home was ordered by this routing on November 25.

Despite American fears, it does not appear the Japanese regularly monitored the travels of either the independent sailing vessels or the escorted convoys. Several personal accounts of voyages speak of sightings of foreign aircraft, often seaplanes. Certainly there were active Japanese patrol squadrons operating from Pacific bases. It is not improbable that sightings were made, reports filed, and even some amount of "shadowing" of vessels accomplished. On the other hand Japanese surface forces were not regularly posted to the central Pacific. Few significant fleet bases were developed in the Japanese possessions in the central Pacific; besides, Japanese naval doctrine favored fleet concentration for potential offensive use, not dispersion to bases that could not be mutually supported. Also, preparations for the offensive planned for late 1941 preempted the routine of most of the heavy surface and underwater forces of the Japanese navy. While some units were deployed earlier in the year off the China and Indochina coasts, by June 1941 the heavy cruiser fleet was being recalled to Japan in preparation for its offensive role.

Most of the Japanese light cruisers were quite elderly, and were generally used as flagships of destroyer or submarine squadrons. A few also were local garrison vessels or used for training. In the mandated islands, the only permanent assignment of cruisers was the three very small light vessels of the Fourth Fleet usually stationed at Truk or Saipan. Japan had also just recently completed three special-built training cruisers. Intended for extended cruising to train midshipmen and other specialist ratings, the ships were not originally intended for organized units of the combat fleet. By the start of the war training cruises were no longer scheduled, and the ships were used as sort of station flagships. Of these, *Kashima* was stationed at Truk, *Kashii* at Saipan, and *Katori* was serving as the flagship for the submarines of the Japanese Sixth Fleet.

Only one encounter between American supply ships and Japanese surface vessels can be documented. First-person accounts and the deck log of *Boise* describe an encounter with a mystery ship on the evening of November 27. Lookouts detected a darkened ship at about 6:40 PM. Challenges for identity went unanswered, and eventually the ship picked up speed and disappeared. Later that same evening, at 10:53 PM, the same vessel appeared again. In this instance *Boise* interposed herself between her five-vessel convoy and the unidentified ship, and went to general quarters. The stranger was assumed to be Japanese, and personnel on one of the convoy's merchant ships mistakenly identified it as a heavy cruiser, as did watchers in *Boise*, according to her deck log. The following day this (or perhaps another) vessel was again spotted, and tentatively identified as an *Atago*–class heavy cruiser.[9]

It turns out that the vessel was in fact the Japanese small training vessel *Katori*. This ship was functioning as the flagship of Vice Admiral Mitsumi Shimizu, commanding the Sixth Submarine Fleet. The command (and thus *Katori*) departed Japan in late November 1941 by way of Truk, which it left in turn on December 2 for Kwajalein Island. The latter post would serve as the advance base for Japanese submarine operations in the eastern Pacific at the start of hostilities. *Katori* encountered *Boise* and her convoy just east of the Marianas. The sighting was duly reported by the Japanese, and passed on to the Pearl Harbor attack task force, where it caused an increase in lookout vigilance. On the other hand, the Americans did not report the encounter until the ships arrived in Manila just a few days prior to the attack.[10]

Besides this mystery ship encounter, the convoy had no other complications on its voyage. It arrived on December 4 in Manila Bay and the ships went to the commercial Manila piers for unloading. *John Lykes* discharged some cargo at Manila on the fifth, but soon proceeded to Cebu. All the other merchant ships were still in Manila when war broke out. Like the previous convoy, plans were made for a quick turnaround of the ships involved. As soon as December 6, the Asiatic Fleet ordered Capt. Stephen B. Robinson of Task Force 15.4 to Cebu, where it was to meet American commercial vessel SS *Gertrude Kellogg* and escort her back to Honolulu. This order, however, was never implemented. *Kellogg* was bombed by Japanese aircraft in Manila Harbor on December 10. Two crewmen were killed and eight wounded, but structural damage was slight. She was partially loaded with coconut oil and soon departed south and eventually returned to New York. *Boise* was soon attached to the Asiatic Fleet, and her movements were thereafter dictated by the needs for war dispositions rather than convoy escorting.

Maintaining a degree of secrecy about the American reinforcement effort to the Philippines was an interesting problem. There were obvious military needs to keep the specific movements confidential. Much of the world was at war, and the Japanese were well known to have begun all of their modern conflicts with surprise attacks. Elimination or capture of a major convoy was within the realm of possibility as an early act of war. Discretion argued in favor of keeping the ships, dates, units, and routes taken as confidential as possible. The peacetime U.S. Army was not really very good at this. Such a movement required lots of people to coordinate, and involved many civilian or public facilities over which direct control was difficult. For example, when the Army used commercial ships, the freight or transport line still was expected to advertise cargo space or passenger bookings in newspapers and other media. For a long time sailings were still posted in maritime registries and port newspapers. The military asked for cooperation, but could not directly control this information. Finally on May 29, 1941 the Army issued orders that there be no release to the press of sailing information on Army transports.[11] Still, many of the ships were commercial vessels to which this order could not apply.

The situation was also complicated by the sheer size of the movements—particularly for the thousands of young soldiers excited about what was probably their first trip abroad. In mid-1941 the Army adopted a code-word system to designate overseas destinations, primarily to avoid directly stating the name of a destination in orders or stamped on packages and freight. For example, Hawaii was referred to in shipping documents as "Copper," Alaska as "Bronze," and Panama as "Mercury." Apparently the translations were not well known, at least at the worker and enlisted-man level, but obviously after repeated usage the destination codes became more widely recognized. For the U.S. forces in the Philippines the destination code word was "Plum." Many a soldier tried to find some rationale for this particular word; attempts at unraveling the word as an acronym appear in personal experience books from the war. For example, some thought the word stood for "Philippines, Luzon, Manila." There is no Army record reference to any meaning whatsoever. There was a separate word for freight assigned to the Philippine Army (the forces of the commonwealth), and that was "Peach."

In Washington the signs were clearly being read that war in the Pacific was imminent. Senior military officers and diplomats began selectively sharing descriptions of the buildup. Secretary of War Stimson found it useful to describe the Philippine reinforcement efforts to a variety of foreign emissaries as a sort of proof of America's commitment to aiding the Allied cause. On November 6 he told Chinese representatives T. V. Soong and Alfred Sze details of MacArthur's reinforcement. On the twenty-fourth of the same month he did the same with Major General Ludolph van Oyen, the Dutch East Indies senior air officer.[12] It is likely that some of these visits were arranged to plead for more physical aid and priority by the visitor, and Stimson could deflect some of the requests by describing how the Philippine buildup helped their cause. Brigadier General Gerow wrote, on behalf of the War Plans Division staff, about the Army's attitude toward Philippine reinforcement:

> Most effective aid to China, as well as to the defense of Singapore and the Netherlands East Indies, is now being built up by the reinforcement of the Philippines. The safety of Luzon as an air and submarine base should soon be reasonably assured by the arrival of air and ground reinforcements. Strong diplomatic and economic pressure may be exerted from the military viewpoint at the earliest about the middle of December, 1941, when the Philippine Air Force will have become a positive threat to Japanese operations. It would be advantageous, if practicable, to delay severe diplomatic and economic pressure until February or March, 1942, when the Philippine Air Force will have reached its projected strength, and a safe air route, through Samoa, will be in operation.[13]

This was one of the "catches" of the situation. The Americans needed to keep the buildup of forces secret in order to both protect them during their vulnerable shipping time, and also to hopefully avoid a preemptive Japanese strike on the Philippines (or other island bases) before the defense was thought ready. On the other hand, at some point the existence of the new forces needed to be revealed to the Japanese if they were to have any role as an active deterrent. The real situation was that the American command did not have the ability to really control either the public information being disseminated or the ability of the Japanese to collect the same information directly.

The press had been actively following the war threat in the Pacific and Far East. Almost every edition of every major American paper had something on its front pages about both the war in Europe and the deteriorating situation in the Far East. The moves of the Allied powers, particularly Britain and her Commonwealth partners, figured prominently. For example, the movement of Canadian troops to Hong Kong was reported in detail in mid-November even to the name and rank of the commander.[14] Other stories from the newspapers during the fall of 1941 talked of the transfer of U.S. combat planes to a secret Far Eastern assignment (the United States had only one Far Eastern country with aircraft basing rights—the Philippines), the expansion of the strength of the Philippine Scouts, the mobilization of the Philippine reserve divisions, the plan for American volunteer pilots and planes to fight with the Chinese, and the withdrawal of the China-based Marines and gunboats to the Philippines. Any astute reader (including one at a Japanese embassy or consulate) would clearly perceive that American forces were being concentrated and augmented in the Philippines during the last half of 1941.

In late October newly appointed Philippine air commander Maj. Gen. Lewis H. Brereton stopped in Washington for his final briefings and orders. General Marshall took considerable time to orient the new commander to the military situation. Among his statements was the newly increased strategic importance of the Philippines. Brereton was fearful that the Japanese had or would soon learn about the significant buildup, and move to promptly knock out the newly arrived B-17s. Marshall responded that the War Department knew the situation was a calculated risk, but were doing all they could to forestall a premature attack.[15] However, even as the two generals discussed the need for interim confidentiality of the situation, the press lost no time in prominently announcing the general's new appointment. The *Chicago Tribune* ran an article on October 26 about Brereton's mission to go to Manila to head the U.S. Air Forces. The article went on to describe how the Philippine aerial defenses had been reinforced substantially in recent weeks, and how munitions shipments to the Philippines had been given the highest priority lately.

A meeting three weeks later is even more revealing. Fearing leaks in the press, Marshall asked seven key correspondents to attend a special meeting at his office in the old Washington Munitions Building on November 15, 1941. Invited were the correspondents covering the subject from the *New York Times*, *New York Herald Tribune*, *Time*, *Newsweek*, and the wire services. Upon arrival they were told that the meeting was secret and none of its subject matter could be revealed. They were free to then leave if they didn't like the conditions set forth—but none did. The chief of staff then made an informal presentation on the situation in the Far East. The audience was told the American position was highly favorable, strength in the Philippines was far greater than the Japanese imagined. He told how tanks and guns were arriving hourly, and that the island would soon have the "greatest concentration of heavy bomber strength in the world." Allowed time, this strength would then be revealed to Japan's moderate leaders. Hopefully the Japanese would interpret the information as an incentive to deter any attack rather than accelerate one. Peculiarly one of the other facts that stood out in the memories of the reporters was the concept that the B-17s in the Philippines could be dispatched immediately to bomb naval bases and set the paper cities of Japan afire. The lack of range of the planes to then return was brushed off with the comment that landing rights would be obtained in Vladivostok, Russia. Both these ideas (the vulnerability of the targets and the landing rights) were in fact fanciful.[16]

Of course, the ultimate effectiveness of the reinforcement effort depended on just when the Japanese would attack. Essentially, how much time would the defenders have to augment their strength prior to the need? No one in the American camp really knew the Japanese timetable, but the estimates formulated were at the heart of the belief that there was indeed going to be enough time. How much (if any) of these estimates were based on any military or political insight versus wishful thinking is unknown. It may well have been that the estimated date for the start of the war was more influenced by when the defenses were felt to be sufficient than when the enemy was likely to move. There doesn't seem to have been any discussion of "if" war was to start, just "when."

Probably the most important opinion-holder on this subject was General MacArthur. It appears that relatively early he fixed on April 1, 1942 as the likely start of hostilities. He is on record as telling Admiral Hart on September 2 that he doubted the Japanese would attack before the spring of 1942. Thus adequate defenses could be developed in the time available.[17] Apparently Hart was less optimistic. In a meeting as late as November 27 between MacArthur, Francis Sayre (U.S. high commissioner to the Philippines), and the admiral to discuss the war message from Washington, the general reiterated that current Japanese movements and alignment convinced him that there would not be an attack before the spring—Sayre's report of the conference states that Hart felt otherwise.[18] When Major General Brereton arrived in early November he received the same message. MacArthur delivered a concise and clear-cut situation analysis to the general. Brereton's autobiography reports MacArthur (and "most informed men") thought nothing would happen before April 1, 1942. The persuasion of this opinion did have an effect. Brereton states that under this assumption he emphasized deployment, training, and equipping his newly arriving units instead of actively planning for imminent combat.

Likewise, the general imparted the same feelings to his most senior field commander, Brig. Gen. Jonathan M. Wainwright. In September MacArthur proffered command of the new North Luzon Force to Wainwright, until then the commander of the Philippine Division. On November 25 MacArthur instructed Wainwright to proceed to his new command quickly but not urgently, and to complete the training of the Philippine divisions under his command. At a personal meeting the Army commander told the leader of his key defensive force: "You'll probably have until about April to train those troops."[19] In none of these reports is there relayed any hint at the source or logic behind MacArthur's opinion. The estimate that the Inland Seas Project would be completed in April, the defense reserves except for a few types of ammunition would be completed by April, and the full mobilization of the Philippine Army would also be completed by that month are suspicious coincidences in timing, indicating perhaps that the April date was the hoped-for timing rather than one based on enemy capabilities.

While MacArthur's opinion was adopted by many, it was not adopted by all. Secretary of War Stimson leaned to January 1942; Marshall's thoughts are less easy to identify. His correspondence and biography do not indicate an expressed opinion—though one has to infer that with his considerable effort to push through reinforcements that he was leaning to sooner rather than later. One of the reporters from the November meeting with Marshall recalled that he stated: "If we [the United States] get past the current crisis, we're okay until February. MacArthur will have plenty in the Philippines by then."[20] Similarly the War Plans Division estimate of October 2, 1941 stated that the U.S. Army in the Philippines would be well equipped with adequate reserves by February 1942.

An inconsistency between MacArthur's defensive organization and Washington's endorsed war plans came to a head in the weeks prior to the start of the war. When MacArthur received his version of the revised Rainbow No. 5 plan in October of 1941 he immediately comprehended that it did not reflect his own current view of the defense. The plan still called for the retreat to and defense of Bataan and the harbor islands, while MacArthur was planning a protracted defense of the entire island of Luzon. His requests for specific reinforcements, and for the Inland Seas Project and Offshore Patrol, were predicated on this wider plan. Right or wrong, the Rainbow No. 5 plan was clearly out of step with the realities of there being a 200,000-man Philippine Army by early 1942. An intensive exchange led to the Joint Board, under Marshall's recommendation, endorsing a revision to the plans along MacArthur's lines on November 21, 1941.[21]

Right after the departure of the *Boise* convoy, the War Department began efforts to substantially accelerate the pace of shipments. Efforts were already in hand for the follow-on convoy (that would become Convoy No. 4002, the *Pensacola* convoy), but planned movements further out were to be pushed forward. In a memo of November 10 Brigadier General Gerow stated that the planned movement schedules for November 20, 29, and December 1 and 17 would remain unchanged; however, those for January 10 and 18 would be advanced to December 17 and 20. Over 1.1 million tons of freight had already been cleared for shipment to the Philippines, and the Quartermaster Corps and Maritime Commission were arranging for seventy-one ship trips involving approximately fifty vessels. To meet the advancing schedule, all the stops would have to be pulled out and additional troop transports located.[22]

Besides units and weapons, stockpiles of key operating supplies had been significantly augmented during the fall of 1941. In June the authorized defense reserve of gasoline had been just over 5 million gallons, but it was thought that most all of this could be acquired from commercial sources locally if a crisis occurred. Since then 9 million gallons of 100-octane aviation gasoline had been scheduled for delivery to the Philippines as a reserve supply—though it is unclear how much was on hand when war began. Brig. Gen. Charles C. Drake, quartermaster for USAFFE, had requested empty 55-gallon drums in mid-summer of 1941. He intended to use these to establish supply dumps around the island. To his surprise, the drums arrived already filled, providing a fortunate 1-million-gallon windfall.[23] This supply was stashed at dispersed depots in Camp Limay, Manila, Camp Stotsenburg,

Table 4. Philippine Ammunition Stores[24]

Ammunition Item	Quantity on Hand January 1, 1940	Quantity on Hand November 1, 1941
.30-caliber rounds	57,100,000	80,000,000
.50-caliber rounds	917,000	3,800,000
37-mm infantry gun high explosive rounds	21,945	97,000
37-mm tank and anti-tank rounds	0	31,500
37-mm anti-aircraft rounds	0	52,000
3-inch & 81-mm mortar rounds	20,680	41,000
2.95-inch gun rounds	38,078	50,000
75-mm field artillery rounds	176,684	599,000
3-inch anti-aircraft rounds	54,617	56,000
155-mm field artillery rounds	28,996	55,000

Fort McKinley, and Fort Mills. Additionally relatively large stocks were confiscated or donated from private oil firms in the islands. Some fuel did make it to Bataan during the retreat, but larger stores were lost or had to be destroyed for lack of transport. About 600,000 gallons made it into the rapidly closing perimeter. Gasoline was heavily rationed during the campaign, with strict restrictions on vehicle usage. With conservation the stocks did last; the final 13,000 gallons in Bataan were ordered not to be destroyed with the hope that they would be used for moving prisoners.

As part of department plans, there did exist substantial reserve food stocks. In accordance with the command's decision to fight on the beaches, four forward depots were developed at Tarlac, Guagua, Los Baños, and Cebu. Dry rations were stocked at these locations; the troops were expected to buy fresh vegetables and meat locally. A central storage of balanced rations was held in Manila, and the harbor defenses had their own storage on Corregidor. Unfortunately two major developments aggravated the food supply situation. First, the number of people to be fed was considerably in excess of the 50,000-man estimate that the strategic reserve was based upon. Counting all USAFFE forces and civilian refugees, something more like 104,000 were in the Bataan perimeter.[25] Second, and more seriously, the sudden collapse and retreat meant that most of the food depots had to be abandoned. The quartermaster worked wonders in the week after December 23. Supplies were immediately dispatched to Bataan from all possible sources, but there simply wasn't enough time or enough transports.

All considered, the ammunition supply situation for the defending forces was not bad. Certainly the total stockpile was less than what was desired, but as it turned out was adequate for the events that unfolded. Steps had been taken to augment the reserves during 1941. A comparison of the inventory of ammunition rounds between January 1940 and November 1941 (twenty-two months later) is instructive of the supply accomplishment.

CHAPTER SEVEN

The Philippine Army

The Tydings-McDuffie Act passed the United States Congress and was signed into law in March of 1934. The act authorized commonwealth status for the Philippines, as a sort of precursor for complete independence to be granted in 1946. During this period U.S. military forces would stay in the Philippines and provide for the defense.[1] The Philippine legislature also ratified the act, and began to organize a constitutional convention and other trappings of international statehood. An integral part was the provision for Filipino armed forces. With a very limited budget and uncertain future financial support from the United States, the commonwealth planners had to make wise choices. They found they could not afford the creation of a modern navy. Likewise, an air force would have to be limited to local defense and support needs. However, a large army, based on the archipelago's substantial population, was embraced as the primary defensive arm. The very first legislative act of the Philippine National Assembly was the National Defense Act passed on December 20, 1935.

Manpower for the new army was not limited. The Philippines quickly established compulsory training—all Filipino males twenty years of age had to register within their military districts; the requirement was generally well complied with. Obtaining officers and technical specialists was a touchier proposition. A few U.S. Army officers were initially detailed to assist in training efforts. Also a military academy and a reserve officers' school were established and soon functioning.[2]

Almost immediately thought was given to the equipment needs of the Philippine Army. Very little—besides some leather goods and transportation animals—was available from local Philippine sources. Almost everything needed would be either transferred from the U.S. Army or bought direct from suppliers. During the summer of 1937 the U.S. Army's chief of staff reviewed a couple of memoranda for the projected equipment needs. The Philippine Army was being trained in staged increments, so the initial concern was to obtain enough equipment to adequately equip these cadres. Each increment would be called to training centers, undergo five and one-half months training, and then return home to become the reserve necessary in time of war. Ultimately the plan was to train all of the men necessary to form the heart of the Philippine Army—thirty reserve divisions by 1946.

The reserve division was to be the basic unit of the fully mobilized Philippine Army. Eventually there would also be an army and corps headquarters (with their attendant attached units), supporting independent units (including independent field artillery, coast artillery, anti-aircraft artillery, engineer, signal, transport, medical, ordnance, and quartermaster functions), a small regular Philippine Army, a Philippine Offshore Patrol (navy), and Air Corps. But still, it was the thirty reserve divisions that would make up the fighting strength of the army. Each division would be raised from one of ten military districts defined geographically. The first from each district was to be available for mobilization by early 1942. The division's organization changed slightly between 1936 and 1941, but its essential design was fairly consistent. Representing strength of 520 officers and 7,881 men (in a 1941 plan) it was to consist of:

Division headquarters with Headquarters Company
Transport Company
Engineer Battalion
Signal Company
Medical Company
Field Artillery Regiment:
Total of two battalions each of three firing batteries
Twenty-four 75-mm field artillery pieces (four per battery, or twelve per battalion)
Three infantry regiments:
Each with three infantry battalions
Each battalion with three infantry companies and one machine-gun company

The most significant change between 1936 and 1941 in division design was the incorporation of an anti-tank battalion. Also some later versions had the transportation unit rated as a battalion of two companies rather than just a single company.

In September 1937 it was estimated that this army would require within the next three years: one thousand light machine guns or automatic rifles, 180 3-inch trench mortars, and 120 field artillery pieces (thirty batteries of four guns each).[3] It is important to understand that the training and equipping of this force had the clear and active support of the local U.S. Philippine Department. After all, the Philippine Army was assumed to be essentially an in-depth reserve for the U.S. forces in the islands, at least during the ten years of shared defense responsibility. Prior to the eventual withdrawal of American forces the Philippine Army could be asked to directly serve with the Americans during an emergency. Consequently in this same 1937 memo it was found that twenty-four trench mortars, thirty-two 75-mm guns, and twenty-four 2.95-inch mountain guns were available for "loan" to the Philippine Army from the Philippine Department. Other material such as mess kits, shelter tents, and first-aid pouches were authorized for sale by the department to the Filipinos. At this stage the initial phase of the training program would involve about 32,000 trained Filipino soldiers. This was approximately one full infantry regiment, one artillery battalion, and parts of other units for each of the first ten reserve divisions. It was calculated that the value of the material supplied amounted to a little under $6 million.[4]

The first identified need was for rifles. Of all the basic infantry needs imagined, clearly a standard small arm for the line soldier was the most important—and the one that virtually every soldier would require. A large supply of rifles was needed for the first class of recruits in 1937 and thereafter. Eventually a supply to arm the entire reserve army was needed if it was to have the capability of being mobilized for active service. The rifle had to have two important characteristics: it had to fire the standard American .30-caliber model 1906 ("30-06") ammunition, and for the stretched Philippine budget it had to be cheap. The Philippine Constabulary had purchased Springfield Model 1903 rifles in the past; however, the unit cost of almost ninety pesos was far too expensive for the entire army. After all, the need was for 90,000 rifles per year between 1936 and 1939. General MacArthur in this instance performed precisely the task for which he was hired by President Quezon as military adviser. MacArthur, using influence within the War Department's bureaucracy, managed to stir up the Ordnance Department in looking for solutions.

The final solution was to secure surplus First World War rifles initially at just eight pesos apiece. These were American-built guns patterned after the British Enfield rifle (properly known as the U.S. Rifle Model of 1917), but chambered to fire the standard American round. Ultimately an agreement was made to secure 100,000 rifles in 1936, with more available later, for eighteen pesos each. The gun had some troublesome problems, but it was immediately available and affordable and thus the only viable solution to the problem.[5] The first Model 1917s arrived in August of 1936, and enough were on hand to completely arm the Philippine Army through the 1941–1942 conflict.[6] Shortly before the start of the war MacArthur attempted to upgrade this arm to M1 Garands, but the story of this request will be dealt with later.

President Quezon secured legislative approval for the plan, with an impressive annual budget of $8 million. Training started for the reserve divisions in 1937, though the budget allowed only for a class of reduced size, particularly as training camps had to be funded and constructed. As might be expected there were many start-up problems. The goals had been ambitious in the first place, and the costs underestimated. The diversity of the Filipino population with regard to tribal and language groups was formidable. In some cases basic hygiene and elementary skills had to be taught prior to military instruction. With no predecessor organization, instructors themselves were difficult to locate and train. The training program never did progress to large-unit exercises. While MacArthur continued to be enthusiastic about the progress, his aides in the Philippines and the War Department had serious reservations about the readiness of the Filipino forces. Also, in 1937, the Army chief of staff refused to directly fund ammunition and arms for the Philippine Army that it could not afford with its own budget. In fact, by 1938 the expansion and training goals had outgrown their financial underpinnings. A $16 million annual expense was now predicted against the government's expected $8 million budget. Quezon became disillusioned with the program's progress, and with the legislature cut the budget by 14 percent in June 1939. After a declared limited state of national emergency funding was restored, but progress in the years of 1939–1940 was not what had been hoped.

In April of 1941 Brigadier General Grunert recommended that portions of the Philippine Army be mobilized and called into the service of the United States. Washington wasn't quite as sure that the moment for this action was right, and furthermore didn't have congressional support for the expenses required to equip and train these men. After all, once called into U.S. service, these expenses would become an American, not a Philippine Commonwealth, obligation. One item was approved (although not until early July): the request for 425 reserve officers of the United States Army to act as instructors. Initially the Philippines Commonwealth paid for its own expenses—construction of training facilities, purchase of weapons, and payment of the army's salary. As the war approached, and particularly as the army was called into U.S. service in July 1941, the expenditures quickly outran the ability of the commonwealth to fund them. An initial $10 million was made available on August 23, 1941 and another $5 million on November 29. Both of these came from the U.S. president's emergency fund. Once war started the problems with getting congressional funding passed, and the final $53,333,377 was appropriated and released to the Philippines on February 14, 1942.[7]

The adopted timetable called for ten regiments (the first from each reserve division) to be called up on September 1, the second set of regiments on November 1, and the third and final infantry regiment on December 1. Artillery, engineer, signal, transportation, medical, and other smaller components of the division began with early cadres, but full manpower would follow in early 1942. It was hoped that there would be time to call up and train additional divisions later in 1942. Roughly forty American officers and twenty experienced American (including Philippine Scout) non-commissioned officers would be assigned to each division as instructors. As it turned out, many of these ultimately served as commanders to the formations they were assigned to. Commensurate with the mobilization was a large construction project. The need for room to quarter and continue the training of 70,000 soldiers was considerably in excess of the facilities already built for training annual contingents of about 20,000. Many of the original training camps were simply enlarged, several to full divisional-sized capacity.

Many practical problems plagued the mobilization, and other problems that had been ignored or tolerated during the preceding training courses re-emerged. One of the chief of these was language. In 1941 the Philippines were still very much a multilingual nation. Dozens of major dialects were in use, with enough difference between each other to make conversation impossible in units with mixed backgrounds. The organizational plan tried to regionalize where units were raised, and with smaller-sized units that usually worked. Still, many of the whole divisions and even regiments operated on several different languages. Officers and many NCOs spoke passable English, but the average recruit did not. Issuing of orders almost always necessitated one if not two or more verbal translations. Even literacy was lacking in some cases. One American adviser found that there were many first sergeants and company clerks who could neither read nor write.[8] It was also found that the previous training had not really been very effective. Even those soldiers who had gone through the total five and one-half month training program were capable of close-order marching and drill—and that was about it. Suffice to say that glaring deficiencies in the preparedness of the Philippine Army emerged. On top of the training, equipment standards were also marginal. The one major positive attribute of the army was its overall loyalty and morale. Despite its considerable handicaps, the Philippine Army fought loyally and generally with steadfast resolve throughout the upcoming campaign, in stark contrast to some of its counterparts in Southeast Asia.

The expansion and training program for the Philippine Army encountered several setbacks as war approached. A continuing problem was encountered with pay levels. Ordering the Philippine Army into U.S. service did not mean that it was federalized. The soldiers continued with their previous organization, uniforms, and pay. And in pay there was a considerable difference. In 1941, for example, a U.S. corporal received an equivalence of 1,008 pesos per month, an American Philippine Scout corporal 444, and a Philippine Army corporal just 264. Just whom you worked for made a significant personal difference, and discrepancies in pay and benefits during and after the war were issues to be dealt with.[9]

The first of many lengthy requests by the newly activated Far Eastern command for equipment for the Philippine Army was made in a radiogram from Manila on August 15, 1941. To provide arms for the ten reserve divisions then being trained and organized, a request was placed for: [10]

337	.30-caliber Model 1917A1 machine guns and tripods
326	.50-caliber heavy anti-aircraft machine guns and mounts
449	37-mm M3 anti-tank guns
217	81-mm mortars
1,837	.45-caliber pistols
84,500	M1 semi-automatic rifles
248	75-mm field guns
100	M3 scout cars
300	½-ton ambulances, 80 sedans
6,820	various types of trucks

Notes accompanying the message allowed room for a single substitution: the command was willing to accept the use of 37-mm Model 1916 infantry-support guns for the anti-tank guns. The M1 semi-automatic rifle was requested as a replacement to the already-adopted Enfield rifle (65,000 pieces) and for general command reserve (19,500).

Besides the actual weapons for the first ten Philippine reserve divisions, the most urgent single item in demand from American sources seems to have been motor transport. Even with the large expansion in manpower as represented by the reserve divisions, the defense plan for Luzon still depended on the concept of quickly deploying strength at any potential enemy landing site. While the Philippines did have a respectable level of domestic motor traffic that was available for requisition, ideally the divisions would be equipped with a fairly high organic level of vehicles. In the large-scale funding request by Grunert in June 1941 were four hundred to five hundred small ½-ton pickups or weapons-carrier type trucks. It was recognized that the road conditions were such in the Philippines that a preference existed for a large number of smaller vehicles versus the other way around. Also it was necessary that the various units of the Philippine divisions should be able to operate independently, and to supply themselves without recourse to higher echelons. Still, in general the division would depend on the majority of its motor transport coming from expropriation of civilian vehicles, and when off-road would move by foot or native animal transportation.

In a study of mid-August 1941 it was recommended that the organic transportation of a Philippine Army reserve division be 479 vehicles, with a "minimum" of 316.[11] This forecasted requirement changed several times over the next few months, but in general is a pretty good description of what was envisioned in late 1941. A follow-up War Department analysis of early September summarized the vehicle requests coming from MacArthur. By his most recent radiogram, he had requisitioned a total of 4,040 vehicles and 1,770 trailers. Altogether the cost of this transport amounted to about $5.2 million, not counting maintenance and reserves. By comparison the U.S. garrison of the Philippine Department then had just over one thousand vehicles.[12] Of course, the start of the war intervened long before any division got anywhere close to this number of cars and trucks. In fact, besides a few trucks, wreckers, and 150 staff cars that the American forces held in excess to requirements, the only vehicles ever obtained by the Filipinos were through civilian confiscation. None of the American-supplied requisitioned vehicles ever made it to the islands.

In the late summer of 1941 the requests from the Far Eastern Army command continued at an unimpeded rate. After the initial request for vehicles on August 15, MacArthur clarified the list in more detail (and requested yet more trucks!) on August 23. On August 28 in a radiogram, the general provided a revised list of sixteen types of critical ordnance and fire-control items. On September 10 helmets, gas masks, engineer, and signal items were requested. On October 22 the U.S. Army's surgeon general was told to come up with ten 150-bed hospitals for the divisions and 180 sets of regimental infirmary equipment—all to be obtained and shipped no later than December 5. The types and quantities of items requested were huge; after all, an entire field army of a quarter-million men was to be equipped in a matter of months. October saw additional ordnance and signal corps supplies requested, November asked for airplane bombs and ammunition. On November 7 even construction supplies for the new Philippine Army camps were needed—eight thousand kegs of various nails, roofing paper, pipes, hinges, and hardware. Some of the requisitions were almost comical—a type of canned foot powder hadn't been manufactured in the United States since 1918. For one request MacArthur was radioed that no serviceable horse gas masks were available anywhere, and that he'd have to wait until Edgewood Arsenal manufactured 2,600 specifically for the Philippines.

Dialogue continued into September on the U.S. Army's ability to comply with the lengthy requests for equipment coming from Manila. In mid-September the War Department agreed as a first step to supply 20 percent of the equipment request, but with several key exceptions. The scout cars were either all issued or obligated to lend-lease; none would be available for some time for the Philippine Army. No 75-mm guns and carriages with high-speed adapters were available; however, the forty guns already with the Philippine Department could be released to Philippine forces once they were replaced by 105-mm howitzers, and similarly forty-eight such guns in the Hawaiian Department could also be obtained in the same fashion. No additional 37-mm anti-tank guns or .50-caliber machine guns were available either, but new production of these types could potentially fill at least part of the requests by the end of the 1941 calendar year. The offer by MacArthur to take the older 37-mm in place of the modern anti-tank gun was acknowledged, and thirty-five such guns were located and prepared for immediate shipment via San Francisco.[13]

The demand for more anti-tank weapons for the Philippine Army forces continued to bedevil the supplying agencies. The mission of the anti-tank units recently added to the organization of the Philippine reserve divisions also included a role for beach defense. Army planners tried to patch together a supply strategy attempting to give the Filipinos at least partial coverage of their beach defense needs, even if the anti-tank role could not be satisfied until the new M3 guns were produced. They calculated that the self-propelled 75-mm mounts, the old 37-mm infantry guns, and the 20 percent allocation of the M3 anti-tank gun need could be supplemented by another 123 .30-caliber machine guns then surplus and available in Hawaii. Worthless in the anti-tank role, the guns could at least be used to defend beaches against landing parties and also be a way to productively use the gun crews being mobilized and trained at various camps in the Philippines.[14]

Another key requirement for the new Philippine Army was to be its anti-aircraft capability. However, with the need to get the training and equipping of the basic reserve divisions off to a good start first, the organization of anti-aircraft units lagged seriously. In hindsight this was a serious error by MacArthur's command. It was the one defensive element that would be called upon for maximum effort starting on the very first day of war. Finally, in November, MacArthur and the War Plans Division began to address this deficiency. In fact, in late September MacArthur had asked for the priority shipment of the equipment for additional 3-inch and 37-mm gun battalions, but the requisition did not receive that attention, perhaps because the intended units were not yet recruited or formed and no training centers yet established. Then in mid-November the War Department suggested that due to the urgency and lateness of the hour, complete units should be requested instead of just unmanned equipment. General MacArthur complied and sent a formal request to Marshall dated December 1 for the equivalent of about six regiments of U.S. anti-aircraft troops.[15] MacArthur then finally admitted that a Philippine Army anti-aircraft training center would begin construction and go into operation by February of 1942. He would also need the equipment for eight new Philippine anti-aircraft regiments. Of course, all this was too late—none of the requested units even made it to the port of embarkation much less the Philippines themselves.

Of all the requests for equipment made by General MacArthur in the immediate reinforcement period, only two item types were specifically denied. Others were in short supply and requisitions had to be delayed or delivered in smaller quantities due to juggling of production. Only the 90-mm anti-aircraft gun and the M-1 semi-automatic rifle were directly refused, and for the latter it was a matter of policy on quantity rather than utility. As early as January 29, 1941 the office of the chief of coast artillery expressed concerns that the production of the three necessary elements of the 90-mm "system" (guns, ammunition, fire-control devices) wouldn't coincide enough to allow the guns to be deployed to an overseas garrison. Also, the War Department definitely turned down the request for M-1 rifles. On September 23 MacArthur was told that in view of the M1917s on hand in the Philippines, no additional M-1s could be supplied. While they were issued to the regular combat units of the Philippine Department, regular U.S. Army units in the United States had priority over the department for issue of newly produced rifles.

It wasn't just the ten reserve divisions that needed equipment. MacArthur's staff soon began to think of how these divisions would be integrated with the U.S. forces into corps or commands. A variety of units would be needed to equip the new operating formations besides those just available as divisions. Artillery, engineer, and signal units were envisioned—most made up of Philippine recruits but armed and equipped with U.S. matériel. On November 7 the adjutant general approved sending 45 motorcycles, 450 trailers, and 411 trucks specifically for corps and army units. A variety of specialized signal and chemical equipment was being prepared for shipment when the war began, and several of the artillery units designed to help fill out corps artillery (in this case involving American troops in addition to just their equipment) were at sea on the *Pensacola* convoy or soon to follow from San Francisco.

The beginning of hostilities found the Philippine Army in the midst of mobilizing, training, and equipping. This process was far from complete, and virtually all units had only a portion of the weapons and military supplies required. Many of the records of the army were destroyed during and after the campaign; no good equipment rosters exist that can tell us today the precise armament of these units. However, Brig. Gen. Clifford Bluemel did write a good report on the wartime activities of one of the Luzon-based divisions, the 31st. While this was probably one of the better-equipped reserve divisions, his description of it as published in Louis Morton's *The Fall of the Philippines* provides a useful record:

> The 31st Division, like the other Philippine Army divisions, suffered from shortages in personal and organizational equipment. Every man was equipped with a rifle, the .30-caliber Enfield rifle used by American troops in World War I. The stock was too long for the small Philippine

> soldier and the weak extractor often broke and could not be replaced. There was one Browning automatic rifle for each infantry company and eight .30-caliber Browning water-cooled machine guns for each machine-gun company. Each infantry regiment had two .50-caliber machine guns and six 3-inch trench mortars, 70 percent of the ammunition for which proved to be duds. Artillery equipment for the division consisted of eight World War I model 75-mm guns that were delivered on the evening of 7 December, without sights or fire-control equipment. The 31st Field Artillery, therefore, could only organize two of the six firing batteries it was authorized.
>
> Organic transportation was virtually nonexistent. Division headquarters and the motor transport company could muster only one sedan, one command car, one bantam car, one 1½-ton truck and one ½-ton truck. The 31st Infantry had only one command car and eight 1½-ton trucks, which was more than the other regiments had. The division was deficient also in communications and engineer supplies, office equipment, spare parts, and tools.
>
> The personal equipment of the Philippine soldier in the 31st Division left much to be desired. His uniform consisted of shorts, short-sleeved shirt, and cheap canvas shoes with a rubber sole that wore out in about two weeks. Some of the men were fortunate enough to draw leather shoes. For warmth and protection against mosquitoes, the Filipino wore his blue fatigue uniform.[16]

In early 1941 MacArthur began to promote what became known as the Inland Seas Project. Basically MacArthur and his advisers believed that a relatively small coast artillery-like force in the Philippine Army could seal off many of the important straits between the various islands. This could help deny to an enemy some landing sites, and also provide safety to interior supply lines. On February 1, 1941 MacArthur sent a personal memo to Marshall about steps he was taking to increase the capacity of Philippine defense prior to the 1946 independence date. The archipelago's connecting waterways could be secured by blocking the narrow straits with mines, coast defense guns, and motor torpedo boats. For coastal defense MacArthur needed only the equipment; he was willing to rely entirely on Philippine Army soldiers to man his prospective units and batteries. Twelve identified positions could be defended using 155-mm guns in pairs. In addition to the twenty-four 155-mm guns, he calculated he needed seven heavier, longer-ranged 12-inch guns on barbette mounts. Always the salesman, MacArthur added a note to his request: "The cheapness to the U.S. of such a significant increase in defense potentialities makes the project doubly attractive."[17] He wanted Marshall to personally approve the scheme and then present it on his behalf to Stimson and the president. The equipment could be transferred to the commonwealth on a deferred payment basis.

General Marshall was predictably receptive. While there were some exceptions, coast artillery forces did not depend on weaponry in short supply. The president also supported the recommendation, particularly as it did not affect the present commitments of matériel to the British government. As to specifics, Marshall replied to MacArthur that the 12-inch gun carriages were simply not available until early 1943, but that substitute 8-inch railway guns might be immediately available. The 155-mm guns were in stock and could be issued; the searchlights would have to be manufactured, but that could be done early in 1942. Also, some fire-control equipment was short, but acceptable substitutes could be sent or improvised locally. For MacArthur, the heavy-gun substitution was the hardest to accept. The 12-inch type gun he needed had a range of 29,000 yards, the substitute 8-inch only 21,000 yards. Still, the project moved ahead. There was a little confusion concerning the urgency of shipment, Marshall thinking it would take a little time to prepare the installations and train Philippine Army troops, but MacArthur wanted an early dispatch of equipment if at all possible. The War Plans Division issued a go-ahead on March 19 with an urgent supply status. Army transport USAT *Liberty* took eight 155-mm guns, 12,000 high-explosive rounds for 155-mm, and all seven 8-inch mounts on a journey starting June 3. The remaining sixteen 155-mm guns were placed as contract freight on the commercial SS *American Leader* departing San Francisco on June 16. The 8-inch ammunition followed later in the fall, along with part of the fire-control equipment.

Despite General MacArthur's own sense of urgency and the relatively quick supply response by Washington, it did take some time to get this project going. A coast artillery training camp was established at old Fort Wint on Grande Island in Subic Bay. This had been an American coast artillery post, but was unmanned with just a small caretaker detachment watching over the guns and emplacements still at the fort. About 365 Filipino trainees started their instruction here, but when war started they were organized into the 2nd Coast Artillery, Philippine Army (the similar 1st Coast Artillery was organized on Corregidor with trainees there). Most of these men were ultimately attached to the Bataan force, though one battery of Filipino artillerymen went to Fort Frank in the Manila Harbor defenses. A staff officer with recent coast artillery experience, Maj. Stephen M. Mellnik, was placed in charge of constructing the gun emplacements of the new program. The first concrete was poured at the Cape Santiago 8-inch battery location on December 8, 1941. Needless to say not much else was achieved; most of the guns and other equipment were eventually turned over for the general defense.

Simultaneously with the Philippine buildup, American foreign policy supported supplying munitions to the Chinese. Both .50- and .30-caliber ammunition was needed for the P-40s being supplied to the Flying Tigers (AVG). The urgency of a request for machine-gun ammunition led to a plan to supply it from Philippine stocks. The Philippine Department was ordered to ship to Singapore 100,000 rounds of .50-caliber and 500,000 rounds of .30-caliber ammunition (which would then be transshipped to Rangoon on coastal freighter). As the Americans were careful to not use military-owned or military-operated transports for these missions, *President Harrison* shipped out of Manila on August 21 for Singapore with this ammo as part of her cargo. Soon there was a second transfer made with more of the .30-caliber machine-gun ammunition needed for the AVG airplanes. This time 4 million rounds were needed, and were duly supplied from Philippine stocks. The ammunition was indeed replaced; it was in the manifest of SS *Yaka* that left San Francisco on September 17 and arrived in Manila a month later.

Yet another ally was similarly supplied in the fall of 1941. The Dutch East Indies government had been anxious to acquire American war production for their home defense. Unlike some of the other nations who made requests of the United States in this time frame, one thing the Dutch did have was money. Their oil production was widely coveted and earned for the local East Indies government the means to pay in full for war matériel acquired. Despite considerable sympathy, the administration had not looked favorably on Dutch requests. Roosevelt and the lend-lease staff were firm on supplying only those nations actually fighting the Axis, which at that moment the Dutch were not. A personal appeal to General Marshall in August 1941 urgently requested, among other things, 25 million rounds of .30-caliber small-arms ammunition. The Dutch feared that without the ammunition (they already had the rifles and machine guns) their local defense force morale would decline and potentially even disintegrate. Marshall personally approved a transfer of 7 million rounds. It came from decreasing the stocks allocated to the Marine Corps for the summer's Iceland deployment. The Philippines were ordered to ship 4 million rounds immediately to the Dutch; replacement came from San Francisco as soon as shipping could be arranged.

A wider proposal for supplying the Chinese came from the staff of the War Plans Division on November 3. In most of these cases one of the issues was timeliness of supply. Getting matériel ordered in the United States, arranging shipping already in short supply, and taking a six-week journey across the southern Pacific to Rangoon where it had to make it by road to southern China was a very long pipeline. Using Philippine stocks could get equipment and supplies to the Chinese much quicker, and shipping was already flowing at a considerable pace to the Philippines. The memo in November recommended that 50,000 rifles, 10 million rounds of .30-caliber ammunition, and fifteen 2.95-inch mountain guns with 15,000 rounds of ammunition be sent to China from the department.[18] As the Philippines on paper had an excess of 66,000 rifles at this moment, they would not need replacement. The replacement ammunition, however, would come immediately from U.S. depot stocks. The guns would be replaced with new 75-mm pack howitzers from Panama and 40,000 rounds of ammunition for the same would come from domestic stocks.

MacArthur came down on this idea forcefully. For rifles, he was going to be raising new Philippine non-divisional units and a home guard for local defense, and would need all the rifles then in the Philippines.[19] As for the artillery, one of his most pressing requests was for additional guns, particularly as arms for the newly forming Philippine divisions. He needed all the 2.95s on hand, in addition to any 75-mm pack howitzers available. Obviously if he kept the rifles and guns, he also needed the ammunition that went with them. Washington quietly withdrew this idea in deference to the commander in Manila.

CHAPTER EIGHT

B-17s and the First Air Ferry Route

Deploying heavy bombers to the Pacific outposts had not been part of the pre-war planning. Of course, the development of the four-engine heavy land bomber itself had been fairly recent—only since the mid-1930s had the Air Corps and major engineering firms like Boeing begun serious work on the type. This led eventually to the introduction of the B-17, America's first long-range strategic bomber. Simultaneous with the aircraft's technical development were a new strategic doctrine and significant improvements in navigation and bombing accuracy. The limited numbers of B-17s initially procured led busy lives. In addition to being active test beds for the technology of the aircraft itself, the planes were needed both to help work out the tactical concepts of long-range bombing and as public relations vehicles for the growing capabilities of the Air Corps and America's rearmament. Through the late 1930s into 1941 small groups of planes participated in a number of spectacular flights. A flight to Brazil by seven bombers commanded by Maj. Gen. Delos Emmons in September 1939 was a well-publicized event.[1] Other Caribbean flights and several "intercepts" of offshore passenger liners clearly helped define the plane's potential for both coast defense and long-range operation. The enthusiasm publicly and within the War Department for this weapon system convinced many that the airplane could be a potent strategic deterrent.

Preceding the military's use of long-range aircraft in the Pacific had been the commercial development of planes and routes. The 1930s were in many ways the golden years of commercial aviation. Individual entrepreneurs led both the aircraft and air traffic industries forward, repeatedly breaking barriers. The first stirrings of what would become international air travel started when newly developed flying boats acquired the range to cross first the Atlantic and then the Pacific Oceans. The American side of this development was aptly demonstrated with Mr. Juan Trippe and his Pan American Airways. Finding himself shut out of the Atlantic trade (by British reluctance to provide landing rights in England), Trippe turned to the Pacific. In 1934 Pan American began in earnest to develop a stepping-stone approach to trans-Pacific travel. The driver of the trade would be the ongoing traffic between the West Coast and the Philippines.[2] Passenger flying boats were a very specialized type of aircraft that actually saw a rather narrow time frame of use in the 1930s and early 1940s.

For the potential Pacific route, the challenge was to find adequate intermediate stops to allow the aircraft of the age to "skip" along the course intended. Pan Am first investigated the great northern route, but weather conditions for a good part of the year quickly eliminated that alternative. Eventually the airline chose a more direct western course across the widest part of the ocean; this was farther, but less problematic in terms of weather and had the additional benefit of being entirely based at U.S. territories. That in turn meant less difficulty in acquiring the needed leases and permits, and also more cooperation with the U.S. military, which potentially meant less expense and not insignificantly more security against a foreign government's actions. The route's anchors were obvious. San Francisco was to be the base on the West Coast, and the first leg would connect to Hawaii.

Even though that route was perhaps obvious, it was by far the longest leg of the journey; in fact, for many years it would be the longest commercial air route in the world. It was not just the 2,400 miles, but the Hawaiian Islands as a group is just about the most physically isolated spot on earth; there would be no emergency landing spots between the Golden Gate and the islands themselves. Only in 1933 had six Navy P2Y patrol bombers (also flying boats) been able to make the twenty-five-hour journey on anything resembling a routine flight. However, once at Honolulu there was plenty of sheltered water and land-based facilities to serve as an adequate stopover. Except for this one leg, all the others were day-trips, allowing the passengers to overnight at hotels along the route and restrict travel to just the bulk of the daylight hours. Manila Harbor at the arrival end was the obvious destination. No problems were encountered in using the calm waters of sheltered Manila Bay, and likewise there was a good infrastructure locally in this American territory to serve all the needs Pan Am could envision.

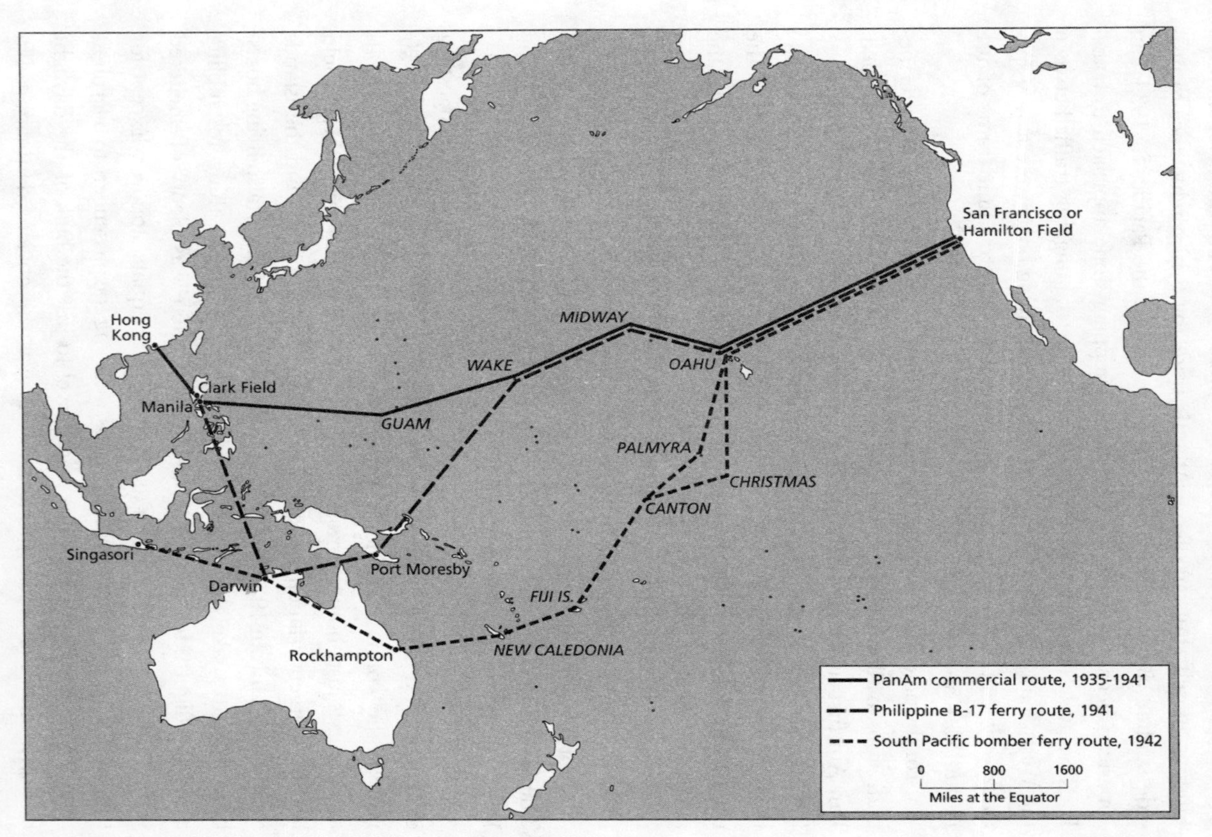

Map 2. Pacific Aircraft Commercial and Military Routes, 1941–1942

In mid-1934 Pan American sent C. H. "Dutch" Schildhauer to collect information on the needed intermediate stations. Midway, Wake, and Guam were the American territories selected for the necessary trans-Pacific stops. Guam was the simplest. While it was not nearly as developed as either Manila or Honolulu, Guam had an existing Navy and commercial presence. Apra Harbor provided enough sheltered water, and the Navy base had the seafront for an adequate docking ramp, plus hotel and dining facilities could be leased from the Navy. Labor was also not a problem; in fact, as it turned out the service crews and hotel attendants at most of the other bases were primarily Guamanian Chamorros. Midway had been an American possession since 1867. It had been little used over time, but did have a small station for the commercial trans-Pacific cable. At only 1,380 miles from Honolulu, it would be the easiest of the progressive steps in the network. An atoll, the lagoon would offer shelter for landing, but work would be needed to build a landing wharf and to cut an entry through the coral reef. Wake Island on the other hand was an isolated collection of three small islets surrounded by the usual reef located some 1,260 miles farther to the west. An 1899 acquisition of the Spanish-American War, the islets had never been settled and served no commercial or military use in the mid-1930s.

Pan Am actually had to lobby hard with both the Navy and other government agencies to get both Midway and Wake put under Navy jurisdiction (in fact, the actual custodian for Wake wasn't even known by government officials). In December of 1934 the president signed an order giving the Navy jurisdiction over Wake, Johnston, Kingman Reef, and Sand Island at Midway. Within months the airline had been given approval, and in some instances a five-year lease, to operate its facilities at all of the route's proposed locations. These actions weren't one-sided. The Navy and state departments were both worried about Japan's use of its island outposts, and increasing the commercial presence on American islands was deemed highly desirable on several levels. The physical erection of facilities presented its own problems. Where there was no presence and no commercial construction infrastructure—at Midway and Wake—Pan Am had to do it all alone. Work started in the spring of 1935, and soon adequate facilities were in service.

In the summer and fall of 1935 Pan Am began progressively testing the runs between stations. Initially there was no passenger traffic, just freight destined for Pan Am's own developing facilities, but in the fall of 1936 successful passenger flights began.

Early in 1941 the Army began to address the relative weakness of the Hawaiian air defenses. Deteriorating relations with Japan had moved the Navy to permanently base the Pacific Fleet at Pearl Harbor, and the Army's obligation to defend the port and fleet demanded it redress the deficiencies. At the start of 1941 only 117 Army Air Corps planes were based in the Hawaiian Islands, all of them considered to be obsolescent. Fighter planes were shipped out using Navy carrier USS *Enterprise.* The decision was also made to send heavy B-17 bombers, for what would be their first opportunity to be based outside the continental United States. Despite apprehension about the length of the flight (and potential adverse reaction from the public if disaster occurred), plans were crafted to directly fly twenty-one bombers to the islands.

The planes and flight crews came from the 19th Bombardment Group commanded by Lt. Col. Eugene L. Eubank. This unit was about the only relatively complete, manned, and trained heavy-bomber unit in the Air Corps. The plan was that after the planes had been taken to Oahu, just a small cadre of experienced flight crew would remain in Hawaii. After a couple of weeks training airmen of Oahu's own 11th Bombardment Group, most of the men would ship back to their home station, and the planes were to be incorporated into the squadrons of the bomb units already in the islands—in other words, this was just a movement of aircraft, not a transfer of an organization. Considerable pre-flight study of the route and potential weather, along with testing of aircraft components and fuel endurance, was needed before any plane could be certified for the flight.[3] Finally twenty-one B-17Ds were qualified and ready for the flight by the target date of May 13, 1941.

The Army asked the Navy, in a memo dated April 11, to supply guard vessels along the expected route. Navy Secretary Frank Knox personally committed to active compliance with this request.[4] Navy vessels were positioned about every five hundred miles along the route, and all ships in the vicinity were asked to supply weather information. A communications net was established using the facilities of both services and Pan American Airways. For this and subsequent flights commercial radio stations in San Francisco and Honolulu provided homing signals by staying on continuously during the flight.[5] After all the preparation the flight itself turned out to be quite smooth. Taking a little over thirteen hours, all twenty-one aircraft arrived on the morning of the fourteenth within just five minutes of their expected arrival time.

In 1941 the heavy strategic bomber was one of the few weapons systems the United States military was genuinely proud of. A long line of vocal champions had promoted the long-range bomber as being of unique benefit for America—a nation geographically removed from most potential enemies. The development of the plane and its enabling, technologically advanced bombsight was seen as a military breakthrough. Unfortunately a sort of cult developed around the system, one that had a difficult time admitting problems once the planes and squadrons began being produced. Early training exercises exaggerated results, leading to a belief in some circles that the B-17 with the Norden bombsight was capable of uncanny, "pickle-barrel" accuracy. The planes' rugged construction was capable of considerable resistance against damage, but it also initially lacked adequate defensive firepower. In particular the lack of nose and tail guns was a significant early design flaw. Even when the British created a sort of test squadron of twenty B-17Cs (Fortress Is) in the fall of 1941 the truth was ignored. The British did not have much success, losing many of the planes because of mechanical difficulties, the inadequate armament, and admittedly poor employment doctrine. However, even Secretary Stimson continued to preach that the planes had "achieved great success" in Europe.[6]

Within the highest levels of the War Department staff, the Army Air Corps, and even the administration there was an exaggerated belief that the strategic bomber was a weapon that could inflict tremendous damage at great distances. Perhaps based more on wishful thinking than actual facts, great feats were anticipated from relatively small numbers of planes. In hindsight it seems that expecting either a significant deterrence or wartime results from several dozen early-model B-17s was naïve, but that is precisely what occurred. The contagious optimism for the strategic bombers in the Philippines should not be underestimated. In discussions of the reinforcement of the Philippines within the administration and with Allied dignitaries, reference to the buildup of B-17 strength in the islands was repeatedly mentioned. While just a part of the reinforcement plan, they were deemed, at least by some in high command, disproportionately important.

The recommendation for basing heavy bombers in the Philippines appears to have originated in the Army Air Corps command structure. It may well have been discussed, but General MacArthur and the Philippine Department appear to have made no formal request for this type of aircraft. Of course, MacArthur had made his career thus far as a ground warfare officer and staff commander. He was never a flier, never commanded air units in his combat experience (until this upcoming campaign), and had the usual skeptical view of the potential of air warfare shared by many of his contemporaries. MacArthur himself was not one of the champions of strategic airpower mentioned above. However, he did strongly support the enhancement of his air force in the Far East, gladly passed along recommendations from his air officers, and was excited about what he eventually received, but the concept of strategic air capabilities was foreign to him. The idea for basing B-17s in the Philippines was clearly not his. Soon after the "plan" got started for the heavy-bomber reinforcement, Stimson and Marshall became enthusiastic supporters. From the dates of surviving memoranda it seems that Air Force Maj. Gen. Hap Arnold championed the idea, Stimson and Marshall sold the senior staff and the president on it, and MacArthur was thankful for any weapons of any kind he received.

Arnold advocated that four heavy bombardment groups (272 planes, not counting reserves) be allocated to the Far East Air Force sometime in July 1941.[7] In February 1941 the Army general staff had listened to a proposal from the Air Corps for developing a ferry route for heavy bombers across the Pacific. The staff disapproved the proposal on the basis that there was then no approved plan to deploy such bombers in the Far East. Obviously a major change occurred sometime between February and July. On July 24 Secretary of War Stimson urged Roosevelt to take all practical steps to increase the defensive strength of the Philippine Islands, including sending B-17s.[8] Regardless of the strategic rationale, this plan was only made possible by the sudden increase in production planned for the fall of 1941 at Boeing's plant. Even then the relative size of the Philippine allocation can be seen in the numbers—the islands' defenders were to get 165 of 220 planned new-production aircraft by the end of February 1942.[9] Marshall and Stimson together made a tour of the Boeing plant in Seattle in late August and both came away deeply impressed with the bomber's capabilities and Boeing's plans about production.[10] In a little over two weeks the planned transfer of twelve bombers from Hawaii to Luzon was under way, thus providing the potential of getting this weapon to the islands outside of the shipping bottleneck. The Army had a powerful new weapon now coming off the production line that could be supplied to the Philippines relatively quickly. All these facts combined as an irresistible opportunity. Moving with speed (oftentimes not the case with the pre-war staff), the newly pioneered trans-Pacific ferry route was to be firmly established as a top Army priority.

The movement of these planes was also planned and executed in a relatively short time. The two heavy bombardment groups already in Hawaii were thought essential for that island's strategic defense, and the only other unit potentially usable stateside—the 19th Bombardment Group (Heavy)—in Albuquerque, New Mexico, was not quite ready in training or equipment. As an interim step, the 14th Bomb Squadron was provisionally organized from the crew and equipment in Oahu and ordered to prepare to permanently transfer to the Philippines. Commanded by Maj. Emmett O'Donnell Jr., the flight crews were all experienced members of the B-17 contingent that had been based at Hickam since May. This independent squadron would take almost half the bombers then in Hawaii (nine of twenty-one in service).[11] At about this same time the 19th Bomb Group was alerted to finish training and gather equipment for an intended permanent transfer to the Philippines.

Considerable planning and logistical efforts had to be made prior to any actual flight. Foremost among these was the preparation of the actual landing and refueling stops. Two were American territories (though not necessarily prepared for this function), and three were Australian fields where diplomatic, administrative, and physical requirements needed to be addressed. In early August of 1941 the Army discovered that telephone conversations alone weren't adequate for making arrangements at the Australian and New Guinea aerodromes. Brigadier General Spaatz, of the air staff, asked the Navy to make a special PBY flight, with a small detachment of expert Army officers from Honolulu, to survey Port Moresby, Rabaul, and Port Darwin immediately.[12] One officer was to be left in each location even after the on-site inspection and negotiations for facilities were completed. Ultimately it was decided to use Port Moresby rather than Rabaul as the primary landing site in New Guinea, utilizing the latter as an emergency strip along the intended flight path, and plans for the deployment were adjusted accordingly.

Steps were taken to maintain a relatively high level of security about the upcoming flight. On September 3 (two days prior to planned departure), the chief of naval operations was informed of the specifics of impending movement and route (now settled as Hawaii, Midway, Wake, Port Moresby, Darwin, and Clark Field). The Air Force requested that Navy units along the route be notified, but that the trip be kept secret even after the flight had been concluded. During the flight itself, once approach had been made to the Japanese mandates a strict discipline of lights-out at night and radio silence was to be maintained. Also the normal cruising altitude of eight thousand feet would be changed to 26,000 for the leg from Wake to Port Moresby that came closest to Japanese territory. The actual flight schedule would be timed to allow the crossing of mandate territory at night, when it would be least likely to encounter Japanese aircraft.

The nine bombers of the 14th Bomb Squadron departed Hickam Field at 5:55 AM, Honolulu time. The first leg to Midway took seven hours and ten minutes and logged in at 1,132 nautical miles. This portion of the trip encountered some clouds and rain but was generally uneventful. The flight used the Pan American radio beacon from Midway, and found the coral-packed runway very satisfactory. Midway had good refueling pits, but drummed gasoline was also used in order to give the men experience in handling fuel that way, which would be the norm until Clark Field was reached. Overnight the officers quartered at the construction contractor's facility, while the enlisted men slept under their planes on cots and ate at the Marine mess. Early the next day the flight took off for Wake, crossing the International Date Line and arriving at 11:20 AM on September 7. This leg took only six hours and forty minutes, was calculated at 1,035 nautical miles, and was flown at the standard eight-thousand-foot altitude. Wake was not quite as developed as Midway. The crews were hosted and fed by the construction contractor on the island. Only three hours of rest were allocated before leaving at 11 PM for Port Moresby—so as to pass over the Japanese mandated islands during night hours.[13]

On the eighth the flight proceeded at 20,000 feet toward the mandates. The first serious mechanical problem forced one plane back to Wake, but repairs were made locally and this B-17 followed the other eight by about an hour and a half. Only about one hundred miles from Ponape, the planes climbed to 26,000 feet, extinguished all lights, and observed strict radio silence. This was the only time in the entire flight that oxygen was needed. Also at this time a major equatorial warm front was encountered. This (and all the subsequent flights) found this almost permanent front of warm, moist clouds on the Wake to Port Moresby leg. Varying in intensity, it often broke up the formation and sometimes contained considerable turbulence.[14] Getting close to New Guinea the plane commanded by Lt. Edward Teats lost one engine due to lack of fuel. He considered landing at the emergency field at Rabaul, but after being advised that it had just a soft field, he decided to stretch on into Moresby. Teats' plane, along with the other eight, all made it down safely on the eighth after twelve hours and forty minutes' flying time and traveling 2,176 nautical miles. The planes refueled again at Port Moresby. However, this site did not have enough 100-octane gas so a mixture had to be used with the more abundant 90-octane fuel the Australians generally used.

At Port Moresby the Australians were found to be enthusiastic hosts. A detail of Royal Australian Air Force men and local labor did the refueling.

The territory administrator personally met the flyers, informing them that this was the first U.S. Army unit to ever set foot on Australian territory. As not many hours of sleep had been obtained since leaving Midway, the ninth was taken at Moresby as a day of rest. Some local sightseeing and a meeting with an Australian Air Board commodore from Townsville were about as ambitious as the day got. On the tenth the flight took off at a respectable 8:45 AM for Darwin. No problems were encountered during the flight of just six hours and thirty minutes, and 934 nautical miles. Landing was a little more problematic. Runways were large, but the infamous Darwin dust created difficulties for landing. However, all the planes made it without incident. Darwin was a rather small town, but the facilities were among the best of the trip. The Australian air forces quartered and messed their corresponding numbers quite enthusiastically, including hosting a gala party where virtually all of the American collar and shoulder insignia were lost to souvenir hunters.

The final leg to Manila started at 4:25 AM, cruising at nine thousand feet. Nearing the Philippines the weather worsened; apparently Luzon was being near-missed by the trailing edge of a typhoon. Upon contacting Clark Field the flight was advised to try to land at Del Monte Field in Mindanao. This came as quite a shock to the crews, as they had never been informed about Del Monte; in fact, they had been told that Clark was the only place a B-17 could land in the Philippine Islands. The flight, still in relatively good order, pushed through to Clark in increasingly bad clouds and rain. It took most of the airplanes three or four passes to find and correctly line up to the field for landing. All made it in with only one mishap—the rudder of one B-17 was damaged when it hit the wingtip of a parked B-18 it could not see in the driving rain. Finally at 4 PM on September 12 this inaugural flight ended. The final leg was two thousand miles long and took eleven hours and forty minutes. Remarkably (future flights would not be able to match this performance) all nine planes took off together and landed together at their destination.

O'Donnell submitted a report a week after the flight containing several pages of comments and recommendations. He was not pleased with the lack of good information provided prior to the flight. In particular current weather information, but also good charts, photos, and descriptions of emergency fields were chief among his concerns and recommendations for improvement. He conjectured that the extreme secrecy of the mission had contributed to the lack of current data—several of the locations were not informed of the precise arrival time. Also, the Philippine Department had prepared detailed airfield information and sent it to Hawaii on a Pan Am clipper. Unfortunately this plane wrecked on the reef at Guam on August 16 and didn't arrive until after the B-17 flight left. Additionally O'Donnell specified some necessary navigational and logistical equipment the planes should carry with them. Particularly handy were the motor-driven gasoline pumps they brought with them, along with strainers and water-siphoning tubing.

One of the most crucial logistical concerns was the provision of aviation fuel for the various stops. It was anticipated that almost two hundred bombers would use the route over the six months following the next October flight. Each plane cruised at about 140–150 mph, consuming something like 157 gallons of gasoline per hour. The requirement for fuel at remote locations of Midway, Wake, Rabaul, Port Moresby, and Darwin was considerable, and the logistical arrangements to provide it consumed much thought and time. Additionally, American high-performance engines had been constructed to utilize 100-octane fuel, which was not readily available from the Allies or commercial vendors. The route had already been subdivided between the existing command structures for logistical responsibility. The Hawaiian Department under Lieutenant General Short was responsible for the facilities and supplying of Midway and Wake (and of course Hawaii itself, which was not a major problem). MacArthur's command would be responsible for supplying the New Guinea and Australian ferry bases.

The shortage of tankers in mid-August led to the waiving of provisions of the Buy America Act and allowed petroleum products to be purchased directly in the Far East and carried on ships of foreign registry. Soon commercial tankers (of any registry) in the employ of the Standard Vacuum Company were delivering cargo in Manila from a variety of sources. By October aviation gasoline was being supplied from the Dutch East Indies by commercial contract—Standard Vacuum was given a contract for 6.3 million gallons to deliver in Manila over the next four months.[15] Tankers were scarce, but ultimately that scarcity did not limit the contract's fulfillment. In late November a report indicated that some 2 million gallons of 100-octane aviation fuel was in storage in the Philippines. The total requirement was almost 19 million gallons, and the projected monthly consumption was 1.8 million gallons. The plans to rectify the significant shortfall were never fulfilled; however, the massive loss of aircraft in early December made the supply issue moot. While the overall situation for supplying Luzon fuel was being addressed, the logistics of supplying some of the outlying fields were more complicated. At the end of September the Army decided that the building air power in the Philippines could benefit from having alternate support fields throughout Southeast Asia.

Advance placement of fuel, oil, bombs, and ammunition for several missions would allow the Air Force to operate over a very wide area, particularly to aid America's allies. Many of the selected bases already were being used as ferry bases and had an American presence; only Singapore had to be added as a new operating location.

A plan was cast to pre-position two missions' worth of fuel, bombs, and ammo at two bases (Singapore and Port Darwin), one mission's worth at two others (Port Moresby and Rabaul), and to have an air depot on the Australian mainland (at Rockhampton). The missions were sized for a bombardment group of thirty-five heavy bombers. MacArthur's Far Eastern command was charged with getting the supplies to the bases, while Washington would obtain any diplomatic permission and replace the supplies with new shipments. The Philippine-registered motor ship MV *Don Esteban* was bare-boat chartered on October 25, 1941. This handy small ship was not a tanker, but the fuel to be delivered to Mindanao, Darwin, Port Moresby, and other island airfields would be drummed.[16] On October 8 the War Department started SS *Hawaiian Planter* west with drummed fuel, expecting to make delivery starting with 1,020 drums for Rabaul on November 12. Unfortunately the war started before she ever had a chance to make a delivery and the ship and cargo were diverted to Australia.

The specially acquired MV *Don Esteban* was scheduled to depart on her first supply mission on November 4. She was to carry the bombs and .50-caliber ammunition for four places—Singapore, Port Darwin, Rabaul, and Port Moresby. For some reason the ship's capacity was found to be much more limited than anticipated; she was incapable of carrying this size load and had to return after delivering just the Rabaul and Port Moresby quota. However, in addition to her supplies, she also delivered at each place a small Army detachment of one non-commissioned officer (NCO) and four enlisted men. Still needing a ship to take bombs and drummed fuel to the remaining ports, Manila took advantage of the recent arrival of USAT *Liberty*—which had been scheduled to spend time in the Dutch East Indies and Singapore to pick up strategic cargo anyway. The ship departed Manila on November 18 and was scheduled for Port Moresby with 1,275 drums of gasoline and Port Darwin with 525 drums. Singapore's allocation of bombs was delayed until December 18 (for the second trip of *Don Esteban*), and in any event Singapore never did get either the bombs or see American bombers in the upcoming campaign. As of December 17 Darwin held a stock of 560 500-pound bombs, Port Moresby 280 bombs. Apparently Rabaul only received gasoline and no munitions or an American detachment.[17]

An Army memo of October 13 describes the impending fuel needs for the bases actually used in the pending B-17 flight. As of that date the anticipation was for sixty-one bombers to make the transfer across the ferry route beginning October 25 and ending at the end of November. Actually only the twenty-six bombers of the second wave made the trip, though the rest would have gone in December if war had not interrupted plans. In any event, to service this plan would have required 80,000 gallons of 100-octane aviation gasoline and 1,600 gallons of engine oil at both Midway and Wake. Subsequent to this movement another one hundred airplanes were due to make the transit, requiring another 120,000 gallons of fuel and 2,400 gallons of oil. Pan American Airways was asked to supply fuel for this first flight from their island stocks, but this would soon have been exhausted, and their supplier (Standard Oil Company of California) had the fuel, but not the tanker availability to resupply. The Navy was requested to help the Army establish the necessary fuel reserve for these two locations.[18]

The large second bomber transfer to the Philippines began on October 12. Due to the accelerated timing of the movement, some of the planes had just arrived at the Sacramento Air Depot. The short notice actually meant that some of the aircrews experienced considerable hardship, and were physically fatigued. Some aircraft actually arrived as late as 7 PM and were scheduled to depart on the long, exhausting flight to Hickam at 8:30 that same evening. One aircraft in fact had to make the flight on its own after the others had departed due to lack of time for it to complete its flight evaluation. The post-flight report by Maj. David R. Gibbs is quite critical of this short-notice schedule.[19] The other consequence of this late arrival was that all cohesion of the two squadrons included was lost. The flight actually became a "flow" of twenty-six bombers, starting from California and ending up in the Philippines, accomplished by small contingents. From the very beginning the idea of succinct flights or batches of bombers flying together was lost. Thankfully though, this was not yet war, and all of the aircraft eventually made it to their destination.

One of the practical aspects impacting this situation was the existence of physical limitations at some of the landing sites. Beyond Sacramento, Hickam, and Clark, often there simply wasn't enough space on the intermediate bases to properly receive, park, and service (refuel and/or repair) twenty-six airplanes at once. Additionally there frequently weren't facilities to provide sleeping and eating quarters for this number of crewmen at once. The optimal size flight seems to have been calculated at about nine aircraft, though that exact number was rarely seen in practice. Twelve planes left Hamilton Field, near San Francisco, on October 17, flying in two elements of six planes each. Planes took off at two-minute intervals, and the second element followed the first by thirty minutes. The procedure had each pilot report his position to the element leader every hour, and each element reported every hour to headquarters (HQ). Over West Coast waters the radio-silence protocol was not yet in practice. Three days later, on October 20, the next thirteen planes departed. The last plane (the one delayed by its late arrival in California) completed the journey one day later. By late morning of the twenty-second all twenty-six airplanes were at Hickam Field. Navigation was judged excellent and no mechanical problems were evident, though that good fortune wouldn't persist for long. It was planned to send the planes farther along in batches of eight to nine aircraft, but breakdowns, weather problems, and base capacity made that plan impractical.[20]

The usual precautions about alerting the Japanese were observed. Radio silence over the mandated islands was practiced. Also, unlike the preceding flight, the bombers were armed and issued one hundred rounds per gun as a precaution against interception. It is almost impossible to describe the individual flights that proceeded along the planned route. A better way to provide a picture of the aircraft movement is to use the same approach Gibbs did in his report, just to mention where planes were located as of given dates. Planes began leaving Hawaii on October 22, and all but the last plane arrived on November 5. An abbreviated reported position of the planes was given as:[21]

October 24:	7	planes at Wake
	1	plane departed Wake for Port Moresby
	10	planes departed Hickam for Midway (1 returned)
	1	plane at Midway
	7	planes at Hickam
October 28:	8	planes at Darwin
	10	planes at Wake
	8	planes at Midway
November 1:	8	planes at Clark
	6	planes departed Darwin for Clark

	1	plane departed Rabaul for Port Moresby
	11	planes departed Wake for Port Moresby (1 returned, 2 diverted to Rabaul, 2 departed Port Moresby immediately for Darwin)
November 5:	24	planes at Clark
	1	plane at Darwin
	1	plane departed Darwin for Clark

A constant occurrence of relatively minor accidents and mechanical problems plagued this flight more than the previous one. Gibbs' description is useful:

> Several minor incidents occurred on the entire flight from Albuquerque to the Philippines. At Hickam Field one airplane scraped the wing tip of another while taxiing, due to a sudden loss of brake pressure. The wing tip was repaired locally. One airplane had an engine changed at Hickam Field and another had a broken oil tank replaced. At Midway Island one plane was held up a day with a flat tail tire. A spare arrived in the following flight. At Wake a truck backed into the aileron of one plane causing considerable damage. The broken aileron and two sections of cracked engine cowling from two other ships were repaired at Wake with the aid of Pan American and the contractors. The battery charger at the marine detachment on Wake was also used. Three airplanes returned to Wake Island after starting for Port Moresby. One returned because of weather and the other two returned because of ignition trouble encountered at high altitudes while trying to fly over the equatorial front. At Darwin two airplanes developed trouble in the internal blower sections of one engine each. This necessitated sending two replacement engines from Manila. One of the two airplanes took a good engine from the other and continued to Clark Field. The airplane which remained at Darwin had both bad engines replaced and at present is held at Darwin because of poor field conditions due to rain.[22]

The report's evaluation of the various fields is also instructive. Midway was judged excellent—it now had hard-surfaced runways and parking areas, and could accommodate up to twenty-five planes and crews. Wake had one good crushed-coral runway and adequate parking, but was more constrained for crew accommodation. Nine-plane flights were recommended for transit to Wake unless special advance preparations were made. Rabaul was suitable only as an emergency field. Its one strip was of soft material, and surrounding hills made certain landings and takeoffs dangerous. Local facilities were lacking, probably only adequate for six planes. A side note also mentions that the crews that did have to go into Rabaul on this flight contracted intestinal difficulties. Port Moresby's field was hard, but relatively small with a dangerous approach in bad weather. Only soft ground off the field was available for aircraft parking. It was not calculated to be able to host more than ten crews at once. Darwin had no less than four runways, but at that time they were dirt and presented dust problems when dry and mud problems when wet. Facilities to house and feed up to twenty-five crews were available.

Recommendations were also made to substantially increase the radio and communications capabilities along the route, particularly homing and radio direction finding. Wake Island specially stood out as needing improvement. Compliments were made to both Navy and Pan Am facilities for their work, but it was recognized that the Army should place its own equipment and personnel at these fields if it were continuing the flight schedule as contemplated. As was mentioned in the September report, there was an insatiable need for more and better weather forecasts all along the route, to the point of suggesting that qualified weather officers be sent to Wake and Midway a week before any flight to monitor the weather and prepare the needed forecasts. As to be expected a request to pre-position certain equipment (energizers, jacks, spare oxygen, and the like) along the route was also made.

The third wave of B-17s beginning the trip to the Philippines was scheduled for early December, but got caught up in the Pearl Harbor attack and never made it. Sixteen bombers were planned to take the usual route westward from California. These planes originated with the 38th Reconnaissance Squadron from Albuquerque, New Mexico, and the 88th Reconnaissance Squadron from Fort Douglas, Utah. Each squadron had eight planes, though a mixture of types (four B-17Cs and twelve of the very first B-17Es). The B-17E was a significant improvement over the older "C" and "D" models. It featured a newly redesigned and enlarged vertical fin, but for combat the greatest enhancements were in defensive armament. The new model was fitted with an upper and belly dual .50-caliber gun turret, plus another pair of these guns in a tail position. The Japanese had already identified the defensive weaknesses of the plane, and their first encounters with the newest model came as quite a shock.

While these two squadrons were designated as reconnaissance rather than bombardment squadrons, at this time in the Air Force there was little practical difference. Bombardment groups were usually composed of one reconnaissance unit and several bombardment squadrons, the original logic being that one squadron would specialize in its training for long-range scouting and patrol while the others were held back until a target was designated. In this period of early organization and widespread exchange of crews and equipment between units, the different designation virtually meant nothing but a name. These two squadrons had the same exact capabilities and duties as the other four squadrons already in the Philippines. These planes were destined for the new 7th Bombardment Group as compared to the 19th Bombardment Group now in the islands. This was to be the first aircraft increment for this unit, while the majority of the ground crew and support units had shipped out on the vessels of the *Pensacola* convoy over two weeks previous. Follow-up squadrons would be dispatched later in December to bring the group up to its full complement.

Once the sixteen planes reached Hamilton Field, California, the usual procedures took place to prepare for the ferry-route transfer. Additional extra fuel tanks in the bomb bays were installed. Guns would be carried, but as usual no ammunition would be shipped in order to further release weight for the fuel necessary on the first long flight to the Hawaiian Islands. It was to be a group night flight (composed of both squadrons, all sixteen airplanes), but was delayed a couple of days due to the presence of strong headwinds over the initial course. Finally on the evening of December 6 the planes departed. Almost immediately four aircraft had to scrub the mission, either at takeoff or soon after. Two planes from each squadron developed engine problems and stayed behind at Hamilton Field. Most of the journey was routine, but that changed when they approached Hawaii. Unfortunately this flight arrived precisely during the Japanese air attack upon Pearl Harbor at 8 AM the morning of December 7, 1941.[23]

As usual the radio stations stayed on during the night of the sixth so that their music broadcasts could be used by the bombers as a homing beacon. Incidentally the Japanese attack formation found it useful for the same purpose. The most famous story about the arrival of the flight concerns the mistaken identity of the Japanese attack formation for the B-17s. Inexperienced Army radar operators at the Opana Station in the morning prior to the attack reported a large flight of aircraft approaching from the north about 7:30 AM; 2nd Lt. Kermit Tyler at the joint control center assumed that this must be the

B-17 flight. Of course events proved him wrong; it was the Japanese formation heading in for its initial attack. In Tyler's defense, he was not informed of the size of the flight (and the early radars weren't very good at determining this anyway), he knew the B-17s were expected due to the night radio music, and he had not received any specific warnings or alert. Still the radar installation had done precisely its job in detecting a potential attack, and an opportunity to at least meet it with an alerted defense was lost.

The twelve B-17s sighted Oahu at 8 AM and began their descent toward Hickam Field. As the B-17s prepared to enter into their landing pattern they ran directly into the Japanese. Initially the enemy was identified as escorting or at least friendly aircraft, but that soon changed when Japanese fighters immediately took on the large, undefended planes. Five of the six planes of the 38th were attacked, and two were lost. The bomber piloted by 1st Lt. Robert H. Richards had to abort its landing and make a barely controlled landing at Bellows Field. Richards came in too fast and ran off the end of the runway, essentially damaging the aircraft (and it was subsequently strafed also) to an extent that it was a total loss. Capt. Raymond T. Swenson did land at Hickam, but he was also soon strafed. The enemy fire ignited the flares on board, burning the plane neatly in half. Also destroyed, the engines were later salvaged. The squadron's only casualty occurred when the flight surgeon, 1st Lt. William R. Schick, died on this plane. The remaining four aircraft were soon repaired and ready for action.

The 88th Reconnaissance Squadron followed the 38th for its arrival in Oahu, and basically shared the same experience. While existing records conflict with eyewitness reports, it appears that two B-17s managed to land at small Haleiwa Field. One came down on an uncompleted airfield near the Kahuku golf course. Three wound up at the end of the day at Hickam, though it appears one may have originally landed at Wheeler Field.[24] In any event the squadron had planes shot up, but none totally destroyed. Luckily the 88th also avoided any casualties.

The story of one other air mission needs to be recounted. In late November of 1941 plans were finalized to send two specially equipped B-24 bombers to the Philippines for photo-reconnaissance duties. Apparently discussed for a while by the Joint Board, the need to gather information on Japanese military preparations was becoming acute as tensions escalated. Major General Brereton had requested better information on Formosan airfields and embarkation ports if he was to prepare missions for the B-17 force being deployed there.

Similarly the Navy was desirous of aerial photos of several of the mandate island bases reportedly being reinforced by the Japanese. On November 26 the board was advised by the Air Force that two planes were preparing to leave Dayton, Ohio, for permanent assignment in the Philippines.[25] Originally of the 44th Bombardment Group, the early model B-24As were provisionally assigned to the 1st Photo Group. The plan was for the planes to travel the proven northern route through Oahu, to Midway, Wake, Port Moresby, and eventually to Clark Field. On the way out they would pass over and photograph Japanese bases in the Marshall and Caroline Islands (Jaluit and Truk). Once in the Philippines they would carry out missions initially over Palau and Yap.

Aware of the potential dangers in penetrating Japanese air space, specific instructions were issued. If possible, photographs would be taken of gun positions, air fields, barracks, camps, ports, and Japanese naval vessels. This all had to be done in one pass, the planes were not authorized to circle or remain in the vicinity once an original pass was accomplished. The run would be at high altitude; that and the aircraft's speed should help them avoid interception. Still, they were both to be fully armed and carry a full ammunition load. The pilots were requested to confer with Admiral Kimmel at Pearl Harbor for advice prior to departing, and both the Army and Navy in Hawaii and the Philippines were to get copies of the photographs.[26]

In late 1941 the B-24 bomber had yet to make an operational appearance outside the Air Force in the continental United States; this mission would be their first such deployment. As often happened with these early plans, the inevitable delays pushed the start date of the mission back. Only one of the two selected airplanes made it as far as Hawaii. On December 5, 1941 the first B-24 arrived at Hickam Field, where it was to have its guns installed. On the morning of December 7 the transient was parked outside of Hangar 15, where it suffered the fate of most of the bombers on the ground that morning. The plane was totally destroyed. Three crew members were wounded, and unfortunately 2nd Lt. Louis G. Moslener Jr. and Pvt. Daniel J. Powlowki were killed during the attack.

CHAPTER NINE

Marine Corps Base Defense

The Navy demonstrated only limited strategic interest in the American Pacific islands for most of the early years of their possession. For example, Guam was desirable as a coaling station and way-stop to the Philippines and was retained in the peace treaty at the end of the Spanish American War. But beyond the utility of the big islands with functioning harbors (Guam and American Samoa), it took the potential of military airpower to attract attention to places like Wake, Midway, Palmyra, and Johnston. With the worsening international situation developing in the late 1930s, a belated effort was made to address the need for new American naval stations.

A congressional act of May 17, 1938 authorized and directed the secretary of the Navy to appoint a board of officers to investigate and report upon the need for new submarine, destroyer, mining, and naval air bases. It was soon called the "Hepburn Board" in recognition of its chairman, Rear Adm. Arthur J. Hepburn.[1] Appointed on June 7, 1938, the board of experienced naval officers enthusiastically commenced work. They logged over 20,000 miles of travel inspecting existing and new facilities on the continental Atlantic, Gulf, and Pacific coasts, in addition to traveling to several key Caribbean sites. They certainly did not neglect the Pacific Ocean islands. The title of the report submitted to the House of Representatives on December 27 included "[the] need of additional naval bases to defend the coasts of the United States, its territories, and possessions."[2] The act that created the board had in fact been part of a significant naval expansion bill. Clearly events were demanding the growth of the U.S. Navy, and that growth was supported strongly by the administration. The new bases to be recommended were linked to the increased forces soon to become available. Also Rear Admiral Hepburn (and most of the other board members) was strongly air-minded. Whether it was the original intent or not, the board aggressively addressed the need for new air bases. The need for destroyer, submarine, and mine facilities occupies only a small portion of the published report. The final report is essentially a plea for new runways and seaplane bases. Finally the board was not charged with developing cost estimates; it was solely to address perceived needs.

The recommendations did indeed address certain critical land facilities on the East Coast (for example, the huge Quonset Point, Rhode Island, base was created by the report's direct advice). Facilities along the southern Atlantic, for expansion of bases to protect Puerto Rico, Roosevelt Roads, and the approaches to the Panama Canal were included. A concern for the lack of presence in Alaska led to the beginnings of new bases in Seward, Sitka, Kodiak, and Unalaska (Dutch Harbor). Two Pacific locations presented political complications. The board simply refused to address the need for new bases for the Philippines, explaining in the report that this omission was due to reasons of national policy. The situation in Guam was more problematic due to a long and complex history.

Since Guam was seen as both an essential link in any air bridge and as being the only potential refuge for the Asiatic Fleet outside of Luzon, the board advocated the development of a full fleet base there. The essential element was the need to develop a deep-water port. That involved the construction of a new breakwater and extensive dredging operations, besides the supporting airfields, seaplane ramps, and supporting shops and offices. Politically the defense of Guam had been a hot potato for virtually all of its American existence. Realizing that important support in Congress was lacking, the request for authorization to develop the island seesawed regularly in the last half of 1938. The formal recommendation was removed to a "strictly confidential" portion of the report, until newspapers released the content. Though eventually retained in the board's official report, when it came to appropriation money, Guam failed to gather enough support to ever get much of a start for new defenses.[3]

For the mid-Pacific area, the board was emphatic about the importance of a secure base in the Hawaiian Islands (Pearl Harbor). Tied to its defense was the necessity of patrol bomber scouting that could be conducted by basing seaplanes at the various islands encircling Oahu to the west. Essentially development of such facilities could provide almost continuous coverage of the Pacific Ocean east of the 180° meridian. In summary the board's recommendations were:

1. Expand facilities on Oahu—fully develop Ford Island in Pearl Harbor as a major air base, and also expand capabilities by developing Kaneohe Bay as a seaplane base.
2. Midway Island from a strategic standpoint is second only to Pearl Harbor. Need to dredge a channel, erect a breakwater, expand fuel storage, and construct facilities for permanent basing of two patrol squadrons and two divisions of submarines with a tender.
3. Wake Island should be developed by constructing a pier, channel, turning basin, and facilities for permanent assignment of a patrol squadron and one division of submarines with a tender.
4. Four islands or atolls—Johnston, Palmyra, Canton, and Rose—should be developed to permit seaplane tenders to be based there supporting the temporary assignment of patrol bomber squadrons.

Once these recommendations were submitted, it took additional congressional action to authorize construction work, and then an actual appropriation bill to provide the money. The Navy Bureau of Docks and Yards provided an estimate of $326 million (including $80 million just for Guam) to the Naval Affairs Committee. The late 1930s was a period with considerable American public and political isolationism sentiment, or at least resistance to significant rearmament. It took the adroit maneuvering of the Navy's longtime supporter, Georgia representative Carl Vinson, to produce the Air Base Bill of April 1939. Once again Guam was cut from the final proposal. Several key concepts did emerge in the bill's text. Work was to be done by private contractors, but the nature of the work in faraway, isolated places put a real demand on competency. Consequently the Navy would not use competitive bidding, but rely on its own judgment to select firms. As there was not the time available to estimate costs (and frankly nobody really knew precisely how much work would be required at several of the sites), contractor fees were to be paid on a cost-plus-fixed-fee basis rather than as a percent of the work.[4]

Next was the effort to get an actual appropriation bill passed. As this involved yet another congressional committee and set of players, many of the issues had to again be debated. Finally on May 25, 1940 a bill passed the House of Representatives. It authorized $63 million for new bases, $15 million of that for the Pacific outposts. Work was to proceed on Oahu, Midway,

Johnston, and Palmyra, but the House thought Guam and Wake were too close to the Japanese and potentially provocative. After organizing itself internally to supervise the work, the Navy's Bureau of Yards and Docks created contract No. NOy-3550. A consortium of three large, experienced engineering firms would form a new corporate organization to be known as "Contractors, Pacific Naval Air Bases," or CPNAB (often shortened slightly to PNAB).[5] This initial contract was signed on August 5, 1940.

The largest number of individual projects was understandably directed at naval facilities on Oahu. Most notable was the full development of Kaneohe Bay into a serviceable seaplane base. In fact, this bay and the island outposts had many similarities in the actual work needed. Seaplanes needed a long stretch of clear, protected water to land on, frequently requiring something like a space one thousand feet wide and two miles long. What's more, a depth of eight feet unobstructed by rocks—or, in the mid-Pacific, protruding coral heads—was required. Work at all the seaplane bases required varying degrees of blasting and dredging to secure this clear landing space. As this water needed to be sheltered from waves and storms, this usually meant the inside or lagoon of a coral atoll. For those bases receiving permanent patrol squadrons (Kaneohe Bay, Midway, and eventually Wake), adequate facilities on a neighboring island would be needed—ramps to haul the seaplanes ashore, repair and supply shops, munitions and fuel storage, radio and weather stations, garrison barracks, mess halls, hospitals, and the other necessary habitat buildings. Even for those locations just hosting an occasional seaplane tender and squadron (Johnston and Palmyra), ramps, fuel storage, and a smaller land-based facility were required.

In the case of the four outlying islands, the absolute isolation and barrenness of the sites was a major obstacle to work. On all four there was no local population or habitation. Midway and Wake were relatively recent recipients of the small Pan American stopover hotels and refueling facilities. Midway also had been a site for the Pacific Commercial Cable Company station since early in the twentieth century. On none of the islands was there any fresh water. All were exposed to swells and at times heavy surf on the windward side, all had problems with coral heads, and all eventually required more dredging and underwater work than initially projected. They were not pleasant places. The first reconnaissance parties usually worked from an anchored ship, commuting to the lagoon and islands by small boat through the heavy surf daily. Later the advance parties worked out of small tent facilities. Even after semi-permanent contractor camps had been built, the intense equatorial weather, almost total lack of recreational facilities, and limited chance for rotation led to problems of morale and more than an occasional complete breakdown.

Of the four island bases, work got under way on Johnston Island first.[6] Johnston had only occasionally been used for PBY landings, and had a preexisting small boat channel and water tank. In September 1939 the PNAB surveyed the island, and followed with a fifty-man pioneer group and 650 tons of construction freight transferred by the Navy on USS *Wright* on November 6. Though the contractor was an independent business and worked under a contract, the nature of the task demanded a high level of cooperation between the Navy, Pan American Airways, and the PNAB. Most transportation was organized and provided by the Navy. Over time several ships became totally dedicated to the routine supply runs to the various islands, at first working to get the contractors and supplies out for construction, and then later also assuming a similar role for the Marine Corps defense units. The ships were generally based and operated out of the commercial port of Honolulu. Serious work began on Johnston Island in early 1940; eventually a channel one hundred feet wide and twenty feet deep, a turning basin, three cleared seaplane runways, and minimal land facilities were constructed.[7]

Palmyra was a somewhat different animal than the other atolls. Relatively large, it had a high rainfall of two hundred inches per year, and consequently much more vegetation. Indeed for the workers it resembled the traditional notion of a tropical island, whereas the others were almost desert islands. In November 1939 the PNAB survey was conducted, transported by the Navy destroyer *Preble* from Johnston Island. On January 27 there arrived a pioneer group of twenty-four men and materials ferried from Honolulu. Dredging a supply channel was the first order of business, but that also provided the opportunity to get fill material necessary to link several islands together and eventually find the space for a runway.

Midway was the most civilized of the island bases, having a longer history of military usage and at least some permanent facilities. The initial contractor pioneer group arrived on March 13, 1940, in USS *Sirius*, a follow-up to the January 1940 survey. Ninety workers and supplies were delivered. Some work had actually been under way on Midway; the U.S. Army Corps of Engineers had been operating since 1938 to cut through the reef and provide a boat channel, although progress had been slow and mechanical breakdowns frequent. Like the other locations, contractor camps had to be constructed for the workers. The workforce needed was considerable: here at Midway there were 312 men in the fall of 1940, but that grew to 1,500 by the summer of 1941. Midway is famous even today as the home of the gooney bird (albatross). The birds proved particularly irksome to construction superintendent A. C. Gallagher, as described in the narrative of the Pacific Naval Air Bases:

> For one thing, they were having gooney trouble. The men soon tired of watching the birds but they couldn't get rid of them. Everywhere a man drove a cat or a bulldozer. The vast population of birds stood in the way, bowing and whacking beaks or simply staring off to sea. Small gray babies nestled in little hollows made for them by their elders and refused to move out. They didn't dare, for they got roundly scolded whenever they left the nest. Washington had sent word that the goonies must not be hurt, so for a while Gallagher had to detail an extra man to walk in front of every vehicle, awkwardly requesting the birds to step aside, setting the young out of harm's way one at a time.[8]

Wake was the last of the four island bases to begin development, as a result of its political sacrifice in the first round of congressional funding. A new appropriation bill, passed in June of 1940, provided $706 million for the Navy's Pacific bases—including new funds for Wake, Guam, Samoa, and the Philippines. Two new partners were invited into the consortium to help with the increased work.[9] As the base contract grew, with annual appropriations and supplemental change orders, the work eventually became one of the largest construction contracts ever undertaken. More work in 1941 meant that three final partners were added to the contractors' consortium.[10] By 1943 when the military took over much of the work itself, well over $300 million in work had been prescribed and performed. It is almost impossible to describe the scope and depth of the work, with hundreds of individual projects in dozens of locations involving thousands of workmen.

Work on Wake, the farthest and most exposed of the new air bases, was given priority to help make up for its late start. The Navy assigned transport USS *William Ward Burrows* exclusively for the initiation of the job. She arrived at Wake with the first party on January 9, 1941. Making monthly trips of supplies and men, the workforce quickly rose to almost 1,200 under the supervision of Morrison Knudsen executive Daniel Teters. To supplement the transport, a small local fleet of tugs and four special large barges was also regularly employed. When December 7 (the eighth on Wake) occurred, it was estimated that the work stood at 65 percent complete. Initiation of construction projects on the other new sites was slower in coming.

At Samoa work began just before Christmas of 1940 by a reconnaissance party brought out on a regular Matson liner journey. In January work started—but rather than dredging, the first assignment was the construction of concrete positions for naval 6-inch defense guns. Later in 1941 an $11 million project was added for a runway and a small naval air base. Eventually 1,500 men were utilized in construction on Samoa, though three-quarters of them were locally hired. There was difficulty in maintaining adequate supply to the base; eventually a small, chartered freighter was assigned to directly supply men and materials from the Alameda logistical center of PNAB, bypassing the warehouse and shipping crunch at Honolulu. At Cavite in the Philippines work started in April 1941 even prior to the summer appropriation bill. Dredging, seaplane ramps, hangars, fuel and ammo storage, powerhouse, and living quarters were to be built for a new naval seaplane base. Work had not progressed much when the start of war pre-empted the construction. A party arrived in Guam in July 1941, to assess the work for a permanent breakwater enclosing Apra Harbor. It was found that coral heads had to be removed in the anchorage, and the small naval base at Piti (its inadequacy led to an obvious pun heard frequently in this regard) would have to be considerably expanded. As on Samoa, the workforce for Guam would consist of American supervisors with local labor—and a significant number of Filipino workers.

In 1933 the U.S. Marine Corps had organized the Fleet Marine Force, specifically those forces available for the seizure and temporary defense of advance bases.[11] By 1937 the concept of a Marine Corps Security Detachment for garrison duties emerged. By 1938 it was conceived that these detachments were to be deployed on or before the outbreak of war on Midway, Wake, and Johnston Islands, as well as be available for new bases to be taken in any future Pacific advance. Designed to repel minor naval raids and landings by small parties (it was well recognized that a full assault on any of these small bases could not be stopped by anything less than the actual presence of the U.S. Fleet), they were envisioned as roughly battalion-sized units with organic medium-caliber seacoast guns, anti-aircraft batteries, searchlights, and machine guns for both anti-aircraft and beach defense. While an existing unit could theoretically be set down about anywhere, once emplaced the detachment was relatively immobile.

Another advantage with these units was the ability of the service to get them approved. Congress and some members of the administration were still leery of approving the expansion of the military's offensive capabilities—both due to significant public opinion, and to the potential of provoking negative Japanese reactions. It was better to create these as purely "defensive" elements, or at least call them such whether they could be productively used in an offense or not. By the late summer of 1939 the organizational design and equipment allocation had crystallized. Each battalion would contain about eight hundred enlisted men. Seacoast armament was to consist of three two-gun batteries with the naval 5-inch/51-caliber gun. Firing a 50-pound projectile, it had a useful maximum range of 15,850 yards.[12]

The battalion would normally have three four-gun heavy anti-aircraft batteries armed with the Army's 3-inch/50-caliber M3 gun on mobile mount M2A2. The gun fired a 12.8-pound projectile to a maximum ceiling of 31,300 feet. The mount allowed an elevation from −1 degree to +80 degrees, meaning the unit was useful in a supplementary anti-ship role to augment the battalion's 5-inch guns. The excellent Browning .50-caliber heavy machine gun was usually used on a light anti-aircraft mount, and had a range of 7,400 yards. Lighter .30-caliber guns were usually deployed to cover beaches and landing zones. Searchlights and aircraft sound locators rounded out the proposed armament. Altogether this was a fairly powerful armament suite for a battalion. While not of the most recent models, it was up to the task of its assignment and not inferior to the weapon types the Japanese were likely to use.

The first defense battalions were organized and ready in early 1940. Four were created in San Diego, and three others in South Carolina. On January 17, 1941, in view of the worsening international developments, the Navy moved to deploy its new defense battalions to the islands being developed as seaplane bases. Midway was assigned the entire 3rd Defense Battalion (one-third of the unit's troops were already on the atoll). The 1st Battalion, still in San Diego, was transported to Pearl Harbor and subsequently divided between Johnston and Palmyra. The 6th Battalion was also in San Diego, but still awaiting some of its heavy armament and other equipment. It was to move to Pearl to act as a reserve and replacement unit. Even this early it was anticipated that the isolated garrisons would require periodic rotation of personnel.[13] Work was finally just beginning at Wake Island; it would not be ready for its first defensive garrison until August 1941. On the East Coast the 5th Defense Battalion, without its heavy seacoast armament, was deployed in Iceland in June 1941.

The initial garrison selected for Midway was the 3rd Defense Battalion. Organized and trained in South Carolina, the unit boarded the venerable *Chaumont* for the voyage to Pearl Harbor, arriving at that port on May 7, 1940. Meanwhile the commanding officer of the unit, already on Oahu, made the first preliminary reconnaissance of the island. In September USS *Sirius* and two destroyer minesweepers returned with the initial contingent of the 3rd Battalion. These eight officers and 143 men with their heavy equipment and guns went ashore on September 29 after the usual struggle with barges and small landing boats in the surf. They did carry with them the first of the heavy guns for the island—one battery of 5-inch seacoast guns and one heavy 3-inch anti-aircraft battery. A second, smaller contingent of the 3rd arrived in January 1941. The bulk of the battalion stayed at Pearl Harbor, with occasional rotation of officers and men to its detachment on Midway. In early 1941 the CNO directed that one entire defense battalion be concentrated on Midway as its permanent garrison. Consequently on February 9, 1941 the balance of the battalion (twenty-eight officers, 565 men, and most of the remaining heavy equipment and guns) boarded USS *Antares*. Escorted by Cruiser Division 8 and Destroyer Division 11 they arrived at Midway on February 14.

By the middle of 1941 the defense battalions represented a considerable portion of the total strength of the Marine Corps. In a report at the end of the fiscal year (June 30, 1941) there were just 50,571 Marines in service. A little under half (22,595) belonged to the Fleet Marine Force (FMF). Of that segment, a little under 16,000 were serving in one of the two Marine Corps divisions. Another 1,553 Marines were in the FMF's aviation units. The final 5,045 (10 percent of the total strength, or over 20 percent of the Fleet Marine Force strength) were in the organized defense battalions.

On Midway the initial concern following the February deployment plan was for living quarters. In late February there was barrack accommodation for 250 on Sand Island. Tripling the garrison would require obvious expansion, plus adding a smaller facility on Eastern Island to allow troops to have easy access to the weapons to be mounted on this island.[14] Of course, cold storage, fresh water, and messing facilities would be needed also. Cooperation with the construction contractors was generally good: the lending of heavy equipment from the contractor to the Marines was frequent, and at times even housing facilities were shared. And everyone pitched in when supply ships arrived or special activities were undertaken. In general harmony existed between the various contingents, though they usually kept focused on their own responsibilities. In August the island was sufficiently developed to be officially declared Midway Naval Air Station.

By May of that year the permanent armament of the defenses had been emplaced. For Midway this consisted of six 5-inch guns—two dual batteries on Sand Island and one on Eastern Island. They were sited to provide at least some coverage on every approach. Four three-gun batteries of 3-inch anti-aircraft guns were in fixed emplacements. Original plans had called for another three guns (either 3-inch or 37-mm) to be available for boat defense; the local command was still requesting these weapons. Thirty each .50- and .30-caliber machine guns were on the island. Four searchlights had positions, directors, and generators installed and it was thought the coverage was good. However, the CNO was not entirely satisfied with the seacoast defenses. In his letter of May 2, he requested that four 7-inch/45-caliber guns be shipped to and installed at Midway, in addition to sending four more 3-inch guns having a primarily anti-boat role.

As outpost life was pretty harsh, it was always intended to provide periodic relief of the units assigned. In the late summer of 1941 the 6th Battalion, then in training at San Diego, was selected for replacing the 3rd on Midway. The first advance party of the 6th was sent to the island in cruisers *Chester* and *Astoria*.[15] Ten officers and 130 men arrived there on August 11. The main body of the 6th under Col. Raphael Griffin arrived a month later, and the 3rd took their place on board the ships for their (no doubt highly anticipated) return to the civilization of Oahu.[16] Of course, this sort of exchange could avoid much of the equipment. The guns, stores, equipment, and supplies were left on the island for the next occupants—and the same thing was done in return at Pearl for the unit arriving back at its base. On December 7 Midway's ground complement was about completed; it reported on station 843 men of the 6th Battalion. Also on the island was a small Army contingent of one officer and four enlisted men, who had just arrived in October. Their mission was to operate a small radio facility for communications with the transient bomber ferry flights anticipated for the next several months. Then in mid-November the advance echelon of the intended land-based Marine Corps air squadron arrived. This consisted of one officer and sixty enlisted men to support the Marine bomber squadron (VMSB-231) expected in early December.

While perhaps it originally had been assumed that each of the Pacific island bases would get a defense battalion, it had been realized early that several of these small stations just could not support this large a force. The situation at Palmyra illustrates the physical limitations of these islands. On this island, facilities at that time (February 6, 1941) could only accommodate 130 men. Water was obtained solely from rainwater catchments—but the high rainfall on the island was theoretically projected to be able to support five hundred men.[17] Consistent delivery of quality rations for the men was also a concern, particularly perishable meat, fruit, and vegetables. Sometimes elaborate shipping schedules were built around the availability and transfer of large refrigerated food canisters universally known as "reefers." In June it was decided to permanently split the 1st Battalion between the bases of Johnston, Palmyra, and Wake, with some adjustment of the armament available.

Based on the orders of January, the advance detachment of Marines for Johnston left San Diego on February 1941. The 1st Battalion was subsequently subdivided between Johnston and Palmyra, with a portion kept at Pearl for later use. *Antares* delivered a small detachment of just six enlisted men, two Navy corpsmen, and two 5-inch seacoast guns to Johnston Island on March 3, 1941. Twenty additional Marines came at the end of the month on board destroyer minesweeper *Boggs.* While the seacoast gun battery was emplaced on Johnston Island and serviceable fairly quickly, it took until July to receive and begin work on the first anti-aircraft guns. The island's garrison grew by just small increments (in some ways Johnston was the least hospitable of the island outposts); another batch arrived on October 18. By the time of the Pearl Harbor attack the defenders on Johnston consisted of just seven officers and 155 men of the 1st Defense Battalion equipped with a single battery of two 5-inch guns, one anti-aircraft battery with four 3-inch guns, and eight each .50- and .30-caliber machine guns.

Palmyra Island also received its first garrison troops as a result of the CNO's directive in early 1941. Drawing from the 1st Battalion troops arriving in Pearl Harbor in February, a detachment was dispatched on USS *Antares.* Stopping first to deliver a similar advanced unit to Johnston, *Antares* arrived at Palmyra later in March. Three officers and forty-five men went ashore, but they had to build their initial crude barracks from spare materials supplied by the contractors already present. They were joined by ninety-seven more Marines who arrived in April, along with more equipment. Initial armament in these early shipments consisted of four 5-inch seacoast guns, one battery of four 3-inch anti-aircraft guns, and four each of the .50- and .30-caliber machine guns. No additional heavy guns were received before the Pearl Harbor attack, but the garrison was slightly increased over the course of the following months. Palmyra reported a Marine strength of seven officers and 151 enlisted men on December 7, 1941.[18]

On June 23, 1941, work on Wake was considered far enough along that the CNO directed that elements of a defense battalion be dispatched for defense. The contingent for Wake used most of the remaining men of the 1st Defense Battalion. For guns, Wake received those allocated to the 6th Battalion, which would not be needed when that unit went to Midway to replace the men of the 3rd Battalion assigned there. By this time plans called for Wake to get an entire battalion suite of armament—all six 5-inch guns and twelve 3-inch anti-aircraft guns. However, while there was room (and need!) for all these guns, it was another matter for the men. Wake was to receive about half a battalion's manpower, roughly four hundred Marines. It was realized that this meant all defenses and guns could not be manned simultaneously, but it would prove easier to send in additional manpower when needed. The advance detachment of the 1st Battalion arrived on August 19, 1941 on regular supply ship USS *Regulus.* On September 1 the island's defenses were stated as 172 Marines (five officers, 167 enlisted), and four attached naval medical personnel. All six 5-inch guns were present (though two were still without fire-control gear), as were the twelve 3-inch anti-aircraft, eighteen .50-caliber anti-aircraft machine guns, and thirty .30-caliber guns for beach defense. The six searchlights were there with power plants, but no sound locators or radar were yet present. Dry provisions for the garrison to last an estimated sixty to ninety days were stored.

In mid-October Maj. James A. Devereaux (executive officer of the 1st Battalion) arrived on a routine supply run to become the permanent commander of the Marine defenders. The final, major allotment of the 1st Battalion arrived in early November in USS *Castor*, escorted by destroyers *Blue* and *Jarvis.* Disembarking November 2 were nine officers and two hundred enlisted men of the unit, bringing total Marine strength on the island to just fewer than four hundred men. On November 29 Maj. Robert J. Conderman arrived with forty-nine Marines of the ground component of the Marine fighter squadron destined for the islands. Also on this ship (USS *Wright*) was the first allotment of two naval officers and fifty-eight men needed to establish and run the newly commissioned Wake Island Naval Air Station. This included Cdr. Winfield S. Cunningham, sent as the new commander of the station. As the senior officer present, he would be nominally in command of all military forces, including Devereaux and his defense battalion, which subsequently led to some confusion and conflicts when action started. Like Midway, Wake also received a small Army communications detachment meant to support the expected continuous flow of Army bombers in the near future.

As mentioned previously, the Navy made available a number of excess 7-inch guns for fixed defense. These guns had been mounted as a heavy tertiary battery on American pre-dreadnought battleships in the early 1900s. After spending years in storage, twenty-nine otherwise unclaimed guns were allocated in 1940. Four were earmarked for training facilities, twelve were put into reserve for the Marines at Charleston, South Carolina, and the last thirteen were sent to Pearl Harbor. Four of these Pearl Harbor guns were immediately allocated to Midway; sites for two 2-gun batteries (one each for Sand and Eastern Island) had been authorized on October 24. These new weapons moved to Midway relatively quickly. On November 29, 1941, USS *Regulus* took three of the four guns from Pearl Harbor to Midway, arriving just on December 4.[19] The final gun followed within several weeks.

Right before the war the battalions were ready and deployed, if not up to what the Navy viewed as optimal strength. Midway was thought in relatively good shape with its full battalion and pending emplacement of the 7-inch guns. Wake was almost fully armed, though missing some fire-control equipment and still much under strength in men. It was hoped that living facilities, storage facilities, and a new water distillation unit for the full garrison could be completed by February 15. Likewise Johnston was still a little below its target garrison of 185 men, and Palmyra its 240-man allocation. These last two islands still needed power, water supply, sewage, and refrigeration facilities.

Guam was not one of the projected Army ferry bases, though it was an early and active stop for the Pan Am clippers (and also hosted the transfer of the Navy patrol bombers from Pearl Harbor to Cavite in 1940), was a relay point for the Pacific cable, and had a functioning naval radio facility. The Five-Power Treaty (also known as the Washington Naval Treaty) had banned the addition of new fortifications in much of the Pacific. Japan announced its withdrawal from this treaty in 1934, to be effective in 1936. Legally there was a window of several years prior to the war when Guam could have received defensive fortification, but congress never approved such a move, and the Navy itself waffled on its desires. To be sure this was indeed naval turf—the Navy administered the island and had the only military presence; the U.S. Army was not present. A small local supply ship, USS *Gold Star*, was used regularly to bring perishables and coal for the island's power plant from the Philippines.

The Navy's General Board issued a report to the secretary of the Navy on October 23, 1941, concerning the further fortification of Guam. The report attempted to settle the policy about the military development of the island, and tried to consider national policy along with military priorities. Weighing factors like the impending independence of the Philippines, the stretched American resources for lend-lease and a Europe-first strategy, and the natural limitations of the island's harbor and likely facilities, the board recommended that Guam not be fortified. They did recommend continuation of the relatively small-scale harbor and seaplane facility improvements. Admiral Stark endorsed the report and forwarded it to Secretary of the Navy Frank Knox.[20] Guam had not been favored, and would not at any time of the pre-war period receive more than a token military presence.

In 1941 Guam's defenses depended on two small organizations. There was a small Marine Corps detachment based at Sumay Barracks near Apra Harbor. While the size of this unit fluctuated somewhat in the 1930s, on December 7, 1941, it had a total strength of just eight officers and 145 enlisted men.[21] The second unit was an auxiliary volunteer force of local Chamorro soldiers known as the Insular Force Guard. The men of this unit were to receive rudimentary training on the island and be used essentially as an auxiliary reinforcement to the Marines in times of need. The Guard's authorized strength was increased to 230 by regulation in early 1941; however, enlistment and training restrictions resulted in a partially trained force of about eighty men.[22] In terms of armament, at the time of war these forces had at their disposal 170 Springfield rifles, thirteen Lewis .30-caliber machine guns, and fifteen Browning automatic rifles. No artillery, mortars, or other heavy weapons were present. The largest single weapon was a 3-inch gun on the deck of USS *Penguin*, an old minesweeper that was the Navy's sole armed warship at the station.

Samoa was acquired by the United States as part of a three-nation treaty in 1899. The principal island, Tutuila, had a well-protected though small harbor. The Navy had developed this harbor at Pago Pago into a coaling station from the early 1900s. Consisting generally of coal sheds (two 55,000-gallon fuel oil tanks were added in 1922), storehouses, a small dispensary, and an adequate concrete wharf, the station was a small though acceptable refueling stop for America's interests in the South Pacific. Also, fresh water was not a problem here; fine supplies were available for any garrison or for ship boilers. Through most of the 1920s and 1930s it sustained a complement of about

150 sailors. As on Guam, the commander of the naval station was also the island's governor. A small native guard, known locally as the Fita Fita, of fifty to one hundred men, provided a sort of militia-like armed defense. Tutuila is a relatively large, mountainous island rather than an atoll. Large hills directly adjacent to the naval base prevented it from being developed initially as either a land or seaplane base. Samoa did not appear as a base recommendation of the Hepburn Board, but was funded in the follow-on appropriations for harbor and base improvements in 1940 and 1941.

Along with the first contractor assignments came an effort to augment the defensive capabilities of Pago Pago. In the summer of 1940 a small party of Marines from the 14th Naval District surveyed Samoa. This was followed by an order from the CNO to immediately implement defensive plans, including the mounting of seacoast armament on November 29, 1940. An advance party of the Marine Corps 7th Defense Battalion arrived at Pago Pago direct from San Diego on December 21, 1940. It journeyed in a regularly scheduled Matson liner. The guns for projected batteries were already in storage, and consisted of four 6-inch/50-caliber seacoast guns and four 3-inch/50 caliber anti-aircraft guns. On February 1, 1941 it was reported that two officers and twenty enlisted men of the 7th Battalion had custody of the recently mounted guns. The Navy then moved the balance of the 7th Battalion to Samoa. The ships arrived on March 15, 1941 with the designated troops. Transport USS *William P. Biddle* with escorting light cruiser USS *Concord* brought out twenty-four officers and 405 enlisted men. A routine unloading followed, and the small convoy departed again on the twentieth. The balance of the unit's strength was to be completed by the attachment of the roughly 250 men of an expanded local Fita Fita guard.

It wasn't until November of 1941 that the Navy finally felt ready to substantially augment the aircraft assigned at its two most critical forward bases—Midway and Wake. Of course, both had been used commercially by Pan Am as a refueling stop for the clipper route the previous five years, and the Navy had temporarily based PBY squadrons at Midway. For Midway, new patrol bombers were transferred from Hawaii. Additional supplies of bombs were sent to the island to be able to support extended patrol schedules.[23] Patrol squadron VP-21 moved to Midway on December 1 in order to provide anti-submarine warfare (ASW) patrols and scouting for the journeys of *Enterprise* and *Lexington* bringing the Marine squadrons to the island bases. On December 7 that squadron had twelve PBY-3s deployed at Midway. Seven were in the air, four on ten-minute standby, and one was under repair. Some of the PBY-3s of the squadron had flown to Wake on December 2 to help screen and guide the arriving fighter squadron in from *Enterprise*, but they returned to Midway. One of the bombers was subsequently destroyed in the night bombardment at Midway by Japanese destroyers, and two were damaged while trying to take off at night.

It took completion of the hard runways previously started (but accelerated by the Army's bomber ferry plan) and the building of base facilities by the contractor before it became practical to actually assign land-based aircraft squadrons to these islands. Much discussion ensued about whether the defensive fighter squadrons should be provided by the Army or by the Marines. The Army had more resources to spare and one of the key reasons for the islands' defense was their use as ferry bases, but the Navy administered virtually all of the rest of the activities on the islands and was already operating an active supply system. Eventually Marine Corps aviation units were selected. On November 10 the Navy command recommended that aircraft be based at these two new naval air stations in order to meet the emergency defense requirements. Wake was to be prepared for a squadron of twelve Navy patrol planes and a unit of either twelve Marine scout bombers or fighters. Midway was to get a second patrol bomber squadron (another twelve planes) and a squadron of eighteen Marine planes.

Both the urgency of deployment and the logistical situation affected the arrangements for these squadrons. The patrol bombers could fly direct, and plans were made to have the single-engine fighters or bombers taken by carrier to the islands to be flown off by their pilots. (Marine aircraft were naval types with all the required capabilities to operate from carriers, and the pilots were trained for carrier operations.) Follow-up delivery of key ground personnel, parts, fuel, and munitions would then be scheduled. Even with the rapid progress in new construction, at Wake the personnel would be accommodated at contractor's camp No. 2 or in a tent camp next to the runway. At Midway there was some room at the naval air station for the patrol bomber personnel; the Marine fliers and ground personnel would need a tent camp on Eastern Island.

Marine Fighter Squadron VMF-211 was selected to go to Wake. It consisted of twelve relatively new Grumman F4F-3 fighters, known popularly as the Wildcat. The squadron was based in San Diego, and would be brought out on aircraft carrier *Enterprise.* From Pearl Harbor, Task Force 8 was organized. In addition to *Enterprise* and her cargo were escorting cruisers *Chester*,

Northampton, and *Salt Lake City*, along with Destroyer Squadron 6. The task force was to proceed to two hundred miles from Wake and fly off its planes at approximately 7 AM on December 3. PBYs from Wake and Midway were to cover the movement and help escort the planes into Wake. The patrol bombers sent were stationed at Midway at the time, being detached for Wake on December 1.

Marine Bomber Squadron VMSB-231 was selected for deployment to Midway. This unit was based at Oahu's Ewa Field and consisted of twenty-four SB2U-3 dive-bombers. Known as the Vindicator, this older model aircraft was just passing into the category of obsolete. Scheduled for replacement by the much better SBD dive-bomber in the Marine Corps inventory, it was one of those events that just hadn't yet occurred. The squadron (or rather most of it—eighteen planes) embarked on USS *Lexington* at Pearl and departed with a heavy escort on December 4.[24] *Lexington* and the rest of Task Force 12 were scheduled to arrive at a point four hundred miles off of Midway to commence flying off the eighteen dive-bombers on the morning of December 7. The task force was recalled to Pearl Harbor with the news of the Japanese attack, before the fly-off of the air contingent of VMSB-231 could be made. The planes went back to Ewa.

Navy seaplane tender USS *Wright* was used to transport the ground personnel and attendant equipment of the airplane squadrons being deployed. She arrived at Wake first from Pearl Harbor on November 28, depositing one officer and forty-nine enlisted men of the ground-support echelon of VMF-211.[25] Proceeding, she left one officer and forty enlisted men at Midway from VMSB-231 on December 4. A stockpile of bombs was created at both places, as were protected magazines to store them. Plans had developed to anticipate that the Hawaii Army B-17s might be called upon to operate from these bases, and bombs and limited amounts of matériel to allow temporary operation of twelve such planes were at each island. The Army was experiencing a critical shortage of bombs, but with minor modifications they could use the Navy bombs already stored on the islands.

Right before the war a discussion began about replacing the Marine island outposts, or at least those at the air ferry bases, with Army detachments. Apparently stemming from a Marine Corps desire to concentrate its forces for offensive purposes, and from the Army's to assume responsibility for bases for which it was the primary user, the discussions became fairly advanced. The concept was for the Army to organize battalion-sized units roughly mimicking a defense battalion. Generally speaking this was to be a coast artillery battalion (separate) of about one thousand men. Due to lack of extra equipment, they would take over the fixed seacoast guns and anti-aircraft guns on the islands—in fact, all heavy weapons except .30-caliber machine guns and Browning automatic rifles. Each island would also get a pursuit squadron to replace any Marine Corps aviation unit. The islands involved would be Palmyra, Johnston, Wake, and Midway. The Army had already committed to the provision of such units for Canton and Christmas Islands.[26] The Army garrisons would come from the Hawaiian Department, but additional coast artillery units, and six field-grade officers as task force commanders, would be needed from mainland resources.

Once the proposal was put together, the Navy and Marines had second thoughts. In the first place the Marines still wanted their deployed equipment; they would need seacoast and anti-aircraft guns for any future base, and realized the Army could not replace these items, at least in the short term. Also, Navy-directed construction work was still going on at most of the four original islands; it would complicate supply, command, and coordination to mix services in these small locations. It might be better to wait until construction was finished before turning the sites over to the Army. Finally Admiral Kimmel concluded that with current war tensions, the Marines were already trained, acclimated, and deployed for this mission. He suggested the Army prepare three battalions and three eighteen-plane pursuit squadrons with as much equipment as possible for use at a better time, or even with new island bases that might need garrisons. Another issue arose in regard to the air squadrons. Army fighters, because of training, usually couldn't operate more than about fifteen miles from land—a real handicap for island bases.[27] Also, because they couldn't land on carriers, the short-ranged fighters would be stuck at a base, and not capable of movement or concentration elsewhere without a lot of work. While the Army did go on to garrison a number of Pacific bases, the Marines stayed on Midway, Johnston, and Palmyra through the war's duration.

CHAPTER TEN

Pensacola Convoy Begins

Many of the requests of the new command in the Far East had been favorably met during the late summer of 1941. On September 17 MacArthur dispatched a more detailed radiogram to Washington outlining additional needs a little more specifically.[1] Units of American troops were desired to help in the further reorganization of the Philippine Division, for anticipated Army and corps troops, and in the continuing augmentation of the Air Forces. After analysis the War Department plans staff gave priority to various field artillery and air units for the next successive convoy. Eventually allocated the heavy cruiser *Pensacola,* this convoy departed Hawaii at the end of November and was a week at sea when Pearl Harbor was attacked. Subsequently diverted to Australia the troops, equipment, and even the conveying vessels of the convoy experienced the full onslaught of the American early war experience in the Pacific. Torn between constantly changing strategic goals and faced with daunting tactical situations, many of the men, ships, and airplanes of this convoy were tragically lost in early 1942.

The Far Eastern command was keen on substantially reinforcing its field artillery capability. In event of war the ten Philippine reserve divisions would be incorporated in the combined Filipino-American forces. Higher echelon corps and Army structures would be required. Normally these formations managed a few artillery regiments to be used in support of divisional artillery for major operations. The September request included a complete field artillery brigade—the headquarters and three regiments totaling six battalions. Two of these battalions were to have 155-mm howitzers and four the 75-mm light field gun. Altogether the artillery requested totaled two brigade HQs, three regiment HQs, and eight field artillery battalions. Another complicating factor in the artillery request was the problem of acquiring field guns for the Philippine reserve divisions. At twenty-four per division, a total of 240 75-mm guns (plus reserves and training center weapons) were going to be required, of which only a portion was available at the time. Some of the thinking in selecting American field artillery units was influenced by the idea that their guns would eventually be replaced by more modern 105-mm howitzers and the older weapons would be handed down to the Philippine Army.

On October 15 orders were issued by the adjutant general's office to various field commands to start the movement of the selected artillery units as a permanent change of station. Selected for transfer to the Philippines on this date were the 26th Field Artillery Brigade Headquarters, the 147th Field Artillery Regiment, and the 2nd Battalion of the 131st Field Artillery Regiment. These units were to arrive in San Francisco for shipment no later than November 20, 1941. Three days later the 148th Field Artillery Regiment (less its 2nd Battalion) was also notified to prepare for shipment by November 29.[2] Ultimately these units would all be selected to ship out on vessels eventually composing the *Pensacola* convoy. Despite the fact that a brigade headquarters and two regimental headquarters were part of the shipment, it is important to note that the Army simply considered these units components to be reassembled any way the Philippine Department desired. Thus the 2/131st was not assigned as the "missing" battalion to the 148th, and the two regiments were not sub-units of the brigade.

The reorganization of the American field army into the triangular division format facilitated the finding of these units. The reduction in size of the National Guard artillery brigades made available most of the pieces that were sent to Manila. The other practical advantage was that these parent units had been organized for some time and many had participated in the extensive Army maneuvers of 1940 and 1941. The regiments and battalions selected for this particular shipment came from the National Guard forces of three states—Idaho, South Dakota, and Texas.[3]

The 26th Field Artillery Brigade headquarters and headquarters' battery was a regular Army unit. It had been activated at Camp Roberts in California on June 1, 1941. Basically just an artillery command unit, it consisted of a small headquarters staff with a commanding brigadier general and the administrative headquarters' battery. It contained a wire and radio communications section, a maintenance section, and a command post with survey section. Total personnel of the 26th Brigade HQ were just twelve officers and eighty-nine enlisted men.[4] The largest unit selected for this shipment was the entire 147th Field Artillery Regiment. This was a South Dakota ex–National Guard unit that had been inducted into federal service on November 25, 1940 at Sioux Falls. The unit's personnel roster at time of transfer consisted of sixty-one officers and 1,107 enlisted men. In addition, a medical detachment of seven officers and thirty-eight enlisted men was attached for overseas service. The formation's commander was Col. Leslie Jensen, one of the more senior officers of the pending shipment.[5]

Also part of the original artillery selected for transfer was the second battalion of the 131st Field Artillery Regiment. This was part of the Texas National Guard 36th Division. It had been inducted into federal service on November 25, 1940 at Camp Bowie outside Brownwood, Texas. The battalion was one of those found in excess of requirements when the parental 36th Division changed to a triangular organization. It did actively participate in the General Headquarters (GHQ) Louisiana maneuvers in August, and shortly after returning to Texas received notice to move. The battalion commander was Lt. Col. Blucher S. Tharp, who had been with the regiment for several years. Prior to movement overseas it brought its strength up to prescribed levels by transferring men from other batteries of the regiment. The unit and its complement of 531 men (twenty-six officers and 505 enlisted), plus fifteen attached medical staff, was ordered from its home station to San Francisco. This unit departed Texas on two trains, leaving on November 10 and 11 for the Pacific coast. Ten days later they were boarding USS *Republic* at San Francisco's Pier 57.

Although originally scheduled to leave slightly later, the majority of the 148th Field Artillery Regiment was included in the pending convoy. This was an Idaho National Guard unit inducted at Coeur d'Alene on September 16, 1940. Like the 2/131st it became excess when the division assumed a triangular configuration. As a way of getting a high proportion of headquarters in the shipment, several regiments were scheduled to ship with the headquarters and just one of their two armed battalions. At the time of the movement order this configuration left the unit with 637 men plus an attached twenty-nine medical personnel and one chaplain. It had moved from Idaho to Camp Murray, Washington, on September 24, 1940. An early schedule had placed the unit to depart San Francisco on November 28 on *Bliss*, but its departure was moved up to *Holbrook* leaving November 22. The unit left Washington for San Francisco in a motor convoy on November 17.

Another issue facing the shipment organizers was the matter of gun armament. At that time, all four field artillery battalions were each armed with twelve "French 75s." Left over from the First World War were a number of guns of two Allied designs—one British and the other French. Both were chambered to utilize the same-sized 75-mm ammunition. The French design was both purchased in France and licensed for manufacture in the United States, and was produced in considerable numbers. The British design (designated the Model 1917) was acquired in fewer numbers, but several hundred persisted until early in the Second World War. The 75-mm guns in the battalions' inventories were actually thc model 1897A4—essentially the First World War French-type gun tube and carriage modified with new axels and wheels to allow high-speed towing. A more radical modernization had also been developed, designated the 75-mm model M2A2 or M2A3: the old gun tube sat on an entirely new carriage with a modern split trail, increased elevation, and improved traverse. These were more expensive to produce, and their numbers were still limited. Of course, simultaneously with these improvements the Army had developed the new 105-mm howitzer that would soon become the standard armament of the light artillery battalions.

A decision was reached on November 13 (just nine days prior to sailing) that in order for the Philippine Island garrison to be more completely equipped, the four battalions were to all be armed with the newest models of 75-mm guns. While there was no problem otherwise considering the 105-mm howitzer, its lack of adequate ammunition supply argued against the deployment to the Philippines, at least for a short while. The older 75-mm M1897A4, which the units carried at that time, was slated for modernization. So as not to have to backhaul it in the immediate future, the Army thought it was prudent to not allow this type to go to the islands. Orders were quickly issued to have units in close proximity to the artillery battalions exchange their modernized guns for the older models. For some of the artillerymen this exchange was not the ideal solution. Clyde Fillmore of the 2/131st recalls: "We took our 75 millimeter guns with us but with no enthusiasm because we were to pick up the newly adopted 105's in San Francisco. Somehow, they never made their appearance."[6] It also appears that this replacement schedule was a little too tight. Richard Cropp of the 147th stated that his unit received its new, modernized 75-mms just three days before moving out to Fort McDowell, which was the holding area for troops awaiting embarkation.[7] Receiving the new field guns on November 13, there was time only to coat them with rust-preventative and prepare them for shipping. In fact, for all but these small work details the artillerymen did not lay eyes on their new charges until unloading them in Australia or Java. In any event, the ships of the convoy managed to carry less than half of the specified light artillery pieces. Four 75-mm guns were on *Republic* and sixteen on *Holbrook*. Well over half of the motor vehicles normally assigned to the artillery units also were not shipped with the troops, though most of the equipment needed sailed within a few days on one of several freighters. The remaining twenty-eight field guns, for example, shipped on the freighter *Jane Christenson* just three days after the troops left.

The four field artillery battalions were not the only significant enhancement to the Philippine artillery. Also carried in the convoy were another forty-eight 75-mm guns destined for use by the Philippine rather than American army forces. A significant reserve of 75-mm guns had been carried in the Philippine Department for some years. To simplify maintenance and parts supply, guns tended to be concentrated by type in the overseas departments. On June 30, 1941 there were reported a total of 173 75-mm Model 1917 (the British 75) in the Philippines.[8] Virtually all of the small 2.95-inch mountain guns were also there. The actual needs of the Philippine Scout battalions, as then organized, were just forty 75-mm guns and twelve 2.95-inch mountain guns. The balance was available for a variety of uses: training, beach defense on the harbor forts, and for issue to the mobilizing Philippine Army. In the MacArthur radiogram of August 27 it was reported that forty-eight pieces were on hand for the Philippine Army, leaving a deficit of 240. A later request dated in mid-November listed the need at 276. In the words of the commanding general, Far East (MacArthur): "Unstable situation in Far East requires the early shipment of suitable supporting artillery."[9]

While precise numbers vary by source, a plan soon emerged to free up a significant number of artillery weapons, even if not the most modern, for the Philippine Army. All along they had planned to eventually replace the light artillery of the Philippine Division with the newly developed 105-mm howitzer. In July a plan was adopted that authorized the forty Model 1917 guns carried by the U.S. Army to be replaced with these new howitzers—when production and priorities allowed.[10] Early in the fall it was stated that the Army's policy was to distribute 105-mm howitzers to units *least* likely to go into combat. That was based primarily on ammunition availability. On November 10 the chief of ordnance approved the immediate shipment of the required forty 105-mm howitzers, and also 66,000 rounds of ammunition that had been set aside as a reserve for the emergency task force. In turn when these arrived (they never did, war came sooner than the shipment), the 75s replaced would be turned over to the Philippine units.

The second source of 75-mm guns would be a series of direct shipments from the United States. Modernized 75s were being released from non-task force infantry divisions and from a reorganization of equipment of the fledgling anti-tank units. It was calculated that 130 such guns could be made available for immediate shipment to the Philippine Army.[11] Like the previous source, none of these newly found guns made it to the defenders before hostilities, though several ships were loaded with them at the time shipments were interrupted.

Finally a third source of weapons was found in Hawaii. Like the Philippines, the Hawaiian Department carried a considerable excess of artillery pieces in its inventory—in fact, so many that they could not be manned in the event of a true emergency. Besides the organic artillery of the two Hawaiian divisions, forty M1917 75-mm guns with high-speed modernization were provided as a pool for beach defense. On November 11 the Hawaiian Department was ordered to ship these guns and others to the Philippines on the first available transport. All forty beach defense guns and eight from the divisions were contributed. Department commander Short quickly complied, but simultaneously registered his request that they be replaced with 105-mm howitzers or at least modernized M2s as soon as possible.[12] Additionally 123 excess machine guns were made available for the same shipping schedule.

Initially Hawaii only prepared to send along the fire-control sights mounted on the carriages, but the War Department urged that all additional fire-control equipment suitable for use be supplied. In compliance, the following material was loaded with the guns:[13]

67 gunner quadrants M1918 MILS
70 panoramic telescopes M6
57 aiming posts M1
25 battery commander's telescopes M1915A1
28 aiming point lamps
6 firing tables 75 x 3
18 range-finders, 1-meter base
54 rocking-bar sights
26 aiming circles M1918 French
4 bore sights, 75-mm
54 panoramic telescope carriers
67 bracket fuse setters M1916

This detailed list is at odds with accounts by various veterans of the artillery battalions. Virtually all postwar accounts mentioning these "British 75-mm" guns insist that they did not have any sights or fire-control equipment. Perhaps this equipment was physically separated from the guns and not located quickly enough by the troops to be of use.

A few new 37-mm M3 anti-tank guns also accompanied the four artillery battalions (the tables of equipment called for each battalion to have a small section of such guns). For at least two units the first glimpse they had of this weapon was on this trip—during the previous year's maneuvers stand-in substitutes or even mock weapons had played the role of anti-tank guns.[14] It appears also that there was a total lack of ammunition accompanying these guns. This particular weapon was also in very short supply for the Philippine defenders. Up to the time of the Pearl Harbor attack only nine guns of this type had been supplied to the islands (although in this case with their allotment of ammunition). Total combined requirements for both the American and Filipino forces were 449 such guns. As one of the roles for the anti-tank gun was for beach defense against light boats, older 37-mm infantry guns partially substituted for the required anti-tank guns. The same authorization that released the 75-mm Hawaiian guns for shipment was used to also obtain 123 excess .30-caliber machine guns to serve as temporary 37-mm replacements. These were also placed on *Meigs* in Honolulu in late November.[15]

One unusual Army service unit was slated for this convoy. The 3rd Chemical Company (Lab) was issued orders on October 22, 1941 to report to San Francisco for sailing on November 20. Only one small Chemical Warfare Service unit was actually present in the Philippines (the 4th Chemical Company of the Philippine Department), and with stories of Japanese use of toxic agents in China widespread, there was a strong desire to augment this service. A recent request for a full chemical battalion had to be turned down, but a smaller unit was offered as a substitute. The laboratory unit's primary mission was to identify enemy chemical weapons and design countermeasures. It also was useful in actually researching and manufacturing limited quantities of chemical agents (including things as diverse as insecticides, disinfectants, uniform dyes, and food preservatives). The lab unit was stationed at the Edgewood Arsenal in Maryland, and was just one of two such labs that existed in the Army's roster. While the unit consisted of only seventy-nine men, a high proportion (thirteen) were officer/scientists. A considerable-sized laboratory and equipment locker accompanied the unit as it moved cross-country on its way.[16]

Virtually every major shipment to the Philippines in 1941 contained at least some air assets. The *Pensacola* convoy was no exception; in fact, it carried more troops for air units than it did for the ground combat forces. Significant cargo space was allocated to carry the ground echelon of the 7th Bombardment Group and its supporting service units. The 7th was to be the second of two heavy bomber groups for the islands, intended to supplement the B-17s of the 19th Bombardment Group already fully established at Clark Field. The actual aircraft for the group's squadrons (and of course aircrew) would fly out on the Pacific ferry route in batches during December.

Air Force groups, despite their large numbers of ground personnel, were not self-supporting. Groups usually had a considerable number of attached, specialized ground units. The Air Force had by this time developed a pretty good sense of what was needed, the attached complements being fairly well standardized. The chief two specialized units were a matériel squadron and an ordnance company. The 8th Matériel Squadron with attached medical (totaling eleven officers and 211 enlisted men) received its orders on October 15 at Fort Douglas. This type of unit was essentially a heavy maintenance company, filled with specialized mechanics, welders, painters, electricians, and parachute riggers, and maintained a considerable inventory of spare parts. It specialized by the type of aircraft supported. The 453rd Ordnance Company, Aviation (Bombardment) was an ordnance department unit specializing in supporting bombers. It had responsibility for maintenance and repair of gun armament and handling and the loading of bombs. From Salt Lake City, Utah, the unit mustered six officers and 181 enlisted men when orders to transfer were received on October 15. Finally forty-eight individual pursuit aircraft pilots and two navigators, mostly destined for the 21st and 34th Pursuit Squadrons, were provided transport. However, it seems they lacked many of the preferred hours of training. Some were subsequently described as little more than cadets, and more than a few serious accidents occurred while they were training or transferring aircraft.

Two significant loads of aircraft also were in the manifest. *Meigs* was loaded with fifty-two A-24 "Banshee" Army dive-bombers in a partially knocked-down condition. These were the complete complement of light bombers destined for the three squadrons of the 27th Bombardment Group. The aircrews (this was a two-man, single-engine aircraft) and complete ground echelon for this unit were already in the Philippines, awaiting their aircraft. Ultimately this separation of men from planes would cause great consternation, and attempts to unite the two would be a considerable part of Army efforts over the next two months. Originally the shipment of the airplanes and personnel had not been that far apart—*Meigs* left San Francisco on November 2, while the crews left on *President Coolidge* just the day before. Differences in the speeds of the vessels and Navy delays in organizing a second convoy conspired to separate the two shipments by more than a month.

The A-24 was an Army-purchased Douglas dive-bomber for all purposes identical to the Navy's SBD-3. The Army had been slow in adopting close-support aircraft for ground units, and it was only by watching the success of German operations early in the European war that enthusiasm for a U.S. dive-bomber grew. An order for eighty-two A-24s was issued on June 26, 1940, with delivery stipulated by August 1941. The only changes from the naval version were the deletion of arrestor and flotation gear, and carrier crash hook. From this lot fifty-four were delivered to the 27th Bombardment Group stationed at Savannah, Georgia. This unit was the Army's first dive-bomber unit, and consisted of the 16th, 17th, and 91st bomb squadrons.[17]

There was also an allotment of fighter planes in the convoy. On the Dutch vessel *Bloemfontein* were eighteen crated P-40Es. This was to be the full strength for the 34th Pursuit Squadron. That unit's ground crew and about half the pilots had been delivered to Manila on *President Coolidge* in late November. The unit had initially been issued P-35s handed down from the established fighter squadrons pending the arrival of their own airplanes. While these were obsolete, worn-out planes, at least the squadron had something to fly, unlike the 27th Bombardment Group!

One item that didn't make it into the manifest was PT Squadron 3's six motor torpedo boats waiting in Pearl Harbor for transportation to Manila Bay. The first six boats of the squadron had been transported on the deck of the naval tanker *Guadalupe* in late September. The next six were now waiting for a ride. It was found impossible to transport PTs on *Holbrook* or *Republic*. *Republic* was already overloaded and *Holbrook* could only take them stored athwart ship and it was doubtful the sheer legs at Cavite could lift them from that position. Pearl Harbor requested that a *Chenango*–class oiler be made available for the trip. Even one of the officer passengers of an artillery battalion got wind of this proposal, but reported: "The captain refused, stating that he considered such a load dangerous to the stability of the ship."[18]

For those departing, the five weeks or so between notification of an assignment change and physical departure must have rushed by. Final leaves were taken; for some of the National Guard units this meant saying good-bye to the only communities they had ever really known. Units were brought up to wartime strength. Often that meant simply asking for volunteers from sister units sharing the same post. For the 147th about fifty men were brought in from other units. For the 2/131st men were shifted from the "B" battery (staying behind with the 36th Division) to "E" battery scheduled for departure. At other times drafts had to be accepted. New equipment was supplied also. In particular, a full allocation of vehicles was made, and Army orders stipulated that only new model 1940 or 1941 makes were to be taken. Items that in peacetime were relatively scarce flowed in during these final weeks—things like gas masks, small arms, radios, and even full allocations of tropical clothing.

USS *Republic* started her voyage on November 5, 1941 from Boston following her employment taking troops to the American garrison in Iceland.[20] After stops at New York, New Orleans, and Los Angeles she stopped in San Francisco on November 17. By far the largest vessel of the convoy, *Republic* was fully outfitted as a troop transport, though with a useful cargo capacity. All the Air Force units totaling about two thousand men were taken on *Republic*. Also, the small artillery brigade headquarters and the separate 2nd Battalion of the 131st Field Artillery Regiment were found homes on board. The other large troop transport was USAT *Willard A. Holbrook*. Formerly operated by the American President Lines as SS *President Taft*, she had only been obtained by the Army the previous year, and already had made several Army voyages to the Philippines. On board were the balance of the artillery units—the 147th Field Artillery and the 148th Field Artillery minus its second battalion.

USAT *Meigs* was a well-used Army freighter that had seen many years of Army supply missions. With virtually no facilities for troops, only four Army soldiers were on board. Freight, some of the most critical, it had aplenty. From San Francisco it had numerous types of ammunition (including the only rounds for the 75-mm guns—and just 460 of those). On deck the fifty-two A-24 Dauntless dive-bombers were carried knocked down in crates; parts for them were stored separately below deck.[21] At Honolulu space was found to place the forty-eight 75-mm field guns destined for the Philippine Army, as well as the fire-control equipment and the machine guns.

USS *Chaumont* was attached to the convoy at the request of the Navy. Regular supplies, mail, replacement parts, and personnel were to be taken to both the shore stations and the Asiatic Fleet; returning personnel were to accompany the vessel back to San Francisco or Pearl Harbor. Two smaller, private commercial vessels were also instructed to join the convoy out of Oahu for Manila. SS *Admiral Halstead* was carrying a considerable cargo of

Table 5. Convoy No. 4002, November-December 1941[19]

Convoy/Ships/Speed/Escort/Dates/Route	Units and Major Cargo Items
Convoy No. 4002	147th Field Artillery Regiment
	148th Field Artillery Regiment (–2nd Battalion)
USS *Republic*	
USS *Chaumont*	2nd Battalion of 131st Field Artillery Regiment
USS *Niagara* (PT-boat tender)	
USAT *Willard A. Holbrook*	HQ and HQ Battery 26th Field Artillery Brigade
USAT *Meigs*	
SS *Admiral Halstead*	7th Bomb Group HQ and HQ Squadron
SS *Coast Farmer*	
MV *Bloemfontein* (Dutch)	88th Recon Squadron (H)
	38th Recon Squadron (H)
9–10 knots	8th Matériel Squadron
	36th Signal Platoon, AB
Escort: USS *Pensacola*	Company A, 91st QM Battalion (LM)
	453rd Ordnance Company (Avn) (B)
Ships departed SF between 11/02/41–11/21/41	Pilot officers 21st and 34th Pursuit Squadrons (of 35th Group)
Ships departed Hawaii 11/29/41	Limited number of casual fillers
Due to arrive Manila about 1/04/42	
Arrived Brisbane, Australia 12/22/41	Total of 4,690 officers and men
Southern route through Torres Strait	With above units 340 vehicles, 20 75-mm guns, 6 37-mm anti-tank guns, small arms, etc.
	52 A-24 dive-bombers, 18 P-40E fighters
	48 Model 1917 ("British") 75-mm and 123 .30-cal machine guns, 680,000 rds .50-cal, 3 million rds .30-cal, 9,600 rds 37-mm AA, 460 rds 75-mm shrapnel, 5,245 bombs, 6,000 drums aviation oil, 2,953 drums aviation gasoline, general stores and supplies, troop property, steel helmets, blankets, tires, gas masks, exchange supplies, torpedoes, mail, Christmas parcels

drummed gasoline for the Army in the Philippines. SS *Coast Farmer* had only a relatively small quantity of military cargo, consisting of 150 tons of letters and Christmas parcels for the personnel in the Philippines.[22] Both freighters did carry quantities of government and contractor cargo destined for Manila and Guam. Also on board these ships was a considerable amount of commercial cargo. The only foreign registry vessel included was MV *Bloemfontein*, a Dutch vessel that had been serving the Dutch East Indies for several years. She was chartered to carry a large Army cargo, including no less than 172 trucks for at least twelve separate units on the way or already in the Philippines.[23] Eighteen crated P-40E fighter planes destined for the 34th Pursuit Squadron were on board, along with sixty-seven American volunteers for China.

Additionally among the various units and weapons were large quantities of routine supplies. Tons and tons of crates, boxes, drums, and barrels of stores, supplies, and equipment were sent, and certainly this convoy had its share. Samples of items listed from the manifests of the convoy include:

blankets	trailers	clothing
helmets	merchandise	wire
gas masks	lockers	ship stores
torpedoes	propellers	baggage
gasoline	small arms	pipe
canned goods	oats	beef
spinach	hay	lima beans
aluminum ware	khaki	bed springs
searchlights	batteries	radios

The vessel selected as escort for the convoy was heavy cruiser *Pensacola.* For the voyage she would be designated Task Force 15.5. While of an older design (being the name ship of the first class of American "Treaty Cruisers"), the cruiser would have provided adequate protection from surface raiders, but could use little more than her speed for protection from submarines. Initial orders forming the convoy were issued on November 12. Following the sequence begun with the previous convoy, this sailing was designated Convoy No. 4002. Orders of this date, issued by the commandant of the Twelfth Naval District, were for USS *Chaumont*, USS *Republic*, and USAT *Willard A. Holbrook* to form a convoy with USS *Pensacola.* These ships were to depart Oahu on November 28 and proceed at fourteen knots to the Philippines. *Chaumont* had freight and personnel to drop along the way, so she would depart two days earlier on November 26 and go alone to Wake, joining the other three ships on December 4 near that island. The convoy would assume a basic western course and next travel to Guam, where *Chaumont* would again deposit supplies and exchange personnel. Together the four vessels would then make for Manila via the San Bernardino Straits. The three transport vessels would each carry signalmen and radiomen to maintain the necessary watches on communications.[24]

These orders did not stand long, for they were canceled just two days later. The biggest change was for the routing. On November 25 the Navy ordered all commercial traffic to take a southern route to the Far East. Then the famous November 27 "War Warning" message from Washington was dispatched to Hawaii and Manila.[25] On this same day the commander of the Fourteenth Naval District issued new orders for the convoy. *Chaumont*, *Holbrook*, and USS *Niagara* would depart Pearl Harbor while *Meigs*, *Republic*, *Admiral Halstead*, *Coast Farmer*, and *Bloemfontein* would put out of Honolulu starting at 7 AM on November 29. They were to meet escort commander Capt. Norman Scott with *Pensacola* a few miles out at sea and subsequently proceed on the prescribed routing. That would lead south of Suva in the Fiji Islands where vessels could take fuel or water as needed. Then the convoy would go to Port Moresby, and pick up a pilot for transiting the Torres Strait, eventually making Manila via the Molucca and Sibutu Passages.

After arrival and discharge of cargo in Manila, the ships would receive new routings for their return voyages. Presumably those vessels traveling on would depart on their own, such as *Bloemfontein* with its passengers for China. Also, it seems likely *Chaumont* and the freighters with contractor supplies for Guam and the other islands would take the direct route back to Hawaii, though that is not spelled out in the remaining correspondence. Of course, security-sensitive information about destination and routing was not routinely shared with most passengers on board. The average soldier was left to guess—and this they did. Sgt. Frank Fujita wrote home from Fort McDowell that there were rumors about going to Singapore or even helping with the defense of the Burma Road.[26] Crates and documents were marked for destination "Plum," but most soldiers could not break the military code word substitute for the Philippines.

Ships assigned to the convoy made their own unescorted way to Hawaii from San Francisco. As mentioned previously, *Meigs* sailed first, back on November 2, and essentially waited for the others in order to justify a convoy. Of course, that also gave *Meigs* the time to load the artillery and machine guns donated by the Hawaiian Department to the defense of the Philippines. *Chaumont* departed on the thirteenth. *Admiral Halstead* left San Francisco on the fifteenth, probably about the same time as *Coast Farmer*.[27] *Bloemfontein* and *Republic* sailed out under the Golden Gate on the twenty-first, followed by the

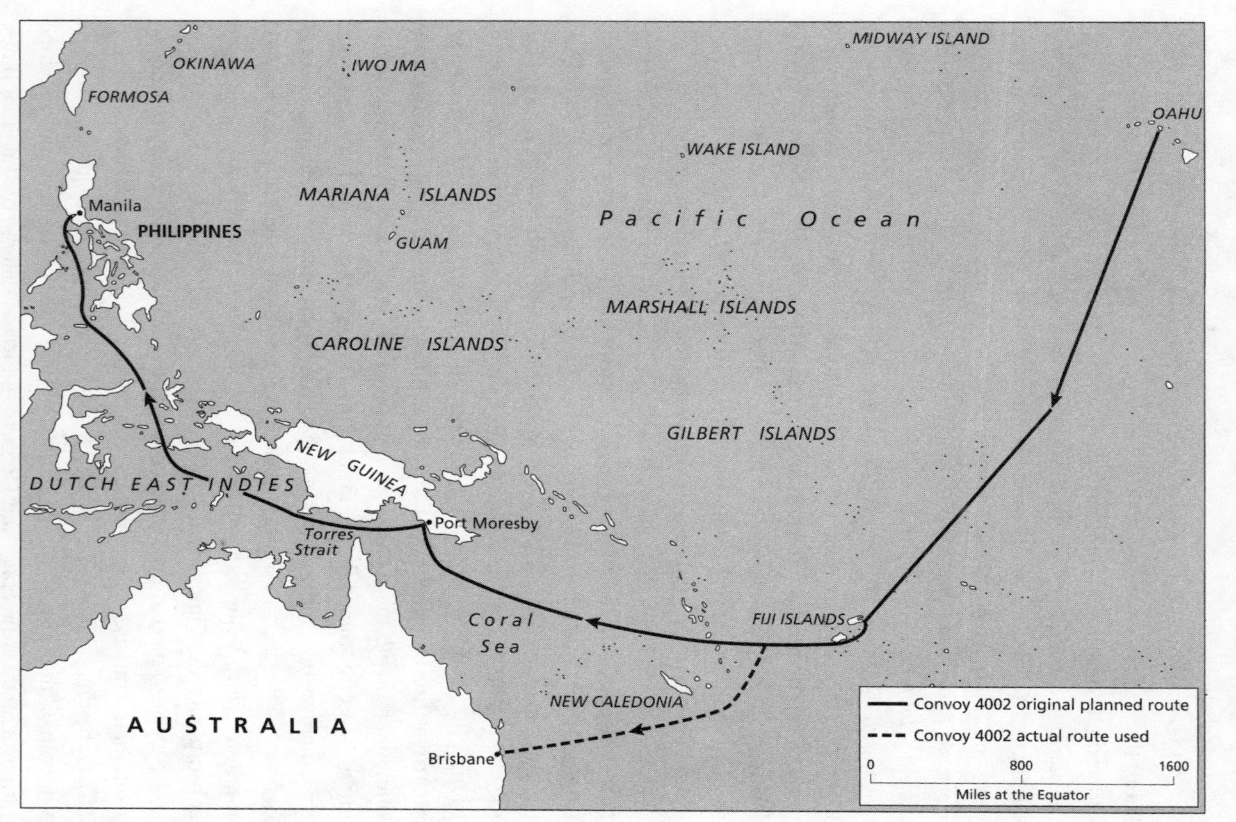

Map 3. Route of *Pensacola* Convoy

last San Francisco departure—*Willard A. Holbrook* on the twenty-second. Of course, *Pensacola* and *Niagara* were Pearl Harbor–based ships, and only joined the convoy in Hawaiian waters. *Holbrook* soon found herself delayed at Pearl Harbor in order to correct a mechanical defect that developed on the trip.

Departure of the convoy from Oahu was scheduled for November 29, and started precisely on time at 7 AM. *Republic* was a little slow in leaving and joined with the waiting *Pensacola* and other vessels a few hours late. More seriously delayed was *Holbrook* due to her repairs at Pearl Harbor. During the journey security precautions were in place. Ships observed signal and radio discipline. Twenty-four-hour watches were posted, and guns were manned (some Navy gun crews on *Republic* were glad to accept volunteer relief by the Army troops). Normal lifeboat and evacuation drills were conducted on each ship. Blackout was ordered from the first night out as a routine precaution.

Shipboard activities for the first days were what one would expect. Men explored their new home, traded sleeping quarters, tried to find place on deck for sun or shade. Organized recreation wasn't much more than evening movies. Recreational reading was common and of course the ubiquitous soldier card and dice games were everywhere. Films were shown on the troop transports—veterans of *Republic* recall seeing the 1940 film *Waterloo Bridge* starring Robert Taylor and Vivian Leigh. Normal celebrations for crossing the equator were held on all the troopships on December 6.[28] Actually, it wasn't quite normal. Many of the participants record this as the largest contingent of American servicemen to have yet undergone these ceremonies. In the recorded memoirs of the soldiers, even dozens of years after the events, the ceremonies by shellbacks, pollywogs, and King Neptune stand out starkly in their memories.

Meanwhile, in Washington, D.C., anxiety about the safety of the newest wave of reinforcements for the Philippines was mounting. After the warnings issued in late November to the Pacific commanders, it seemed evident that war could erupt any day. The concern was not specific to the safety of the convoy, but rather if there would be enough time to get the significant quantities of men and matériel in the *Pensacola* convoy to the Philippines to help deter or destroy a Japanese invasion. On December 6, Stimson noted in his diary: "We are mainly concerned with the supplies which are on the way to the Philippines and the additional big bombers which we are trying to fly over there and which are to start today."[29] And then time ran out.

CHAPTER ELEVEN

Pensacola Convoy after December 7

Back at sea the day following the equator crossing a starkly different event is equally etched in the memories of those who were on board. Received by *Pensacola*, the radio message about the attack was quickly disseminated to the troop passengers—reaching *Republic* at 11 AM on December 7 (the dateline had not yet been crossed). The transports used their onboard loudspeakers to relay the message: "Attention all hands. A state of war exists between Japan and the United States. Pearl Harbor has been attacked. Good luck."[1] Most everyone thought war with Japan was inevitable, but nobody knew when or where it would start. Obviously the exposed condition of the convoy, with important military cargo not packed or loaded with a thought of immediate usage, became a concern. Both the occupants on board and those in Washington were highly interested in the fate of the voyage.

The week between the attack on Pearl Harbor and the convoy's arrival at Fiji was a period of confusion. In Washington conferences were held and decisions were made at the highest levels concerning the fate of the convoy. Options ranged from returning to Hawaii or the West Coast, to proceeding to the Philippines, or stopping at an intermediate location. The Navy, Army, and even the president had opinions. Generally the Navy was the most conservative; they were the advocates for canceling or returning in the face of what appeared to be Japanese air and naval superiority. The Army (including long-distance input from MacArthur) usually voted to try and push the convoy and its valuable contents through to the Philippines.[2] Another option appeared to be letting the convoy get to the Fiji Islands or to Australia before making a final decision on disposition.

At this point the convoy commanders themselves were simply following directions, though these changed considerably over time. It is constructive to look at a summary of the daily orders to Convoy No. 4002:[3]

Dec 7: Direct *Pensacola* convoy report arrival and wait orders.

Dec 8: Japan declared war on United States. TF-15.5 (*Pensacola* convoy) proceed to Sydney.

Dec 8: MacArthur message to Barnes: Desire convoy (less air corps units landed and ferried north) to proceed to P.I. by most expeditious route.

Dec 9: Direct *Pensacola* and convoy return Honolulu, course east of Christmas I.

Dec 10: Disregard all previous orders; proceed with convoy less *Niagara* to Brisbane. Direct *Niagara* proceed Honolulu passing east of Christmas Island.

Dec 12: All previous instruction cancelled. Return Honolulu with convoy. If water needed make Suva.

Important discussions occurred at the meetings of the Joint Army Navy Board. This board acted in 1941 and 1942 as a sort of precursor to the general staff, usually addressing issues that affected both services or in those where inter-service cooperation was deemed most important. Official members included the chief of naval operations (Stark), the Army chief of staff (Marshall), their deputies (including Deputy Chief of Staff for Air Hap Arnold), and directors of the services' war plans divisions. Normally meeting every two weeks, the board's schedule changed to daily on December 8 and the few days subsequent. On the eighth Stark advised the board that there was no indication that the Japanese had picked up the convoy's presence in the South Pacific; the board agreed to direct it to Suva in Fiji to await instructions. The next day's discussion was more extensive. Rear Adm. Richmond K. Turner stated that it was now impossible to get shipping to the Philippines, and since the Oahu situation was still dangerous, the planes and ammunition should be returned to the Hawaiian Islands for use there (additionally mentioning that the personnel and some of the equipment might be useful to defend either Port Darwin, the Dutch East Indies, or even Samoa). The board approved the return to Hawaii—though later statements by Marshall indicate that the Army members agreed reluctantly.

Another interesting note crept into the orders, one reflecting the high anxiety over the perceived Japanese rampage in the Pacific. The orders of December 9 for the convoy contained directions for the return to Hawaii on a course east of Christmas Island. The escort and convoy commander were both told to take positive measures to assure the scuttling of the ships to avoid their capture if enemy forces were encountered. This action was countermanded within a few days. It does not appear that the message was further disseminated among the crew or passengers of the convoy.

The discussions about the convoy's ultimate destination reached and involved the highest levels of government. Washington's major military figures—Stimson, Stark, King, Arnold, and Marshall to mention just a few—all refer to the controversy over the convoy in their memoirs. Even President Roosevelt was personally consulted. Roosevelt's involvement apparently came as a result of an impromptu White House discussion with Secretary of War Stimson, Admiral King, Secretary of State Hull, and Navy undersecretary James Forrestal. According to Stimson's diary, the discussion about the decision to return the convoy to Hawaii was taken by all as a very serious proposition. The president said that it would be better not to stop the convoy but allow it the chance of getting to Australia where the men and matériel it carried could probably be gotten by air or other routes to the Philippines. With a hearty urging by Stimson, the president personally ordered the board's decision overruled and to allow the convoy to proceed to Australia. Stimson (and Marshall and MacArthur when they were informed) was greatly relieved by this decision.[4]

Interestingly enough, on another occasion not long after this the president got involved not just to save the convoy's assets but to hand them over to an ally. During an informal session between Roosevelt and British prime minister Winston Churchill at the December conference the president offered the convoy's contents (conditional to a finding that it could not be gotten to MacArthur) to help bolster Singapore's defense. Fortunately he backed off when his advisers vehemently opposed that offer.[5] Marshall learned of this offhand offer during a session at the joint U.S.-British conference on December 25. Concerned that such a move could be interpreted as an abandonment of the Philippines in favor of Singapore (and a blow to the morale of the defenders even now engaged in a desperate struggle), Marshall, Arnold, Eisenhower, and Stimson managed to back the president off his offer.[6] General MacArthur was elated when he received news that the convoy was once more being turned around after its initial change of course was ordered by the Navy. Stimson wrote that one bright spot in an otherwise gloomy day was the news that the convoy had achieved a safe arrival in Australian waters.[7] Not only did the convoy have just about the only ready reinforcements for the western Pacific, but it also represented American action in a period otherwise marked by widespread indecision.

The orders listed above clearly indicate the convoy was instructed twice to return to Hawaii. The personal accounts of half a dozen passengers make no mention of changes or reversal of course; however, the logbooks of the Navy escort vessels and the two Navy transports in the convoy indicate otherwise. At noon on December 9 the convoy changed from a southwest heading of 225 degrees to 145 degrees or southeast.[8] Eight hours later the change was made back to a southwest heading. Then again a day later on December 11 (the tenth was lost in crossing the dateline) for five hours the same changes to about the same headings were made between 6 AM and 11 AM. It is clear that while the convoy and escorts for short periods were moving away from their course line, they did not simply turn around and attempt to retrace steps to Pearl Harbor, which of course was where the enemy was still thought to be lurking.

Perhaps the need for fresh water (for the boilers of the freighters) determined that the convoy must press on to Fiji before making a permanent course change. While the course alterations went largely unnoticed, what was noted was a distinct change in onboard procedure. Radio silence had been observed all along, but now lifejackets had to be with passengers at all times. Strict restrictions on use of lights at night were enforced. General quarters drill was conducted every morning at an early hour. Abandon-ship exercises were conducted by everyone. The convoy began zigzagging as a way to thwart potential submarine torpedo attacks.

Efforts were also made to further organize the disparate units in the convoy, particularly as it appeared they might soon have to enter combat. On December 12 General Order No. 1 created the newly designated "Task Force—Southern Pacific" and appointed Brig. Gen. Julian F. Barnes (senior officer on board) as commander.[9] General Order No. 2 followed on the next day and created a temporary structure. A staff was organized and named to support the new task force. Anticipating potential early combat by the embarked forces, four temporary organizational elements were formed:

1. A provisional field artillery brigade under Col. Leslie Jensen (commander of the 147th Field Artillery Regiment) would consist of the four artillery battalions and brigade headquarters.

2. An Air Force command under Capt. Roscoe Nichols. It included personnel of the 7th Bombardment Group, 88th Reconnaissance Squadron, and 8th Matériel Squadron.
3. An infantry detachment, under the command of Col. John A. Robenson (senior unattached officer in the convoy). Assigned were all available personnel not otherwise organized, placed into rifle and machine gun companies.
4. Special troops also under Colonel Robenson. Composed of the highly specialized service ordnance, chemical, signal, and quartermaster units.

Julian F. Barnes was a professional artilleryman. He was born in Washington, D.C., on October 14, 1889, and was fifty-two at the time of these events. His most recent permanent promotion was in October 1940 to colonel, though he became a temporary brigadier general on September 29, 1941. His career was entirely in field artillery; as usual in the Army he served at many posts, including Camp Stotsenburg in the Philippines in 1913–1915. He did not see overseas service in the First World War, but had assignments in training roles stateside. In early 1941 he moved to Camp Blanding, Florida, to command the 35th Field Artillery Regiment. His final pre-war assignment was as commander of the 26th Field Artillery Brigade headquarters and posted to an unannounced overseas station. A professional soldier long on organizational and training experience, Barnes found himself in an awkward command situation. As senior commander present he was thrust into a leadership role he surely didn't foresee. For a period of about six weeks he was the commander of all U.S. Army forces in Australia and an important adjutant to generals several levels above him. By February of 1942 a new command structure was in place. He returned stateside in October 1942, served a variety of positions in the United States, and retired in 1946.[10]

Also on the thirteenth Barnes' task force command was now enlarged. General Marshall sent a directive (entrusted to the Navy to deliver at sea) naming him commander of USAFIA—United States Army Forces in Australia. Succinct directions as to his immediate mission were enclosed: "Take charge of all troops and supplies. Report to commander U.S. Forces in Far East, Manila for instructions. Prepare airplanes in cargo for combat. Make every effort get them to Philippines. Incur financial obligations using agent on transport. Unlimited credit from treasury. Full instruction sent military attaché Australia."[11]

For those in the convoy, the self-defense capabilities of the ships suddenly became important. Besides the heavy cruiser *Pensacola*, only half the ships had any means of defense. As a longtime commissioned naval transport, *Chaumont* was armed with four 3-inch guns and *Republic* had been recently armed when sent to Iceland as a Navy-crewed transport. The most heavily armed of the transports, she carried four 3-inch guns, four .50-caliber anti-aircraft guns on the four corners of the upper boat deck, and a single 5-inch gun near the stern. *Niagara* was lightly armed as a Navy auxiliary, carrying only two 3-inch guns. Of the freighters only *Bloemfontein* was armed. As the Dutch had been at war since being invaded by the Germans, their merchantmen were routinely armed as protection against German submarines and surface raiders. The ship's single stern 3-inch gun was readily apparent to the American soldiers who observed her.[12]

With the perceived threat of omnipresent Japanese underwater, air, and surface forces, the passengers on the transports scurried to locate and mount whatever expedient defensive armament they could find. On *Republic* members of the 2/131st (naturally it would be the artillerymen who were assigned the task to locate and mount additional guns) located 75-mm guns. The guns were brought up from the hold and lashed to the railings.[13] The situation on *Holbrook* must have seemed even more desperate—the Army transports did not yet mount any defensive armament, and *Holbrook* with its valuable cargo was no exception. Lieutenant Stensland of the 147th Regiment took an expedition into the cargo spaces and located some 75-mm guns and even a pair of 37-mm anti-tank guns to bring up and mount temporarily. The 37-mm guns had no ammunition, but their presence probably helped improve morale.[14]

Passive means of defense were also not neglected. On *Pensacola* all flammable wooden furniture was pitched over the side, as was most of the linoleum flooring. Even though at sea, on several ships the peacetime paint job came off. Large American flags painted on the vessels to mark them as neutrals for the benefit of German observers were suddenly liabilities. In *Republic* and *Holbrook* soldiers remember being organized into work crews to chip off the old paint and apply a new coat of Navy gray.

Late in the afternoon of the thirteenth the convoy arrived at Suva. Though an originally scheduled stop, it assumed more importance as a place to get reliable information and to get a glimpse of new allies. Fiji was a British crown colony, with New Zealand troops operating a small naval and air base along with beach defenses. This was the first time since war broke out that between-ship communications was possible. The opportunity was taken for Barnes to reorganize his staff, and for the manifests of the various ships to be checked out.[15] Only a few officers were allowed ashore during the brief stop (total time was just a little over twenty-four hours). Personal accounts describe the sharp-dressed appearance of the British and New Zealand troops, along with the strange garb and hairstyle of the local Fijian native police guard. At 5:30 PM on the evening of the fourteenth the convoy departed. One vessel, *Niagara*, set a course back to Hawaii. She had been appointed as a tender for the PT boats to be stationed in Manila Bay, but with little prospect of getting to that harbor, there was no further utility in sending her on the next leg of the voyage.

More serious discussion occurred as the convoy traveled from Fiji to Brisbane. MacArthur (Barnes' nominal superior, though Barnes was getting much more direct communications from Washington than from Manila) waded in with a memo sent on December 18. He desired that the convoy less Air Corps elements proceed to the Philippines. MacArthur was convinced that the route was not yet fully blockaded by the Japanese and the convoy had a reasonable chance to make it. Active assistance would be needed from the Navy and Allies, and he asked for Washington's help in arranging this. The Air Force ground elements were to be held in Brisbane or other Australian bases, while the aircraft in the convoy would be erected and prepared for ferrying as quickly as possible. Also on the eighteenth, Barnes was notified that Maj. Gen. George H. Brett was arriving in Darwin on December 19 and would assume command of all U.S. military troops in Australia. Brig. Gen. Henry B. Claggett had been ordered to fly to Australia from the Philippines and act as assistant to Brett, but assumed command of forces in Australia from Barnes under General Order No. 5 of December 24.

The messages urging the quick dispatch of the seventy warplanes in the convoy grew in frequency and intensity over the next two weeks. By now the disaster that had befallen the Far Eastern Air Force was fully apparent and the Philippines needed modern bombers and fighters more than anything else. Obviously they also offered the capability to be flown in quickly vs. needing to run a blockade in an eleven-knot ship. As early as the twelfth the Joint Staff issued instructions to: "Immediately on arrival have . . . prepared for combat all planes. Make every effort to get these planes to Philippine Is."[16] Six days later (on the eighteenth) instructions were added to send vessels with remaining cargo (after the air assets had been removed and hopefully forwarded north) to any favorable port to place in position to aid the Philippine Islands.

On the twenty-fourth Barnes was told: "The War Department directs you and authorizes you to do anything necessary to effect the delivery of arms, equipment, and ammunition to the islands (Philippines). . . . Your authorization includes the incurring of necessary financial obligations."[17]

The convoy's final 1,700-mile leg of the journey proceeded without encountering hostile forces. Around noon on December 19 general quarters were sounded, but the approaching vessel was found to be the New Zealand light cruiser HMNZS *Achilles.* Later the same evening two Australian cruisers found and began escorting the convoy, and on the twenty-first two Australian corvettes also joined. Early on the twenty-second the convoy did experience its first casualties. An SOC-1 scout floatplane from *Pensacola* on anti-submarine patrol failed to return to the ship. Aerial searches were performed but no trace of this aircraft or its crew was ever found. There were no enemy vessels of any sort in the vicinity of the convoy and weather was calm. It can only be presumed that the loss of the aircraft and its three-man crew was due to an accident or malfunction.

While no specific cooperation had been requested prior to the war, after hostilities started both southern navies attempted to locate and provide additional escort for the *Pensacola* convoy. Sailing independently, *Achilles* spotted and joined the *Pensacola* convoy early on December 19. For the Australian part, HMAS *Perth* and *Canberra* left port on the fifteenth to try and locate the American convoy. That contact was made on the evening of the nineteenth after extensive use by both cruisers of their Walrus scouting planes. The radio-silence of the Americans was effective, and the Australians had searched for several days with some frustration before finally finding the convoy. By the twenty-first the assembled convoy and "guest" escorts were close enough to the mainland that Australian Hudson bombers could provide air anti-submarine cover. The final augmentation to the escort was made with the arrival of Australian sloops *Swan* and *Warrego* on the twenty-first.

By the time the convoy reached Australia it had almost as many warship protectors as it did ships to protect. *Pensacola* and her charges arrived at Moreton Bay—the outer roadstead of Brisbane—on the early afternoon of December 22. Trouble was immediately encountered when it was found that *Republic*'s deep draft would not allow her entry. *Chaumont* and a local tanker took off fuel to lighten her enough to tie up at the wharf. American military attaché Van Merle-Smith took a boat immediately to meet Brigadier General Barnes. Hand-delivered were a number of dispatches and details of the preparations made in Brisbane for the arrival of the convoy. Headquarters staff moved off their vessels in the afternoon and occupied temporary facilities at the Lennons Hotel. The Australian army erected quarters for the disembarked American troops. Tent facilities were erected in two large, local racecourses—Ascot and Doomben racetracks.

Immediately the process of offloading troops and cargo began for most of the ships. As all had been loaded in peacetime, cargo was stored mostly with the thought of maximizing load, rather than for combat. Consequently virtually everything had to be unloaded and checked against manifest lists (and if these were missing, they had to be created). American troops and Australian labor all worked feverishly to unload the vessels. While an adequate port, Brisbane was not a huge harbor; wharf and adjacent warehouse space was severely limited and congestion quickly occurred. Originally supplies were stored dockside, but eventually facilities were found in the vicinity of Ascot Racetrack. After essential supplies were dispatched for points north, the resulting supply "dump" on the docks at Brisbane had to be addressed. In order to assist its movement, the unusual step was taken to have the Australian government requisition all these supplies in order to clearly be able to use, move, or dispose of them. It was also found that considerable pilfering had occurred—some no doubt by units desperate to get what they needed for their next assignment, others for less noble motives.

Even with security concerns, it was decided that moving the troops to their new encampments would be accomplished as a formal military march—complete with a full complement of flags and unit bands participating. At their new home the 4,600 American troops had to be fed, supplied, and adequately equipped. Fortunately the Australian forces agreed to furnish rations if the units would do the cooking. Memories, usually unpleasant, about Australian mutton vividly survive in the personal accounts of many of the soldiers on the receiving end.[18] However, over the next few weeks the general reception of the Americans was outstanding. Many Americans found themselves invited into Australian homes to enjoy the Christmas holidays. Others claimed they could never pay for a drink in a local watering hole. There was even amusement with the Aussie habit in referring to each American as a "Yank." It took some time for the surprised troops of the 131st Field Artillery Regiment—proud Texans barely two generations removed from the American Civil War—to get used to this title of affection![19]

Even before their arrival, plans were cast to get the forces on the move again. On December 19 CinCPac ordered *Pensacola*, after unloading the convoy aircraft at Brisbane, to proceed inside the barrier reef and through the

Torres Strait to Darwin. Arrangements were being made to hand off the convoy to the Asiatic Fleet, which would escort it from that vicinity.[20] Plans were to have the most critical freight and troops moved north on the two fastest transports—*Willard A. Holbrook* and *Bloemfontein.* On Christmas Day General Marshall expressed the War Department views on the situation in the southwest Pacific. Now there was doubt that the previous plan to stage short-range airplanes to Luzon could be executed. The retreat in the Philippines might leave no fields available. However, the vigorous buildup of strong forces in Australia was to be strenuously pursued. These were to be primarily air forces, deemed essential to either any future defense or offense. Even while preparations were being made to get the airplanes and artillerymen to the Philippines, realistic doubts about the practical ability to do just that were being voiced.

Finally on December 28 *Pensacola* pulled out of Brisbane again, escorting just *Chaumont* and *Willard A. Holbrook.* The Navy transport had not even docked, and retained most if not all her original cargo and personnel. *Holbrook* again carried the parts of the two artillery regiments she had brought all the way from San Francisco. During the Brisbane stay opportunity was taken yet again to add to the self-defense of the vessel, the ship winding up with four 75-mm and a couple of .50-caliber anti-aircraft guns and temporary Army gun crews for this next journey.[21] When departure was made on the twenty-eighth, the official destination of *Holbrook* was still the Philippines, though one has to wonder how seriously the military thought this could be successfully achieved.

In fact, this brings up an interesting question: when did the Army realize that reinforcement of the Philippines was not going to happen, and focus its efforts on defending the Malay Barrier and in running in emergency supplies to MacArthur? MacArthur himself argued vehemently for weeks that efforts should be made for direct convoys, with a high likelihood of success. Stimson was probably one of the first to come to a negative conclusion. As early as December 8 he confided in his diary: "The news continues very bad. . . . We should be unable to reinforce him probably in time to save the islands. However, we have started everything going that we could."[22] Meanwhile the Navy's attention was focused on the situation in Hawaii. A strongly worded letter from Stark to Marshall on December 11 outlined a very realistic, and pessimistic, analysis of Japanese capabilities. The chief of naval operations was very worried about the security of Hawaii and argued that they (the Army *and* the Navy) make every effort to augment the security of the islands and the naval base. Marshall agreed, with the caveat that everything, short of jeopardizing the security of the continental United States or the Panama Canal, should be done for Hawaiian security.[23]

A new young colonel was called to Washington from Fort Sam Houston on December 12 to become the deputy on the War Plans Division staff for Pacific and Far Eastern theatres. This was Col. Dwight D. Eisenhower. Marshall asked Eisenhower on their first brief visit, after an equally brief orientation to the situation: "What should be our general line of action [relative to the relief of the Philippines]?" After giving it a couple of hours of thought, Eisenhower prepared a short memo, titled "Assistance to the Far East." After concluding that it would be a long time before reinforcements could get to the Philippines (in fact, longer than that garrison could probably hold out), it was still necessary that reasonable efforts be made. American actions were scrutinized by Asian allies (the Filipinos, Chinese, and Dutch). To use the words of one of Eisenhower's biographers, "they could excuse failure, but not abandonment."[24] Essential to any such effort, and incidentally not without its own strategic value, would be the development of a strong base in Australia, particularly for air power. Marshall agreed with Eisenhower's position, and left him with orders to do his best to aid the garrison *and* build up the new base.

What then developed was a sort of strange dichotomy. Everyone seemed to agree that significant help couldn't be sent to the Philippines in time. There simply were not the resources available, particularly with demands elsewhere and the universal agreement that Germany had to be defeated first. Resources were not just hardware, but also trained troops, leadership, and shipping just were not available in the quantity needed and the time available. And the military situation was not favorable. After Pearl Harbor the U.S. Navy did not have the strength to break the Japanese blockade of the Philippines in a sustained manner. Even if forces did make it through, what then? Could they be adequately supplied indefinitely? It was not reasonable to think that the Philippines could be used in 1942 for a major counteroffensive against Japan.

However, at the same time it was not considered wise to be forthright about the situation. For the benefit of allies, and particularly for the morale of the fighting troops, no admission of lagging effort was permitted. Publicly Washington continued to communicate its efforts to do everything possible to reinforce and resupply the Philippines. Words and promises were carefully chosen to positively comment about the efforts being made to dispatch forces to Australia, but neglected to mention that there was no immediate plan to forward them onward. A look at the actual messages sent to MacArthur from Marshall (often actually written by Eisenhower for him) is instructive in understanding the positioning taken:[25]

December 18, 1941: "Following summary of resources already in process of execution for your immediate support is for your information. . . . Fifteen heavy bombers carrying their own spare parts only will reach you on schedule of three per day with movement completed around New Year's."

December 22, 1941: "We are doing our utmost to organize in Australia to rush air support to you. Fifty-five pursuit planes 4 days at sea and 55 more sail in 3 days. President has seen all of your messages and directs Navy to give you every possible support in your splendid fight."

December 23, 1941: "The routes and methods already adopted and described to you for supporting you with air strength are the only practicable ones under the existing strategic situation. It is expected that the fighter and dive-bomber planes now in Australia will quickly determine feasibility of route from Darwin to Luzon for transmitting small fighter planes. These planes are now being rushed to that base by fast ships. Navy sea train which is particularly suited for the transport of planes is being obtained from the Navy for additional shipment. The heavy bombers beginning to flow from this country via Africa to your theatre should be able to support you materially even if compelled initially to operate from distant bases. So far as possible critical items listed in your recent messages are being shipped to Australia for delivery as quickly as circumstances will permit."

January 2, 1942: "Replying to your [messages] there is here a keen appreciation of your situation. The President and Prime Minister, Colonel Stimson and Admiral Knox, the British Chiefs of Staff and our corresponding officials have been surveying every possibility looking toward the quick development of strength in the Far East so as to break the enemy's hold on the Philippines. Previous losses in capital ships seriously reduce the capability of the Navy to carry on indispensable tasks including convoys for heavy reinforcements for the Far East."

January 7, 1942: "Navy Department has directed CINCAF: 'Get ammunition into Corregidor via submarine or other available means.' Brett at Melbourne requested Hart to furnish transport, either air or submarine, and will report action."

Note how the messages begin with statements of positive action—what was being done even if a little lacking on just how things were supposed to get to the Philippines. Then the message on the twenty-third is more forthright on the problems with getting a seaborne convoy through and on new bombers based only from a distance. Eventually in early January the messages began covering what is being done to defend the Malay Barrier, and any efforts to directly support the Philippines is in the context of critical blockade-running activities.

A joint Army-Navy conference on December 16 concentrated on efforts to move airplanes to Hawaii and Australia. Eisenhower represented the Army, and he met in the office of the chief of naval operations with Stark and other Navy personnel. The Navy's position was that its few carriers were badly needed for active operations, and could not be spared for any ferrying of Army aircraft. However, they did offer two new vessels specifically converted from seatrains to aircraft transports. Both *Hammondsport* and *Kittyhawk* could carry over one hundred crated fighter aircraft, and they could be ready for aircraft shipment to either Hawaii or Australia in early January. The Navy was about to order the Asiatic Fleet to assist escorting the *Pensacola* convoy through the Torres Strait as far as Darwin. The message makes no mention of any further destination, such as the obvious one of the Philippines. A careful reading of the Navy's communications indicates it had already come to the conclusion that movement by sea to the Philippines was impractical.

The actual events in the southwest Pacific conform to these dates. The last dispatch of forces with a clear destination of the Philippines was the *Holbrook* and *Bloemfontein* convoy that left Brisbane at the end of the year. The Navy changed the destination to Darwin on January 1, 1942. Thereafter efforts clearly continued to build up and re-deploy air and land forces in Australia and the Dutch East Indies. Also, strong efforts were continued for several months to get urgently needed supplies to the fighting forces on Luzon by blockade-runners, submarines, and aircraft. However, these were not reinforcements, but more like relief amounts of the most critically needed supplies—later in the campaign they more and more became food and medicines and took on the aura of being almost humanitarian supply runs.

Back in Brisbane in late December, efforts continued with this last attempt at transferring troops to the Philippines. More extensive rearrangement of cargo was needed for the third transport headed north. The Dutch *Bloemfontein* would now carry the 2nd Battalion of the 131st Field Artillery Regiment and the Headquarters and Headquarters' Battery of the 26th Field Artillery Brigade. Personnel of the battalion even recall helping move their equipment and trucks from *Republic* to *Bloemfontein* just the day after their arrival.[26] Also the forty-eight Model 1917 75-mm guns and the bulk of the .50-caliber ammunition desperately needed by MacArthur were moved from *Meigs* to this ship. Most accounts say that the 75-mm guns were without sights or fire-control equipment for this journey, though they would have certainly been useful at arrival and were on the manifest as originally packed into *Meigs.* The precise manifest of other supplies on the two Army transports on this new convoy has not come to light. Later documents do declare that in addition to the artillery units and spare 75-mm guns, ninety casual officers and cargo of ammo, gasoline, oil, food supplies, and, curiously, clothing were included on the ships.[27]

Problems were encountered in obtaining use of *Bloemfontein*. This was a privately owned Dutch-flag vessel, belonging to the Holland African Line. It had been chartered by the U.S. Army for the delivery of cargo in Manila, but under maritime law the ship was released from further obligations once cargo was discharged instead in Australia. The ship's master was wary of further commitments in dangerous waters now that war was declared. The confusion led to the intended passengers boarding, debarking, and then boarding again. After a two-day delay finally agreement was made between the U.S. Army, the Dutch military in the East Indies, and the captain. She belatedly sailed on the thirtieth of December with orders to rendezvous with the rest of the convoy off Thursday Island. When she sailed at 7 AM on the thirtieth it was with Surabaya as a destination, with simultaneous instructions to the Asiatic Fleet to find a means to get the ship escorted on the last leg to Java. While events would change the final disposition of these units, it seems a sincere effort to get all the artillery outfits and the additional .50-caliber ammunition quickly to Manila was attempted in late December.

The military situation in and around the Philippine Islands continued to quickly deteriorate. By the end of December the general retreat of the American and Filipino forces into the Bataan Peninsula was ordered. Marshall asked Brett on the thirtieth for a recommendation of action relative the convoy in view of the situation in the Philippines. He replied on New Year's Day that Glassford was being directed to take the convoy (*Holbrook*, *Bloemfontein*, and *Chaumont*) into Darwin and forgo the direct run to the Philippines.[28] The ships were to discharge cargo and troops in Darwin pending decisions on their ultimate destination. The little convoy, under the protective guns of the Asiatic Fleet, arrived at Darwin on January 5. *Holbrook* discharged her two artillery regiments into local camps. USS *Chaumont* promptly began delivering her supplies and replacement personnel to the ships of the fleet. Meanwhile *Bloemfontein* anchored in the harbor's protective waters for a few days (with no shore time for her passengers—though some casual officers on board received orders to depart the vessel here), before proceeding to Surabaya. The men and guns of the 2/131st and the 26th Brigade Headquarters were soon to begin the next phase of the American ground forces' story in the southwest Pacific.

Just what ammunition was available for the four artillery battalions is an interesting question. As originally shipped, the entire *Pensacola* convoy carried just 460 rounds of 75-mm shrapnel (on *Meigs*), not even ten rounds per gun for the full armament of forty-eight artillery pieces. Of course, originally the units were not dispatched anticipating a combat need for ammunition along the way—adequate stocks existed in the Philippines. Rushed supplies of additional ammunition were made on the very first new scheduled sailings to Australia. A memorandum for the president drafted on Christmas Day by General Marshall described the artillery forces in Australia as "elements of 2 regiments of 75-mm artillery. No ammunition available until about January 8."[29] *President Polk* carried five thousand rounds when it departed San Francisco on December 18, and *Mormacsun* carried 3,442 rounds when it left eight days later. However, neither of these shipments arrived prior to the dispatch of the units (now boasting their full complement of guns with the arrival of *Jane Christenson* in Australia the day after Christmas). Just how the meager supply was divided between the units is not known. Ammunition arriving in early January could have been sent to Darwin to supply the battalions of the 147th and 148th, but there was not time available to do that with the 2/131st on board *Bloemfontein*. Likely the entire American stock of 75-mm ammunition in early January was sent to Java with the 131st. It was one thing to send artillery pieces on a voyage where they would marry up with ammunition at the destination; it is quite another to send these troops into harm's way with not even enough ammo for a single engagement.

Some explanation should be made about the various names mentioned for command in Australia. Altogether there were four commanders of American forces in the southwest Pacific area who served a total of six times in December and January. The rapid changes in command reflect a number of factors, including the overall confusion of the moment, the physical availability of appropriate officers, and the conflicting needs to also adequately contribute command officers to ABDA. Originally Brigadier General Barnes had been appointed commander of Task Force South Pacific, which became, upon arrival in Brisbane, the United States Forces in Australia. Plans were actually made before landfall for the command to be taken by Major General Brett, who was then on an inspection tour in China, orders of that intent being issued on December 17. Pending his arrival in Brisbane, temporarily command title was assumed by Brig. Gen. Henry B. Claggett. Claggett was a senior air staff officer for MacArthur, and was sent from the Philippines to Australia specifically for this assignment. On December 22 Claggett arrived in Australia, and relieved Barnes on the twenty-fourth. He only lasted a short time until succeeded by Brett on January 5, when the command was more accurately renamed United States Army Forces in Australia (USAFIA). Barnes stayed on, first as Claggett's and then as Brett's chief of staff. Claggett soon returned stateside. On the third of January headquarters of USAFIA moved to Melbourne. When Brett moved on to an ABDA assignment, Major General Brereton took command on January 12. Confusingly enough Brereton became the American-British-Dutch-Australian Air Operational Command (ABDAIR) deputy commander on January 27, being replaced in USAFIA again by Barnes. Finally Barnes was replaced by Brett again in late February when the ABDA command was dissolved.[30]

A significant challenge was encountered in trying to set up an efficient organization in Australia. The contents of the convoy were never intended as a self-contained expeditionary force; they were simply what was next in line for shipment to the already established Far Eastern command. Lacking were headquarters units, communications equipment and personnel, quartermaster and maintenance depots, military police, and even the right staff officers. For almost a month USAFIA had to assemble a working organization without substantial help. A very few officers were assigned and brought in by airplane, but the first shipload of Americans and supplies sent after Pearl Harbor did not arrive until January 12.[31] Even then the emphasis was on getting matériel (primarily pursuit aircraft, .50-caliber ammunition, and rations) to Australia for transshipment to the Philippines rather than on supplies and organizational units suitable to set up a substantial base in Australia.

What was most lacking was the engineer, ordnance, quartermaster, and signal units needed to operate a base. Those few units of these technical services were quickly split up and asked to perform tasks far outside their normal routine. As an example, for the first four weeks after arrival the 453rd Ordnance Company was the sole Army ordnance unit in Australia. By necessity it was scattered in detachments all over the country to support the various airbases used for assembling and ferrying aircraft. The home station of the company was in Brisbane performing port ordnance duty, but other platoons were stationed in Darwin and Melbourne. Three small detachments were even taken to form transport guards for blockade-runners to the Philippines; on one such mission the company suffered its first casualty due to enemy action when 2nd Lt. Joseph F. Kane died of wounds after the ship he was on was bombed and sunk.

The importance of Darwin as a clearinghouse for military cargo heading north to the Philippines and Dutch East Indies was apparent early. On December 21 the Joint Board agreed to the establishment of a limited American base at Darwin. A few Air Force service units were transshipped from Brisbane to Darwin in mid-January to begin operations at this base. Company "B" of the 33rd Quartermaster Regiment (Truck) and much of the Air Force's 8th Matériel Squadron arrived on January 22.

The various ships used in the *Pensacola* convoy had different experiences on their way back home. *Republic* was most urgently required to return home for further troop-ferrying duties; a dispatch concerning her disposition was sent as early as December 24. After a trip to Sydney (from which she departed on the eighth of January), *Republic* made a stop at Wellington and arrived at San Francisco on February 7. After her successful run to Surabaya, *Bloemfontein* departed that city on January 30, also for Wellington. Eventually she arrived back in San Francisco on March 4. *Pensacola* herself returned to Brisbane to refuel after her previous escort mission. She refueled and returned to Hawaii independently with some urgency on January 19, 1942.

Willard A. Holbrook spent a long period serving the needs of the Army in the southwest Pacific, touching at Melbourne, Fremantle, Colombo, Karachi, Bombay, Adelaide, and Wellington. Her next immediate major voyage involved the sealift of Air Force personnel from Brisbane to Fremantle and India as part of convoy MS-5 in mid-February 1942. Eventually she returned to San Francisco on June 25, 1942.[32] The commercial freight on *Admiral Halstead*

Philippine Commonwealth President Manuel Quezon and military adviser Gen. Douglas MacArthur in Manila during the late 1930s. These two men would create the new Philippine Army, called into U.S. service in July 1941 after the Japanese occupation of French Indo-China. (National Archives, Still Photos Branch, College Park, MD)

U.S. Army Chief of Staff Gen. George C. Marshall (left) and Secretary of War Henry L. Stimson at the Washington Conference in January 1942. These two men were instrumental in approving and facilitating the reinforcement of the Philippines just prior to the outbreak of war. (National Archives, Still Photos Branch, College Park, MD)

The decision to base the Pacific fleet at Pearl Harbor resulted in the first significant new Army reinforcements for Oahu. Thirty-three B-18 medium bombers were sent to Hickam Field in early 1940. Here all thirty-three are shown in formation over Diamond Head on April 6, 1940. (National Archives, Still Photos Branch, College Park, MD)

The band of the 31st Infantry Regiment greeting a ship arriving in pre-war Manila. The 31st was a longtime constituent of the regular Philippine Division, and the only all-white American infantry unit in the islands. All units arriving in the last half of 1941 witnessed similar scenes. (National Archives, Still Photos Branch, College Park, MD)

The Marine Corps garrison on Palmyra was gradually increased to a total of 310 officers and men at the time of the Pearl Harbor attack. The garrison was quickly reinforced in January and February of 1942. This photo in early 1942 shows the Marines' ordnance storehouse, stocked mostly with Model 1903 Springfield rifles. (National Archives, Still Photos Branch, College Park, MD)

Army transport *President Coolidge* arriving in Manila Bay in August 1941. On this journey she carried the Philippine Air Warning Company with the first radar sets for the islands. On departure she carried 250 Americans stranded in Asia by the worsening diplomatic situation. (National Archives, Still Photos Branch, College Park, MD)

The U.S. Navy's *PT-32* at high speed in a pre-war photograph. This boat was one of six Elco-built, 77-foot PT (patrol torpedo) boats carried to the Philippines in late 1941. She served in Manila Bay with PT Squadron 3 until she joined in the evacuation of General MacArthur and his staff and family in mid-March 1942. (National Archives, Still Photos Branch, College Park, MD)

USS *Boise* escorted five commercial ships to Manila, arriving on December 4. Along the way she experienced the only pre-war convoy contact between American and Japanese naval forces when just east of Saipan. This photo dates from November 5, just two weeks before the start of this mission. (National Archives, Still Photos Branch, College Park, MD)

On the night of November 27, 1941, the *Boise* convoy twice spotted the Japanese cruiser *Katori*. This ship was the flagship of Admiral Mitsumi Shimizu, commander of the submarines of the 6th Fleet. Journeying to the submarine base at Kwajalein, the ship's course inadvertently encountered that of the convoy. (Naval Historical Center)

Twenty-one B-17s of the 19th Bombardment Group were dispatched in a mass flight for the first time from the mainland to Hawaii on May 13, 1941. All the planes arrived safely. This photo is dated May 19 and features two of the planes and most of the crew members of that inaugural flight. (National Archives, Still Photos Branch, College Park, MD)

The Army forces in the *Pensacola* convoy were organized into an emergency task force when word of war was received mid-journey. The senior officer on board, Brig. Gen. Julian F. Barnes, was designated commander, Task Force South Pacific, reporting directly to General MacArthur. (National Archives, Still Photos Branch, College Park, MD)

After the start of war efforts were made to put guns on unarmed Army transports. At times troops temporarily placed their own weapons on deck for use. This photograph, from December 23, 1941, of USAT (U.S. Army transport) *Tasker H. Bliss* shows soldiers with a .30-caliber machine gun temporarily lashed to the ship's railing. (United States Army Museum of Hawaii)

The ex-Matson liner *Monterey* in San Francisco on January 1, 1942. She had just returned the day before from an emergency high-speed run to Oahu, taking the first reinforcements to the island since the attack. She returned with 804 Army casualties and dependents. She is already painted gray all over and shows no name. (National Archives, Still Photos Branch, College Park, MD)

Besides troop transports, freighters were also extensively used to carry military cargo to the outposts. Longtime Army freighter USAT *Ludington* was actually at sea delivering vehicles and equipment to bases on Canton and Christmas Islands when the war intervened. This shot was taken after her return on January 8. (National Archives, Still Photos Branch, College Park, MD)

The largest ship of the *Pensacola* convoy was USS *Republic*. The Army had acquired the ship in the early 1930s, though she started life as the German-built SS *U.S. Grant*. As a Navy ship she left Boston on November 5, 1941 and carried 2,730 men for Army postings in the Philippines. (National Archives, Still Photos Branch, College Park, MD)

Three ex–President Line transports were operating in the Pacific for the Army in late 1941. This is USAT *Hugh Scott*, the former SS *President Pierce*. In late August 1941 she took part of the 200th Coast Artillery and the 194th Tank Battalion to Manila. She made another trip in October, and took reinforcements to Hawaii in December and to Australia in January and April 1942. (National Archives, Still Photos Branch, College Park, MD)

Another Army freighter active in the Pacific was USAT *Liberty*. After a Manila voyage in October 1941, she was diverted to make a fuel-supplying run to the new bomber ferry bases and to pick up strategic cargo. The freighter ran afoul of a Japanese submarine off Java on January 11, 1942. (National Archives, Still Photos Branch, College Park, MD)

In the rush to employ the few remaining commercial liners, both services initially made only the most necessary changes to ship's quarters. Here, a photo of USS *Lurline* in early 1942 shows new tiers of military bunks crowding a ceiling still ornately decorated. (National Archives, Still Photos Branch, College Park, MD)

Deployed for the first time to the Far East in the fall of 1941 was the A-24 dive-bomber. Fifty-two of these planes meant for the 27th Bomb Group were sent on USAT *Meigs* in the *Pensacola* convoy. Within months these were lost either in operational accidents or in combat in Java. (National Archives, Still Photos Branch, College Park, MD)

To support the Far East buildup, the U.S. Navy significantly reinforced the submarine strength of the Asiatic Fleet. Pictured are eight fleet submarines tied up at base—probably in San Diego—prior to the fall of 1939. The Asiatic Fleet received at least six of these subs prior to the war. (National Archives, Still Photos Branch, College Park, MD)

After the First World War the United States had a large inventory of M1917 75-mm field guns of a British design, most assigned to the overseas departments. Hawaii was stripped of many for transfer to the Philippines. This could have well been one of those guns, as the photo was taken in Oahu maneuvers in March 1941. (National Archives, Still Photos Branch, College Park, MD)

To make up for the lack of anti-tank guns, the ordnance department placed a special order for T12 gun carriages. This mated the familiar 75-mm field gun with the standard half-track. Later the type was standardized for production as the M3 gun motor carriage. Pictured is one of the early T12 types at Fort Hood trials. (National Archives, Still Photos Branch, College Park, MD)

The heavy cruiser USS *Pensacola* was selected as escort for Navy Convoy No. 4002. Departing Hawaii on November 29, 1941, the convoy consisted of this escort, the Navy's PT-boat tender USS *Niagara*, four military transports, and three commercial freighters. The convoy was mid-journey at sea when the war began. (National Archives, Still Photos Branch, College Park, MD)

Struggling to supply troops to fill the increased demands in the Pacific, the Army hoped to use new formations of African-American soldiers. MacArthur cautioned about their acceptance in the Philippines, but was open to their use in Australia. These soldiers were boarding a transport in San Francisco in early 1942. (National Archives, Still Photos Branch, College Park, MD)

and *Coast Farmer* was also unloaded at Brisbane. The ships' agents were notified that some of this freight was required by the Army and was thus confiscated. The Army's Australian command asked on the twenty-ninth to be able to keep *Admiral Halstead*, *Coast Farmer*, and also USAT *Meigs* for use in transshipping personnel and cargo locally. Only the last mentioned was an Army-owned vessel; the other two were private ships that were "appropriated" for their subsequent usage. In fact, there was a substantial legal entanglement over the loss and compensation of *Coast Farmer* that lingered for several years. *Meigs* was given a cargo and sent off to Darwin on January 8, and arrived at that port on January 19. She was subsequently bombed and lost during the attack on Darwin on February 19.

CHAPTER TWELVE

Caught at Sea

When Pearl Harbor was attacked, there were many more vessels at sea than just the *Pensacola* convoy. Eight independently sailing freighters with significant military cargoes were already near or west of Hawaii on their way to the Philippines. A message was sent to American merchantmen immediately following the attack. The text was short and to the point: "War exists between United States and Japan. Proceed closest U.S. or friendly port immediately."[1]

Army transport *Ludington* actually departed San Francisco prior to most of the ships making up the *Pensacola* convoy. On November 11 the ship left port for a series of stops including Hawaii, Canton Island, Christmas Island, and ultimately the Philippines.[2] As one of the few Army-owned/Army-operated transports of the service, her cargo was entirely for the military or the contractors constructing bases on the two smaller islands. For the two island bases she carried heavy construction materials. For the Philippines she had twenty knocked-down P-40Es, and 11,010 drums of aviation gasoline. *Ludington* had completed her voyage to Hawaii and Christmas Island (where she successfully discharged her cargo for the contractors) and was just leaving for Canton Island when war broke out.

For a while she was trapped in the communications confusion of those days. One report indicated she was in the vicinity of the Tokelau Islands on December 8, and subsequently heavy gunfire and explosions supposedly heard in that area by local natives implied that she was lost to enemy action. On schedule she should have arrived at Canton on December 12, but the Army issued orders for her to proceed immediately to Samoa with the ultimate destination being Brisbane. Cargo was to be made available to General

Table 6. Freighters for the Philippines in December 1941[3]

Ships/Speed/Dates/ Route	Major Cargo Items	Diverted/Fate
USAT *Ludington* 10.5 knots Depart SF 11/11/41, LA 11/19/41 Due Manila about 1/10/42	Construction material and supplies for Canton and Christmas Islands 20 P-40E, 16 boxes machine guns, 11,032 drums gasoline, ammunition, 92 vehicles, trailers, 1,200 spools barbed wire, gas masks, nails, shoes, signal wire, 35 searchlight trailers 2 motor mine yawls (26-foot)	Ordered diverted to Samoa from Christmas Island. However, returned directly to Los Angeles (arriving 12/23/41) and then San Francisco subsequently.
SS *Mauna Loa* 10 knots Depart SF 11/21/41	214 vehicles, 8,089 barrels airplane gasoline, medical supplies, subsistence, troop property, ordnance, 15 .50-cal machine guns, ammunition, oats, blankets, shoes	Diverted to Sydney, arriving 12/29/41. After some offloading relocated to Darwin, Australia.
SS *Joseph Lykes* 14 knots Depart New Orleans 11/23/41	141 trucks Engineer equipment, including power shovels and graders, general engineering supplies	Diverted to San Francisco.
SS *Jane Christenson* 10 knots Depart SF 11/24/41	28 75-mm guns and 275 vehicles for units on *Pensacola* convoy 4,583 drums gasoline, concrete mixer, subsistence, helmets, pipe, mattresses, mail, mixed general supplies and stores	Diverted to Sydney, arriving 12/26/41. Relocated to Brisbane, arriving 12/31/41.
SS *Portmar* 10 knots Depart SF 11/26/41	314 vehicles, 5,939 barrels gasoline, 129 boxes small-arms ammunition, bombs, machine-gun mounts, 26 .50-cal machine guns, blankets, clothing, ordnance stores, equipment, parts	Diverted to Suva and then Sydney, arriving 12/31/41. Relocated to Brisbane, and eventually Darwin.

Table 6. Freighters for the Philippines in December 1941[3] (*Continued*)

Ships/Speed/Dates/ Route	Major Cargo Items	Diverted/Fate
USS *Jupiter* 15 knots Depart SF 11/26/41	89 trucks, general engineering supplies and tractors, medical supplies, ordnance equipment, 634 boxes small-arms ammunition, gas tanks, asphalt, steel, general supplies	Diverted to Hawaii after Pearl Harbor attack. Returned to San Francisco.
SS *Montgomery City* 11 knots Depart SF 11/27/41	105 vehicles, troop property, ordnance supplies, subsistence, bombs, canisters, general stores and supplies	Diverted to Hawaii after Pearl Harbor attack. Returned to San Francisco.
SS *Malama* 9 knots Depart SF 11/29/41	Signal corps equipment, including seven radar sets, 116 vehicles and trailers, subsistence, troop property, CWS supplies, including 181,000-lb demustarding agent, chlorinated paraffin, acetylene tetrachloride, airplane parts, oxygen, mine cables	Diverted to Hawaii after Pearl Harbor attack. Left Honolulu 12/12/41 on southern route to Australia. Intercepted and sunk by Japanese raiders 01/01/42.

MacArthur. However, instead of making for Samoa the ship returned to the mainland. She sailed east along the equator to Panama and Mazatlan and subsequently north along the Mexican coast to Los Angeles. *Ludington* arrived the night of December 22, but stayed offshore during the night due to a local submarine scare, and entered Wilmington Harbor the next morning. In Los Angeles both the planes and gasoline were sent to San Francisco and thence back to Hawaii on different ships of a subsequent convoy.

The next freighter sailing independently was *Mauna Loa.* This vessel was time-chartered by the Army from the Matson Line, and left San Francisco on November 21. The items making up the majority of the manifest seem to have been trucks and aviation gasoline. She was sailing independently southwest of Hawaii when war broke out, and was apparently diverted for a few days to Samoa.[4] Soon she resumed a new course for Australia and arrived at Sydney on the twentieth. The third independently sailing freighter was SS *Joseph Lykes*.[5] This ship had a cargo loaded before the war's outbreak. She had started from New Orleans, and most recently had departed on November

23 from Panama, but was ordered back to the West Coast after the start of the war. *Jane Christenson*, as previously mentioned for carrying the additional 75-mm guns of the artillery units of *Pensacola* convoy, was the fourth freighter proceeding on her own to the Philippines. After the attack she was too far out to be recalled to Hawaii, but was instead diverted to Samoa until the scope of the Japanese attack became clear. After a few days she was sent on to Australia instead of the Philippines.

Portmar departed the Golden Gate on the twenty-sixth.[6] Chartered by the Army, the Calmar Steamship Corporation ship carried vehicles and other equipment for the units sailing in the *Pensacola* convoy. Apparently not scheduled to stop at Honolulu, the ship was steaming the southern route and well south of Hawaii when the attack of December 7 occurred. She was ordered to put in to Suva, Fiji Islands, but after a few days was released to resume her voyage, now with Australia as her destination. On the last day of 1941 she arrived, probably docking initially in Sydney and then moving to Brisbane on January 2.[7] After unloading her valuable cargo, the Army virtually commandeered the ship and she became a de facto U.S. Army transport, initially at the command of the local USAFIA command and then its successor Southwest Pacific Area (SWPA). She was ordered to Darwin on February 9 to participate in the projected Timor expedition.

Two cargo freighters left San Francisco on November 26 and 27 for the Philippines, but never made it farther than Hawaii. USS *Jupiter* was the former Matson vessel *Santa Catalina*. The vessel was part of the Navy's effort to substantially increase the service's role in overseas supply; unlike many other Navy freighters in 1941, she did not exclusively serve the needs of her service, but was actively used to carry Army freight. Docking in Hawaii just prior to the Pearl Harbor attack, she soon returned to San Francisco and never made it to western Pacific waters. Her next assignment was with a large convoy leaving the West Coast on January 6 to reinforce Samoa. Army-chartered freighter *Montgomery City* departed San Francisco on November 27. Apparently docking in Honolulu on December 6, her onward voyage was delayed after the attack. She was one of several vessels escorted by destroyer out of the port on the twelfth. However, she subsequently returned to San Francisco (perhaps together with USS *Jupiter*). Soon she accompanied many freighters in a convoy to carry military supplies to Hawaii in mid-January.

The next freighter of this wave left San Francisco on November 29, and was the only ship of the November reinforcements to come to grief trying to get west. SS *Malama* was another chartered Matson Line vessel. She carried a heavy Army cargo out of California, plus on board the ship with her crew of thirty-three were five Army Air Force enlisted men.[8] Besides regular Army stores, she had a considerable amount of chemical warfare supplies. However, the most important component was twenty-five tons of signal corps equipment. Included were seven mobile radar sets, the SCR-270 destined for the Philippine defenders.[9] *Malama* was close to Hawaii when the war started. She was ordered to take refuge in Honolulu, and consequently docked there on December 8. While in port the commanding general of the Hawaiian Department was offered her cargo, if needed—though he declined it. After a few days the ship was released to resume her travels, though now with an intermediate route stop in Wellington. The ship was totally unarmed, as she had been since leaving San Francisco. In fact, her captain, Malcolm R. Peters, had asked permission to carry a pistol but was refused by the military governor!

After several days of wondering where the Japanese striking force was going, the Navy began releasing ships for voyages leaving Oahu on the twelfth. On the next day SS *Lansing* departed for Vancouver, SS *Haleakala* for Kahului on Maui, and ammunition ship USS *Pyro* for the West Coast. A day later the Navy ship reported being attacked by an enemy submarine eighty-five miles from Oahu, but she was not hit or otherwise damaged. On the sixteenth of December the Navy released six merchantmen to depart together with local escort at noon. After a few hours they split for destinations in California, the Panama Canal, Australia, and New Zealand.[10] The concern was to get them through the worst of any Japanese submarine concentration. Unfortunately this batch of freighters managed to hit the high point of Japanese efforts against shipping around the Hawaiian Islands. Three of the six ships never made it. *Manini* was lost on the seventeenth and *Prusa* on the eighteenth to Japanese submarines. At 8:30 PM on the sixteenth *Malama* began her solo voyage, which managed to take her through the submarine patrols safely. However, on December 31, she was spotted by a Japanese floatplane from the auxiliary cruiser HIJMS *Aikoku Maru*.

The Japanese had organized a special raiding unit designed to be released at the start of the attack on the Allies. Impressed with the accomplishments of their German ally in this field, they similarly modified two fast merchantmen to use as surface raiders. Selected were two new large liners under construction for the Osaka Steamship Company's service. *Aikoku Maru* and *Hokoku Maru* were 10,500–gross ton ships with twin-screw diesels capable of a speed of 21.5 knots. Taken over prior to completion at their building yard, they were armed at the Kure Naval Yard, each with four 152-mm Vickers guns, two 76.5-mm and four smaller anti-aircraft guns, and two 21-inch torpedo tubes. Each had one Type 94 E7K2 reconnaissance seaplane plus a spare.

The twin raiders were organized into a unit designated the 24th Sentai—roughly the 24th Division. *Hokoku Maru* was outfitted as a flagship, and carried Rear Admiral Moriharu Takeda as squadron commander. He was worried about the state of preparation and origin of his crew. The yard where the modifications and arming of the ships was conducted wasn't privy to the secret start date of the war, and seemed to lack urgency. Nonetheless the ships were completed on time for their first mission. Much of the original Osaka Steamship crew was already in the naval reserve, and transferred directly into the navy to serve the ships' new master. Original orders were quite simple—at the start of war they were to attack the enemy lines of communications and destroy shipping. The ships departed Kure together on November 15 already blacked-out and observing radio silence. They left Jaluit on November 26 for their first patrol. The admiral had to combine intensive training with this first operational sortie. Coincidentally this was also the departure date for Vice Admiral Chuichi Nagumo's Kidō Butai. Takeda avoided the shipping lanes so as not to be observed prior to the start of hostilities. He generally sailed southeast, to position himself along the Panama-Canal-to-Australia route. However, for the six days after being notified to begin active operations, he searched in vain for targets. Finally on December 12 the raiders encountered the American SS *Vincent.* At the time they were just six hundred miles northwest of Easter Island.

Vincent was a maritime commission freighter operating on a long itinerary that started in New York on July 2, 1941 and went all the way to Manila, Shanghai, and Brisbane. Starting back to the Panama Canal she departed Australia on November 25. Her returning cargo was wool, wood, and chrome ore. Both raiders closed at high speed in the darkening dusk to about three thousand yards. The Japanese used signal lights to order the ship to stop. There was little master Angus MacKinnon and his crew of thirty-seven could do except destroy confidential papers, prepare the boats, and get off a radio distress message about the interception. The two warships fired twice across the ship's bow, and the crew of *Vincent* abandoned the ship in boats; all were soon taken on board *Hokoku Maru.* After an inspection by a Japanese prize crew, who found it not worthwhile to capture *Vincent* as a prize, the raiders used both gunfire and torpedoes to sink the ship.[11] Interestingly the ship was the single farthest east American war loss in the Pacific, it being actually farther east than San Francisco or Los Angeles.

On December 31 the two raiders, now in waters near the Society Islands, launched their seaplanes to search for targets. The plane from *Aikoku Maru* spotted SS *Malama*. She attempted to get the ship to stop. Personnel in *Malama* reported at first that the approaching plane had no markings (although they thought it might be a New Zealand plane), but it was unable to answer an identity challenge. The ship then tried to take evasive course action. The plane disappeared for a while, but then returned. Apparently this floatplane had an operational accident, as it never returned to *Aikoku Maru*. *Malama* was unarmed, and could not have shot it down. On the next day an attempt to locate the missing plane resulted in the aircraft from *Hokoku Maru* spotting *Malama.* Eventually it had to bring the two raiders physically to the unfortunate freighter. The enemy floatplane allowed the crew to man its boats, before dropping bombs. Several hits were scored, including one that started a major fire among oxygen cylinders. The Americans had abandoned the ship in the meantime, scuttling the ship by dismantling the condensers to allow seawater in. When the raiders showed up most of the action was over. The Japanese were unable to inspect the ship; it was fortunate that they did not acquire, nor apparently ever knew about, the secret radar equipment that was on board. The crew of *Malama*, master Malcolm Peters, and the small military contingent were all safely taken on board the Japanese ships.

Though the raiders remained in these waters for several days, they could find no additional ships. The 24th Sentai sailed to Truk, arriving on February 4. On the way they narrowly missed crossing paths with Vice Adm. William F. Halsey's carrier task force just then starting a surprise attack on various Japanese island bases. Leaving Truk within a couple of days they returned to Japan, arriving in Hiroshima on the thirteenth. The crews of the two American freighters were sent to prison camps; subsequently two from each vessel died in captivity. This cruise was the only attempt on the part of the Japanese to use raiders in the Pacific. However, the squadron with its two ships did make a foray into the Indian Ocean later in 1942. Considerable success in destroying Allied commerce was achieved; the 24th Sentai is credited with sinking twenty-one ships in June and July of 1942. *Hokoku Maru* was sunk on November 11, 1942 in the Indian Ocean, and sister ship *Aikoku Maru* was lost to a U.S. carrier raid on Truk while serving as a transport in 1944.

Of course, in addition to the ships preparing to head or actually heading west to the Far East were those already out there or heading back. The ships of the previous two convoys were thus also caught by the start of the war.

Fortunately USS *Louisville*, with Army transports *Hugh L. Scott* and *President Coolidge*, was fairly far along on the return voyage from Manila. Leaving the Philippines on the first of December, they passed the Torres Strait on the southern route on December 3; the three ships were just east of the Solomon Islands in the South Pacific when word of the Pearl Harbor attack was received. In close formation and observing the tightest security precautions, Convoy No. 6002 was initially ordered to Samoa to await further orders. On the ninth they returned to Honolulu but by a route going one hundred miles east of Christmas Island. Instructions were given to prepare for scuttling to avoid capture. *Louisville* was welcomed back to the fighting force of the fleet, and the two transports played an important role in returning civilians and the wounded back to the mainland.

Light cruiser USS *Boise* and her convoy mates were all still in Philippine waters—they had only arrived on December 4, after all. *President Grant*, *American Leader*, *Cape Fairweather*, and *Doña Nati* were still in harbor, either awaiting or actually undergoing unloading. On the eleventh *President Grant*'s master, Captain Emmett Tyrell, was told by a Navy officer that Manila Bay was no longer safe. Heeding the advice, the ship left quickly, leaving all passengers and even fifty-seven members of her crew ashore. The transport made quick time to Darwin, where she picked up 250 women and children evacuees for the trip south. She eventually arrived at Sydney on January 14. Keeping just her strategic hemp load taken in Manila and adding wool and passengers in Sydney, she sailed on an independent return to the United States. Three of the other freighters were soon on their way. *Cape Fairweather* discharged all of her cargo except some lumber and flour in Manila before heading to Melbourne on the eighteenth. *Doña Nati* made her way starting on December 11 safely, first to Fremantle and then to Sydney, where in late January the U.S. Army took over her control. *American Leader* departed Philippine waters, going south to Australia (unloading most of the rest of her cargo in Sydney) and then east. *American Leader* was not as fortunate as the other two freighters. On another voyage later in 1942 she fell prey to the German raider *Michel* in the Indian Ocean.

The fifth convoy member, American flag freighter *John Lykes*, discharged part of her cargo (Navy freight, U.S. mail, and some commercial apples and potatoes) in Manila. Because of dock congestion and the deteriorating situation in China on December 6 she was ordered to go to Cebu City on the island of Panay to unload the cargo destined for Shanghai. She arrived on the seventh and began unloading just when war began on the eighth. The Lykes agent in Cebu arranged for all remaining cargo to go to local warehouses. Included were foodstuffs, medicine, radios, tobacco, shoes, refrigerators, spirits, and motorcycles. Items of immediate use to the Army were requisitioned by the Cebu Quartermaster Depot, following orders issued by Brig. Gen. William F. Sharp of the Visayan-Mindanao Force.[12] The food items included canned goods, dried fruits, flour, crackers, potatoes, and chocolates. Though they don't sound exactly like valuable items, as it would turn out food supplies were ultimately precious commodities, though unfortunately it proved almost impossible to transfer much food to Luzon. Other commercial goods were put into storage, and either taken over by the Army or destroyed when the Japanese occupied the island on April 10, 1942. The freighter herself was ordered to leave on December 19. She got away safely and survived the war.

Boise herself was scheduled to escort tanker SS *Gertrude Kellogg* on her return trip to Honolulu. This vessel had been on a commercial voyage to the Orient, and arrived in Manila on November 27. While she was not leaving with a military cargo (coconut oil bound for New York), the Navy's mission was still to protect American-flag vessels in potentially dangerous waters.[13] Orders for *Boise* were not issued by the Asiatic Fleet until December 6, and obviously other events intervened before the voyage could continue. *Gertrude Kellogg* was lightly damaged with two killed and eight wounded by bomb fragments during the air attack on Cavite on December 10, but eventually got away safely. *Boise* was already under way from Manila to Cebu to make her rendezvous for the escorting when she was ordered on the eighth to meet instead with USS *Houston.* The light cruiser *Boise* was being temporarily incorporated into the Asiatic Fleet. Six weeks later she hit an underwater reef in the Dutch East Indies, and suffered damage significant enough to force her withdrawal to a dockyard in India. *Boise* survived the war with distinguished service.

Commercial freighter SS *Admiral Cole* had brought out a cargo of engineer equipment and supplies in late October, and had apparently made other stops in the Far East or picked up a return cargo. In any event, she was still in Philippine waters when the war started. The Sixteenth Naval District received word on December 8 that the ship had been attacked by a Japanese airplane off of Iloilo in Panay Island. Three bombs were dropped, but missed. The ship did receive some strafing damage, but Capt. C. F. Bryant managed to bring her to temporary safety at Zamboanga. From there she eventually made it on to Brisbane, Sydney, and finally Los Angeles on February 16.

Army transport *Liberty* was used in the early October transfer of troops and matériel to the Philippines. Arriving in Manila on November 11, she unloaded quickly and then prepared for a supply run in the Far East prior to returning to the United States. *Liberty* was to be used both to deliver supplies of aviation fuel to the southwestern bomber ferry strips and to collect a strategic cargo for the return. On the seventeenth she loaded 1,800 drums of aviation gasoline and lubricating oil for Port Moresby and Port Darwin. Leaving Manila on the eighteenth, she proceeded without escort and arrived at Port Moresby ten days later. Problems were encountered with a lack of dock space and stevedoring help, but the delivery of fuel was made and she went on to Darwin on December 5. On December 15 *Liberty* then shuttled to Batavia in the Dutch East Indies to load rubber. On January 3 orders were received for her departure; due to recent Japanese submarine activities in the Java Sea, Dutch authorities recommended she take the long route along Java's southern coast to Surabaya before leaving. Unlike virtually all of the other U.S. Army and commercial transports mentioned in this chapter, *Liberty* was armed. Somewhere along the line the transport was given guns, probably on the West Coast earlier in 1941.[14]

On January 7 *Liberty* departed Batavia for Surabaya, via the Sunda Strait. It was on this leg that the ship's lengthy voyage came to an unfortunate end. At 3:15 AM on January 11, while she was entering the Badung Strait a submarine torpedo slammed into the vessel on the port side abreast the No. 1 hold. The explosion was forceful, blowing off hatches and flooding the forward deck. Just a few seconds later a second torpedo hit by the No. 4 hold. The ship began taking on water, took an immediate list, and lost both engine power and the use of her radio transmitter. Within a few more minutes the master ordered the ship abandoned; the two boats on the high side of the ship were launched, soon followed by a third from the port side. All the crew was able to get away, with important papers and confidential signal books. At 8 AM a Dutch East Indies flying boat rescued the crew of the three boats in two trips. On the twelfth the men were received in Surabaya, while *Liberty*, still afloat, was towed to Bali Island by the American destroyer USS *Paul Jones* and the Dutch *Van Ghent*, and beached. It was possible to salvage some of the instruments and equipment of the ship, along with explosives stored on the shelter deck. Eventually the crew of fifty-three made it out of Java to Australia, returning to New York in early April 1942.[15] Today it is considered one of the premier diving wrecks in Indonesia. The torpedoing of USAT *Liberty* on the eleventh is credited to Japanese submarine *I-66*.

One of the ships preparing to leave the United States for the Philippines in early December was loaded with a very special cargo. The first new shipment of poison gas for the islands' defenders was prepared for departure from Baltimore on December 8 on the chartered motor vessel *Roamer*. A refrigeration ship (recommended in order to keep the gas cylinders at a constant, cool temperature to forestall expansion and leakage), she had been made available by charter on December 2.[16] Baltimore was the port of choice due to its proximity to the Army's chemical warfare depot at Edgewood Arsenal, Maryland. On board were both offensive and defensive chemical warfare supplies for USAFFE. Included were one thousand tons of mustard gas, five thousand 155-mm gas-loading howitzer shells, six thousand smoke candles, and thirty-seven portable M1 flamethrowers.[17] A 20-ton gas filling plant from Panama was to be transshipped to the Philippines in a separate voyage.

War Department discussions about the potential need and use of poison gas for the Philippines (and other overseas departments as well) had been periodically held since the First World War. At this time, in 1941, there was no treaty or international law that in any way prohibited the use of this weapon. Only national policy and international opinion governed its military use. While considerable stockpiles were accumulated in Hawaii (one 1934 Army report claims that this was "the largest known concentrated reserve of lethal gas in the world"), no similar quantity was in the Philippines prior to the war.[18] Apparently only a small reserve quantity of one or two agents was present during 1941.[19] Of course, defensive items were present, such as gas masks and smoke dischargers, and there was a small chemical warfare unit of about company size in the Philippine Department. The Joint Board in 1934 approved preparations to use chemical warfare from the outbreak of any future war, but only if or when an opponent used it first. Army Chief of Staff Gen. Douglas MacArthur reinforced the board's decision by stating that the use of chemical warfare was authorized, subject to any international convention. However, nothing was done to improve the chemical warfare supply in the Philippines—a review of requested supplies was answered in 1939 with: "It is not the intention of the War Department at this time to authorize any additional chemical ammunition or weapons for the Philippines."[20]

The Philippine Department itself had also studied where and how poison gas could be useful to the defense. In mid-1941, at about the time the decision was made to significantly augment the defensive forces in the islands, the department reminded Washington that they had consistently advised stocking mustard gas. It would be very effective in defending landing beaches, particularly if available in a land-mine form. The War Department's objection to filling the request was based on political concerns. A large quantity shipment might well become publicly known, and create serious complications in American positions concerning the European war and Asian situation. The secretary of war withheld approval for the stocking, though again mentioning that the strategic positions in Hawaii and Panama were different.[21]

In mid-November the opinion in Washington changed. Secretary Stimson began to actively advocate and support a different supply situation. In his diary, the secretary notes that on November 21 he advised the president that it was thought the Japanese had used poison gas on the Chinese at Ichang (killing an estimated seven hundred). He stated that he didn't want to get caught without gas in the Philippines, and that it was time to make the shipments despite the risk that if they came to light it could negatively affect negotiations. Stimson directed the War Plans Division to prepare the facts for possible shipments, and to exercise all care for the secrecy of any movement. Subsequently a memo of requirements was drawn up and preparations made for the shipment from Baltimore. An enhanced chemical warfare service staff for the Philippines was to include the company already stationed there, a chemical laboratory dispatched on the *Pensacola* convoy, and then a chemical depot company, maintenance company, two decontamination companies, another lab, and an impregnating company were to be organized by the Philippine Army with U.S.-supplied equipment. The nine ex-Thailand A-27 ground support bombers were already equipped for spreading gas, as would be the fifty-two A-24s shipped on *Meigs*.[22]

When war broke out, the subsequent voyage of *Roamer* was cancelled. For a few days she remained fully loaded at anchor in Baltimore, but then the cargo was offloaded between the sixteenth and nineteenth of December. Modern refrigerator ships were scarce, and she was needed to take perishable food items for the garrison in Iceland. No subsequent attempts were made to get gas to the islands in this phase of the war. MacArthur actually issued a memo in early January to field commander Wainwright to abstain from *any* use of chemical munitions—regardless of whether they were filled with white phosphorus, smoke, or tear gas. Without any capability to respond in kind, he obviously did not wish to provide any excuse for the Japanese to employ such weapons. As it turned out, no poison chemical weapons were used by either side in the Philippine campaign. Still, the potential retaliatory usage remained an American tactical option—on March 27, 1942 shipment of mustard gas to an Australian depot was approved.[23]

CHAPTER THIRTEEN

Aborted Convoys from San Francisco

The units to go to the Philippines began to accumulate a backlog in San Francisco as the fall of 1941 progressed. A complicated mix of whole units, filler personnel, technical and command advisers, and a vast quantity of supplies were being requested. In fact, MacArthur and his staff had a delicate balancing act to perform. Shipping became the limiting factor, forcing commanders to make choices as to what to send when. The large number of troops demanded was most limiting—human traffic required more space, comfort, and coordinated naval escort than did bulk supplies.

For the Philippine Army, which General MacArthur now directly commanded in the United States Army Forces in the Far East (USAFFE), supplies were urgently needed, but manpower was to come almost exclusively from Filipino recruitment. The American forces were also to be expanded, but the situation here was more complex. In addition to the 19,000 American troops in the islands there were 12,000 Philippine Scouts.[1] These were U.S. Army soldiers recruited from Filipinos and mostly concentrated in a few segregated units (though generally led by American officers).[2] Expanding the Philippine Scout numbers had a certain appeal; for one thing, the expense was less—they were paid on a lower scale vs. Americans and did not require the same shipment and periodic replacement schedule. However, the Philippine Department recognized that further expansion of the Scouts would come at the detriment of recruiting, or even require the cannibalization of the new Philippine Army. MacArthur was politically locked into keeping the number of Scouts static while expanding the regular Philippine Army. His only source of reinforcement for the U.S. forces was to ask for the transfer of units or fillers from the United States.

The American Philippine units were normally kept at a manpower state somewhat below what was authorized in the official Army tables of organization. For a peacetime army this was not a bad practice. Units were established ahead of time, and they were brought up to full strength by mobilization, recruitment, or conscription when needed just before or after an emergency. In overseas garrisons this remedy was more problematic. While the units in the Philippines were at a higher troop-strength (and had most of their allocated heavy weapons) than most of their stateside counterparts, virtually all were substantially below authorized level. Typically the infantry regiments of the Philippine Division had only 1,500 men of their authorized strength of about 2,500. The harbor defenses were also seriously short of manpower. Another drain on existing American manpower was the need to allocate officers, senior NCOs, and technicians to the fledgling Philippine Army as advisers.

Combining these needs for American personnel created a demand for "fillers." These were personnel who were fully trained in their field or specialty, but were otherwise unassigned and could be used to bring understrength units up to wartime readiness. The Far Eastern Army designed a phased plan to address its unit strength problem. As a first step the command wished to disband a couple of Philippine Scout units—taking the personnel thus released to bring the other Scout units up to strength. With the Scout personnel level fixed by law, this was the only practical solution available to bring some units up to full strength. Then entire full American units would be brought in to replace the disbanded Philippine Scout units. Finally, additional stateside units would be assigned with the sole purpose of being disbanded once in the Philippines to provide trained fillers for the remaining American units. Of course, where possible and for certain key functions a limited number of available fillers from training centers would also be dispatched.

A key element of the plan depended on a major reorganization of the original American Philippine Division. During the First World War America had adopted a rather cumbersome division organization known as the square division. In addition to the division headquarters it had two brigade headquarters each commanding two infantry regiments. The artillery also had its own brigade structure managing three regiments with a total of six battalions. The engineers rated an entire regiment. Dating from 1917 the huge unit (originally 28,000 men, reduced to 22,000 by 1939) may have been fine for

Table 7. Plan for Units to be sent to the Philippines, December 1941[3]

Units Requested by USAFFE	Intended Purpose	Units Selected for Shipment
2 Infantry Regiments	One for Philippine Division One to disband for filler personnel	161st Infantry Regiment 34th Infantry Regiment
2 Artillery Battalions (155-mm howitzers)	For army and corps troops	218th Field Artillery Regiment (−2nd Battalion) 2nd Battalion 222nd Field Artillery Regiment
2 Artillery Battalions (75-mm guns)	One each for Philippine Division and for army and corps troops	145th Field Artillery Regiment (−1st Battalion) 2nd Battalion 138th Field Artillery Regiment
1 Cavalry Recon Troop	For Philippine Division	"E" Troop, 115th Cavalry Regiment
3 Signal Companies	For army and corps troops	101st Signal Battalion (two companies) Operation Company, 54th Signal Battalion
1 Signal Intelligence Company	For army and corps troops	102nd Signal Radio Intelligence Company
6 Sections Signal Repair (two wire, four radio)	For army and corps troops	6 Repair sections of 176th Signal Company
1 Section Signal Depot	For army and corps troops	3rd Section, 202nd Signal Depot
1 Military Police Company	For army and corps troops	41st MP Company
2 Military Police Platoons	For Philippine Division	2nd and 3rd Platoon, 40th MP Company
1 Engineer Regiment	Requested unit	47th Engineer Regiment GS

Table 7. Plan for Units to be sent to the Philippines, December 1941[3] (*Continued*)

Units Requested by USAFFE	Intended Purpose	Units Selected for Shipment
1 Air Warning Battalion	For Department	557th Air Warning Battalion, formed from: Philippine Air Warning Company 5th Interceptor Command Signal Corps recent trainee fillers
2 Ordnance Ammunition Companies	Disband for ordnance filler personnel	67th Ordnance Company 68th Ordnance Company
1 Medical Supply Depot	For army and corps troops	5th Medical Supply Depot
1 Medical Laboratory	For army and corps troops	3rd Medical Laboratory
1 Pursuit Group HQ and HQ Squadron	For Air Force	35th Pursuit Group HQ and HQ Squadron
1 Pursuit Squadron	For 35th Pursuit Group	70th Pursuit Squadron
1 Air Corps Intercept Control Sq	Requested unit	24th Air Corps Squadron (interceptor control)
1 Bomb Squadron (H)	For 7th Bomb Group (H)	32nd Bomb Squadron (H)
1 Recon Squadron (H)	For 7th Bomb Group (H)	38th Reconnaissance Squadron (H)
1 Matériel Squadron	Requested unit	59th Matériel Squadron
1 HQ Airbase Group	Requested unit	HQ 45th Airbase Group
1 Aviation Signal Company	Requested unit	415th Signal Company (Avn)
2 Aviation Ordnance Companies	Requested units	693rd Ordnance Company (Bomb) 711th Ordnance Company (AB)
1 Aviation Signal Platoon	Requested unit	8th Signal Platoon (AB)

static trench warfare, but for maneuver warfare of the Second World War it was both too large and had too many levels of command. Army chiefs of staff from Pershing to Marshall had worked to have the basic division streamlined; eventually that was achieved through thoughtful study and field maneuvers. Starting in 1939 the Army began converting its few regular divisions to a new design.[4]

Known as the triangular division, the new organization eliminated the awkward brigade structure. Three infantry regiments would report directly to headquarters. Likewise just four artillery battalions (three with field guns, one with heavier howitzers) would provide artillery support. Engineers were reduced to a single battalion and other division services likewise pruned. Additionally, more infantry support weapons were shifted down to the infantry, and the final vestiges of the horse-drawn era disappeared with full divisional motorization. This resulted in a smaller, more controllable unit that utilized limited manpower much more efficiently. This type of division, and similarly streamlined armored divisions, would serve with success throughout the upcoming war. When the older-pattern divisions were being converted in 1940–1941, a number of excess units became available for other use. A relatively large number of infantry regiments, headquarters organizations, and artillery battalions were released from the various National Guard infantry divisions being converted—and some of these units became available for helping meet the Far East's expansion plans.

At the same time the Philippine Division itself would be reorganized. This division in the immediate pre-war years was a hybrid with an organization partially belonging to each standard. It only had three infantry regiments, and no infantry brigades. Likewise it had no artillery brigade, but did have two artillery regiments assigned, though only containing a total of three battalions. The engineers were a much understrength regiment. Only one entire sub-unit, the also much understrength 31st Infantry Regiment, was totally a white American unit; the other infantry regiments, all of the artillery, and engineers were Philippine Scout organizations. Efforts were made to reorganize some of the units in order to bring them closer to the triangular design, and also to fill out the roster with needed manpower.

The department's plan was to first disband one of the Philippine Scout infantry regiments of the division—the 45th Infantry (PS). The Scouts released were to be used to bring the remaining Scout regiments, a cavalry, and two Scout coast artillery regiments up to strength. As a replacement, the department requested a fully equipped U.S. infantry regiment. The department division would thus have two white American regiments (the 31st Infantry and the new regiment) and one Philippine Scout regiment (the 57th).[5] While this plan fixed the shortage of men in the major Scout units and would provide a full-strength infantry regiment, it still left the American 31st Infantry Regiment and other U.S. units far below combat strength.

By early November the department requested, and Washington granted, a second American infantry regiment as a source of manpower. Lacking enough qualified men from training centers, Washington was forced to select an entire three-thousand-man unit to send as a source of fillers. Apparently, the primary need was for 1,576 infantrymen for the 31st Infantry, prejudicing the selection of an infantry unit as a source. So by early December 1941 two infantry regiments—the regular Army 34th Infantry and the ex–Washington National Guard 161st Infantry were being sent to San Francisco under shipping orders for the Philippines. The 161st was earmarked for the Philippine Division, the 34th for disassembly into smaller detachments or as fillers for the American parts of the Philippine Division and to bring the two American coast artillery regiments (the 59th and 60th) up to strength.

For field artillery, authorization was made to send a total of eight field artillery battalions to the Philippines, along with a brigade headquarters and four regimental headquarters. As already mentioned, four battalions (and the brigade HQ and two regimental HQs) had already been dispatched in late November on the *Pensacola* convoy. Four more battalions were either waiting in San Francisco to board or actually in transit when war broke out. Two more battalions were armed with 75-mm field guns, but the last two were medium battalions with 155-mm howitzers. These would be the first heavy field artillery units the island defenders had seen in many years. The exact intended disposition for these artillery units is more difficult to reconstruct today. In fact, it may be that units were simply being sent and it was intended that the Far Eastern command figure out their best utility once they arrived.

Two other units were requested for the reorganizing Philippine Division. First was a reconnaissance company. The new triangular division had a recon company equipped with armored scout cars attached to the division headquarters, and such an organization was requested for the Philippines. Selected to be transferred was Troop E of the 115th Cavalry along with its M3 scout cars. Also, an additional military police (MP) platoon of sixty-seven officers and men was needed. Two small platoons of the 40th MP Company (from the 40th Division) were notified for transfer. Various other deficiencies in manpower for select technical services, medical battalion, and the division's headquarters itself were addressed. Either fillers shipped directly or qualified personnel taken from the 34th Infantry or signal and ordnance units being sent were to supply these men.

Another key unit requested was an addition to help the Philippine Air Warning Company manage the radar sets being installed. Ordered to be assembled and at the San Francisco Port of Embarkation by December 3, 1941 were additional equipment and personnel needed to form a new composite air-warning battalion. These various units and pieces of equipment would be combined and incorporated in a new unit to be known as the 557th Signal Aircraft Warning Battalion. Activated on December 1 specifically for this assignment, it was to have a headquarters and headquarters' company, a plotting battalion, two companies of aircraft warning/reporting, and ten distant reporting platoons. Equipment sent was to be at least six more SCR-268s and SCR-270s.[6]

The normal process for alerting commands of orders for movement was utilized for these shipments too. However, there was a geographical concentration: many of the units being sent to the Philippines were drawn from the 41st Division—the Washington State National Guard division. The 161st Infantry Regiment, several of the field artillery battalions (and the 148th Field Artillery Regiment previously sent), and even a military police company were from this organization. The usual filling-out of understrength units was accomplished prior to embarking. Also in the 161st, thirty-six soldiers of Chinese or Japanese ancestry were transferred out of the unit, some with tears in their eyes at being separated from their service buddies.[7] On December 6 the troop trains carrying the 161st and other units left the siding of Fort Lewis for San Francisco. One soldier described the experience like this:

> Troop trains are a life all by themselves, kitchen in baggage car, magazines and littered papers all over, a thick blue cloud of cigarette smoke. Here and there, a poker game, punctuated by a burst of profanity or a surprised chuckle to accompany an unexpected full-house. The night of the 6th passed on with a world outside and world of our own moving along on steel tracks. Towns flashed by in the dark of midnight as the Southern Pacific clicked along—Portland, Springfield, the Willamette River. The morning of December 7th dawned.[8]

A long list of specialized units also appeared on MacArthur's shopping list. Some make rather more sense when the nature of his challenge is appreciated. What he did have was a large amount of relatively poorly trained, but willing, manpower in the Philippine Army. Little technical expertise, much less equipment, was available for the technical services. If modern military capabilities like engineering, radio and radar operation, ordnance and vehicle maintenance, chemical warfare, and medical services were to be provided, they had to come from either trained American specialists or through supplying equipment and allowing sufficient time to train recruits. And time was the commodity most lacking.

The requests from the Philippines were for much more than units, impedimenta, and filler personnel. Equipment in large quantity was scheduled for shipment. Three simultaneous expansions added to the equipment shortage problem. Not only did the new units need their full quota of equipment and supplies, but also the expansion of the authorized war reserves from 31,000 to 50,000 dating from June 1941 had still not been fulfilled. This may not sound like a lot, but supplying six months' worth of every type of supply for another 20,000 men was a significant demand. And of course, finally, the supplying of much of the equipment and supplies to a force of approximately 120,000 Filipino army troops was by far the largest demand. In September efforts were approved to supply 20 percent of this Philippine Army initial equipment, but that was increased to 75 percent in just a couple of weeks. In a memorandum of October 31, 1941 Brigadier General Gerow estimated that these multiple demands (just to date; they were increasing at a regular pace) exceeded 500,000 ship measurement tons.[9] A November breakdown calculated that 150,000 tons were for the units to be sent and their equipment, 82,000 tons for the war reserves, 220,000 for the Philippine Army divisions, and no less than 350,000 for the miscellaneous Philippine Army corps and army organizations.[10]

The problem was that there simply was not the capacity in the Army's transportation fleet—particularly with ongoing demands to also supply garrisons in Alaska, Hawaii, Panama, Iceland, and the recently acquired ex-British bases—to deliver these supplies and new units in anything like a timely manner. In early November the Army's War Plans Division staff began looking for resources to break the logjam of shipment. An oral request to the Navy got a negative reply; no help for this movement could be made available from that quarter. The Army had asked for the use of USS *Henderson* for one trip, but was told the ship was already scheduled to capacity for Navy purposes.

On November 10, 1941 a conference was held at the Supply Section offices of the War Plans Division (WPD) in Washington, D.C. Attended by representatives of the Army chief of staff, Maritime Commission, Navy, and Quartermaster Corps, the subject was the challenge of obtaining additional shipping to expedite the movement of troops and supplies to the Philippines. The backlog accumulating and scheduled to arrive at the San Francisco Port of Embarkation was simply outstripping the resources of the U.S. Army Transportation Service to carry it. At the conference the WPD reiterated that the Philippines should have priority over movements to Hawaii, which could be deferred accordingly. After discussion it was decided that troop movements scheduled for late November and early December would not be changed, but that those proposed for convoys on January 10 and 18 would be advanced about a month to December 17 and 20. To do this the troop capacity on *Coolidge* would be increased by about eight hundred, and military transports USAT *Etolin* and USS *St. Mihiel* would be taken off the Hawaiian run and rescheduled for the Philippines. By the fourteenth arrangements had been started to charter three large liners from Matson Navigation Company (*Monterey*, *Matsonia*, and *Maui*) and three from American President Lines (*President Garfield*, *President Johnson*, and *President Taylor*). The biggest immediate problem was finding the $2.25 million to pay the charters within the quartermaster's budget.[11]

As to freight, at this date approximately 1.1 million tons had already been approved for release for shipments to the Philippines (though some of it was not yet present at the port). It was estimated that it might take seventy-one trips, involving some fifty ships, to move this quantity. There seemed to be general agreement that enough military and commercial vessels for cargo would be available for this movement, if care were provided for the scheduling and certain arrangements expedited. Freight carriers were not quite as limiting as troop transports. Starting on November 8 the Army began negotiations for chartering at least ten commercial freighters for the upcoming surge. Finally, at the November conference a revised troop sailing schedule was also approved and published.[12]

Within a very few days even this accelerated schedule was again reviewed and yet another speed-up requested. At another conference on November 13 at the Quartermaster General's office it was determined that the last units (of those scheduled at that time) should depart San Francisco about December 8, rather than the seventeenth or twentieth. The Matson Navigation Company was notified on November 29 that *Matsonia* would be required for a single round-trip to the Philippines, and *Monterey* for a one-way voyage (in other words she could continue onward to wherever her owners desired).

Meanwhile *Maui* was sold outright to the Maritime Commission in San Francisco for conversion to an Army transport on December 3. Next, the Army maximized the use of its own transports by allocating no less than five troop transport vessels to the effort—*Republic* and *St. Mihiel* (technically operated as commissioned naval vessels, but still under direction of use by the Army), and finally USATs *Willard A. Holbrook*, *Tasker H. Bliss*, and *Etolin.* This "maximum effort" required some significant maneuvers on the part of the Army. In order to provide enough berthing space, contingent modifications had to be made to the vessels involved. While there was not enough time for major conversion, local officers on the West Coast were permitted to acquire six thousand bunk bottoms and 2,500 standard berths on the local market at local costs to equip the vessels for the intended troop load.[13]

Additional air units also arrived at San Francisco or were in transit. As usual, additional aircraft for the Philippines were included in the manifests for early December shipment. On December 7, 138 airplanes were on board ships on their way to that garrison—seventy on the *Pensacola* convoy, twenty with USAT *Ludington*, and another forty-eight recently departed or waiting on board ships about to depart San Francisco.

In late November the movement of authorized U.S. Army and Army Air Force personnel totaled 20,786 officers and men—a virtual doubling of the strength of American forces in the islands. Also, this was without the majority of the requested infantry and other combat unit fillers; only 902 filler personnel were included in the most recent agenda—mostly Air Force and specific medical and signal specialists. The *Pensacola* convoy was the first increment of this transfer, but even after its departure from San Francisco on November 21, well over 16,000 men awaited their turn for transfer to the Philippines. Something of this scale demanded careful juggling of ships and timetables. There were some units like the 34th Infantry, which was on maneuvers, and to give it time to repack, fill vacancies, and relocate to San Francisco it was put on the tail end of the shipment schedule, for December 8. All movements to Hawaii were postponed until the Philippine shipments could be made. The unusually heavy shipment load created problems logistically for the San Francisco Port of Embarkation. To make room for all the units arriving, the Presidio's resident 30th Infantry Regiment was ordered to temporarily vacate their quarters. Even returning casuals were ordered quickly cleared and sent on their way in order to free up rooming space at the port's facilities.

It was planned to have the various transports form into convoys with naval escort upon arrival at Oahu. To accomplish this with ships of different

Table 8. Initial Convoy Assignments for Philippine Movement, Early December 1941[14]

Convoy/Ships/Speed/Escort/ Dates/Route	**Units and Major Cargo Items**
Convoy No. 2002	First two ships (*Tasker H. Bliss* and *President Garfield*)
USAT *Tasker H. Bliss*	
USAT *President Garfield*	145th Field Artillery Regiment (–1st Battalion)
SS *President Polk*	101st Signal Battalion
	3rd Medical Laboratory
Garfield departed SF 12/06,	24th Inter. Squadron
Bliss and *Polk* departed 12/07/41	5th Inter. Command HQ
Due Manila about 1/15/42	54th Signal Battalion, Operations Company
Recalled to SF 12/07/41	
	Total on first two ships of 2,839 officers and men
	25 P-39s, 9 P-40s
Convoy No. 2003	First two ships (*Etolin* and *President Johnson*)
USAT *Etolin*	218th Field Artillery Regiment (–2nd Battalion)
USAT *President Johnson*	
	2nd battalion of 222nd Field Artillery Regiment
Etolin and *Johnson*	
Departed SF 12/05/41	5th Medical Supply Depot
Due Manila about 1/20/42	32nd Bomb Squadron, 38th Reconnaissance Squadron
Recalled to SF 12/07/41	
	35th Pursuit Group HQ and HQ Squadron
	45th Air Base Group HQ and HQ Squadron
	70th Pursuit Squadron
	59th Matériel Squadron
	Total on first two ships of 3,937 officers and men

speeds and states of readiness, a schedule for departure from San Francisco was organized. *President Johnson*, *Etolin*, *Tasker H. Bliss*, and *President Garfield* would depart from the fourth to the sixth of December. *Maui* would depart on the seventh, and finally four more about the ninth—*President Taylor*, *St. Mihiel*, *Matsonia*, and *Monterey*. In accordance to recent policy, the freighters were to sail independently without escort. An exception was the small Union Oil tanker *Paul M. Gregg*, which was to go with the slower convoy.

There are some surviving notes that contain descriptions of the intended convoy organization planned to depart from Honolulu. On November

27 the Navy notified large light cruiser USS *Helena* that it would probably escort five relatively fast seventeen-knot troop transports starting about December 15. This convoy, to be formed in Hawaiian waters, would have included USAT *Tasker H. Bliss*, USAT *President Garfield*, SS *Matsonia*, SS *Monterey*, and the mostly commercial-loaded SS *President Polk*. As mentioned above, three of the ships actually left the docks prior to the start of the war. Both *Tasker H. Bliss* and *President Garfield* left San Francisco at 6:30 PM on the sixth. At noon on the seventh another ship was in the stream at San Francisco and ready to depart. *President Polk* was not really one of the Army-managed vessels of this movement. Rather, she was still on a commercial schedule for the American President Lines. No Army units or personnel were embarked, but she was used to carry twenty-three aircraft (nine P-40s and fourteen P-39s.) The final two ships intended to join the five-ship fast convoy were SS *Matsonia* and SS *Monterey*. No record has been located for their specific intended cargo, but as their large troop capacity was used to take the two infantry regiments to Hawaii a couple of weeks later, it is likely that too was the case for this shipment.

At the same time a slower convoy of six fourteen-knot ships was being prepared. The vessels of Convoy No. 2003 would also leave singly for Honolulu, be formed into a convoy, provided escort, and sail the southern routing through the Torres Strait to Manila. Composing this convoy were *Etolin* and *St. Mihiel*, and recently chartered *President Johnson*, *Maui*, and *President Taylor*. Sailing with the convoy was the Union Oil vessel *Paul M. Gregg*, carrying drummed gasoline. The other three transports and freighter with fuel were to follow within the next few days. While this convoy would have been escorted from Honolulu, the name of the cruiser appointed that task has not been identified.

Several freighters were in the San Francisco Bay terminals preparing for their role in getting supplies to the Philippines. Freighter SS *James Lykes* had sailed on the sixth with ten thousand ship tons of organizational equipment. SS *Will H. Point* was due to sail from San Francisco on the seventh with steel piling, trucks, sandbags, small-arms ammunition, autos, and one dismantled C-53 transport airplane. She never left the dock. Neither did *W. R. Gibson* from Pier 45, whose further loading was suspended. Three freighters were loading at Oakland—*Sterlingville*, *Iowan*, and *American Star*. One ship, SS *Steel Exporter*, departed New Orleans on the seventh for the Panama Canal transit and then eventually on to Manila. She carried commercial cargo for California, and 5,300 tons for the Philippines. Included were forty-two vehicles, engineer and quartermaster supplies, thirty-seven 60-inch searchlights for the Inland Seas Project, and forty-two 75-mm artillery pieces for the Philippine Army.

As impressive as the list of units and equipment scheduled was, it was not the end. The requests from MacArthur's command relentlessly continued. Another seven thousand men were scheduled for shipment to "Plum" between December 24 and February 1. For late December, enhancements to the defense's anti-aircraft deficiency were to be addressed. Two anti-aircraft brigade headquarters and headquarters batteries were slated for movement—the 33rd and 39th Brigades, as well as three anti-aircraft regiments. In January they were to be followed with the 122nd Separate Battalion, and the first battalions of two semi-mobile anti-aircraft regiments—the 94th and 95th—were to prepare for a February 1 departure.[15] Of course, these movements were never implemented, but the units figured heavily in early war deployments elsewhere overseas.

Four transports departed San Francisco for Honolulu in the days prior to the start of the war. On board were 6,775 officers and men and the forty-seven fighter airplanes mentioned above. Another thirty transports or freighters were scheduled to leave within a few days, all to arrive by the end of January 1942. None of them completed their intended mission. When word was received about the Pearl Harbor attack, the transports that had just departed San Francisco were immediately ordered to maintain radio silence and return. All came back into port on the eighth or ninth. Back in port, *Matsonia* and *Monterey* (the latter just received at 9 AM from her dockyard modifications) were at Pier 45 for loading. USS *St. Mihiel* arrived at Pier 7 the morning of the seventh from Mare Island Navy Yard, and *Maui* was at the same pier loading for Manila. *President Taylor* was berthed at Pier 45A, loaded, ready to sail on the eighth. *President Polk* was anchored in stream waiting to leave when the Army commandeered her and ordered her back for unloading. Freighters were involved too; all those that were loading and preparing had their journey cancelled.[16]

From December 9 to 14 the ships returning to or already loaded at San Francisco debarked their troops and in most cases their cargo. Local facilities to house and care for 16,000 soldiers were not available, so many of the units were dispersed to other California or West Coast posts pending a decision on where they were destined next. No unit was larger than regimental strength, and many were sort of miscellaneous bits-and-pieces meant to complete the parent organizations being mobilized in the Philippines. Thus, many did not have divisional homes or immediate assignments to return to. The two infantry regiments were quartered locally; of the other larger units, the 557th Aircraft Warning (AW) Battalion went to Ft. Lawton, Washington, the 47th Engineers to Fort Ord, California, and the bomber and support units went to March Field near Riverside.[17]

As it turned out, the rapid availability of ships, units, and supplies in greater San Francisco directly facilitated the quick reinforcement of Hawaii following the Pearl Harbor attack. The two larger Matson liners (joined by their sister *Lurline* with naval cargo and personnel) left San Francisco for Oahu just nine days after the attack—and six others went to the same place later in the month. *President Polk* was the first transport dispatched with Australia as an original destination on December 18. Many of the Army units originally slated for the reinforcement of the Philippines went on these same new journeys to Hawaii. The two infantry regiments, two of the artillery outfits, the engineer regiment, and the signal battalion were all transferred to Oahu during the post–Pearl Harbor December reinforcement of the Hawaiian Islands. While they were unable to perform their original missions, they provided valuable service in the time of national need.

Another crucial issue facing the two armed services was the arming of transports and freighters engaged in carrying military cargo. The Navy had regularly armed its commissioned transport ships. When it acquired several Army vessels in mid-1941 (like USAT *Republic*), the ships were routinely armed with several small-caliber deck guns and anti-aircraft weapons. Work was usually done in naval dockyards where an adequate store of spare weapons was on hand. Of course, provision was made within the naval crew for serving these guns. On the other hand, U.S. merchant ships were not armed. In fact, a specific prohibition of this was contained in the Neutrality Act of 1940. A modification of that act with the urging of the administration passed in November 1941. Still, the first American merchant ship wasn't actually armed until November 26—just eleven days prior to Pearl Harbor. Other defensive preparations were also called for—such as degaussing the ship to protect it from magnetic mines, provision for blackout lighting, improved radio and signal capabilities, and repainting to remove names, nationality, and eventually provide camouflaged paint patterns. Just a very few merchant ships, those all in the Atlantic, actually received protective guns prior to the Pearl Harbor attack.

The situation with Army-controlled vessels was a little more complicated. In general, the practice followed the rules for commercial merchantmen rather than those of the Navy—even though the Army was not legally bound by the Neutrality Act. The Navy had urged the Army to prepare its ships by degaussing and arming in November 1940, but funds weren't appropriated and practical limitations prevented this up until the time of the war's start. However, immediately following the outbreak of the war, steps were taken to remedy this deficiency. USAT *President Garfield*, immediately upon her return to San Francisco from her aborted early December sailing, was the first Army transport to be armed after the start of the war.[18]

Pending the adoption of a standardized arming and crewing system, the Army strove to put a few light guns on all of its transports and freighters. The perceived threat was from either submarines or aircraft, and thus light guns would appear to suffice for the time being. In some ships already at sea and set to sail in the immediate weeks after Pearl Harbor, opportunity was taken to "borrow" field Army equipment from the holds or units on board. The *Pensacola* convoy, the subsequent voyage from Brisbane of *Willard A. Holbrook* and *Bloemfontein*, and the first sailings to Australia (*President Polk*) and Oahu (*Monterey*, *Matsonia*, and *Lurline*) after the Pearl Harbor attack all had instances where field artillery, anti-tank guns, or machine guns were lashed to the railings for impromptu defense. The chief quartermaster ordered all Army ships to be repainted on December 8—particularly to remove marks, names, flags, or other possible identification signs. On December 19 the various Army ports were ordered to arm all Army-owned and chartered vessels. Following close on the heels of this were more ominous orders for rigging demolition charges in all vessels to allow quick scuttling.

CHAPTER FOURTEEN

War Commences

In the early morning hours of December 7, just minutes before daybreak, the Japanese mobile striking force (Kidō Butai) under command of Vice Admiral Chuichi Nagumo began launching aircraft. It is doubtful that many of the young crewmen had gotten much sleep the night before; surely the excitement of participating in the single most momentous air raid of the war was on every mind. The first wave, composed of 183 airplanes from six different aircraft carriers, departed together at 6:30 AM from a spot 250 miles north of Oahu. At 7:15 AM a second wave of 168 aircraft was launched from the same carrier group. At 7:51 AM the first bombs of the first wave were dropped. This day, December 7, 1941 (December 8 back in Japan and in the American territories lying west of the International Date Line), would change the entire complexion of the world war and with that the military, economic, and political events of the rest of the twentieth century. From this day hence the effort to reinforce the American garrisons as a deterrent to Japanese aggression was a moot point. Rather it now became a matter of throwing something in the way of an enemy's impressive string of conquests. The story of the attack has been well told in numerous historical accounts. The interruption and changes to the flow of men and supplies to Hawaii, the Philippines, and other Pacific outposts is, however, pertinent to the present account.

None of the vessels at Pearl Harbor that had recently participated in the shipment of reinforcements to American outposts were lost to attack. However, the next cruiser designated for TF-15 escort service, USS *Helena*, was one of the victims. She had been scheduled to escort the fast convoy of transports planned for departure on December 14. *Helena* was moored at Ten-Ten pier with minelayer *Oglala* just outboard. A torpedo was released against the pair; it passed under *Oglala* and hit *Helena* in the port engine room. Serious flooding of the engine spaces ensued, but quick action by the crew prevented sinking. Casualties were relatively heavy; thirty-four crewmen lost their lives in that explosion. The ship was moved to brand new dry dock No. 2 for temporary repairs, before being sent to the West Coast for more permanent work.

USS *Curtiss*, which had participated in a supply mission to Midway in October, was tied up at berth X-22 the morning of the seventh. Like most of the harbor's ships, she was in reduced material condition with just one boiler lit and missing sixty-four officers and men on liberty. Crew sighted one of the Japanese midget submarines that had entered the harbor for the attack. *Curtiss* scored several hits on the small conning tower, which helped sink the submarine. During the attack *Curtiss* was struck at 9:05 AM by a damaged Japanese airplane. It crashed into the starboard side No. 1 crane, causing localized fires, but the vessel remained seaworthy and was in no immediate danger. The ship reported twenty killed, fifty-eight wounded, and one missing.

Fleet oiler USS *Ramapo* was moored that morning at the starboard side of Dock No. 12. She was in the process of loading the six PT boats earmarked for the Philippines to complete the organization of Motor Torpedo Boat Squadron 3. Four boats had already been loaded onto deck in cradles (*PT*s *27*, *29*, *30*, and *42*), and two more were dockside (*PT*s *26* and *28*) in cradles waiting to be lifted on board by the adjacent immense hammerhead crane. While not targeted specifically by the Japanese during the attack, the ship and her covey had a great front-row seat to the action. *Ramapo* herself quickly brought her anti-aircraft guns into action. The PT boats were immobile due to the insertion of carbon dioxide in their fuel lines as a safety precaution for the journey, but that did not affect their machine guns. Even though the guns were being maneuvered by hand, over four thousand rounds of .50-caliber machine-gun bullets left the guns of the boats, apparently with some effect.[1] Ship's captain Cdr. Duncan Curry Jr. was so frustrated with the situation that he was seen standing on the bridge, firing his .45-caliber pistol at the Japanese while tears streamed down his face.[2]

And we should not forget lowly Navy store-ship *Antares.* The ship, under Cdr. Lawrence C. Grannis, was just approaching Pearl Harbor after completing a successful supply run to Canton Island, towing an empty 500-ton lighter. On the morning of December 7 the anti-submarine nets to Pearl Harbor were opened early to allow two minesweepers to transit. They were left open during sunrise to allow Navy tug *Keosanqua* to exit Pearl in order to take

Antares' tow and bring the barge into port. At about 6:30 AM crewmen on *Antares* noted an odd shape following the towed barge and proceeding at about five knots. Even though no such beast existed in the U.S. Navy, it was soon assumed to be a hostile miniature submarine. Inshore patrol ship USS *Ward* was notified, and at 6:45 the first American round of the new Pacific war was fired when *Ward* let loose a well-placed 4-inch round into the conning tower. *Antares* herself watched the attack from a distance, though not entirely safe based on her reports of several strafing attacks. With no useful armament on board, she was eventually directed to berth out of the way at nearby Honolulu.[3]

The Navy's seaplane bases were also priority targets for the enemy. They were essential for any American attempt to locate and attack the Japanese carrier fleet, and thus targeted for neutralization. In this the Japanese succeeded. Six squadrons were on Oahu, with each nominally having twelve planes, though with a few out for repairs only sixty-eight patrol bombers were active with the Navy that morning.[4] Only seven of the Navy's PBYs were actually airborne at the time of the attack. The others—twenty-eight operable planes at Ford Island and another thirty-three at Kaneohe Bay—were caught on the water, ramps, or hangars of these bases. At Ford Island enemy dive-bombers of the first wave attacked. Bomb hits were reported at 7:57 AM. One patrol plane and a couple of utility planes managed to get into the air during the attack and survived. *All* of the other planes here were put at least temporarily out of action, but emergency repairs readied four for duty later in the day. At Kaneohe Bay the enemy attack was equally deadly. Of the thirty-three patrol planes here, twenty-seven were destroyed completely and the other six seriously damaged.[5]

The Marine Corps squadrons on Oahu also paid a heavy price this day. Marine Air Group 21 was concentrated at Ewa Field. It had forty-nine planes here. Suffering several attacks, fortunately just four Marines were killed (another died later from wounds), but the planes themselves were devastated. Nine fighters, eighteen SBD dive-bombers, and all six utility craft were lost, and fourteen others sustained major damage.[6]

In the first wave, enemy units targeted both the fighter base at Wheeler Field and the bomber field at Hickam. After discovering that there was little airborne American air defense, the escorting Japanese fighters also turned to strafing American airfields. Many of the American planes were in hangars or lined up as prevention for sabotage. More than a few were on a four-hour alert status and thus fueled. At Wheeler the first Japanese appeared at 7:51

AM and attacks continued sporadically until 9:15 AM. About thirty-five bombs from D3A dive-bombers hit the hangar and aircraft line; strafing was accomplished from both the bombers and fighters. At 9 AM seven enemy planes from the second wave also strafed the field. Of the 145 planes actually present at Wheeler, a total of forty-two planes were destroyed and fifty-six were damaged. The story was similar at Hickam. Japanese planes attacked beginning at 7:55 and the last attack was recorded at 9:20 AM. Fourteen American bombers were destroyed, another nineteen were damaged, and twenty-two others survived. Heavy damage was done to the facilities, the air depot's mess hall, and several hangars, and some barracks were destroyed. Immediately after the attack the base could offer only the most limited repair and service capabilities.[7]

At the time of the attack the Hawaiian Air Force under Maj. Gen. Frederick L. Martin boasted some 231 airplanes, supported and flown by 754 officers and 6,706 enlisted men. A full bombardment wing, a pursuit wing, and an observation squadron held twelve B-17Ds, twelve A-20s, twelve P-40Cs, eighty-seven P-40Bs, thirty-three B-18As, thirty-nine P-36As, fourteen P26-As and Bs, seven O-47s, and a few miscellaneous aircraft.[8] While not quite as modern an inventory as would have been liked, this was still a considerable concentration of aircraft. Of the 231 planes, 152 were either permanently or temporarily disabled; just seventy-nine were deemed flyable. In casualties the Army lost 226 killed and 396 injured (mostly Air Force personnel). A few American fighters did make it into the air, and gave a creditable performance against the odds. Several flights of P-36s and P-40s managed to get off from Wheeler, Bellows, and Haleiwa fields. They accounted for several enemy losses, though suffering considerable loss themselves.

The Japanese did not target, and no incidental attacks were made on, the commercial dock and harbor facilities at Honolulu. As usual, a considerable number of ships were either at the harbor's facilities or in the process of approaching or leaving. MV *Jagersfontein* sailed into port to dock at 9:30 AM, even while the second wave of Japanese attackers were still working over Oahu's air and naval bases. Three ships arrived on the eighth—freighters *Malama* and *Manini* and tanker *Pat Doheny*. Two more freighters arrived on the ninth, and another three on the tenth, including Norwegian freighter MV *Roseville* from Los Angeles. Temporarily, several ships in the immediate waters of the eastern Pacific were required to divert to Honolulu, and for six days no sailings were permitted until the situation on the island and its immediate waters was determined.

One of the special units dispatched in late November from Japan was the Midway Neutralization Unit, commanded by Captain Kanamo Konishi. Destroyers *Ushio* and *Sazanami*, accompanied by a refueling tanker, were specially assigned the job of putting Midway's airfields and seaplane facilities out of commission.[9] They were to perform a thorough surface bombardment on December 7, allowing the Kidō Butai to retire from the Pearl Harbor attack undetected or at least unmolested from what would surely soon be strenuous American efforts to locate it. The destroyers made the atoll about 9:30 PM on the seventh (local time). The Marine defenders observed flashing lights southwest of Sand Island, along with a radar signal, and eventually they even observed the ships themselves with night glasses. The searchlights were refused permission to illuminate as the command wished to delay giving away positions as long as possible. Bombardment started at 9:35 PM; at first shells were short, but soon they walked over the position of Battery "A," and then the power plant. No return fire was yet offered; the destroyers briefly stopped shelling and closed range.

With one exception, this first barrage did little damage. A lucky hit placed one of the 5-inch Japanese shells directly through an exhaust port of the small power plant. As one of the few concrete-protected buildings on the island, it was doing double duty as a command post on Sand Island. Three enlisted men and 1st Lt. George H. Cannon were all wounded or stunned by the shell's explosion. Cannon, though mortally wounded, stayed at his post in order to organize evacuation of his wounded. He died soon after. The lieutenant became the first Marine Corps Medal of Honor recipient of the war.[10] The destroyers reopened fire at 9:48 PM and quickly hit the Sand Island seaplane hangar. The roof burst into flames. Finally at 9:53 orders were issued for the American searchlights to illuminate, and begin firing. Three-inch anti-aircraft Battery "D" under Capt. Jean H. Buckner did open fire, along with Battery "B" on Eastern Island. The enemy ships were even well in range of several of the .50-caliber mounts and they opened up as well. There is no confirmation of any significant damage or casualties on the destroyers, but we know that the 6th Defense Battalion suffered two killed and ten wounded, and the Navy also lost two killed. One PBY was lost in the destroyed hangar on Sand Island.

Midway Island was also a popular target for Japanese submarines. At least four separate bombardments were recorded after the first of the year. On January 23 fleet submarines *I-18* and *I-24* conducted a bombardment. Two nights later *I-173* used her 100-mm deck gun against the island but quickly submerged after being spotted and fired upon by an American 3-inch gun. On February 8 a submarine hit an American 5-inch magazine, but did not detonate any of its contents. On February 10 a sub fired just two rounds that missed entirely and landed in the atoll's lagoon. At best these can be described as nuisance raids, and no doubt exposed the submarines to risks much greater than the results obtained.

The Japanese Fourth Fleet was assigned responsibility to quickly neutralize and then capture the small American outposts on Guam and Wake. Even though the opposing strength of the two American garrisons was not dissimilar (at least in terms of personnel count), the Japanese resources utilized were significantly different. Guam, with no heavy guns and no resident aircraft, was allotted a landing force of over five thousand men, while Wake—with seacoast guns, machine guns, beach defenses and a dozen fighter planes—was initially assigned just a small naval landing force of roughly five hundred men. The actual experience in early December suggests that the Japanese would have been better off in switching the two assault groups assigned these tasks.[11]

Specific orders were issued on November 8 to Major General Tomitara Horii to prepare his army South Seas Detachment in the Bonin Islands to invade Guam. The convoy of nine ships departed base at 9 AM on the fourth, and waited at Rota for the word to begin the assault. The naval contingent was the Fourth Fleet (sometimes called the Mandate Fleet due to the location of its bases). It supplied a small contingent of naval infantry for the assault, the post-conquest garrison, all of the air support, and of course ocean transportation. Guam was to be bombed for two days before an attempted landing. The Japanese naval air force available for this task was the 18th Naval Air Corps based at Saipan. The 18th had only obsolete two- and three-seat single-engine reconnaissance floatplanes. Under other circumstances these small, slow aircraft would not have been used for a bombing campaign of an enemy base. They were poorly armed with just a couple of 7.7-mm light machine guns and could carry two to four 60-kilogram bombs. Fortunately for the Japanese the Americans had no aircraft of any type on Guam, and no ground anti-aircraft guns whatsoever. Saipan was notified to begin attacks just forty minutes after the Pearl Harbor attack. Nine planes began bombing Guam at 8:30 AM. For the invasion itself considerable naval forces were utilized. There were nine transports, the minelayer *Tsugaru*, and an escort of four destroyers. Supporting cover was provided by the 6th Cruiser Division with four heavy cruisers. Like the ground forces this was an overwhelming allotment of strength, particularly as there was intelligence indicating no shore batteries and thus no Japanese plan for bombardment.

The main assault force was to be a regimental combat team known as the South Seas Detachment. Its core unit was the 144th Infantry Regiment and the 1st Battalion of the 55th Mountain Artillery Regiment with twelve guns. Overall the 55th Infantry Group headquarters directed command. The Japanese estimate of American strength was approximately correct at three hundred men and maybe 1,500 native soldiers. The navy contributed a unit drawn from the Saipan navy base's 5th Base Force, composed of Japanese naval infantry. These four hundred men were referred to as the Hayashi Detachment for its leader—Commander Hirashi Hayashi. After securing Guam, the army would move on to other assaults in the Bismarcks, while the navy base unit would remain as Guam's permanent garrison force.

The invasion was made in the early morning hours of the tenth. The small navy unit went ashore as planned at Apurguan, near Tamuning. The much larger army South Seas Detachment encountered other problems. Initially planned to go ashore at Merizo and then to travel via Agat to the Orote Peninsula, it was found at the last minute that no road existed along this route.[12] The landing site was switched at the last minute, but the delay incurred meant that the army component did not arrive until the U.S. forces surrendered. The naval landing team was ashore by 3:30 AM (local time). The only resistance it encountered was when, about 5:30 AM, it neared the plaza outside the American government house. Three small machine-gun squads manned by the Insular Guard engaged and stopped the advancing Japanese in a short but sharp action. Casualties occurred on both sides, the local, partially trained but patriotic Chamorro guard unit acquitting itself well. The Navy governor, Capt. George J. McMillan, surrendered the American forces at 7 AM. Total casualties for the Americans to this time were seventeen dead military (thirteen American, four Guamanian) and four dead civilians (one American civilian, three Guamanian). Total wounded casualties of the defenders, military and civilian, were calculated at forty-two. Japanese casualties were ten dead.

Japanese air attacks to neutralize Wake began promptly with the start of war. The principal land-based unit used was the Chitose Air Group, a constituent of the 24th Air Flotilla deployed in late 1941 to the Marshall Islands specifically to participate in the opening combat of the offensive. Based on Roi in the Kwajalein atoll, the unit had a strength of thirty-six G3M2 navy land bombers and a complement of A5M fighters. Also, a number of flying boats were at Marshall Island bases belonging to the Toko Kaigun Kokotuai and used on several occasions to also bomb Wake. The first air raid occurred just before noon on December 8.

Four of the recently arrived F4F Wildcats of VMF-211 were on combat air patrol; the other eight planes were deployed around the airfield roughly one hundred yards apart. The next flight of four was fully gassed and armed. Without encountering the American fighter patrol, the Japanese bombers emerged from a low bank of clouds almost directly over the airfield. At least eighteen of the planes bombed the airfield with numerous small bombs, and followed with an extensive strafing.[13] Seven of the eight F4Fs on the ground were destroyed; the eighth was severely damaged but was eventually cannibalized for parts. This was a devastating blow to the defense—losing two-thirds of its airpower in the very first attack without a chance to strike back. Three officers and twenty-one enlisted men died at the airfield attack. Upon arrival one flight (probably nine planes) split off and hit the Peale Island seaplane base. Contractor Camp No. 2 and the Pan American facilities were hard hit. The hotel was burned and virtually all the clipper support buildings destroyed or heavily damaged. Five Guamanian employees of the airline and fifty-five civilian workers were killed.[14] The four airborne fighters, at the time a ways distant from Wake, arrived back only to see the enemy formation departing.[15]

Immediately following the first air attack renewed efforts were made to disperse the remaining personnel, food, water, and fuel. Protected revetments for the planes were pushed to completion, though there were only four now to protect. The following day (the ninth) another raid occurred at 11:50 AM. An estimated force of twenty-five planes approached at eight thousand feet and heavily struck Construction Camp No. 2 and the Naval Air Station. This time the defenders downed two bombers with the remaining flight of fighters. With a couple of exceptions, air attacks continued on an almost daily basis. Fortunately little damage or casualties were experienced in these subsequent attacks. Some of this was due to the fact that only the first two attacks (those of the eighth and ninth) were conducted at low level and utilized heavy strafing in addition to bombing. The air attack on the tenth caused just slight damage and few casualties on Wilkes Island. The morning of the eleventh brought the expected amphibious attack.

The first attempted Japanese landing on Wake was entrusted to a small naval and even smaller landing force. A task group of only 450 special naval landing force troops was allocated. These were carried in two transports and two patrol boats that towed barges. Close escort was provided by six older destroyers. Shore bombardment and general naval coverage was assigned to the Fourth Fleet's heaviest units: three small, old light cruisers, *Yubari*, *Tenryu*, and *Tatsuta*.[16] The enemy task force arrived at 1:50 AM; five ships, commenced a naval bombardment at about 5:30 AM on the morning of December 11. Parading from Wilkes Island toward Peacock Point, at first the Japanese bombarded at six thousand yards without return fire. At 6:10 AM, at just 4,500 yards, the two-gun battery at Peacock Point opened fire. The Japanese received a very rough treatment. The Marine seacoast gunners exhibited excellent fire discipline, not opening fire until their targets were close and clearly registered in the fire-control equipment. Destroyer *Hayate* was hit by the battery on Wilkes Island and quickly sunk. Destroyers *Oite*, *Mochizuki*, *Yayoi*, and light cruisers *Yubari* and *Tenryu* were also reported hit and sustained some damage and casualties. Damage to *Yubari* is difficult to confirm. Certainly the Marines thought they scored several direct hits on the ship, but the Japanese action reports do not confirm this. Damage from the Japanese bombardment was limited: they set some oil tanks afire and wounded only four Marines.

The remaining F4Fs, led by Maj. Paul A. Putnam, contributed one of the finest performances in the aggressive defense. The last four fighters had taken off around 7 AM and at first gained altitude anticipating an enemy air attack coincident to the landing attempt. When that didn't materialize the planes went after the enemy ships (which had no air coverage) with enthusiasm. Armed with only two 100-pound bombs but full .50-caliber gun loads, the planes repeatedly bombed and strafed the enemy. The four planes made ten sorties that morning. Transport *Kongo Maru* was strafed and took a bomb on its stern. Light cruiser *Tenryu* was again damaged. Then Lt. Henry T. Elrod, on his fourth flight about 7:30 AM, hit the trailing destroyer *Kisaragi*. At first put afire, eventually the ship's depth charges exploded, and she quickly sank. Virtually the entire crew was killed. For the attack the Americans claimed that one light cruiser and one destroyer were definitely sunk by the seacoast guns, plus losses to the air attack.[17] Actually lost were only destroyers *Hayate* and *Kisaragi*, but crew losses probably amounted close to four hundred. Unfortunately two fighters were damaged sufficiently to put them permanently out of action.

The days following the attack were relatively calm for the defenders. On the twelfth only a single seaplane attacked (and was claimed shot down by the defending aircraft). A daylight raid on the fourteenth did manage to kill two enlisted men and destroyed one of the two remaining fighters. A nighttime seaplane attack was made again on the fifteenth. A summary of cumulative damage to date reported: "The majority of the dynamite had been destroyed; fifty percent of the heavy digging equipment and transportation including trucks had been destroyed; the principle storehouses with spare parts and construction material had burned; eighty percent of the diesel oil had been destroyed; the machine shop, the blacksmith shop, and the garage had been destroyed."[18] An interesting exchange of messages occurred on December 17. Authorities in Hawaii radioed the post to ask how progress was coming on the dredging of the channel. They wanted to know when that work, along with other projects, would be completed. Apparently the message had originated with Rear Adm. Claude C. Bloch of the Fourteenth Naval District late on the sixteenth. While otherwise a pertinent question, particularly when Pearl was in the midst of organizing a relief attempt and needed to know the status of certain work, it obviously hit Commander Cunningham and the defenders wrong. Showing amazing restraint he responded that with air raid damage, half of his trucks and equipment were lost, and most of his fuel and dynamite were gone. A supplemental report added apologetically that the men on the base had been busy defending the atoll and keeping themselves alive. It had been impossible to keep up the work due to the noise, inability to use lights at night, and poor morale of the civilian contractors.[19] Also on the seventeenth Cunningham was advised to organize an evacuation of the civilian workers, but to retain 250 to complete the most essential construction.

The Japanese used their submarine force in Hawaiian waters on a number of occasions to try and bombard the ferry bases. Many of the Japanese fleet submarines were armed with one or two 140-mm deck guns with twenty ready rounds each, a relatively heavy armament compared to that carried by most nations' submarines. Numerous bombardments occurred in December and January; few, if any, were effective. Johnston was bombarded on both December 15 and 22. The first attack by *I-22* managed to puncture the 50,000-gallon water tank and set another oil tank afire. But altogether there was limited damage and no casualties reported. Navy transport *William Ward Burrows* was at the island, but was not sighted and got away unscathed with a valuable barge in tow. Palmyra was hit on the twenty-second and the twenty-fourth and the Army dredge *Sacramento* was slightly damaged.[20] Samoa's turn came on January 11, again with little damage, but a shell did wound a Navy officer. In mid-December long-ranged seaplanes bombed Canton Island, but caused no damage. Little Howland Island, which did not have an American base on it, was bombed on the ninth of December by Mavis flying boats of the Yokohama Air Group, followed by a bombardment by three subs on the eleventh.[21] Apparently the Japanese thought there was more of an American military presence here, but in fact there were just some shacks inhabited by a very few Hawaiian teenagers who had participated on and off in a sort of youth-group colonization of the island since 1935.

The Pearl Harbor attack was to be the signal for the rest of the Japanese armed forces to spring into action. The initial attacks on the Philippines were no exception. On December 8, 1941 there were nineteen B-17s at Clark Field belonging to the 28th and 30th Bomb Squadrons. One was having storm damage repaired; two were in a hangar getting their first application of camouflage paint. Of the sixteen operational planes, fifteen were in the air—one off on a reconnaissance mission and the other fourteen in response to an alert posted at 8:30 that morning. Also at Clark was the 20th Pursuit Squadron with its eighteen P-40Bs. Around 11 AM the circling airborne bombers began to land to refuel and prepare for potential assignments. There were many questionable actions and decisions taken by the Americans in the first few days of the war (and the timing of the first Japanese attack on Clark Field is a good example), but there also were several instances of just plain bad luck. Two American fighter squadrons, the 17th and 21st, were at Nichols; each had eighteen P-40Es. At Iba Field northwest of Clark was the 3rd Pursuit Squadron with its eighteen fully ready P-40Es, and finally at Del Carmen was the 34th Pursuit Squadron. This unit had not yet received its intended P-40s, and was thus left with the outmoded—and worn—P-35s.

Early on the morning of the eighth most of the Japanese attack squadrons on Formosan airfields were seriously delayed by thick fog. An army strike had managed to attack Baguio at 9:30 AM, and light bombers hit Tuguegarao airfield shortly after. American airplanes were scrambled again to intercept; both the 17th and 20th squadrons from Nichols and Clark respectively went up, but failed to contact the enemy and returned. Running five hours late, the Japanese navy planes finally started their mission to Luzon at 10:15 AM with 192 airplanes. If they had gotten off at or just prior to dawn the Americans would have been better prepared—the fighters would have been flying combat patrol and most of the bombers out of harm's way. But to refuel the American planes returned briefly, precisely at the moment when the belated enemy bomber formations roared into position overhead. Unfortunately at

12:35 AM local time the attack caught all but perhaps two to three American bombers and fighters at Clark.

The P-35s at Del Carmen were about all that was available for intercept, but thick dust at the field delayed takeoffs and the fighters arrived too late to attack the enemy. The Japanese formations, largely unaffected by either American fighters or bothered by anti-aircraft fire, were quite accurate. Thirty-four enemy fighters escorting fifty-four bombers plastered Clark for over ninety minutes. The three B-17s preparing to take off on a photo mission were hit and destroyed. Nine other parked B-17s were completely destroyed, and five damaged but deemed repairable (over the next few days some never got that chance). Only the two bombers actually in the air survived without damage. Carnage among the precious P-40s was also severe. Virtually all of the 20th Pursuit Squadron was destroyed. The bombing and strafing attack of Clark Field killed fifty-five officers and men and wounded more than one hundred. The attacks cost the Americans twelve B-17s, another five damaged, and twenty P-40Bs.

Iba was attacked by a formation of fifty-four bombers about the same time. Most of its 3rd Fighter Squadron was in process of returning from the failed intercept. Eight P-40Es were destroyed on the ground, five more were shot down in the air, and three had to ditch due to lack of fuel. Along with the planes, the defenders lost the only installed radar set that was functioning at the time. This one action basically wiped out the entire squadron, though a few lucky planes managed to land at Camp O'Donnell a few miles to the east.

Nichols Field received its attention early on December 9. At 3 AM just seven older Japanese navy Type 96 bombers hit the field. Due to the relatively light attack force, damage was limited—but the Americans did lose two B-18s and an O-52, and one hangar of the air depot was heavily damaged. One American was killed and twelve wounded.

Steps were taken on the ninth to reorganize and enhance the anti-aircraft defenses. The 200th Coast Artillery Regiment (AA) at Clark was ordered to dispatch a cadre of 524 officers and men (out of a roster strength of about 1,800) to form a new anti-aircraft regiment. It generally duplicated the two-battalion/eight-battery organization of the 200th. Under the command of the 200th's executive officer, Lt. Col. Harry M. Peck, it was for a short while known simply as the 200th Provisional Coast Artillery Regiment (AA), but was re-designated the 515th Coast Artillery Regiment (AA) on December 20.[22] Fortunately most of the needed equipment was available, for the unit took over the assembled "kit" of anti-aircraft guns, directors, searchlights, and trucks that had been stored in the Manila depots for several months pending the creation of a Philippine Army anti-aircraft regiment. All twelve of the required 3-inch and twenty-three of the twenty-four 37-mm anti-aircraft guns were in storage. Fifteen searchlights were located, along with most of the directors and range-finding equipment, but there were no radar sets or communications gear available. Some trucks were also in storage; in fact, the veterans of the 200th were surprised to even find a couple of their "old" trucks (with the unit's designation still on them) that they had turned in for new ones prior to shipping out to the Philippines.[23]

The equipment for the new regiment was issued on the ninth of December, and by midmorning of the tenth some of it was firing at Japanese aircraft attacking near the docks. Most of the new unit was dispatched for airfield protection at Nichols and Nielson fields. Additionally a battery was sent to cover oil storage facilities on the Pasig River and another got the plush assignment to protect the Manila Hotel. With the quick demise of American airpower in the Philippines, both regiments received new assignments in two weeks to help cover the retreat of Fil-Am forces into the Bataan Peninsula.

One of the more farsighted actions prior to the war was the development of Del Monte Field on the southern island of Mindanao. The decision to build this field occurred at a mid-November Brereton staff meeting. The biggest problem was that none of the war plans, even MacArthur's aggressive defense scenario, advocated deployment of ground troops for any sort of defense for this island. Investing in a major airfield that would not be defended thus might appear as a poor decision. Still, the need to disperse air power in the islands (both for defending from air attack and also to physically have the room to properly service the planes) was critical. Del Monte already had a rudimentary commercial airfield, and the soil there was hard and easy to develop. The decision was made to complete the single strip of a size to handle the big bombers, pending locating a facility somewhere in the Visayan Islands. The interim field at Del Monte proved to be extremely useful.

The pending arrival of a second B-17 bomb group prompted the decision to place it at Del Monte. The 5th Air Base Squadron was selected to go to Del Monte, and within a week after arrival in Manila, under the direction of Maj. Ray T. Elsmore, it was there. Joining the 5th was a detachment of the 7th Matériel Squadron—in all about 250 Air Corps personnel. These men found a usable strip but practically nothing else—no barracks, hangars, shops or other items of an airbase infrastructure. Just a few wooden temporary buildings formed the entire community around the field. The units had only a fraction of their equipment. They went to work using native labor, but understandably not much could be done in the ten days left before war began. Constructing crew quarters and auxiliary dispersed fields were among the unit's first priorities, but no radar or air defenses were available.

It was not long before the first planes arrived. Two full squadrons flew down from Clark on December 5. The 14th Bomb Squadron (under Maj. Emmett O'Donnell Jr.) and 93rd Bomb Squadron (under Maj. Cecil Combs), totaling sixteen B-17s and two B-18s, were soon at the field. The planes were quickly dispersed and camouflaged with branches and palm fronds. The single paint spray-gun was given non-stop use in changing the planes' exterior from shiny aluminum to olive drab. To be sure, this was considered a temporary field assignment. At some point the planes would return to Clark Field where they were to join the rest of its permanently assigned 19th Bomb Group. The 7th Bomb Group of B-17s would be the permanent resident at Del Monte. But on the fifth of December the ground echelon of this group was still on board USS *Republic* in the *Pensacola* convoy, and the bombers of the first two squadrons were in California preparing for their flight.

Staging back to Clark, the sorties flown on the tenth represented the first attacks by the Americans on the enemy. Early on that day a fighter tried to maneuver across the damaged airfield to take off and hit a B-17, causing its loss. At 5:30 AM yet another recon mission to Formosa (now Taiwan) was attempted, and then half an hour later five bombers lifted off for an attack on the enemy landing at Vigan. The attack was coordinated with strafing runs by P-40s and P-35s. One Japanese transport was hit and forced to beach, but two of the P-35s were lost. Other small flights went to a later attack at Vigan and Aparri. At Aparri, Capt. Colin P. Kelly Jr. dropped three 600-pound bombs on what he thought was a Japanese battleship. The crew claimed a hit squarely amidships. Later the plane was credited in the American press with sinking the battleship *Haruna*. It was later found that no battleships were used in this operation. Kelly apparently dropped his bombs on heavy cruiser *Ashigara*. Even then no hits were made. A pair of Japanese fighters jumped the B-17 when nearing Clark to land and with its pilot it was shot down. It was the first B-17 lost in aerial combat of the war. A second B-17 had to be ditched when it ran out of fuel. Starting with just thirty-five bombers, and losing a dozen in the first attack, an attrition rate of three for one day of combat was ominous. At this rate the bomber force would not last long. At the end of the tenth, just nineteen bombers were left.

The errors in descriptions of enemy ships were common. Despite reconnaissance patrolling being one of the missions of the B-17 squadrons, the American crews were not well trained in ship recognition and identity. Even the PBY crews of the Navy made many identification mistakes during the campaign. Likewise, the evaluation of hits from the participating aircraft was problematic. To be sure, there was damage from the December air strikes by B-17s on Japanese convoys and landing attempts. Two minesweepers were sunk and several transports were hit and damaged, a couple needing to be beached to prevent sinking and considered a total loss. Still, the Japanese losses were light from a military standpoint. In fact, they were minimal and no strike prevented or even slowed down an enemy landing.

Also on the tenth the remaining fighter force attempted to intercept very large Japanese formations over Manila heading for Nichols Field and the Cavite naval station. The Japanese bombers were flying high—about 20,000 feet—and were well screened by numerous fighters. A handful of fighters were lost through air combat on both sides, but numerous other American fighters were lost when they ran out of fuel. The bomber formations were not intercepted and generally flew above the range of the few anti-aircraft guns. By the end of this day, only the third of the war, the American fighter strength was reduced to just twenty-two P-40s and eight P-35s. Of the ninety-two P-40Bs and P-40Es in the Philippines at the start of the war, over three-quarters were now lost or damaged beyond repair. No further attempts would be made to try and intercept large enemy forces in the air. The Japanese had achieved air supremacy by the third day of the war. The lack of American planes severely hampered further operations, and certainly had a negative effect on the morale of the ground forces. It also spurred renewed efforts to supply replacements.

For the first couple of days of war the Navy in the Philippines had escaped any big attacks, but that changed on the tenth of December. On that day the heavy bombers of the Japanese navy delivered a major bombing on the facilities at Cavite. At 12:30 PM, fifty-four enemy bombers made an almost perfect attack. Taking their time, the enemy bombers had no fighter opposition. No Army anti-aircraft guns were anywhere near Cavite, though the Marine Corps did man a handful of short-ranged 3-inch guns on the base, and a few of the ships undergoing repair still had guns available for action. The enemy's accuracy was phenomenal, as almost every stick of bombs landed on the facilities or the ships under repair. USS *Bittern* and submarine *Sealion* were total losses and destroyer *Pillsbury* was damaged. One PBY was shot down in the air returning to Sangley, and two at the base were badly shot up. One of the most devastating results of the Cavite attack was the loss of torpedoes. A barge holding forty-eight Mark 14 torpedoes—a full load for both *Sealion* and *Seadragon* under repair—was hit and lost. Altogether 233 torpedoes were lost, though some were later salvaged. For many months subsequently submarines were sent on patrol with less than a full load of torpedoes, and captains were urged to expend them sparingly. The shortage of torpedoes for the submarines of the Asiatic Fleet made the retrieval of the remaining stockpile in the Philippines a significant priority. When submarines were sent into Manila Bay to deliver supplies or extract personnel, they almost always picked up a full load of torpedoes for the voyage out.

On the twelfth the Japanese caught a large section of the Navy's Patrol Wing 10 at Olongapo. A squadron of the Asiatic Fleet's PBYs was at this station following a search for a falsely reported Japanese surface force. All seven of the PBYs were caught on the water and strafed to destruction. While personnel losses were happily light, the lack of safety for these vulnerable patrol craft was now obvious. By now ten PBYs had been destroyed and four had major damage—fully one-half of the total force. On the thirteenth, just five days after the start of war, Patrol Wing 10 with Captain Wagner was ordered to safer waters in the East Indies. A few planes remained to be patched up to try and fly out, and a few others would make a trip specifically to pick up critical naval personnel, but the patrol planes would no longer be routinely based in the Philippines. Altogether the Navy lost fifteen PBYs in the Philippines, and had to leave fourteen pilots and 140 enlisted men of the patrol wing behind when they moved south.[24]

The submarines of the Asiatic Fleet were intended to make any enemy seaborne landing heavily contested, but that did not happen. Admiral Hart had been given the flexibility to deploy his subs as he thought best, with the caveat that they be withdrawn to help defend the Malay Barrier when the right time came. On his own initiative he decided to keep the subs and tenders in Manila Bay during the tensions of late November and early December.[25] At the start of the war there were two subs under repair at Cavite, and nine at or under way to designated war stations. Eighteen were with their tenders in Manila Bay, and within hours of the war message they were departing for patrols.[26] However, after the attack on Cavite the Navy realized both its facilities and ships in the Philippines were too vulnerable. It began its exodus from the Philippines. Tender *Otus* headed south, while *Holland* went initially to Darwin. Much of Patrol Wing 10 departed in mid-December. The short-ranged aircraft of the utility squadron did not have the range to fly out of the Philippines themselves, and continued for a while to serve the needs of the Sixteenth Naval District. However, on January 5 four Japanese A6Ms caught the squadron on the water in Mariveles Harbor. In short order two SOCs, two OS2Us, and a J2F "Duck" were destroyed and left sinking in the harbor's shallow water.

Among the supplies potentially available to the defenders in the Philippines were those contained in ships inadvertently in local waters at the outbreak of war. So sudden was the Japanese seizure of air and naval control that dozens of ships in Manila Harbor just didn't have the time to safely escape. Among these was the Philippine-flag SS *Don Jose.* A relatively large steam freighter of Manila's Madrigal Company, the ship was under charter for a voyage from Vancouver, British Columbia, to Hong Kong. Along with a general cargo was a special shipment of military vehicles. Canada was asked by London in late 1941 to contribute a small reinforcement to help augment the defenses of Hong Kong. It consisted of two second-line battalions. The total contributed force amounted to almost 1,700 men. After a hurried trip by train to Vancouver, the units embarked in the Canadian transport *Awatea*, escorted by the armed merchant cruiser HMCS *Prince Robert.* These ships departed Vancouver on October 27, passing through Manila on November 14.[27]

Unfortunately the motor transport for the battalions arrived in Vancouver too late for inclusion on the ships carrying the troops. Arrangements were made to forward this cargo in *Don Jose*. Altogether 212 vehicles, with spare parts and collateral equipment, accompanied this ship on its November 4 sailing. *Don Jose* arrived safely in Manila Bay on the twelfth.[28] Soon her cargo manifest became known to American military authorities and inquiries were made as to its availability. In relatively quick order the Canadian cabinet approved the transfer of the equipment. Financial arrangements were to be finalized at a future date. MacArthur was informed of the arrangements and moved quickly to add this small but valuable quota of vehicles to his army. Taken over were forty-five Harley Davidson motorcycles, thirty-nine 3-ton trucks, sixty-three ¾-ton vans, two ¾-ton water-tank trucks, fifty-seven universal gun carriers, six Ford sedans, and boxes of parts and tires.[29] No actual weapons or ammunition were with the vehicles. For an army desperately short of motor transport, relying mostly on indifferent appropriated civilian trucks, buses, and cars, this was a real windfall. In particular, the universal carriers (sometimes referred to as "Bren carriers" in British military lingo)—as full-tracked lightly armored vehicles—proved valuable to the defenders. About twenty of them were distributed to the 26th Cavalry and a couple of Philippine divisions, and another twenty went to the provisional tank group.

Pre-war plans had emphasized the priority of the Luzon-based forces over those in the southern islands. Consequently the supply of military equipment to the divisions mobilizing in those southern islands had seriously lagged behind. Little beyond rifles and just a few rounds for practice were supplied to most of the infantry, and no guns had yet been issued to the artillery regiments of the divisions. Efforts were made immediately at the start of the war to address these deficiencies. Two initial journeys were scheduled. Inter-island transport MV *Samal* arrived in Cebu from Manila on December 12 with signal equipment, small-arms ammunition, eight 2.95-inch mountain guns, and 1,600 rounds for the artillery.[30] The guns soon were transferred to the 101st Division in Mindanao, where they saw action against the Japanese. A second such trip was organized using another Compania Maritima vessel, MV *Corregidor.* Put under contract of the U.S. Army, she put into Manila's Pier No. 1 to take on military cargo. Included were another eight 2.95-inch guns and ammunition destined for Panay's 61st Division. A large number of civilian passengers evacuating Manila were allowed to board if they signed a release. The ship departed Manila late on December 16. In the early morning hours of the seventeenth (about 12:40 AM) she hit an American mine in the northern channel off Mariveles. The vessel quickly sank, taking her precious military cargo and the majority of her passengers under. Of the estimated one thousand people on board, only 283 were rescued from the water. Two supply attempts later in the month also failed. The ferry MV *Panay* began a one-trip charter from Manila on December 28 with arms and ammunition for Mindanao, but was caught by Japanese bombers. Little cargo was salvaged. A trip by MV *Mayan* was slightly more successful. In late December she took eight hundred Air Force service personnel and thirty-one tons of cargo from Manila to Mindanao, though damaged and re-routed along the way.

While the southern islands did not hold much in military hardware or supplies, they were valuable as sources of food. For the first couple of months of the war numerous runs were made by the islands' considerable inter-island transport force to bring food to Bataan. For example, the freighter *Princesa* brought in a large load of locally produced food from Cebu City to Corregidor on February 20. Altogether six runs were successfully made from the southern islands to Corregidor in January and February. Some 5,800 tons of rice and other foodstuffs, and four hundred head of livestock, were delivered in this manner—more than had safely arrived via blockade-runners from outside the islands.

After attempts at other bomb missions in mid-December, it was found necessary to move the bombers out of the Philippines altogether. The Japanese finally located Del Monte Field, which apparently they were unaware of prior to the start of the war. Attacks began and the lack of any fighters or even anti-aircraft guns at the Mindanao base meant it was time to get the precious few B-17s away. In several trips between the seventeenth and twentieth of December the bomber force, now reduced to a total of fourteen B-17s and a couple of B-18s flying as transports, moved to a new operating base at Batchelor Field in Australia.

It was obvious to the American command that the major landing on Luzon would be made in Lingayen Gulf. It featured a long expanse of almost 120 miles of open beaches, and fed into a broad valley with few natural obstacles. For years the defenders had prepared plans based on this being a landing site, so it was no surprise when the Japanese appeared with an invasion fleet here on December 22. The real Japanese surprise was the early date, not the place chosen. MacArthur confided to Admiral Hart on the twenty-first that he had not expected the main enemy stab this soon.[31] The North Luzon Force, under General Wainwright, had positioned two of the Philippine Army reserve divisions—the 11th and 21st—along this stretch of coast. Supporting the northern end of what would be the landing beach was Lieutenant Colonel Ganahl's 1st battalion of 75-mm SPMs. The general reserve of the force near Rosario was the elite but understrength Philippine Scout 26th Cavalry Regiment.

The Japanese Fourteenth Army under Lieutenant General Masaharu Homma prepared 43,000 men for the assault. Five previous small landings on Luzon had established supporting air bases for the Japanese army's 5th Air Group. The convoys that carried the main assault left Formosan ports on December 17, and consisted of three sections utilizing seventy-one transports. The Japanese task forces entered Lingayen Gulf on the night of the twenty-first. Picking their way through the shallow and reef-laden gulf, they attempted to find their positions prior to dawn on the twenty-second. Plagued with communications difficulties and poor sea conditions the Japanese anchored too far to the south, but despite this all landings were made successfully. Only at Bauang did Filipino beach defenses exact a heavy toll on the landing Japanese. Very quickly the Japanese consolidated the landing and struck south to Damortis and Rosario. Lieutenant General Homma landed on the twenty-third to be with his troops.

These landings were the moment when the carefully accumulated assets of the American defense forces should have been called into aggressive use. Two weeks after the start of the war, on beaches where landings had been anticipated for years, the planes, subs, tanks, guns, and men of the Far Eastern Army and Asiatic Fleet were meant for this moment—to destroy the major enemy landing on Luzon. For a variety of reasons they failed. In the case of aircraft, losses had been so heavy that even though the war was just two weeks old, air superiority had clearly moved to the Japanese and there simply weren't enough planes left to mount an effective attack on the invasion forces. For the ground forces losses so far had been minimal, but for more complicated reasons the men and equipment of the North Luzon Force were not effectively used and soon were retreating. The Navy's submarine force, long considered the best tool for use against an enemy landing force, was thwarted in obtaining results by a combination of technical issues and a lack of aggressive handling.

For the Air Force's part, the only effective striking force had to be the B-17 bombers. The tactical situation would have been ideal for the A-24 dive-bombers of the 27th Bomb Group, but those planes were on *Meigs* entering the harbor at Brisbane that very day. After an attempted strike at Davao, nine B-17s just happened to be staging back through Del Monte Field. Overnight the bomber crews learned of the Lingayen landings, so prepared to strike the enemy the next day. Just six planes could be serviced overnight as just a single fuel truck was available. Two flights were prepared—six planes for Lingayen and three that could not be completely refueled for another Davao strike. They were ready for take off at 3:15 AM on the twenty-third. Two of the planes for Lingayen had to abort due to engine problems; only four attacked the invasion fleet. Fortunately they evaded the air defense and bombs were dropped, though apparently without effect. After the mission, all the bombers eventually flew back to Australia. On this shuttle mission through Del Monte each plane had racked up almost 4,600 miles of flight. It is a sad commentary on the survivability of the bombers that this maximum effort could put only four bombers over the enemy's main invasion fleet when there were thirty-five such planes available two weeks previous.[32]

The submarine force of the Asiatic Fleet also failed at the moment of greatest need. The force was composed of both older coastal submarines and the much-improved modern fleet boats. Lingayen Gulf was so close to the

Navy's main sub base at Cavite that every sub was fully capable of participating in action against a landing. Since the start of the war submarines had been sent to patrol stations screening Lingayen Gulf—none of the fleet submarines of the Asiatic Fleet were sent against Japan or targets away from the Philippines during these early weeks. There were sixteen fleet submarines spread out in a general pattern off the northwestern Luzon coast, and two coastal submarines actually in the gulf. One definite problem the Americans had was with the lack of aggressiveness of some of its submarine commanders. On a number of occasions the captains did not press attacks. Some of the captains that had been outstanding in their pre-war duties were not the sort of men you wanted when the shooting started. The problem was that you couldn't tell that in advance; it took the war patrols to help sort out the personnel situation. America would produce many outstanding submarine captains by the end of the war, and there already were a few among the participants in this campaign—but not enough.

Only one submarine spotted the approaching Japanese task force. Lt. Cdr. Ray S. Lamb in *Stingray* observed an enemy convoy on December 21. Lamb duly reported it and tried to maneuver for a firing position. However, when the enemy began to move into shallower water Lamb broke off contact and did not press this attack, or attempt another approach. Upon his return to Manila, Lamb was relieved of command. Unfortunately command experience was not the only practical problem with the American submarines. Early in the war technical difficulties with torpedoes were a major handicap to submarine success. The older Mark 10 torpedo carried in the *S*-class boats often ran too deep. Then on the more modern Mark 14 torpedo the new, secret magnetic fuse often malfunctioned and the torpedo would not detonate. It took many months to correctly identify and fix these problems. The problems sabotaged dozens of attacks that otherwise would have been successful.

Six submarines were detailed to immediately approach and attack the enemy convoys. USS *S-38*, *S-40*, *Permit*, *Porpoise*, *Salmon*, and *Saury* were ordered to join *Stingray* and close for attacks. Only a single submarine, venerable old *S-38* under Lt. W. "Moon" Chapple, managed to penetrate close enough to deliver an attack. Chapple was one of the rare aggressive commanders the submarine service needed. Lining up four ships, he fired four torpedoes in rapid succession. All four Mark 10 torpedoes missed, probably due to running too deep. After several more hours he made a determined approach on a single transport and sank *Hoyo Maru*.[33] Freighter *Hoyo Maru* was the only large ship of the main Lingayen invasion force to be lost to American action of any sort. On the twenty-third, submarine *Seal* under Lt. Cdr. K. C. Hurd sank the small 850-ton ship *Hayataka Maru* with two torpedoes just outside the gulf. Totally, of the invasion force just three transports and two minesweepers were lost.

The Army units recently transferred as reinforcements to the Philippines were fully committed to the campaign, and unfortunately all shared the same fate at the end. The aviation engineers of the 803rd Battalion provided outstanding service to the defenders. MacArthur was short of trained engineers, so the aviation engineers wound up being used for all general road, bridge, fortification, and construction work, in addition to maintaining airfields. The Provisional Tank Group was in thc midst of the early campaign fighting. The 192nd was dispatched north from Clark to the invasion area on December 22 to support the North Luzon Force. On its move north, "B" Company of the 192nd Tank Battalion was sent toward the town of Agoo, where late on the twenty-second the first tank-vs.-tank combat of the United States in the Second World War occurred when the platoon ran into a similar force of enemy light tanks. It did not go well for the Americans—the commander's tank was hit and disabled, and the other four tanks were hit, but managed to retreat. Unfortunately all were lost the next day to an air attack. On Christmas Day the 194th was moved up from Manila to join its sister unit in an attempt to delay the Japanese advance. There followed another fifteen days of sharp encounters followed by retreats. In one instance the retreat came too late: on the night of December 26, "D" Company of the 194th (under Capt. Jack Altman) was lost to the enemy when a bridge crossing was attempted too late.[34]

The maneuver campaign was coming to a close: in early January both the American North and South Luzon Forces had skillfully managed to retreat, mostly intact, into the relative safety of the Bataan Peninsula. The tank group provided some of the final screening of the withdrawal before a period of rest and reorganization was allowed. The static lines of the Bataan campaign limited the ability of the remaining tankers to participate much in further fighting. Generally they were employed on beach defense, and held as a reserve against enemy penetrations. Eventually the tanks had to be abandoned when gasoline ran out. The tank group surrendered with the rest of the Bataan garrison on April 9, 1942.

On Christmas Day, Clark Field—where the 19th Bomb Group was still headquartered under O'Donnell's command—was evacuated. The destruction of American airpower in the Philippines during the first days of the war naturally left a considerable number of Air Force personnel with less than full jobs. There were thousands of airmen at airfields with no planes to repair, refuel, arm, or direct. They were evacuated to Bataan, and generally sent to bivouacs in the rear areas of the defended peninsula. A few airmen, mostly pilots and other commanders but also selected technical specialists, were evacuated from Bataan. For example, the 24th Pursuit Group managed during the campaign to get forty-nine of its 165 pilots to relative safety in Australia.[35] One creative solution was to organize airmen without airplanes into provisional units to supplement the defending infantry force—on January 8 the Provisional Air Corps Regiment was formed. The regiment had two battalions. Basically the old air force squadrons retained their personnel but would now function as sort of companies in the new regiment. Initially these units were congregated near Orion on the peninsula's east coast. Morale was good; while not trained or initially expecting to be used as infantry, the men were delighted to be able to do something in their own defense. Several pursuit squadrons were organized a little later into similar units for beach defense in southwestern Bataan. Each man was issued a rifle, and target practice conducted. Machine guns were cannibalized from wrecked planes, and grenades were issued. Total strength varied over the next couple of months, but usually about 1,400 men are credited to the regiment's roster.

The major commanding the 27th Matériel Squadron described the condition of his unit:

> We had 153 men of which an average of about 100 were on the front line near Orion. We had about 44 back at the Philippine Air Depot, some on crash boat crews, some driving half-tracks and tanks. We had on the front line 3 machine guns, of which 2 were water-cooled Brownings and one Marlin machine gun. We had two BARs, the rest of the enlisted men had .30 caliber rifles and officers had 1 pistol each. We had two grenades each, some carried 4 each on patrols. The 1st Battalion had about 34 machine guns. About ⅔ of them were machine guns taken off wrecked airplanes, of the .50-caliber class, and too heavy to carry around. Most of these were in frontline trenches in offsets well concealed and fortified by sand bags and sod.[36]

Col. Irvin E. Doane, an infantry officer from the American 31st Regiment, was assigned as new commander, and some NCOs with long experience in the infantry also were provided the regiment. On the fifteenth of January the unit moved from its assembly area to Orion and then to a position behind the main line of resistance of II Corps. During the final Japanese offensive in early April the provisional regiment fell back when units on either side gave way. It surrendered with the rest of the Bataan force on April 9, 1942.[37]

The Sixteenth Naval District assigned to the port of Manila was not a mobile force that could easily be evacuated or transferred. Rear Adm. Francis W. Rockwell moved himself and his staff to one of Corregidor's Malinta tunnel laterals and continued to supervise local naval operations until he was evacuated later in the campaign. Some specialized personnel, such as the code breakers and technicians of Station Cast, managed to evacuate by aircraft or submarines. Most of the members of the Sixteenth Naval District and the remaining Navy vessels, originally amounting to some 1,600 men, were stranded. As many were now without shops, offices, or jobs, some were organized into a provisional battalion not unlike the Air Force personnel. Cdr. Francis J. Bridget, an officer of PatWing 10, volunteered to organize a naval battalion to provide local security to the Navy facilities and beaches fronting the Mariveles station. Two companies were formed, each incorporating a Marine Corps battery of the 4th Marines at its core and filled out with otherwise unattached naval personnel. Eventually enough small arms were scrounged, though of course the Marines had their weapons. Even two 2.95-inch mountain guns with ammo with a small Philippine Army detachment under Third Lieutenant A. A. Perez, were attached. Other personal gear was lacking, even things like helmets and canteens. The sailors tried to camouflage their white uniforms by dying them with coffee grounds. Instead of khaki, they turned out an off-mustard yellow.

The naval battalion saw extensive action at the end of January. The Japanese attempt to land a force behind American lines in southern Bataan resulted in an action known as the Battle of the Points. Bridget's battalion was about the only force available to contact and contain the Japanese landing force until relieved after five days by the Philippine Scout 57th Infantry. The story goes that a captured Japanese diary recorded the enemy's reaction to encountering the ill-trained, curiously uniformed naval personnel: "Today we have encountered a new kind of enemy. They come walking into the front yelling 'Hey Mac, where the hell are you?'" and "There is a new type of suicide squad, which thrashed about in the jungle, wearing bright-colored uniforms and making plenty of noise."[38] It is difficult today to say whether the diary story is true or not, but the unit did acquire a grudging admiration from the real fighting forces. Following this action the naval battalion was one of the few units transferred to Corregidor in late January. It saw action again as part of the Marine Corps defense on the eastern end of that island before the final capitulation on May 6.[39]

The most notorious unit of the remaining naval force was MTB Squadron 3, still with its six PT boats. After a brief encounter with enemy bombers on the tenth off Cavite, the unit moved its base to Sisiman Cove of Bataan. On the seventeenth the PTs helped rescue the survivors of SS *Corregidor.* On December 18 this Philippine offshore patrol was inducted into U.S. service, but continued to serve with their Filipino crews and commanders. On the twenty-third their base was bombed, and the men and equipment of the little Filipino squadron were moved to Corregidor. On Christmas Eve, as Manila was being evacuated, the boats escorted SS *Muyon* with President Quezon and others of the Filipino government to Corregidor. Both US *PT-33* and *PT-31* were lost in local waters. Also, when Cavite was bombed and abandoned many of the spare engines for the boats were lost. Of course, there was one highly significant mission in March. On the eleventh the four remaining American boats left Corregidor with General MacArthur. Unfortunately when these last boats departed for the southern islands, thirty-two members of the squadron had to be left behind with the other besieged defenders. The boats were all lost by the end of the campaign—they lacked the range to head to safer waters. The original three Filipino patrol boats stayed in Manila Bay until the end.

The end for most of the units sent to the Philippines in the last half of 1941 came with the Fil-Am surrender of Bataan on April 9, 1942. The American forces weakened on little rations and inadequate medical facilities and supplies. Many of the defenders were ill, and all were weakened by the lack of food. On January 5 rations had been cut to one-half, and then to one-third. On March 28 it was estimated that the remaining food (portioned out at ⅓ rations) would have only lasted until April 25. Fuel for vehicles and generators was about gone, though by careful husbanding adequate ammunition supplies still existed. The Japanese had rebuilt their depleted forces and acquired new units after the stalemate actions of February. Launched on April 3, the final offensive took only five days to overcome the American and Filipino forces.

CHAPTER FIFTEEN

Running the Blockade

Immediately after the outbreak of hostilities, attention focused on the resupply and relief of the Philippine forces. During December radiogram messages flew back and forth between Manila and Washington concerning both the needs and the potential methods of delivering supplies. While much of the immediate attention was focused on getting the *Pensacola* convoy men and matériel to the Philippines, there was also discussion about additional follow-on supply.

On December 14 Major General Brereton summarized his immediate needs for the Far Eastern Air Force.[1] By this date, just six days since the start of war, over half of the general's aircraft were already lost. Brereton was adamant that the supply of additional aircraft and specifically .50-caliber ammunition for the fighters was key to the ability to hold the Philippines. However, his estimate of the immediate requirements (available at least by January 1) of ten squadrons of fighters was far beyond the capabilities of the American armed forces. He suggested to MacArthur that Navy aircraft carriers be used to deliver two hundred fighters and fifty dive-bombers. Apparently his suggestion was influenced by a conversation with patrol squadron commander Captain Wagner, who estimated that two carriers just might be able to penetrate the Japanese blockade.

Brereton was especially concerned about the rapid depletion of his existing aircraft ammunition. He described this machine-gun ammunition shortage as his primary "bottleneck." At this date he had only an estimated 800,000 rounds—just slightly more than required for his existing, though depleted, Air Force. By December 15 all the .50-caliber ammunition in the Philippines had been issued from reserve depots to units. The expenditure of ammunition by fighter aircraft was at a level not previously experienced by the Americans. Ten combat missions of a P-40E using its six .50-caliber guns were calculated to use about 250,000 rounds. Brereton's stock would last a total of just thirty-two missions! New aircraft, whether delivered by carrier or flown in via Australia, would need to bring their own ammunition, hopefully also carrying additional supplies. Even then he suggested using air supply to bring in additional rounds. He estimated that the Pan American Boeing clippers could each carry 16,000 rounds. Such planes could also be used to ferry pilots to Australia to pick up the planes soon to be delivered by the *Pensacola* convoy and follow-on shipments.

In the most general terms, the Fil-Am forces on Bataan and Corregidor never did run out of ammunition. The pre-war reserves, combined with some careful efforts at conservation, managed to last the campaign's duration. Some particular items were exhausted. For example, all the 2.95-inch ammunition for the little mountain gun was entirely expended. In this case *all* American reserves of this type of ammunition for an obsolete gun type were in the Philippines, and could not have been replaced even if transportation were found. By February 19 Bataan reported that the ammunition was used up, and the few remaining guns were destroyed. The stock of 3-inch mortar ammunition was also entirely depleted, but the remaining mortars could fire the 81-mm rounds still available.[2] It was a slightly different problem with ammunition for the 3-inch anti-aircraft guns. While the total supply was short (expenditures were much heavier than anticipated pre-war), what were really lacking were fuses. The standard ammunition for the coast artillery 3-inch anti-aircraft gun used a powder train fuse, cut by a fuse-setter on the gun to trigger a detonation at a predetermined altitude. A good portion of the old ammunition proved to be duds, but its most serious limitation was effective height. The maximum altitude the round could be set to was about 25,000 feet—a range the Japanese level bombers could fly above. A newer mechanical fuse was in production that allowed the gun to fire to its maximum vertical height of 32,000 feet. Very few of these rounds had yet arrived in the Philippines, really enough to supply only one four-gun battery on Corregidor. More than additional rounds, what the defenders needed were more of these high-altitude fuses.[3]

The only real possibility to get limited amounts of supplies quickly to the Philippines was by air transport. In the days after the start of the campaign desperate attempts were made to try and use air transportation. On December

18,100,000 rounds of .50-caliber ammunition was released for air transport, roughly half going to the Air Ferrying Command at New York's La Guardia facility and half to Miami for flights on Pan Am clippers to the South Pacific.[4] While this ammunition did get to Australia, it was unloaded there pending a decision on how to get it to the Philippines. Also, the proposal to use aircraft carriers to take relief planes directly to the Philippines was seriously considered by the War Department, but the idea was soon dismissed as impractical. Washington was not convinced that the Japanese blockade was as permeable as MacArthur believed it to be. And ultimately the Navy had to agree to risk its precious aircraft carriers for such a mission, and in late December 1941 that just wasn't going to happen.

Despite pleas from Manila for direct, immediate relief, Washington concentrated on using the supplies on the *Pensacola* convoy for the relief. After all, useful numbers of airplanes, pilots, and ammunition were already nearing Brisbane, where they arrived on December 22. Six days before arrival, supply chief Brig. Gen. Brehon B. Somervell penned a note to new commanding general Brett in Australia with instructions dealing with the relief of American forces in the Philippines. In unequivocal words, Brett was authorized to "do anything that may be required to get supplies, equipment, arms, and ammunition to the United States Army Forces in the Far East." To do that he was expected to obtain local supplies by direct purchasing. Highest priority was to be given to forwarding supplies specifically requested by MacArthur's command. The Australian command was also to manage its own sea transportation requirements to implement these relief efforts. Made available was $10 million to fund the relief effort—primarily to acquire local supplies (mostly foodstuffs) and acquire or contract blockade-runners.

Soon the realities of the tactical situation became obvious. The New Year began with the grim realization in Washington that the effective relief of the Philippines was not possible. A long memo to General Marshall by his War Department staff carefully reviewed the situation.[5] The combat force, of an estimated seven thousand Americans and 30,000 partially trained Filipinos, was running low on water, food, and some munitions. The Japanese had complete control of sea and air and possessed a decisive advantage of initiative on the land. The study concluded that only a major offensive gradually driving north from the Dutch East Indies into Celebes and then Mindanao and finally Luzon could offer effective relief, and the necessary forces available to the Allies in this theatre were not sufficient to achieve this. The sobering conclusions were:

a. That the forces required for the relief of the Philippines cannot be placed in the Far East area within the time available.

b. That allocation to the Far East area of forces necessary to regain control of the Philippines would necessitate an entirely unjustifiable diversion of forces from the principal theatre—the Atlantic.

c. That the greatest effort in the Far East area which can be maintained on strategic grounds is that contemplated by the Chiefs of Staff . . . (hold Malay Barrier, Burma, and Australia, projecting operations to the northward to provide maximum defense in depth).

Recommendations:

a. That operations for the relief of the Philippines be not undertaken.

While this recommendation was of necessity followed, Washington and Brisbane were reluctant to share it in such blunt terms with MacArthur, Quezon, and the fighting forces in the Philippines. To sustain the morale of the fighting troops, communications continued to reassure the fighters that efforts were being undertaken for the relief. However, such memoranda and radiograms were missing details as to plans and specifics. Thus, early in 1942 the supply policy in the Far East subtly changed from actively trying to augment the forces fighting in the Philippines to one of attempting to aid the defenders with small quantities of key items necessary to prolong the defense and improve morale. Washington was adamant about the seriousness of the supply effort. It is apparent in hindsight that they did not fully appreciate the logistical and tactical military problems as well as the locals did. Brigadier General Barnes, who had the fate of being the commander in the hot seat when Washington's attention focused on blockade running, was rebuked and lectured on the urgency of providing the logistical support to the fighting forces still in the Philippines.[6]

Not long after the arrival of American forces in Australia, efforts were made to organize the relief effort. Col. John Robenson, in the *Pensacola* convoy as a casual officer destined for the Philippines, was given command of the American base at Darwin after arriving at that port in early January. On the nineteenth he was directed to go to Java and acquire ships and crews to run the blockade. With six officers, a total clerical staff of one private, and most of the $10 million made available from Marshall's contingency fund, he combed the Indies for supplies and craft to penetrate the blockade. The team arrived by C-39 transport from Darwin. They made a strenuous effort but were not rewarded with much in the way of results. The timely arrival of three American ships provided much of the military supplies needed for the mission.[7] However, locating ships for the onward journey was another matter. Owners were reluctant to take local currency. In fact, Robenson had to be supplied with $2 million in U.S. cash to move the project along. Eight planes left Tampa, Florida, on January 24 with $250,000 each in various denominations of bills. However, the biggest problem was in locating crews willing to risk their lives to run a defenseless ship through enemy-held waters. Most Indonesian and Chinese crewmen refused an offer of any amount of payment.

Several items on the urgently required list were addressed in early January. The continued chronic shortage of .50-caliber ammunition for aircraft (though there weren't many fighters left in the islands) and anti-aircraft guns got immediate attention. MacArthur sent two messages to Washington in early January stating that the supply of anti-aircraft ammunition (both .50-caliber and 3-inch sizes) was so critical that the guns could fire only token bursts at enemy planes. Initially the Navy agreed to use submarines to transport some of this ammunition, but then Admiral Hart objected to tying up one of his few surviving weapons. Marshall had to intervene with Admiral King to re-establish the proposed schedule of submarine trips. After realizing that on the return trips the subs could bring out scarce torpedoes and even the valuable personnel and equipment of the naval radio intercept unit, Hart consented to the plan. The ammunition was available—half a million rounds had arrived in Brisbane on *Meigs*, and more was on board *President Polk* and *Mormacsun*, due to arrive in early January. The Army also loaded the B-17 and LB-30 bombers being sent by both the ferry routes with extra .50-caliber ammunition.

Major General Brereton learned of the Navy's release of a submarine while in Batavia on January 12.[8] Fortunately he was able to meet with Admiral Hart in Surabaya and they agreed to the usage of USS *Seawolf*. In Darwin *Seawolf* offloaded its torpedoes (except those actually in the firing tubes), and was loaded in turn with .50-caliber machine-gun ammunition (675 boxes) and seventy-two 3-inch anti-aircraft rounds. She left on January 16, and arrived on the twenty-seventh, promptly delivering her thirty-seven tons of ammunition. Apparently the .50-caliber ammo was well received, but the garrison thought they had plenty of 3-inch anti-aircraft ammo and were less enthusiastic about this portion. The sub loaded sixteen torpedoes, various submarine parts, and twenty-five men. Actually departing four days earlier, another submarine took supplies to the Philippines, but this one was sent by the Pacific Fleet from Pearl Harbor. USS *Trout* departed Pearl Harbor on January 12 and arrived at Corregidor on February 3. *Trout* delivered 2,750 rounds of 3-inch ammo. She took on torpedoes for the return trip. Additionally much of the financial reserves of the Philippine Commonwealth were put on board in order to move them to safety. Included were 319 gold ingots (thankfully the ship was in need of ballast!), sacks of silver coins, and financial documents. Altogether she took what was equivalent to $12 million in assets. She returned safely to Pearl Harbor on March 3 and transferred her valuable cargo to the cruiser *Richmond* for its next leg to the mainland.

Arriving just one day after *Trout* was *Seadragon*. However, in this instance the submarine was already on war patrol, and was diverted to Corregidor not to take in cargo but solely to transport evacuees and scarce munitions out. She took on torpedoes and key men of the Navy's code-breaking and radio intercept station. Not only were these highly trained specialists of much use to the war effort, their capture and interrogation could be potentially disastrous. The next submarine assignment went to USS *Sargo.* She departed Surabaya on February 5 and took more anti-aircraft shells and one million rounds of .30-caliber ammo to Polloc Harbor, Mindanao. Once in Mindanao she found room to take on twenty-four Army Air Force ground personnel for the return trip. On patrol off Luzon on February 19, USS *Swordfish* was diverted for two pickups of important personnel. In separate trips she took out President Manuel Quezon and his staff, and then returned after a drop-off in Panay to get U.S. High Commissioner Francis B. Sayre and staff and take him to Fremantle.

Early in February Robenson finally managed to acquire the first small freighter. On February 8 Brig. Gen. Patrick J. Hurley arrived in Brisbane. He was to be General Marshall's representative to expedite the movement of supplies to the Philippines. Hurley was an ex–secretary of war: he served in that capacity during the Hoover administration. The blockade-running missions were organized as seen in Table 9.[9]

While Robenson and his team were searching for ships in the Dutch East Indies, efforts to find vessels in Australia were also conducted. Two recent American arrivals, *Coast Farmer* of the *Pensacola* convoy and the independently sailing *Mauna Loa*, which arrived a little later, were offered up for blockade-running purposes. Initial efforts centered on *Coast Farmer*, and her voyage was one of the most successful. The freighter had stayed in Australian waters after

Table 9. Attempted Surface Blockade-Runner Missions to the Philippines, 1942

Ship Characteristics	Place & Date of Departure & Route	Major Cargo Items	Arrival and Fate
Coast Farmer U.S. Flag 3,290 tons 10 knots	Brisbane 2/10/1942 Routed through Torres Strait west of New Guinea	2,500 tons balanced rations 2,000 81-mm mortar rounds 800,000 .30-cal rounds 30,000 .50-cal rounds	Arrived Mindanao 2/19/1942
Florence D. Philippine Flag 2,638 tons	Surabaya 2/13/1942 Routed east past Bali to Bathurst Island, then north	200,000 rations 5,500 3-in AA rounds 1.5 million .30-cal rounds 34,500 .50-cal rounds	Scheduled for Gingoog Bay, Mindanao Sunk off Bathurst 2/19/1942
Don Isidro Philippine Flag 3,261 tons 19 knots	Batavia 2/13/1942 Routed east past Bali to Bathurst Island, then north	225,000 rations (700 tons) 4,500 3-in AA rounds 1.5 million .30-cal rounds 200,000 .50-cal rounds	Scheduled for Gingoog Bay, Mindanao Sunk off Bathurst 2/19/1942
Yochow British Flag 2,810 tons 12 knots	Fremantle 2/17/1942	2,900 tons of rations and ammunition	Mission cancelled Darwin 3/08/1942
Dona Nati Philippine Flag 5,011 tons 15 knots	Brisbane 2/18/1942 Routed east of New Caledonia, then northwest to Philippines	4,000 tons rations 4,000 81-mm mortar rounds 1 million .30-cal rounds 100,000 .50-cal rounds 5,000 grenades	Arrived Cebu 3/06/1942

Table 9. Attempted Surface Blockade-Runner Missions to the Philippines, 1942 (*Continued*)

Ship Characteristics	Place & Date of Departure & Route	Major Cargo Items	Arrival and Fate
Anhui British Flag 3,494 tons 12 knots	Sydney 2/22/42 Routed north to Solomons, then northwest to Philippines	450 tons rations 6,000 81-mm mortar rounds 2.5 million .30-cal rounds Engineer & medical supplies Propaganda leaflets 3 x P-40E fighters	Arrived Cebu 3/10/1942
Taiyuan British Flag 2,994 tons 13 knots	Surabaya 2/26/1942 scheduled, apparently never sailed	1,200 tons rations 10,000 3-in AA rounds	Sunk by Japanese or scuttled before departure about 3/08/42
Hanyang British Flag 2,876 tons	Fremantle 2/28/1942	2,400 tons of rations and ammunition	Mission cancelled Darwin 3/08/1942
Thomas Jefferson U.S. Flag 7,000 tons 12 knots	Honolulu 4/03/1942	3,000 tons rations 700 tons rice, meat, milk 20 tons cigarettes 548 tons ammunition	Scheduled for Corregidor Mission cancelled Midway 4/09/1942
Masaya U.S. Flag 1,174 tons 16 knots	Honolulu About 4/16/1942	600 tons rations 330 tons ammunition 40 tons ordnance, small arms, machine guns Medical supplies	Scheduled for Corregidor Mission recalled 4/21/1942
Matagalpa U.S. Flag 1,174 tons 16 knots	Honolulu About 4/17/1942	Rations Ammunition Anti-tank mines Medical supplies Aviation gasoline	Scheduled for Gingoog Bay, Mindanao Mission recalled 4/21/1942

she unloaded her original commercial cargo. On January 10 she was taken over by the USAFIA command. The original crew remained with the ship with the acceptance of a handsome bonus plan for making the Philippine run. She was loaded in Brisbane and left the port on February 10. Apparently never spotted by the Japanese, she encountered no real difficulty during the nine-day trip.[10] *Coast Farmer*'s cargo was unloaded, and she took on a return load of tin and rubber.

Arrangements were made to put much of the cargo brought by *Coast Farmer* onto smaller, fast inter-island freighters to take from Mindanao to Corregidor. Efforts had already been expended to organize a small fleet of local transports to take food to Luzon from southern islands not yet subject to Japanese occupation. Small freighter *Legaspi* made two successful trips to Corregidor, the last arriving on the sixteenth of February (she was sunk on her third attempt). *Princesa de Cuba* arrived with seven hundred tons of food on the eighteenth. To take the rations and munitions from *Coast Farmer* two other Filipino ships were selected —MV *Elcano* and SS *Lepus*. These ships loaded cargo and then soon moved off toward Corregidor. *Lepus* met a Japanese warship on her journey at the end of February, and had to surrender—crew, ship, and cargo were taken. However, *Elcano* arrived safely at Corregidor on February 26. Her welcomed cargo of 1,100 tons of rations and limited quantities of ammunition was offloaded successfully. As it turns out, these were the only supplies sent from outside the Philippines to successfully reach the defenders of Bataan. While important for morale, the actual quantities carried in by these efforts were negligible. A thousand tons of food lasted the defending garrison only about four days.[11]

The modern Philippine transport MV *Don Isidro* was chartered at Brisbane on January 20. Typical of the arrangement required, compensation (often multiples of regular pay plus a completion bonus), officer and crew insurance, and loss guarantees to the ship owner were needed. The vessel was armed with five .50-caliber guns along with an Army gun crew provided by excess troops who volunteered in Brisbane. After partial loading, *Don Isidro* proceeded to Batavia to take on ammunition for the Philippine run.[12] Both *Florence D.* at Surabaya and *Don Isidro* left on a course set by the Dutch naval authorities east through the Timor Sea and then north through the Banda Sea for Mindanao. Both ships were to go to the northern port of Gingoog, where a commercial lumber company had small dock facilities. By the night of the thirteenth, both ships were on their way. Also carried in the cargoes of these ships were small quantities of canned fruit, jam, jellies, candy, cigarettes, and beer. Robenson even sent a personalized case of the latter as a special gift to fellow cavalry officer Wainwright.[13]

Both ships were traveling on a similar course, not together but relatively close in nautical terms, on February 19. They had the misfortune to be directly in the path of the Japanese aircraft leaving the carriers of the striking force on the way to bomb Darwin. Runner *Florence D.* was spotted first by the enemy. D3A dive-bombers left the Japanese formation and quickly scored two direct hits. The ship caught fire and was abandoned out of control. Three crewmen died in the attack and fourteen were wounded. Just over the horizon the Japanese formation next came across *Don Isidro.* A similar devastating attack resulted in five hits. Seven men of the crew and four Army enlisted men of the gun crew were killed and others, including two officers, were injured. Despite the hits the badly damaged, burning ship managed to return to Bathurst where she was beached. The fire eventually managed to entirely consume the ship and her cargo.[14]

Two other British-owned, Chinese-manned ships were located in Australia and contracted for the blockade run. These ships were in the western Australian port of Fremantle, and took on supplies from *Mormacsun.* The latter ship was purposely routed to this harbor (after unloading her aircraft cargo in Brisbane) just for this mission. SS *Hanyang* and *Yuchow* were small freighters of the British-owned Chinese Navigation Company. They departed separately for northern Australia on or before the middle of February. *Yuchow* got away on the seventeenth, but developed engine problems on her journey north. When she reached Darwin the crew decided they would go no farther. In fact, there was some speculation that the reported engine problem was crew-induced. In any event, there was no crew to take the ship farther. Freighter *Hanyang* left Fremantle about the twenty-eighth of February and put into Darwin on March 8. Even though not having the engine-damage excuse, the Chinese crew similarly refused to continue with the voyage. Left without alternatives, the ships were unloaded in Darwin and returned to their owners, both supply missions being abandoned.

Meanwhile, another two ships were being prepared in Australia. *Dona Nati* was a Philippine 5,011-ton freighter. Cargo was partially loaded at three ports, Melbourne, Sydney, and Brisbane, before departure could be made on February 18, the day before the loss of the two other blockade-runners off Darwin. *Dona Nati* was assigned a routing taking her far to the east around the Solomon Islands before heading to Cebu City. She did make the journey safely, arriving on March 6, offloading in just three days, and scurrying back on a similar course to Australia.[15] Following closely on this schedule was SS *Anhui*, another British-owned freighter chartered for the voyage. One unusual item in the manifest was a large quantity of propaganda leaflets. As deck loading, three crated P-40Es recently delivered in Australia by *Mormacsun* were carried. This shipment represented the only successful attempt at sending aircraft to the Philippines by ship once the war began. When close to Cebu, she ran aground off Bohol Island (just fifty miles from her destination). Fortunately local forces were able to offload the crated airplanes onto a barge and hide them in a mangrove swamp, and a tug sent from Cebu soon got the ship sailing again. The runner arrived at Cebu on the night of March 10–11.[16] Quickly unloaded, the ship departed on with a number of U.S. Navy personnel taking advantage of the transportation. On the return trip she was attacked by aircraft off Bougainville, but no hits were scored and she made it safely back to Sydney in early April.

The team in Java eventually located one final ship. The small Chinese freighter *Taiyuan* was in Surabaya with a British shipping firm. This vessel had actually been in Manila Harbor at the start of the war and was lightly damaged there in early December. She had sailed to Surabaya and loaded a cargo of sugar bound for Calcutta. At this point her Chinese crew mutinied (fearing the imminent loss of the ship), and her master and several other officers took refuge in drink. The ship was obtained by Robenson, but it took a while to recruit an entirely new crew and promote the remaining two officers to take charge. By this time Surabaya was under regular Japanese air attack, and only with hard work and the hiring of dock labor from Madera Island was it possible to ready the ship. Apparently *Taiyuan* never made it out of Surabaya. She was originally scheduled to depart on February 26, but it seems virtually all these missions were somewhat delayed, and she was scuttled when the Japanese captured the port. That happened on March 2.

Unfortunately, in the Philippines the ammunition shortage was substantially relieved by the loss of fighter aircraft. On the other hand, the requirements grew for certain essential ordnance equipment and parts. Most of these were relatively light in weight and size, but their supply could restore an otherwise sidelined weapon. In late January MacArthur supplied a detailed list of required items to Washington, where they were favorably considered. Those items immediately available were sent to Eastern Airlines at the Philadelphia airport for transfer by air to the Panama Canal Zone. From there the cargo would await the next available ship convoy. Only amounting to about 2,500 pounds, the list included quantities of some eighty-four individual items. Included were an AA gun director, spare parts for other directors, height finders, and equilibrators.

The next big supply crisis, and one that would never be satisfied, was food. General MacArthur's plan to defend Luzon in depth had led him to disperse supplies throughout Luzon. While some of the recent shipments of food and fuel (three thousand tons of tinned meat and fish, 100,000 canned "C" rations, plus 300,000 gallons of gasoline in drums) were stored in Bataan; much else was not. Much of the subsistence supplies intended for a lengthy defense were distributed at widely spaced depots throughout Luzon. While heroic and partially successful attempts were made to ship as much as possible to the new perimeter in late December, many other stocks were abandoned and lost. Also, the number of soldiers actually in Bataan was much greater than anticipated. By early February the Far Eastern command began to urgently request additional food supplies. The variety requested was impressive: corned beef, corned beef hash, coffee, canned salmon, tuna and sardines, canned fruits, flour, fresh onions, fresh potatoes, canned tomatoes, dried beans, pepper, salt, baking powder, margarine, polished rice, milled rice, condensed milk, granulated sugar, jam, vinegar, and flavoring extracts. Only when satisfied would other priorities be shipped (mostly ammunition and certain weapons and ordnance parts).

While acquisition of foodstuffs was left to the Australian command to secure locally, the ammunition and ordnance items received the same prompt attention the earlier ordnance parts request had. As soon as the eleventh a reply was sent to MacArthur asserting that many of the items were already on the way. On board *Hawaiian Merchant* sailing January 31 were the anti-aircraft fuses and the 37-mm anti-tank rounds. Hand grenades and 60-mm mortar rounds were in the process of being loaded. Later in the month anti-tank mines, complete 81-mm mortars, and rifle extractors would be made available.[17] Unfortunately this was an order that had to be duplicated—an earlier air shipment of extractors was mistakenly delivered to the Chinese. Several days later the Ordnance Department received a new request for technical supplies. Desired in the Philippines were numerous mainsprings for wristwatches, artillery gas-check pads, one thousand chests for water-cooled machine guns, one thousand wrenches, 25,000 ammunition belts, four thousand rifle and machine-gun cleaning rods, and a like number of cleaning brushes.[18] All of this was available in department inventory, and sent to San Francisco for shipping on the next transport. Unfortunately the supply line was too long. Not until March did most of this arrive, at a time when the Japanese advance into the Dutch East Indies made further transshipment by surface ship almost impossible.

The most valuable cargo coming *out* of the Philippines during March was General MacArthur and his family and staff. Since early January of 1942 Washington had discussed the need to eventually evacuate the general. Everything else aside, the cost to national morale of losing the service of its most popular general, one with actual experience fighting the Japanese, was simply too high. MacArthur himself did not desire to leave, he wished to remain and suffer the same fate as the Army and nation he had dedicated himself to. Only by using the logic that he was needed to organize the relief efforts in Australia (in fact years from being anywhere near ready) was his evacuation made possible. MacArthur was given the flexibility to select the exact date and method of departure, and he eventually decided to use the four remaining PT boats of Bulkeley's command. After departing Manila Bay at night the boats would hide out during the day, and then complete the voyage to Cagayan in Mindanao on the second night. From there the party was to transfer to Del Monte Field for the journey on by ferrying bombers flown in especially for this pickup. On schedule, *PT-41* picked up the general and his family at the north dock on Corregidor. The other three PT boats (*PT-32*, *PT-34*, and *PT-35*) were loaded at Bataan. The passengers all reached Mindanao safely, though having to squeeze onto just three boats when one was delayed during the voyage. From Mindanao just one plane (of the seven sent) actually made the mission and carried out the general and his family as planned. The rest of the staff subsequently was able to depart on a second plane.

The submarine supply and evacuation efforts continued into March and April of 1942. USS *Permit* while on patrol received orders to rendezvous off Corregidor on the night of March 15–16 to pick up an "important party" for evacuation. With MacArthur's decision to use PT boats, *Permit* continued her mission and was able to find room for forty passengers, mostly additional members of the Navy radio intercept organization.[19] *Seadragon* was tapped for a second special mission to Manila Bay. Leaving Fremantle on March 18 for a war patrol, she was diverted to Cebu to take on cargo and arrived successfully at Corregidor on April 8. She unloaded thirty tons of food, and took on twenty-three passengers. Similarly *Snapper* departed Fremantle on a war patrol and was ordered on the thirty-first to Cebu to load forty-six tons of food (mostly rice and flour in 100-pound sacks) to take to Corregidor. She arrived at Cebu on April 4 and unloaded four torpedoes and 185 rounds of 3-inch ammo to make room for the food. *Snapper* followed *Seadragon* closely, but arrived on April 9. In just an hour and a half at night she delivered a little under half her cargo—twenty tons—and took twenty-seven passengers in turn.[20]

Even while the blockade-running effort from Australia and the East Indies was reaching its culmination, MacArthur urgently proposed sending relief supplies directly from the United States. He used the occasion of the safe arrival of *Coast Farmer* in Mindanao on February 19 to make his point. He continued to describe the enemy's coverage as thin, and remained optimistic that the enemy's blockade was not complete. Additionally he made the point that the Australian command did not have the resources at their disposal to properly organize the relief. Many critical supplies were simply not available in Australia. This command was in the midst of its own desperate combat, and the support of the Philippine forces was naturally taking a back seat.[21] MacArthur obviously thought that Washington's direct control of the effort would bring a better sense of urgency and perhaps more resources.

Brigadier General Somervell agreed that direct supply from the continental United States was both practical and desirable. The War Department had identified seven potential ships for blockade running as early as January 12. On February 22 it was reported that they had procured three fast banana boats. Six decommissioned First World War destroyers had been sold to the United Fruit Company in the early 1930s. They were totally disarmed, and even provided without engines. United Fruit had four of them equipped with diesel motors providing a top speed of about sixteen knots and placed them in service to make the fast trip from Central America to American ports. One vessel was lost in 1933; the remaining three were chartered to the Army. One ship (MV *Masaya*, ex–USS *Dale*) was almost immediately available, and the other two (MV *Teapa*, ex–USS *Putnam*, and MV *Matagalpa*, ex–USS *Osbourne*) required repairs that delayed their availability until about March 15. The initial plan was to load each with a balanced cargo and send them from New Orleans to Panama and then Hawaii prior to a direct run to Mindanao.[22]

This plan was to be carried forward independently of the blockade-running effort being mounted by the Australian command.[23] MacArthur was contacted to obtain more precise estimates of his requirements, and efforts in New Orleans moved ahead rapidly to prepare the ships and get cargo shipped there from various supply depots. As usual, the estimate of timeliness proved inaccurate. Numerous delays plagued the effort, most notably repairing the engines, assembling the cargoes, and obtaining the crews. The first ship ready—*Masaya*—left New Orleans on March 2. After a delay for repairs in Los Angeles, she and *Matagalpa* made it to Honolulu for refueling, while *Teapa* left New Orleans on March 18 and was not far behind. The events of early April, specifically the surrender in Bataan, cast a dark shadow on this attempt. General MacArthur himself advised that further efforts were useless, but Washington persevered. *Masaya* left Hawaii for Corregidor, while *Matagalpa* was sent with a destination of Gingoog. Both ships were recalled on April 21 before they passed Midway into enemy waters. While second thoughts revived the schedule at the end of the month, the final collapse of American resistance on Corregidor obviously halted the plan. The two ships at sea were diverted to Australia; eventually they served as coastal steamers in Alaska.[24]

As the campaign advanced in Bataan and Corregidor, one final category of supplies became urgent for the defenders—medical supplies. On March 27 Marshall radioed Australia to request that energetic steps be taken to supply medicine in the next attempted blockade run. Required were 3 million tablets of quinine sulfate for malaria. In fact, the need was so urgent that it was suggested they be sent by airplane. Additionally sulfa drugs, atrabine, vitamin supplements, and topical skin preparations were required. Once bombers had taken the medicine to Mindanao, it was suggested that the three P-40s recently delivered by *Anhui* be used to take them on to Corregidor. Also, a Navy submarine would be requisitioned to take additional supplies as follow-on.

The top command in the Philippines eventually realized that substantial relief or reinforcement was not going to occur. In his memoirs, General MacArthur's aide Sid Huff stated that it was understood that the assignment was to hold out on Bataan and Corregidor until help arrived. Just when doubt began on the "until help arrived" qualifier was difficult to say. Despite optimistic messages from Washington, MacArthur must have soon realized what was likely to happen.[25] That cannot be said of the average combat soldier or his immediate line commanders. One of the most tragic aspects of this campaign was the feeling of abandonment by the troops. Of course, the central premise of the pre-war plans had been the strategy of holding Manila Bay until the Navy could fight its way to the relief of the defending forces. Knowledge of this element of the plan was widespread. It must have occurred to many soldiers, aware of the increased tempo of shipments in the preceding six months, that the supplies and troops assembled in San Francisco had to be going somewhere. Publicly the War Department and the administration talked of the efforts under way to take the war to the Japanese and provide help to the men fighting in the Far East. Rumors were rampant among the Filipino-American forces that supply convoys were imminent—just entering Manila Bay, just over the horizon, or even already arrived at the docks. And in every case these raised hopes were crushed.

Another highly interested participant in the dialogue about relief was President Quezon. At times during the campaign (and probably rightly so) this talented politician became highly frustrated with the actions of his protecting ally. Quezon had tried to do his best to prepare his nation for its defense. For a small economy, very large expenditures had been made for defense, and he had hired America's premier soldier as military adviser. In his mind this war was between Japan and the United States, and the Philippines could be characterized as an unfortunate host to one of the combatants. This logic has some justification for the Philippines, probably more than Malaya or the Dutch East Indies, which had key resources the Japanese needed. While generally not wavering in his ardent support of the fighting forces, the Philippine president was highly perplexed over the lack of effective relief. After listening to a radio speech by Roosevelt that reiterated the Germany-first strategy (and in fact didn't even mention the forces or situation in the Philippines), Quezon sent a direct radiogram to Roosevelt on January 22, 1942. Using tact, he stated: "It seemed Washington does not realize our situation." The American president strangely responded with more assurances. Essentially Quezon was told that while the date of arrival of help was uncertain, ships had been loaded and sent to Manila with necessary supplies. Furthermore, a continuous flow of fighters was crossing the Pacific.[26] Only if one stretches the truth—that the ships and fighters were heading to Australia and that it was hoped that someday they might be used in a campaign to fight the way back to the Philippines—could this even remotely resemble the truth. The continued support and morale of the (mostly Filipino) fighting troops in Bataan was very important to Allied plans in the western Pacific, but one has to wonder about where the line was between encouragement and outright deception.

An interesting story about MacArthur's sometimes sardonic humor is reflective of the situation. On February 13 the Japanese submarine *I-17* surfaced in the Santa Barbara channel of southern California. Seventeen rounds were fired from the sub's deck gun at the oil facilities near Goleta, California. A little damage was done and one man was wounded, but the psychological impact of an attack on the continental United States was much greater. News flowed about the event in the American press and on radio. General MacArthur was preparing for a local Philippine radio speech when he remembered hearing about the incident. After a slight revision by his speechwriter, the message was issued with the statement that the Filipino-American forces had heard about the unfortunate California attack, but help would be sent from the Philippines if the local defenders could manage to hold out for just a little longer.[27] Even the Japanese seemed to be aware of the disappointed hopes of relief. One headquarters officer recorded: "The damned Nips have got a new propaganda program that does not help our morale any. KZRH in Manila plays American songs to American soldiers on Bataan and Corregidor at 2145 hours every night. Theme song 'Ships that never come in' followed by popular records."[28]

Meanwhile, the shipping efforts were resulting in a considerable accumulation of supplies at Cebu. This port was one of the more important cities of the Philippines outside of Luzon. A regional American quartermaster depot had been located here pre-war to store and supply the troops of the Visayan-Mindanao Force. It became the nucleus for relief efforts as the closest well-equipped port to Corregidor and Luzon, which were just four hundred miles to the north. The Japanese did not invade Cebu until April 10, though of course the enemy could bomb the city and observe coastal traffic from the air and sea at will. The cargo from the private steamship SS *John Lykes*, including a considerable quantity of food, had been offloaded at Cebu prior to the ship's departure. Several successful missions early in the campaign ran food from Cebu to Bataan. Two of the three blockade-runners that made it safely from Australia docked at Cebu. Cargo from *Anhui* and *Dona Nati* was dispersed in safe locales pending transshipment to Corregidor.

A final attempt to push through relief stores was planned for April 1, 1942. Eight small ships and one tanker were loaded and laying to either in Cebu or Iloilo waiting to make the run to Corregidor. Cover was to be provided by a carefully planned bombing and escort mission. Using Mindanao fields, the bombers were to temporarily neutralize Japanese airfields on the night of April 1–2. The planes would remain to fly additional ship escort missions. The air portion of this plan was entrusted to Maj. Gen. Ralph Royce, and consequently it was known as the "Royce Mission." He opted to use ten newly arrived twin-engine B-25s and three B-17s. Of course, escorting fighters didn't have the range to fly to the Philippines, so an effort was made to concentrate all the remaining fighter strength in the islands. Fortunately the three recently arrived P-40Es from *Anhui* made it from Bohol to Butuan Bay, sixty-five miles northwest of Del Monte. After the planes were taken off the barge and moved to the inland air base, seventy-five mechanics of the 19th Bomb Group and 440th Ordnance Company hurriedly completed their assembly at the new Maramag Field in central Mindanao. These three planes joined one older P-40 already present. Pilots for these planes were flown south from Bataan. Originally it was scheduled to use the four P-40s available to strafe patrolling Japanese ships and then fly escort to the merchantmen heading north. Finally all the surviving fighters would concentrate on the Bataan airfields. Even the last two surviving U.S. PT boats in Mindanao would participate in the escorting of the supply ships. Considerable secrecy was attempted; the Bataan pilots were not told of the mission until the very last minute.[29]

Eleven B-25Cs (their combat debut in this theatre) of the 3rd Bombardment Group from Charters Towers went to Brisbane to pick up special bomb bay fuel tanks on April 9. Assembled on the eleventh at Darwin were these eleven planes and three available B-17s of the 40th Bomb Squadron. One B-25 aborted the mission, but the remaining ten planes arrived at Del Monte after a twelve-hour flight. On April 12 and 13 a series of attacks was made on Cebu, Davao, and even Nichols Field by the bombers. They claimed four enemy transports and another ten damaged, and lost just a single B-17 by a bombing attack on the runway at Del Monte. The twelve surviving airplanes left on the morning of April 14. Unfortunately the Japanese moved more quickly than the Americans. The bombing campaign was delayed past the Japanese invasion of Cebu on the tenth and Iloilo on the twelfth. All airplanes were evacuated from Cebu on the ninth as the invasion forces approached. The Americans only had two hundred combined Filipino and American soldiers on Cebu Island, and they had to take to the mountains, destroying what they could at the supply depot. All the readied relief ships and their supplies were sunk to prevent them from falling into enemy hands.[30]

One final attempt at a direct surface ship run to Corregidor should be mentioned. Alarmed at the diminishing food situation in Bataan, on March 29 General Marshall requested Lieutenant General Emmons of the Hawaiian Department to secure a ship for immediate duty. Emmons soon located the Navy-chartered *Thomas Jefferson.* Both Eisenhower and Somervell prevailed on Admiral King to release the ship, which he did. A special new Navy crew was selected, headed by Lt. Cdr. J. W. Baldwin, USNR. For security, the ship was rigged with trinitrotoluene (TNT) demolition charges for scuttling if she were about to fall into enemy hands. Loading was completed by the end of the day on April 2, just four days since Marshall's directive to Emmons. After the last-minute mounting of a pair of 20-mm anti-aircraft guns and ammunition, the ship departed Pier 28 in Honolulu about noon on the third. Her sealed orders called for a refueling at Midway and then the long journey across the Pacific. Pacific Fleet submarine USS *Drum* would precede *Thomas Jefferson* by a day, not as escort but as a detector of enemy presence. On the ninth the ship reached Midway safely, but once there received the news of the surrender of the Bataan garrison. The mission was cancelled, and much of the fuel oil and some of the supplies were conveniently added to the Midway garrison before the freighter returned to Hawaii.[31]

Up until the end the Navy still attempted to use submarines to get emergency supplies to the defenders. The last submarine reaching Corregidor was USS *Spearfish*. While carrying only mail and documents for the garrison, the ship's arrival on May 3 allowed it to take out twenty-seven passengers. Three other submarines were at sea on their way to Corregidor with additional supplies—but the missions were aborted when Corregidor surrendered, and the submarines resumed normal patrols. The actual quantity of matériel delivered was insignificant in military terms, but the impact on morale was probably worth the temporary diversion of these ships. Altogether the submarines brought in fifty-three tons of food, 3,500 rounds of 3-inch anti-aircraft ammunition, thirty-seven tons of .50-caliber and 1 million rounds of .30-caliber ammunition, 30,000 gallons of diesel fuel, and smaller quantities of medicine, mail, and specialty radio and ordnance equipment. They evacuated 185 people that would have otherwise been incarcerated as prisoners of war.[32]

And finally another small quantity of supplies arrived by aircraft. Del Monte Field in Mindanao remained within range of Australia throughout the campaign, at least for the long-range B-17 and B-24/LB-30 types. Late in the campaign the journey became more hazardous as the Japanese discovered the location of the field and consolidated their air coverage over the island. Still, a sporadic sort of air service existed between Del Monte and Australia through much of the campaign. Small amounts of freight—often medical supplies and small ammunition items—were taken into Mindanao and essential personnel taken out. A flight of two bombers was made on January 29. They completed the mission successfully and delivered ten thousand morphine doses, 148 ampoules of gangrene antitoxin, and some machine-gun ammunition. In early February another two planes brought in more medicine, including 600,000 quinine and 50,000 atrabine tablets, more small-arms ammunition, and Prestone coolant for the remaining P-40s.[33]

The flights continued into March and April. On March 27 three B-17s left carrying 1 million quinine tablets, surgical instruments, two P-40 propellers, and 6,200 pounds of the scarce radio tubes and electrical supplies requested by MacArthur. As return cargo the planes carried Philippine president Quezon and his staff and family to Australia.[34]

CHAPTER SIXTEEN
Airplanes for ABDA

By January 1, 1942 only eight of the original twenty-eight PBYs of PatWing 10 were left. A few new PBYs were virtually the only naval reinforcements the Asiatic Fleet received from the start of the war until the conclusion of the Java campaign. Eleven PBYs of VP-22 under Lt. Cdr. Frank O'Beirne were flown out from Oahu to the East Indies, along with a handful of recently transferred Dutch planes in need of crews. The American planes were the new PBY-5s, capable of operations from both land and water, though still highly vulnerable to enemy fighters. They left Hawaii on January 3, and arrived at Townsville on the eighth. From there they went to Darwin on January 11. Attrition dogged these few planes. Four were lost in the February Darwin attack, and two others at Broome in early March. Additionally, the Navy acquired five other PBYs from a less anticipated source. In early January the Dutch found they could not man all the PBYs they had acquired, and five of the planes from training schools and reserves were lent to the Americans. However, they lasted no longer than the planes arriving from Oahu.

The surviving B-17s had quit the Philippines as a permanent base by the twentieth of December. By Christmas Del Monte was abandoned even as a bomber staging base, except for runs by individual planes. Several subsequent small attacks were launched from the new base at Batchelor Field near Port Darwin in late December. Very quickly it was apparent that the bomber base in Australia was just too far from the action in the Dutch East Indies. After barely a week of operations, the remaining aircraft of the 19th Bomb Group transferred to Java. Ten surviving B-17s flew to Singosari Airfield five miles northwest of the town of Malang, Java. Headquarters for the Far Eastern

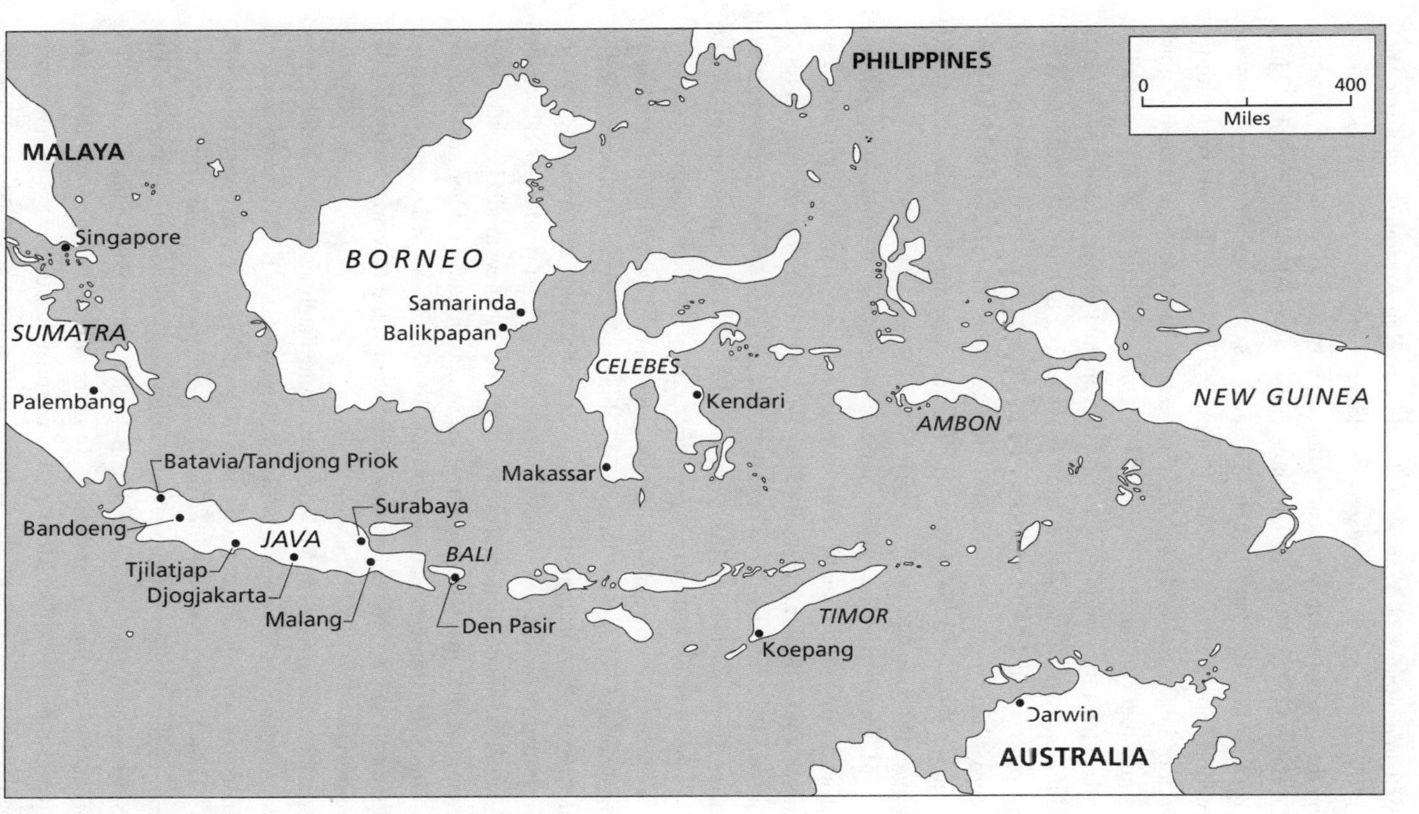

Map 4. Dutch East Indies Features and American Bases, 1942

Air Force under Col. Francis M. Brady stayed in Australia until it relocated on the fourteenth of January to Bandoeng. On January 4 eight B-17s staging through Samarinda in eastern Borneo surprised a Japanese surface force. Coming in at 22,000 feet each plane carried four 600-pound bombs. Three Japanese heavy cruisers, three light cruisers, and a seaplane tender were anchored in Malalag Bay in the Philippine's Davao Gulf. One bomb hit the deck of heavy cruiser *Myoko*. This was one of the most damaging hits made by an American bomber in the campaign. On board, thirty-five were killed and twenty-nine wounded. A second raid on the Japanese landing at Davao in Mindanao was mounted with eight B-17s staging through Kendari. Mechanical problems plagued the flight, just five bombers reached the target, and poor visibility prevented accurate bombing. Other small bombing flights were attempted—one on the eleventh on Tarakan, and another on the fifteenth to Sungei Patani in Malaya.

Meantime the first of the bombers dispatched through both the new African and South Pacific ferry routes began to arrive in the Dutch East Indies. Four LB-30s and four B-17s arrived at Malang from the African route, and two B-17s came in from the South Pacific. This was the first appearance in an American combat theatre of the LB-30. This export version of the B-24 bomber proved to have excellent range and bomb-carrying capacity, but these early versions were under-armed and found to be unsuitable for combat conditions. A few were used in bombing formations, but even in the plane-starved environment of the Americans in Java, they were mostly used for transport missions. The new B-17s were the latest-produced "E" version. As such they had much-improved armament. The new model boasted a dorsal and ventral machine-gun turret, as well as dual .50-caliber guns in a tail position. The rear installation proved to be particularly well received, as a tail approach was a favored Japanese tactic against the otherwise well-defended bomber.

The new arrivals at Malang were immediately used in a bombing mission on January 16. That day three LB-30s and two B-17s headed out for a disastrous strike in Borneo; only one of each type of plane returned to base. The new bomber crews of the 7th Group did not yet have the combat experience of their brethren in the 19th, and lessons were learned the hard way. On the nineteenth a large force of nine B-17s left Malang; three had to turn back because of mechanical problems, but six bombed Jolo Island and landed for an overnight stay at Del Monte. On the return they brought out twenty-three badly needed officers of the group who had been stranded in Mindanao.

Attrition of the bomber force roughly equaled the pace of new arrivals—it seemed that there were rarely more than ten heavy bombers available for a mission. Between January 22 and February 3, fifteen bomb missions were made. While the B-17s were tough planes capable of sustaining a tremendous amount of damage, the odds were overwhelming and losses continued. Also, the planes were being used at a pace that was quickly wearing them out. With no chance for major depot overhauls, the engines and other equipment were being pushed beyond their maintenance tolerance. Even the new planes often had traveled over 12,000 miles with minimal mechanical attention.

The severe losses in the early days of the Philippine campaign led to high hopes that the aircraft actually in transit could be of immediate aid to the defenders. The *Pensacola* convoy transported four otherwise unrelated Air Force assets. The majority of the troops being taken to the Philippines belonged to the command, ground, and service echelons of the 7th Bomb Group. Additionally, forty-eight pilots were transported to fill out the requirements of the 35th Pursuit Group. And then there were two separate shipments of the aircraft themselves. The entire consignment of fifty-two A-24 "Banshee" dive-bombers destined for the three light bombing squadrons of the 27th Bomb Group and finally eighteen P-40E fighters were included. The trained air personnel and the seventy modern planes would have been a substantial contribution to the air capabilities in the Philippines.

Unlike most of the transfers of Army ground units, the complexities of equipment and manpower often resulted in air units being split up during transport. The shipments included in *Pensacola* convoy were good examples of this. At that time, the appraisal of Air Force needs for the defense of the Philippine Islands envisioned five complete Air Force groups. Two (the 19th Bombardment Group and the 24th Pursuit Group) were basically fully equipped and manned by the start of hostilities. The outbreak of war interrupted the transportation of the other three groups. The second B-17 heavy bombardment group, the 7th, was just starting its relocation. The first aircraft had departed California for Hawaii on December 6. The majority of the ground personnel for this unit were on USS *Republic* at sea. The light bombardment group (the 27th) already had sent its ground echelon to the Philippine Islands in November, but the aircraft were on USAT *Meigs*. Finally, the 35th Pursuit Group had already dispatched part of both its personnel and aircraft to Manila also in November, but forty-eight pilots were in *Republic* and eighteen fighters were on *Bloemfontein.* An additional squadron (the 70th), the group's headquarters, and more aircraft were supposed to follow in early December.

The long separation of the aircraft and men of the 27th Group attracted questions and criticism in later analysis of the campaign. As early as December 3 General Marshall himself inquired why the shipments were separated so long. The reply blamed the selection of particular ships—*Meigs* had the cargo capacity but was just a ten-knot ship, while *Coolidge* had the troop accommodations but did twenty-one knots and did not need a Hawaiian stopover. In peacetime the separation of the two elements might have been awkward but only of a temporary nature. Wartime was another matter.

The Air Force ground personnel in the *Pensacola* convoy were mainly assigned to the ground echelon of the 7th Bomb Group headquarters. Upon arrival in Brisbane, men of the 7th Group and 8th Matériel Squadron immediately began the assembly of the knocked-down aircraft carried in the convoy. While the planes being assembled were not the type the unit had been trained on or was designed to support, fortunately both of these outfits were longtime service units containing many professional technicians. They rose to the occasion, putting in long hours and essentially working around the clock. In a little over a week, on the first of January, it was reported that twenty-six dive-bombers and two fighters were ready to fly. By January 9 all eighteen P-40s were assembled. However, only seventeen were flyable: one was found to have been shipped without its tail rudder assembly.

Initially American fighting forces were quartered at Brisbane's Ascot and Doomben racetracks. Royal Australian Air Force stations at Archerfield and Amberley were made available for the assembly of the convoy's aircraft. Archerfield was utilized for the fighter aircraft, Amberley for the bombers. On the twenty-eighth of December a training program was also undertaken at these stations. With the exception of a few pilots flown out of the Philippines to meet "their" aircraft in Brisbane, the aircrew on the convoy was woefully short of the required air time in these aircraft. It made sense to get in additional hours while awaiting completion and forward movement of the fighting squadrons, though as we'll see the skill level of most of these pilots was still below acceptable standards. Tragically, for all the effort made to get these planes into combat, many more were lost due to pilot inexperience than enemy action.[1]

The most significant problem encountered was the lack of several key parts for the aircraft being assembled. The P-40s were mostly intact in terms of mechanical parts (with the single exception mentioned above). However, the planes were shipped without a supply of Prestone coolant. The Allison inline engines on this aircraft had a liquid cooling system requiring ethylene glycol. For the original shipment plan this would not have been a problem, as there was an adequate supply of coolant to cover needs in the Philippine Islands where the airplanes were intended. Australia, however, was a different matter. No readily available supply was located. Only by thoroughly canvassing the country and obtaining virtually all the commercial supply was enough coolant located to allow the first flight north of the newly assembled P-40s. In fact, at one point early in the assembly process the coolant had to be drained from each plane to allow its use by the next when the engines were tested. Eventually adequate supplies were sent to Australia, but initially this issue was a major factor in the delay of making these aircraft available.[2]

Far more serious was the list of critical missing parts for the light bombers of the 27th Bomb Group. Upon assembly it was found that some items were just plain missing. Only twenty-four of the required 104 (two per plane) trigger motors were present. Each trigger motor served one of the forward-firing .50-caliber machine guns of the A-24 bomber. Even worse, all of the solenoids for the machine guns were also missing. Apparently the solenoids were in boxes nailed to the inside of the wooden crates holding the aircraft, and the inexperienced assembly crews inadvertently destroyed them when the crates were thrown on a trash pile and burned. There was even a problem with the rear observer's machine-gun mounts—they were defective and tended to break upon first firing. The planes had apparently been extensively used in the recently concluded General Headquarters' maneuvers. Some of the tires were heavily worn, and the radial engines proved worn-out and in need of servicing. Admittedly it is difficult to understand today precisely why this situation developed. Yes, it was peacetime when the aircraft were shipped—and it was assumed that there would be time and skills to assemble the aircraft properly upon reaching the Philippines. The wear to the tires and engines in order to meet a shipping deadline could be accepted recognizing the availability of extensive repair shops and supplies at the destination. The lack of key mechanical parts for an aircraft not otherwise in service at the receiving end is more difficult to comprehend. It is unclear today whether the problem was the physical lack of these parts or the inability of the ground crews, unfamiliar with these types of planes, to locate them in the jumbled shipments hurriedly offloaded in Brisbane. In any event they were *not* located, causing a serious delay in making the aircraft serviceable. Air Force Major General Arnold sent 104 replacement solenoids by B-17 airplanes across the Pacific, and to be safe sent another 104 by ship and a third complete set by bomber aircraft transiting the Africa route. That was good foresight, as the

B-17 flight through Hawaii was retained at Hickam Field for patrol duty, further delaying the receipt of the critical parts.

The frustrations over this situation with the A-24s must have been agonizing for both those charged with the preparation of the aircraft and those pilots sent down from the Philippines at some risk to pick up the planes. One desperate officer's efforts to locate the missing parts was described as causing "one harassed lieutenant to rush frantically all day in his jeep trying to collect spare parts, and wildly beat his head when none were available."[3] The situation with the solenoids became well known even at high military levels in Washington, D.C. Secretary of War Henry Stimson is recorded as having a conversation with Robert Lovett, the Army's assistant secretary for air, as follows: "Bob, where are those things you need on those airplanes? Those things you need to make the airplanes shoot properly—oh, what's the name—hemorrhoids! Where are those hemorrhoids, anyway, Bob?"[4]

Some P-40 pilots destined for the 35th Group were on the convoy, and a few more found their way from the Philippines to meet the arriving aircraft in Australia. On the last day of 1941 two Philippine Airlines Beechcraft transports brought fourteen pilots to Brisbane. The ferry flight of pursuit pilots from the Philippines has a story of its own. Pilot of the lead transport aircraft was Paul I. "Pappy" Gunn. Gunn had come to Manila in 1939 with his wife and four children from a twenty-one-year stint as a pilot in the Navy and Marines. He combined his own Philippine Air Lines with the older Philippine Air Taxi Company in the year before the war. At the outbreak of hostilities he turned his six twin-engine Beechcraft transports, staff, and personal service over to the Air Force. He personally piloted several of the early transport missions for Army pilots and officers, and eventually helped create the Air Transport Corps for the Southwest Pacific. The initial equipment of this rag-tag command included the surviving Beechcrafts, two old B-18s and one C-39 from the Philippines, and five new C-53s delivered by ship to Australia since the war began. Gunn's zeal in conducting the war was no doubt influenced by the fact that his wife and children had been left in Manila when he evacuated south. Pappy Gunn became an early hero in this part of the world, and an inspiration for the American fighting forces.

These recently arriving pursuit pilots formed the nucleus of the new squadrons forming at Brisbane. The new squadrons were given the same squadron numbers as those destroyed in the early Philippine attacks, but as "provisional" squadrons. The first formed would be the new 17th Pursuit Squadron (Provisional) with its pilots drawn from this transferred contingent of airmen. By the ninth of January all seventeen usable aircraft were prepared for their journey northward. A week later on the sixteenth two flights started on their two-thousand-mile trip to Darwin. The planes staged through the Australian airfields at Rockhampton, Townsville, Cloncurry, and Daly Waters. Two C-39s accompanied the flight carrying a small contingent of mechanics that had just arrived on *President Polk* (there had been no fighter aircraft technicians on the original *Pensacola* convoy).[5]

One P-40 was lost at Rockhampton when a pilot experienced an electrical problem and crashed on landing, while yet another plane was lost to a collapsing landing gear at Townsville. One pilot came down with dengue fever on the trip, finally reducing the number of planes to arrive at Darwin to just fourteen. On the twenty-first Major General Brereton himself told the airmen that Java was their destination. They were told that the Dutch and British had some air units still in the island, but in the end they were to depend on themselves.[6] Fourteen P-40s left Darwin on the twenty-second staging through Penfoei Airfield at Koepang, Timor. From Timor two separate flights were made to Soemba Island, each being guided by Pappy Gunn in one of his Beechcraft transports. Another pilot became ill on Timor, so only thirteen P-40Es reached Surabaya on the twenty-fourth or twenty-fifth of January. Japanese airplanes strafing the Penfoei strip destroyed the aircraft grounded due to its ill pilot.[7] Separate transport flights brought up the squadron's enlisted-man ground crew on the twenty-sixth. With a plane loss during an air cover mission, the squadron had now been reduced from its original seventeen planes to just twelve before it got a chance to fire a round in combat. On the first of February the planes and men moved to their permanent field at Blimbing, sixty miles from Surabaya itself. Later, additional detachments of P-40s would reach Java, but though originating in distinct squadrons, they were all eventually incorporated into the 17th Pursuit Squadron at this single station. Over the next month the serviceable fighter strength of the squadron would range from six to twenty-six P-40Es, with a maximum personnel roster of forty-seven officers and eighty-one enlisted men. This would be the sum total of American fighter strength to actually make it to Java.

The A-24s arrived in Australia without any aircrew whatsoever. However, when the unit's airmen already in the Philippines heard of the arrival, efforts were made to get pilots to Brisbane to pick up the planes. Maj. John Davies, group commanding officer, briefed the selected crewmen on December 17. Twenty pilots (plus one volunteer from the 24th Pursuit Group) went south in two B-18s and a C-39 from Clark Field before dawn on December

19.[8] The pilots were very disappointed in finding their aircraft not yet combat-worthy. However, they set up a flight training school at Amberley for the benefit of the flight cadets not familiar with this plane. Formation training, night flying, and bombing and gunnery skills were all taught. Finally, by January 23 the personnel were ready to be organized in squadrons. At Archerfield was the 91st Squadron (under Capt. Edward Backus), while at Amberley the 16th Squadron (under Capt. Floyd Rogers) and 17th (under Capt. Herman F. Lowery) took shape.[9]

When Major General Brett arrived in Australia, he began to reorganize the air assets of his command to facilitate his mission. To meet the goal of becoming a major air staging base, Brett had been promised four pursuit groups and one light, two medium, and two heavy bombardment groups. Eighty heavy bombers were said to be on the way, though during this campaign the promises from Washington always exceeded eventual deliveries. The plans were to use Darwin as a jumping-off point for short-range aircraft, and as a secondary base for repair and maintenance. Brisbane was to be a larger maintenance depot, and Townsville was to become a supply and transshipment point. Headquarters was staying in Melbourne, where cooperation with the Australians was best achieved.[10] After consultations with the Allies and inspection of facilities, a local ferry route was selected. From the assembly facility at Brisbane, planes would be routed through Townsville, Charleville, Cloncurry, and Daly Waters to Darwin, all in Australia. With Java quickly becoming the most realistic destination, the route continued to Koepang, but then on to Den Pasir on Bali (or alternately Soemba Island) and thence into an eastern Java airfield. Of course, more had to be done than just designate fields. Small ground detachments for operating air traffic control, and radios needed to be supplied. Most importantly proper fuel needed to be stockpiled in advance.

The first vessels since the Pearl Harbor attack carrying supplies to Australia were authorized for release on December 14. Over the next thirty days five important shiploads of airplanes and aviation gas were dispatched to Australia. The first two important ships were the relatively fast *President Polk* and *Mormacsun*. These two were specially designated to carry air reinforcements with the ultimate destination of the Philippines. The Navy agreed that their high speed permitted them to make the journey unescorted—though all parties recognized the risk of that decision. Each also followed a routing and timetable independent of the others. High hopes were vested particularly

Table 10. First Shipments of Aircraft and Supplies to Australia[11]

Ships/Speed/Dates/Escort	Units and Major Cargo Items
SS *Hawaiian Planter* 16.5 knots Depart SF 12/03/41 for ferry bases and Manila Diverted to Samoa Arrived Sydney 12/28/41 Unescorted	24,000 drums aviation gasoline 7,000 drums batching oil 140 drums lubricating oil Portable fuel pumps
SS *Paul M. Gregg* 14 knots Depart SF 12/17/41 Arrived Brisbane 1/12/42 Unescorted	102,000 barrels 100-octane aviation gasoline
SS *President Polk* 16 knots Depart SF 12/19/41 Arrived Brisbane 1/12/41 Unescorted	55 P-40Es and 4 C-53s 20 million .30-cal rounds 447,000 .50-cal rounds 30,000 3-in anti-aircraft rounds 5,000 75-mm rounds 81 cylinders oxygen 5 carloads Navy torpedoes 615,495 pounds rations 233 officers and men (including 55 pilots)
SS *Mormacsun* 16 knots Depart SF 12/26/41 Arrived Brisbane 1/19/42 Unescorted	67 P-40Es and 1 C-53 9.3 million .30-cal rounds 617,450 .50-cal rounds 16,488 81-mm mortar rounds 3,442 75-mm rounds 2,952 300-pound bombs, 13,855 100-pound bombs
USS *Hammondsport* 16 knots Depart SF 1/18/42 Arrived Brisbane 2/05/42 Unescorted from U.S. Escorted by RNZA *Achilles* from Fiji	111 P-40Es, 9 other airplanes Various military cargo

with the cargo of *Polk*; the journey was often referred to as the "P Special." Marshall and Eisenhower each took special efforts to notify MacArthur of the ship's schedule and cargo as proof of the commitment to the supply effort.

On December 16, just one week after the Pearl Harbor attack, an Army conference discussed the priorities for shipping and supplies. Fortunately the buildup of supplies in San Francisco, not to mention the availability of units and matériel that was offloaded from the returning western-bound transports, meant that finding the supplies was not the limiting factor. Mentioned for the initial trip to Australia was SS *President Polk.* This fast, modern vessel was just now available for her maiden voyage. Actually she had recently been acquired by the Maritime Commission, but was immediately placed with the American President Lines to carry out a commercial journey to the Far East already scheduled for December 7. The only military cargo contracted for that voyage was crated aircraft—nine P-40s and fourteen P-39s. Her maiden voyage lasted just a few hours until she returned to port under orders issued at the news of war. After re-loading it was foreseen that the ship could carry fifty-five crated P-40 pursuit planes, the most urgent cargo. The ship's capacity was rounded out mostly with munitions needed for aircraft operations and other specialty items.[12] This conference urged the vessel be loaded and set to sail at the earliest possible date that could be arranged with the Navy.

Aircraft, particularly fighters, were certainly perceived as the single most urgent requirement of the Pacific fighting forces. With several hundred planes lost in Hawaii and the Philippines, the replacement of these was critical. Planes were needed for the Army Air Force on Oahu, and to be delivered to Australia for transshipment to the Philippines or maybe the Dutch East Indies. While some planes were already at hand in San Francisco due to be shipped out in early December, the War Department went through hoops to supply more. A temporary suspension of lend-lease shipments helped, as did an elevation of priority (only shared with the Panama Canal) for these two destinations. Special trains with priority track clearance were loaded with planes from East Coast factories. For example, train MT-167 brought in thirty-four P-40s on December 28; two days later train MT-168 brought another forty while MT-174 brought twenty-five P-39Ds. Amazingly, somehow the planes, trains, and ships were found to facilitate transfer of aircraft in a very short time.

On the nineteenth of December *President Polk*, entirely unescorted by any other vessel, slipped out of San Francisco. She was routed, like most early sailings to Australia, on a course mostly south around the Marquesa Islands and then west. While prolonging the trip, this route obviously provided the path least likely to encounter Japanese air, surface, or submarine forces. For this voyage *President Polk* was virtually unaltered from her commercial combiliner configuration. The ship was provided armament and gun crews by the Army. She had four each 37-mm guns, and .50- and .30-caliber anti-aircraft machine guns. The light cannon were standard Army anti-tank guns, lashed to the rails of the sun deck, their trails being secured with piled sandbags. The Army-supplied gun crew consisted of two officers and thirty-eight men.[13] She arrived at Brisbane on January 12.

In Brisbane *President Polk* quickly discharged some cargo and the men on board. All the aircraft were crated and needed assembling at the same facilities used for the *Pensacola* convoy airplanes. She took on some service troops and then proceeded to the Java port of Surabaya. A small convoy for Java was formed of *President Polk*, *Hawaiian Planter*, and Navy tanker USS *Pecos*. Besides the artillerymen provided by *Bloemfontein*, this was just about the only shipment of Army men and supplies to reach Java during the campaign. On board were the desperately needed ground echelons of the 11th and 22nd Bombardment Squadrons. Moved to Djogjakarta by February 3, they became the mainstays of maintenance for the American heavy bombers operating out of Java for the next critical month. Except for what was needed for the aircraft squadrons and the local artillery battalion, the ammunition and half of the rations carried on *Polk* were turned over to Colonel Robenson for his blockade-running operations.[14]

About a week later a second ship departed the West Coast with even more fighter reinforcements for the Far East. *Mormacsun* was a near-sister to *President Polk*, both being new Maritime Commission C-3 designs. *Mormacsun* had a strict freighter configuration with very little passenger space. Like her sister she was new and could manage sixteen knots and thus avoid the need for escorting. She was to follow the same general routing to Brisbane as her immediate predecessor. Aircraft began arriving in San Francisco on December 23 for loading. It was found possible to place sixty-two P-40s and one C-53 on board while dockside. Once into the stream, at the last moment, another five P-40s were squeezed on deck from a barge alongside.

SS *Mormacsun* departed on what should have been a long but undisturbed journey. Just two days out, on the twenty-eighth about five hundred miles from San Diego, aircraft attacked the ship. The attacker was described as an aluminum-colored patrol plane identified by the crew as a Navy-type PBY. At 5:30 PM the plane made a determined attack out of the sun, and dropped a fragmentation bomb that landed just fifteen feet off the port bow, causing the ship's gun crew to be covered with spray. Attempts to communicate with the aircraft initially failed, but eventually a radio exchange was established.

Mormacsun's reply to the inquiry about destination of "sealed orders" was apparently not satisfactory. Twice during the late afternoon machine-gun fire was exchanged between ship and airplane. Fortunately it seems no material damage was done to either party. Obviously the U.S. Navy patrol bomber did not recognize the vessel as American, and in these nervous days just a couple of weeks after Pearl Harbor they were taking no chances. The ship's master immediately changed course, and the cover of darkness helped the vessel get away toward the Mexican coast. Nothing was seen the following day. A report was filed with the commander in chief, U.S. Fleet, advocating better protocol and instruction on ship identification.[15] The ship arrived safely enough in Brisbane on January 19 and promptly began unloading. While the local command tried to take possession of the ship for a potential run north, the request was refused. Washington was very protective of the few modern and fast freighters it had access to, and they weren't about to risk losing a ship with such a good capacity in hostile waters.

The third rushed fighter shipment, and the largest, was dispatched on USS *Hammondsport.* This vessel was known as a type of seatrain—a transport specializing in carrying large, bulky pieces of equipment. Originally put into service in the early 1930s as SS *Seatrain Havana*, she was acquired in mid-1941 by the Navy and commissioned as USS *Hammondsport.* The ship's design to carry railroad cars in capacious deck hangars lent itself easily to either crated or assembled aircraft. She carried PT boats to Panama and then went to San Francisco on January 7. She arrived safely in Brisbane on February 5. On the latter part of her voyage escort was provided by HMNZS *Achilles* from Fiji. The aircraft and other cargo were quickly unloaded so the ship could make a fast turnaround. She returned to California on March 17.

The quick dispatch of a substantial number of fighters to Australia was an accomplishment of considerable note. Within six weeks of the Pearl Harbor attack, over three hundred P-40s were actually delivered or on their way to reinforce the American forces in the Far East. Thankfully the buildup of planes already awaiting shipment in San Francisco, and the transfer of aircraft being completed at the Curtiss factory, facilitated this response. But the finding of appropriate transport, loading the aircraft (and this time parts, pilots, and fuel), and scheduling the port facilities and Navy cooperation speak to the tremendous effort being made.

Of course, just as important as the aircraft and crews to fly them was aviation fuel. Australia had no domestic production of oil, being totally dependent on imports. There was little beyond emergency supplies to be spared

Table 11. Summary of U.S. Fighter Deliveries to Australia, December 1941–Early February 1942

Ship	Depart SF	Arrive Aus.	Aircraft
Bloemfontein	11/21/1941	12/22/1941	18 P-40E
President Polk	12/19/1941	1/12/1942	55 P-40E
Mormacsun	12/26/1941	1/19/1942	67 P-40E
Mariposa & *President Coolidge*	1/13/1942	2/02/1942	51 P-40E 19 P-39
Hammondsport	1/19/1942	2/05/1942	111 P-40E

for the American buildup, so aviation gasoline had to be shipped from the United States. Fortunately one shipment was already in the supply pipeline. The Matson freighter *Hawaiian Planter* had left Honolulu on December 3 to offload supplies at the bomber ferry bases: 1,020 drums for Rabaul, 7,140 for Port Moresby, 6,000 at Rockhampton, and 8,160 at Port Darwin. *Hawaiian Planter* took refuge in Pago Pago when war was declared. After the usual several days of indecision on the part of the American command about where to send what, the freighter was ordered direct to eastern Australia, bypassing the New Guinea stops. She arrived safely in Sydney only six days behind the arrival of the planes of the *Pensacola* convoy. This fuel was urgently needed and no doubt gratefully received. After making port, *Hawaiian Planter* was off again on January 2, ultimately to take part of her cargo to the embryonic American Air Force on Java.

A follow-up shipment of aviation fuel was soon arranged. This time the chosen vessel was the Union Oil of California tanker *Paul M. Gregg.*[16] This tanker was a new ship, just ordered in 1939, relatively large (8,187 tons) and fast (fourteen knots). The ship had originally been a member of the large stream of ships departing San Francisco in early December. She sailed on the fifth, but just two days out war began and she (like virtually every other ship in this situation) immediately returned to the safety of port. On board was 102,000 barrels' worth of 100-octane aviation gasoline. She stood by until released on December 17 for an independent voyage now routed direct to Australia. A relatively fast ship sailing a southern route carrying an important but non-personnel cargo, it was trusted to send her unescorted. The scheduled arrival date in Brisbane was January 12.

One of the problems encountered by the Allies at this stage of the war was the very rapidity of the Japanese advance. The Japanese plans for the progressive conquest of Southeast Asia had been formulated in advance in great detail. Air, land, and sea units were carefully allocated and progressively shifted from one successful operation to the next throughout the first four months of the war. In fact, a very severe economy of force was achieved—the actual numbers of troops, airplanes, and ships utilized by the enemy in this phase was quite small, and always considerably below the estimates of the defenders. The plans, usually emphasizing the capture of distinct ports, airfields, and commercial centers, were in most respects very well executed. Quite simply the Allies often did not have time to react to a threat or even an attack. This was particularly true during the campaign on the various islands of the Dutch East Indies. The Japanese secured Tarakan in northern Borneo on January 10 and Menado in Celebes on the 11th. The landing at Balikpapan was made on the twenty-third, and Kendari on the twenty-fourth. The last staging field capable of getting small planes to the Philippines, Samarinda in Borneo, was lost on February 7. In less than four weeks all the airfield staging points in the central part of the Indies fell to the enemy.[17]

By February 1 fifteen more B-17Es and four LB-30s had reached Java. Most came by the African route, but three of the LB-30s flew the new South Pacific route. This influx allowed two important organizational moves. Most of the older, worn B-17Ds of the 19th Group were released to go to Australia for a badly needed period of overhaul. The planes wound up being used only as transports. The arrival of ground crews on *President Polk* on January 28 allowed for the development of a second heavy bomber field in Java. The newly arriving 7th Bomb Group would now be based at Djogjakarta, 150 miles west of Malang, where the 19th Bomb Group would remain. By this stage the number of bombers was so few that individual squadron designations of planes or crews meant nothing; all were combined into essentially one understrength unit at each base. It was intended to try and alternate missions between bases, but often even the two groups were combined in a single mission to try and maximize results.

The Japanese were first able to hit Java from Kendari with land-based bombers on February 3. Heavy attacks were reported on Malang, Surabaya, and Madioen, the airfield at the latter suffering badly. Altogether thirty-one Allied aircraft were destroyed in these attacks, including five B-17s. The 17th Pursuit Squadron was finally in place and offered the first American opposition to the Japanese on this day. A flight of P-40s from the 17th hit the Japanese over Surabaya, claiming one enemy fighter and one bomber, but losing a P-40 in the process. Unfortunately the Dutch suffered much more seriously, losing thirteen fighter airplanes and claiming no enemy craft in return. While the Americans were desperately trying to increase the fighter strength in Java, the strategic situation demanded a further dilution of strength when ten of the P-40s were sent west to support the defense of Palembang. They achieved little and lost several aircraft in the process before returning to their permanent base in Java.

The rapidity of the Japanese advance affected the dispatch of the P-40s following the 17th Squadron. The next provisional fighter squadron was organized as the 20th Pursuit Squadron (Provisional), commanded by Capt. William Lane Jr. It was ordered to proceed with eighteen P-40s to Port Moresby in New Guinea on January 24, but then Kendari fell to the invaders, and the squadron's destination was changed to Java. A full quota of twenty-five planes was dispatched along the ferry route to Darwin, arriving on January 31. Due to weather problems the first flight of fourteen planes departed with a B-24 guide, and all but one arrived in Bali on the fifth.[18] While they were in the process of refueling a force of twenty enemy aircraft hit the field, destroying several more fighters both in the air and on the ground. The second flight of the squadron started with ten planes (though losing two quickly to pilot crashes), a couple of days behind the first. It managed to avoid attack, even shooting down a Japanese reconnaissance plane on the journey. Altogether the squadron managed to deliver just seventeen of its twenty-five planes to Java, but unfortunately only eleven were in flying condition.

Five provisional fighter squadrons were formed from the 140 P-40Es assembled in Brisbane between December 23 and February 4. These had been delivered by *Bloemfontein*, *President Polk*, and *Mormacsun*. More planes would soon follow in additional convoys scheduled to arrive in early February. While thus sufficient for five squadrons (usually equipped with from eighteen to twenty-five airplanes), there were not nearly enough trained fighter pilots. The earliest squadrons, particularly the 17th and to a lesser extent the 20th, naturally got the experienced pilots transferred directly from the Philippines plus the few relatively well-trained cadets actually on the transports. The later squadrons were left with the least experienced flyers (many with less than twenty hours' flight time in a P-40), and this really began to show itself in pilot errors and crashes. The third unit organized, the 3rd Pursuit Squadron (Provisional), actually lost seven of its twenty-five airplanes due to pilot inexperience before even arriving at Darwin in early February 1942.[19] Eventually fresh shipments of better-trained pilots from stateside bases, plus the time interval separating the end of the Java action and the real start of the New Guinea and Guadalcanal campaigns, provided a better matchup of planes to operators.

The 3rd Pursuit Squadron (Provisional), commanded by Capt. Grant Mahony, suffered the worst during transfer. As mentioned above, things didn't start well with the loss of seven planes just in the overland transit to Darwin. On February 9 a combined flight of nine of the squadron's P-40s and three A-24s of the 91st Bomb Squadron started out from Darwin for the field on Timor. Due to bad weather the navigating bomber got lost, and except for one P-40 that had to return due to mechanical problems the other eight all crashed when their fuel ran out, though all but one of the pilots survived and were recovered. Two days later the second flight of nine P-40s did successfully make the crossing to Java. This squadron delivered just nine of its twenty-five planes, though just eight to the fighter field at Blimbing. The ninth airplane only made it as far as the small Java strip at Pasirian, where it was damaged on landing and subsequently destroyed by Japanese strafing attacks.[20]

With these piecemeal arrivals, the American fighter strength in Java for a few days was able to keep pace with losses. On February 12 the defenders had twenty-five operable planes under the care of forty-seven officers and eighty-one enlisted men. The maximum reportable strength of the squadron at Blimbing was twenty-six P-40Es available for combat sorties on February 14. By the time the 20th and 3rd squadrons made their transit, it was obvious that the Japanese had a good feel for the routes and fields being used. In addition to the high aircraft (and pilot!) attrition rates due to inexperience, weather, and mechanical failures, the interception and destruction of planes both in the air and on the ground made the loss rate intolerable. There are still two provisional squadron fates to recount, but no planes after the last flight on February 11 would succeed in completing the ferry route from Darwin to Timor, then either to Soemba or Bali, then to Java. The remaining aircraft in Java inevitably declined in numbers as the frantic pace of operations and combat took their toll.

The problems in getting the A-24s into combat service were even more difficult than those encountered with the fighters. The missing parts were more critical, and the lack of adequately trained pilots more severe. A hurriedly constructed field on what had been rice land a few days before at Malang on Java would be the base for the first squadron to arrive. By the first of February enough triggers were completed to allow a full squadron to be equipped, and judicious use of six practice bombs each allowed some measure of crew training. The 91st Bombardment Squadron with eleven A-24s departed Brisbane on February 8. They all arrived at Darwin the next day. On February 9 three A-24s departed Darwin for Koepang with nine P-40s of the 3rd Pursuit Squadron and an LB-30 bomber. The A-24s were more fortunate than their fighter companions and did find Koepang. However, it seems the local Australian anti-aircraft unit had not been advised of the flight, and all three planes were damaged by fire, two so severely that they had to return to Darwin.

On the eleventh another eleven A-24s led by Lt. Harry Galusha left Darwin, and reached Koepang for overnight refueling with far less trouble than the preceding flight. By February 16 ten operational dive-bombers were stationed at the Malang airfield. Plagued by continuing mechanical problems and operational accidents, it took personnel until February 19 to get just seven planes ready for action. However, the field was hit by another air raid, and while most of the planes were returned to their revetments, two managed to get airborne. Taking advantage of cloud cover these pilots found an enemy convoy off Bali and performed the maneuver they were trained for. They both managed to secure either direct hits or damaging near-misses on what was reported to be a transport and a cruiser. Both aircraft returned to Malang without damage. This was the very first dive-bombing attack ever made by the U.S. Army Air Force.[21]

The single largest combined attack of the American Air Force in this campaign occurred the next day—on the twentieth of February. Seven A-24s and three LB-30s, escorted by no less than sixteen P-40s, set out to hit the same Bali-bound convoy. While damage to enemy vessels was reported, the invasion was not stopped, and three A-24s were lost. The airfield on Bali at Den Pasir, once an important link in the Darwin to Java route, was soon being prepared for Japanese fighters. This relative success of the attacks on the enemy Bali-bound convoy was more than overshadowed by two other recent significant favorable developments for the Japanese.

On the nineteenth the Japanese accomplished their landing near Dili in Portuguese Timor. Resistance by local Portuguese forces was negligible. Very soon the island's only airfield at Koepang was under Japanese control. This occupation, combined with the taking of the Den Pasir Field on Bali, essentially cut the aircraft ferry route to Java. Of course, B-17s and B-24s had the range to go to Java direct from either India or Australia, but the shorter-ranged fighters and light bombers (precisely like the P-40s and A-24s being assembled in Australia) could not. From this date forward no additional A-24s would reach Java; the eleven sent there with the 91st Squadron would be all. In fact, part of the group was at Darwin and the rest at Daly Waters when the news of the loss of Koepang was received; the onward journey thus terminated at Darwin.[22] Additional P-40s would eventually reach Java, but they had to be brought in by ship rather than flown in. Now only the heavy bomber pipeline was operational—and that for just another ten days.

On February 19 the Japanese launched a major air raid from carriers and land bases. On this day at Darwin was the next contingent of P-40s destined for Java. A flight of ten P-40s from the 33rd Pursuit Squadron (Provisional) under Maj. Floyd Pell was en route to Java via Koepang when early in the morning poor weather turned them back. Pell ordered five aircraft to land and refuel while the other five provided air cover. As the Japanese land-based contingent of seventy-two bombers and thirty-six fighters approached from the south, Pell got himself and the other aircraft into the air and dived into the Japanese formation. The overwhelming cover of naval A6M fighters intercepted the Americans. One enemy bomber was claimed, but Major Pell and three other pilots and fighters were lost in the combat. With relative ease the Japanese destroyed the airport and many military structures, and sank or damaged much of the shipping in the harbor. By the end of the attack eleven P-40s, an LB-30, an A-24, four Navy PBYs, and three transports were lost by the Americans. Altogether twenty-six Allied planes were destroyed, while confirmed Japanese losses were only five planes. As if the loss of Bali and Timor weren't bad enough, the vulnerability of Darwin clearly indicated that the ability to freely move aircraft in the ABDA operational area was at an end.

After the conquest of Sumatra and further consolidation, Japanese air forces could hit Java from any of a number of directions. Air fields at Palembang (Sumatra), Tarakan (Borneo), Kendari (Celebes), and recently acquired Bali and Timor were all within range of the final Allied bastion. The Allied operating airfields themselves proved adequate, and one talent the Dutch demonstrated well was their ability to camouflage or otherwise disguise these fields from the air. As a good example, the American fighter strip known as Ngoro Field was not discovered by the enemy and attacked until the very end of the entire campaign. However, the aircraft operated were quickly becoming worn. The only way to protect flyable aircraft was to have them in the air as much as possible; crews, engines, and airframes got extremely little rest. Repeated missions with little or no routine maintenance were quickly affecting mechanical performance. Defense of the fields was also difficult. In most cases the interceptor control consisted of little more than a Dutch officer or two with a radio; no active radar or even sound-locating gear was available, at least to the American units. Finally, coverage by anti-aircraft guns was very spotty—there simply weren't enough guns and crews to spread around with good effect.

Very little in the way of ground maintenance personnel had been provided the Americans operating on Java. To begin with, only a very few technicians had been flown into Java by the bombers that arrived with the 19th Bombardment Group retreating from the Philippines. Not only were skilled mechanics needed, but manpower was also needed to maneuver aircraft on a field, to load and sometimes unload bombs, to fuel (sometimes from fifty-five-gallon drums), to operate radios and control towers, and to run some semblance of quarters, mess halls, motor pools, and medical facilities. For a while the same aircrew that flew in the day performed these missions each night, but obviously that could be sustained for just a short time before the crews were as worn as their aircraft. Under these conditions operational losses of planes were as numerous as those from enemy action. On February 20 a Japanese strafing attack on Singosari destroyed another three B-17s and left two damaged. By February 24 the inventory in Java had been reduced to twenty heavy bombers, seven A-24s, and sixteen P-40s.[23]

As the Japanese consolidated their new air bases, losses to the Americans continued to mount. On February 22 an LB-30 was lost on the ground at Djogjakarta, and four B-17s were destroyed at a dispersal field south of Surabaya. Then on the twenty-fourth another three bombers were lost at Bandoeng. The Japanese offensive developed so rapidly and effectively that is wasn't long before officers in the ABDA command reluctantly began the abandonment of the Air Force commitment to Java's defense. Aircraft not used on combat operations began taking non-essential personnel out of Java to Australia in the third week of February. Some key air units and reinforcements destined for Java were subtly rescheduled for India. Even Brereton and his small staff also headed for India. The ABDA command was essentially defunct by February 25. On the last day of February the two Air Force bomb squadron ground crews left Java—though they had just arrived at their base twenty-five days earlier. Boarding the Dutch ship *Abbekerk* at Tjilatjap were about 1,500 men of the 11th Bombardment Squadron from Djogjakarta, the 22nd originally at Malang, most of the 26th Field Artillery Brigade Headquarters and Headquarters Battery, and forty-seven other sick and wounded personnel, some from Navy cruisers *Houston* and *Marblehead.* The ship made it safely to Fremantle on March 5, where the Air Force personnel caught a train for Melbourne.

Local defense of Java reverted to the Dutch, but as a measure of solidarity with their ally a variety of British, Australian, and American units—air, navy and land forces—stayed behind to participate in the final defense. The wisdom of this final decision is debatable in hindsight. Strategically the loss of the Dutch East Indies at this point in the war was inevitable. The resources and time simply weren't available to make the outcome any different. However, totally abandoning the Dutch in their final efforts was politically and morally not acceptable. They had contributed substantially to the defense of Singapore, and freely gave oil, rubber, and access to airfields and other resources in the attempt to keep communications alive with the Philippines. Consequently contingents of American aircraft, ships, and a battalion of field artillery were contributed to the final resistance. All American combat Air Force crews were ordered to remain in Java and operate as long as possible. Lieutenant Colonel Eubank assumed command of the air assets and consolidated his forces at Djogjakarta. On March 2 the final exodus of planes, at least those with the range to make it to Australia, began. Five B-17s and three LB-30s made it out with the enemy ground forces just twenty miles away.

Back in Java, on the twenty-sixth of February the fighter force was down to just thirteen flyable planes. Even fewer bombers were left. Singosari was abandoned, the last few missions being flown from Djogjakarta or Madioen fields. On the morning of March 1 the American Air Force flew its last missions. Only two B-17s were left at this point; five other heavy bombers not airworthy were burned on the field by ground crews to prevent their usefulness to the enemy. The very last P-40s, a few Dutch Brewsters, and five British Hurricanes were caught on the ground at their last airfield and totally destroyed. The remaining air and ground crew—twenty-five officers and sixty men—were taken by truck convoy to Tjilatjap and safely evacuated to Australia at the last possible moment. Even after this, for several days miscellaneous military and civilian aircraft, including some damaged aircraft repaired enough for one final trip, managed to make it out. Altogether the American fighter contingent had claimed forty-six downed enemy aircraft—a very nice return for just eleven P-40s lost in aerial combat. But of course that is just part of the equation: 109 P-40s (and fifteen A-24s) were lost from all causes during the campaign.

On March 1, after the last attempts to bomb the Japanese convoys unloading on Java, it was time for the bombers to leave. First, the remaining airplanes not airworthy (but most being cannibalized for parts) were destroyed—three each LB-30s and B-17s at Singosari, Djogjakarta, and Madioen. Colonel Eubank, commanding the bombers, left in a B-17E at 6 PM on the first. A total of sixteen B-17Es managed to get evacuated from Java during these final days, and just three LB-30s. After much work the Japanese managed to piece together (literally) two B-17Es. They were flown to Japan for study about a year later. The Japanese were impressed with the ease of control of the aircraft and the precision of the construction.[24]

The bomber force had also suffered very heavily in this campaign. In addition to the early model B-17s that had made it out of the Philippines, substantial numbers had made it to Java by either of the two international ferry routes. Altogether thirty-eight B-17Es, twelve LB-30s, and three B-24s (utilized only as transports by the ferry command) had arrived in January and February of 1942.[25] Thirty-eight bombers had been lost, claiming in return twenty-three enemy aircraft in aerial combat. Thus for the Dutch East Indies campaign sixty-one combat bombers had been made available—eleven from the Philippine-based B-17 contingent, thirty-eight new B-17Es, and twelve LB-30s. Of the twenty-three survivors, three were early B-17Ds withdrawn to Australia for transport service, and seventeen B-17Es and three LB-30s went to Melbourne. The remnants of the 7th and 19th Bomb Groups were allowed to rest in Melbourne, while the surviving planes were overhauled at the Laverton Repair Depot. The ground crews evacuated on *Abbekerk* also went to Melbourne, joining men of the 43rd Bomb Group that had arrived on a convoy from the United States on February 26.

There was one other B-17 unit in Australia at that time. After Pearl Harbor a new B-17 unit had been dispatched from Hawaii to Fiji to fly patrols in support of naval operations. The unit's planes had originated with the flight that landed in the midst of the attack on December 7, the 38th and 88th Reconnaissance Squadrons, plus the reinforcing 22nd Bombardment Squadron that flew out from California after the attack. The latter had traveled by the Pacific ferry route in mid-February with twelve B-17Es to Fiji, then after flying missions for a while there, moved on to Townsville. Later that month they began flying missions to Rabaul, and against Japanese targets in New Guinea and the Solomon Islands.

The final force to quit the East Indies was the submarines of the Asiatic Fleet. After leaving their base in Manila Bay at the end of December 1941, the subs had tried to continue to intercept the Japanese. At first they worked from submarine tenders at both Darwin and Surabaya. For a variety of reasons, it was decided to concentrate the resources out of Tjilatjap a month later, on January 29. This port was also found lacking in support facilities, and eventually after mid-February the surviving submarines were assigned to a new base in the western Australian port of Fremantle. Altogether twenty-five submarines survived of the original twenty-nine of the Asiatic Fleet. Unfortunately the torpedo and operational situation did not mean this force was very effective. It had fired 223 torpedoes at ninety-seven target vessels, and only had eleven confirmed kills.[26]

The final Japanese triumph of the campaign came on March 3. An evacuation route for military and civilian refugees had developed, with long-range flying boats, from the southern Java port of Tjilatjap to Perth, Australia, by way of the small harbor of Broome in northwest Australia. While the port of Broome had a usable airfield that could take bombers, its most useful asset was a sheltered anchorage that could sustain a fairly large number of flying boats. At 9:20 AM on March 3 nine Japanese A6M naval fighters arrived, led by a single C5M reconnaissance plane. Just six fighters descended to strafe both the anchorage and airfield. The damage they caused was almost complete. In the harbor sixteen flying boats were lost—two Empire flying boats, three Dutch Dorniers, four Catalinas (two British and two American PBYs), and seven others. At the airfield six planes were destroyed—two B-17s, an LB-30, two Hudsons, and a Dutch DC-3. Another LB-30 was destroyed just as it was taking off, and was lost with thirty-two people on board. Finally the Japanese caught another Dutch DC-3 in the air about sixty miles north of Broome. It too was shot down, the crew killed, and a consignment of diamonds on board—worth $20 million belonging to a Dutch company—was lost. Just one Japanese plane was confirmed lost either to ground fire or running out of fuel.[27]

The loss of two of the few remaining PBYs just about marked the end of the original PatWing 10. There were just three survivors: one PBY-4 worn-out veteran from the Philippines and two PBY-5s from VP-22, the squadron that had flown out to Java in early 1942. These three planes, a couple of single-engine floatplanes left behind in Australia from USS *Langley*, and some very tired sailors were all that was left of the Navy's Asiatic Fleet patrol force. They went to a small base on the Swan River north of Perth to conduct local harbor patrols and begin the road back to rebuilding.

CHAPTER SEVENTEEN

Building the Australian Base

Even while the remnants of the Asiatic Fleet and Far Eastern Air Force were desperately fighting the campaign in the Dutch East Indies, efforts increased to build a major American base in Australia. Of course, the nucleus of this new base was the original components of the *Pensacola* convoy. The supply ships *President Polk*, *Mormacsun*, and *Hammondsport* added their cargoes upon their arrival, though their primary mission was the transport of fighter aircraft and their supplies to the fighting theatre. The first substantial new convoy to Australia arrived in Melbourne on February 2. Considerable thought had been given as to what was needed most—in January 1942 the role of the base was viewed as an advance air depot, as the manifest of the convoy confirmed.

The Army's attempt to locate ships for this convoy is illustrative of the real problems in shipping at the beginning of the war. On the twenty-sixth of December a conference was conducted with the Army's transportation team and the Navy, the latter represented by Rear Adm. S. A. Taffinder of the Naval Transportation Service and Rear Adm. Richmond K. Turner of naval operations. Setting one of the key ground rules, Turner announced that the Navy could escort only one convoy a month to Australia. The Army should plan on this for any troop movements. Freight vessels would not be escorted but would be released to sail individually as best they could. Consequently the Army searched for large-capacity, ex-commercial liners to maximize the number of men that could be sent. However, at the same time the Army was planning this large Australian shipment, the Navy was proceeding with an equally ambitious plan to substantially reinforce Samoa with Marines. They wanted both Maritime Commission ships *Matsonia* and *Monterey* along with

Table 12. Major Convoys for the Australian Base, January–February 1942[1]

Convoy/Ships/Speed/Escort/Dates	**Units and Major Cargo Items**
Convoy No. 2013 SS *President Coolidge* SS *Mariposa* (SS *President Monroe* accompanied for part of journey) 16 knots Escort: USS *Phoenix*, USS *Aylwin*, and USS *Perkins* Later: HMNZS *Leander,* HMAS *Adelaide*, *Australia*, *Perth* Depart SF 1/13/42 Arrive Melbourne 2/02/42	Approximately 7,000 officers and men 39th Pursuit Group (with 7th, 8th, 9th Squadrons) 51st Pursuit Group (with 16th, 25th, 16th Squadrons) HQ and HQ Squadron 35th Pursuit Group 808th Engineer Battalion (Aviation) 4th Air Depot Group 686th, 688th, 693rd Ordnance Companies (Pursuit) 711th, 729th Ordnance Companies (Airbase) 43rd, 54th, 59th Matériel Squadrons 45th, 51st Airbase Group Headquarters "Remember Pearl Harbor" personnel group 51 P-40Es, 19 P-39Ds 200 tons aircraft parts 20 tons Prestone ethylene glycol
Convoy No. 2030 USAT *Tasker H. Bliss* USAT *Hugh L. Scott* SS *Ancon* SS *Hawaiian Merchant* (*President Johnson* and *President Taylor* joined for part of journey) Escort: USS *Honolulu* and two destroyers Depart SF 1/31/42 Arrive Brisbane 2/25/42	9,362 officers and men 22nd Bomb Group (Medium) 38th Bomb Group (Medium) 3rd Bomb Group (Light) Three squadrons of 35th Pursuit Group 35th, 36th, 46th Airbase Groups 15 A-24 dive-bombers Other military supplies, ammunition, rations
Convoy No. 2033 USAT *Maui* SS *Cape Alva* SS *Cape Flattery* MV *Pennant* MV *Perida* SS *Torrens* Escort: USS *New Orleans* Depart SF 2/12/42 Arrive Brisbane 3/05/42	1,593 officers and men 8th Pursuit Group 22nd Airbase Group Other military supplies, ammunition, rations

their own transport *Lurline* for this movement. Of course, the first two ships were those the Army wanted; the Navy would only offer the unconverted sister-ship *Mariposa.* Ultimately the Navy got the use of the ships it wanted, but also sweetened the situation by allowing the Army access to the seatrains USS *Hammondsport* and USS *Kitty Hawk* for one aircraft transport mission each on the Army's behalf.[2]

The Army's convoy was to take the personnel and equipment of several key Air Force organizations to Australia. As many P-40s had already been shipped to Australia on board previous ships, many of the personnel were meant for the planes already being assembled. However, another seventy fighters were scheduled (fifty-one P-40Es and the first nineteen P-39s to be sent to the South Pacific). The usual spectrum of ground support units for the rapidly expanding air force in Australia was also on board. In fact, no fewer than twenty-three individual air support units were included. Some casual officers and administrative personnel destined for the fledgling Australian command structure also embarked, including the officers known as the "Remember Pearl Harbor" group.[3] The total manifest earmarked for Australia amounted to about seven thousand men and seventy aircraft.

Transports selected for the journey were the veteran *President Coolidge* and the former Matson liner *Mariposa*. These were among the largest, fastest American liners in the Pacific, well suited for the duty assigned. Just returned from her last voyage to the Philippines, *Coolidge* needed a short visit to the dry dock to solve a vibration problem in one of her shafts. Even though using fast ships, the importance of the cargo demanded a naval escort. This was provided by light cruiser *Phoenix* and two destroyers. Of course, the short-ranged destroyers could not make the entire trip, and switched over to escorting Convoy No. 2017 (three naval auxiliaries and a merchant ship) onward from San Francisco to Pearl Harbor. Also during the first stage of the trip the convoy included Army transport *President Monroe*, bound just as far as Fiji with an American fighter squadron and lend-lease equipment for the New Zealand troops there. Mid-course the convoy changed its destination from Brisbane to Melbourne.

Meantime the Army was anxious about the safety of the fighter ferry route through Timor, or at least cognizant of the high operational losses being incurred in the passage. The command in Melbourne decided that there were already enough air service forces in Australia, at least to service the immediately available aircraft. Some of these units could be released for Java or maybe the start of a new air force to be created in India. On the twenty-fifth the plan was to consolidate the embarked aircraft on *Mariposa* and perhaps add *Willard A. Holbrook.* They were to run west under southern Australia and then up the west coast to the Dutch East Indies. The Army asked for the continued service of escort cruiser *Phoenix* for this journey. The Navy initially refused the services of this warship beyond Melbourne, but later relented to her use. What had changed was that *Mariposa* was deemed too valuable for use in this capacity, and other ships had to be located to continue the planned voyage west from Melbourne. After arrival *Mariposa* went on to Brisbane and *President Coolidge* went to Wellington. With these new resources a final attempt to bring in more P-40s by sea to Java was undertaken.

In addition to Army transport *Willard A. Holbrook* two small commercial liners were obtained by the Australian navy to add their carrying capacity to the convoy—SS *Duntroon* and SS *Katoomba*. They departed on February 22. Then Major General Brett, in conference with General Archibald P. Wavell, decided that the situation in Java did not warrant additional ground support troops—they decided to divert the convoy to India.

With this convoy departing Fremantle for India were sixty-nine P-40s on three different vessels. Now included was USS *Langley*, the first American aircraft carrier later converted to a seaplane tender in the late 1930s. *Langley* had a very useful cargo of thirty-two fully assembled P-40Es along with thirty-three

Table 13. Convoy MS-5 to Java and India[4]

Convoy/Ships/Escort/Dates	Units and Major Cargo Items
Convoy MS-5	HQ and HQ Squadron 7th Bomb Group
USAT *Willard A. Holbrook*	9th Bomb Squadron (H)
USS *Langley*	88th Recon Squadron (H)
MV *Sea Witch*	36th Signal Platoon
SS *Katoomba*	51st Pursuit Group
SS *Duntroon*	HQ and HQ Squadron 35th Intercept Control Squadron
Escort: USS *Phoenix*, replaced with HMS *Enterprise*	45th, 51st Airbase Group
Depart Melbourne 2/13/42	69 P-40Es: 10 on *Holbrook*, 27 on *Sea Witch*, 32 on *Langley*
Depart Fremantle 2/22/42	
Two ships depart convoy 2/26/42	
Part arrive Tjilatjap 2/28/42	Total 2,953 U.S. Air Force officers and men
Part arrive Karachi 3/13/42	
	Organization equipment, military stores, vehicles

pilots and a few ground crewmen. These aircraft and pilots were with the 13th Squadron and the remainders of the 33rd Squadron that had not been lost in the Darwin attack. The 13th Pursuit Squadron (Provisional) under Lt. Boyd D. Wagner was the last of the five provisional squadrons organized. The fully assembled planes were flown across the continent to Perth and loaded onto *Langley*. These aircraft could not fly off *Langley*, but once offloaded could theoretically be immediately sent into action. Also, MV *Sea Witch* was made available, and carried her twenty-seven planes as crated cargo.

Very soon after the convoy's departure, a change of destination for part of the cargo was made. Major General Brett, making decisions from Australia and assured air cover protection from the Dutch, ordered the two ships transporting airplanes to split off from the convoy and proceed to Tjilatjap to unload their cargo. By now Japanese air superiority had been extended to most of the waters surrounding Java. Due to their difference in speeds, the vessels attempted their missions independently. The choice of Tjilatjap seemed wise based on its geographic location, but it had other handicaps. Unfortunately the town had no airfield, it being proposed to just use an adjacent open field. Also, there were no available ground personnel to haul the planes from *Langley* to such a field from the docks, much less to assemble the crated, knocked-down planes carried by *Sea Witch*. *Langley* left the convoy alone but met up with destroyers USS *Edsall* and USS *Whipple* within a few days for the run into Tjilatjap. The little convoy was sighted by Japanese scouts at 9 AM on the twenty-seventh. The ships were attacked that afternoon within one hundred miles of their destination. The proficient enemy aircrews quickly crippled *Langley*, and she sank that evening after most of the crew had successfully abandoned ship. All thirty-two airplanes were lost with the ship, but none of the thirty-three pilots or twelve ground crewmen was lost.

Sea Witch fared better, though her load of aircraft also never had a chance to participate in the defense. Somehow the ship got through the Japanese watch and arrived in port on February 28. By this time the naval battle of the Java Sea was under way, and news of the impending Japanese invasions swept the streets of every major Java city. The aircraft were offloaded onto barges, but apparently never got farther. There were no personnel to assemble the planes, and no readily available pilots to fly them—time had caught up with the defenders. The Dutch dumped the crates into the harbor's waters in the final moments when evacuating Tjilatjap. Thus the final attempt to bring in fifty-nine P-40s by sea ended with the loss of every single one of the fighters.

After the departure of *Langley* and *Sea Witch* on February 26, Convoy MS-5 continued on its voyage west. Eventually it arrived in Karachi, a port far away in western India, thousands of miles from the front in Burma. The Japanese advance had been so rapid that the Allies feared that ports in eastern India, like Calcutta, would soon be endangered. Consequently a safe haven was sought that might reasonably be expected to still be in friendly hands a few months out. The new American 10th Air Force had been activated for service in Burma, India, and China. Eventually it absorbed Chennault's AVG. When the African air ferry route to the East Indies became untenable, the planes en route were taken over in India. The first ground echelon of air units for the 10th were those in Convoy MS-5.[5]

In early February efforts from Washington began more and more to be concentrated on building a major Australian base of operations. On February 2 a new set of instructions for the supply of Army forces in the Australian area was issued by the adjutant general on behalf of the secretary of war. The commanding general, USAFIA (at that time it was again the recently promoted Major General Barnes), was directed to simultaneously dispatch critical supplies to the Philippines and to build supply levels to ninety days for Australia (five months' worth of aircraft parts and munitions). Also on the second, Brett reported via radiogram his needs for further units to establish air bases in Australia. Urgently required were seven engineer units, eight antiaircraft units, two air warning units, and two mobile air depots.[6]

Mention has already been made of some of the problems encountered with Australian ports. While in general not inadequate, their capacity was sized for the needs of a peacetime nation of a few million people. Docks, wharves, cranes, and most other facilities were not of the capacity to quickly handle the multiple shiploads of war matériel now arriving. In slightly better condition were warehouse facilities: thanks to the extensive wool export business, large warehouses were available. Another chronic problem encountered was with the labor situation. The unionized personnel, frankly of older men not otherwise subject to military service, did not possess the capacity or attitude to handle the sudden increase in workload. An estimate by Army supply officers concluded that the local stevedores did not work more than 50 percent of their paid hours. Work contracts provided for no labor during rain, limits on mechanical equipment, and the suspension of cargo handling on all holidays and weekends.[7] Obviously these rules were at odds with wartime conditions, but the political clout of the dockyard unions was not to be sneered at. Even use of troop labor to supplement the union effort could be applied only sparingly. At an early date the American logistical experts in Australia requested the assistance of quartermaster port battalions to help in Brisbane, Sydney, and Melbourne.

In mid-January a different delicate situation with this request came about. Many of the units of the Army's service branches were being formed with black soldiers.[8] The majority of the non-combat quartermaster, transport, and a considerable number of engineer and ordnance units used black manpower. All the new quartermaster port battalions being formed were to be black. Acting on the request of the command in Australia, two black units—Companies G and L of the 31st Quartermaster Regiment (Truck)—were selected for immediate shipment. At this point the matter encountered a problem with Australian authorities. It was one matter to deal with the recalcitrant local labor unions, another with the country's racial attitude and policies. In the 1940s the country had a "White Australia" immigration policy, and there were fears that a large presence of American blacks would cause domestic problems. They deemed the recommendation of sending a black unit as unacceptable. However, with the urgency apparent, the Australians were ultimately convinced that a black unit would best serve the purpose. Subsequently the 394th Port Battalion (Colored) was issued movement orders for February 7, 1942. Eventually a working policy was established based on temporary assignment; by year's end some eight thousand black American soldiers were serving in Australia.

The Navy's efforts to develop new bases in the southwest Pacific did not really get started until after the early months of 1942. The original forces needing support were mostly limited to the survivors of the Asiatic Fleet. After they left the Philippines, these forces temporarily used either Allied facilities or depended on their own tenders and supply vessels. For short periods Surabaya, Batavia, and Darwin were used as advance bases. After the loss of the Dutch East Indies the remains of the old Asiatic Fleet—now designated Southwest Pacific Naval Force—were removed from the theatre, and the submarine force was based out of Fremantle. In Australia, Sydney was designated a naval base in early February, but depended at first on Australian navy and civilian facilities. Fremantle started submarine operations with the arrival of the tender USS *Holland* in early March, and Brisbane did the same with the tender USS *Griffin* in mid-April. During the first quarter of 1942 the Navy successfully used local resources and mobile tenders; it made no effort yet to establish large shore bases or facilities. Occasional shipments of naval supplies were sent to Australia, and storehouses were managed in Sydney, Brisbane, and Fremantle, but no major naval facilities or substantial reinforcements were received in the southwest Pacific until quite a bit later in 1942.

After the arrival of substantial troops and supplies on board *President Coolidge*, *Mariposa*, and *Hammondsport*, the Army moved to finally admit publicly its presence in Australia. Following the increased sensitivity to security following the Pearl Harbor attack, no public admission of the destination or use of Australia had been made. Now, with tens of thousands of Americans present, Major General Barnes asked the adjutant general for permission to make the existence of the United States Army Forces in Australia public. The restriction was impractical at this point, causing embarrassment to the Australian authorities, and was certainly obvious to the enemy. While discretion was exercised about discussing units and facilities, from early February 1942 troops and public news services could now be officially informed of the existence of American forces in Australia.[9]

Despite the Navy's assertion that only one convoy a month could be escorted to Australia, a second such mission began to be organized later in the month following the successful *Phoenix* trip. Ultimately this movement became a complicated orchestration of four distinct efforts—through ships going from San Francisco to Brisbane, a couple of ships joining the early part of the convoy but bound just for Canton or Christmas Island, a convoy from Charleston, South Carolina, bound for Bora Bora, and finally an entirely separate convoy traveling from the East Coast through the Panama Canal with an ultimate destination of New Caledonia, but joining the Australian convoy and its escort for part of the journey. The shipping scraped together for these late January movements resulted from unprecedented efforts by the Army. Not since the efforts in early December to ship the accumulating forces and supplies to the Philippines had such an impressive schedule been successfully mounted.

The Australian-only segment was designated Convoy No. 2030. Embarked were the usual panoply of Army service units, for both air and ground support. In particular, Air Corps squadrons and service units made up a major portion of the shipment; between these four ships and follow-on *Maui*, 827 officers and 10,128 enlisted men were with the Air Force. Ammunition supplies also figured heavily in the manifest. This was one of the few convoys to the Australian command in these early war days that did not carry a large load of aircraft. Routing took the convoy toward Bora Bora in the French Society Islands, where a sort of hub was developing for the various American convoys moving across the South Pacific. The convoy arrived at its position near the island; the ships did not enter harbor or directly approach the island on February 14. There the convoy incorporated the merchant ships of Convoy BT-200. That convoy had left New York on January 23 and was bound for Australia before most of it was to proceed to Noumea in New Caledonia. *Honolulu* took over escort for the combined force. The convoy duly arrived safely in Brisbane.

The organization of these highly planned convoys prompted a dialogue about the protection of freighters traveling singly on the same routes. In the immediate pre-war period the Navy had been insistent on requiring cruiser escorts for troops and for the most critical equipment, but had still allowed a fairly constant stream of freighters to travel to the Philippines singly, and unescorted. The Army now wanted the same arrangement for shipments to Australia. On January 14 it was attempting to get USAT *Stanley A. Griffiths* (loaded with Army equipment and at the time waiting in Panama) and SS *F. J. Luckenbach* (a chartered ship with heavy equipment of the units on the *President Coolidge* and *Mariposa*, which had already departed San Francisco) to Australia. At first the Navy refused to permit their respective departures without being in a convoy, and the dates of slow convoys suitable to these ships was indefinite. Finally the Navy relented and allowed the independent sailing of freighters to Australia. On January 28 it provided the Army new guidelines for Pacific shipments. It allowed an escort for just one troop convoy a month in each direction from San Francisco to Australia, and five per month for Hawaii. The Navy did request that the Army restrict these convoys to vessels of similar speed and cruising range, and that they be of at least fourteen knots or higher speed. Independently routed freighters to Australia with West Coast or Panama origin were now permitted.

While Convoy No. 2030 was being dispatched from the West Coast, additional troops were moving to Australia in the opposite direction. As part of the recent British-American agreements from the second week of January, several large British liners converted to troop transports were put at American disposal after periods of refit and repair in American dockyards. One of the largest liners in the world—SS *Queen Mary*—was available in Boston in early February. Her high speed (twenty-six to twenty-eight knots) allowed her to make transport runs totally unescorted, as she could easily outrun any submarine or merchant raider in the world, and her size allowed her to carry up to nine thousand soldiers per trip. She was selected to make a run from the

East Coast around the Cape of Good Hope and across the Indian Ocean to Australia. The ship carried the usual variety of American air units and base protection and support personnel.[10] The ship sailed entirely unaccompanied by escort or other transports. Her speed allowed her to take just forty days from Boston to Key West, Rio de Janeiro, Cape Town, Fremantle, and eventually to debarkation at Sydney on March 28.[11]

Hard on the heels of Convoy No. 2030, the Army organized yet another Pacific sailing from San Francisco for mid-February, again despite the Navy's recent ruling limiting the escorts available for Australian convoys to one per month. The mid-February follow-on Convoy No. 2033 originally was scheduled as a slower convoy exclusively of freighters, and included merchantmen *Pennant*, *Perida*, *Japara*, *Cape Alva*, *Cape Flattery*, *Torrens*, and a Navy tanker—USS *Kaskaskia.* On February 12, the delayed *Maui* joined this group, which was provided escort from San Francisco by heavy cruiser USS *New Orleans*. Several of the ships of this convoy had destinations along the routing—MV *Japara* carried supplies just to Canton, and the Navy tanker was to make her delivery at Samoa and then return to the West Coast. The journey was uneventful, and *New Orleans* and her remaining transport and five freighters arrived safely in Australia.

Then just six days after the freighter convoy left San Francisco, yet another escorted convoy departed the same port also for Australia. Large, fast ex–Matson Navigation Company transports *Matsonia* and *Monterey* and new freighter *Mormacsea* left San Francisco on February 18. Many of Major General Brett's recently requested units were on board these transports, including several anti-aircraft units. Yet again the Navy assigned heavy cruiser escort, this time selecting USS *Portland*. Being faster ships (the convoy averaged 16.1 knots), a relatively quick arrival of March 7 was achieved. The ships arrived and unloaded at Brisbane. Thus in about ten days three important convoys reached the east coast of Australia. The combined Convoy No. 2030 and BT-200 arrived at Brisbane on February 25, the freighter convoy (with *Maui*) arrived on March 4, and the fast convoy entered the harbor at Brisbane on March 7.

With the arrival of a large number of air units, Australia was rapidly becoming the planned American air depot confronting the Japanese. A plan approved on January 18 set the strength of the Air Force in Australia to be two heavy, two medium, and one light bombardment group, along with four pursuit groups. The dispatch of fighter aircraft continued at the pace begun in late December. By February 17 the Army was able to report that 326 fighter planes had arrived in the ABDA/Australia area, and another 240 were en route. Scheduled for the month of February were a total of 245 P-39s. Light bombers were also being dispatched by ship. After the initial sixty-seven dive-bombers received in theatre (the fifty-two A-24s on board *Pensacola* convoy and fifteen on Convoy No. 2030), the effort continued with two-engine A-20 light bombers. Forty-two airplanes of this type were scheduled for delivery in February.

B-26 medium bombers were made ready for direct transfer to Australia along the Pacific ferry route. Intermediate in range, these planes had to be shipped to Hawaii by boat, but could then proceed on the island ferry route by flying. It was fortunately found that after a ship journey from the West Coast to Hawaii (always the longest, hardest leg of the ferry program) the planes could be readied with the relatively ample resources in Oahu for further transfer along the southern ferry route. Starting on January 26, 1942, all the B-26s were delivered this way. Initially using USS *Kittyhawk* and other freighters to make shuttle journeys between the West Coast and Oahu, 114 of these medium bombers were scheduled for transfer in January and February. Twenty-eight planes made the flight successfully from Oahu to Australia beginning in late January, with most of the balance making the journey the following month. The ground echelons for these planes were on board the January 31 Convoy No. 2030. With the increased pace of convoys and full utilization of the southern air ferry route, the rapid buildup in Australia became inevitable.

CHAPTER EIGHTEEN

Frantic Efforts to Reinforce Hawaii and Its Outposts

Once the vulnerability of the Hawaiian base was dramatically revealed, little time was lost in replacing losses and reinforcing the garrison. One urgently required element that could be easily replaced immediately after the attack was naval patrol bombers. They were relatively abundant elsewhere in service and were being produced at an acceptable rate by Consolidated Aircraft in its San Diego plant. Of course they also had the range to fly directly to Oahu without risking interception by Japanese submarines or surface ships, which would have been the case if they required transport by ship. As soon as December 8 the Navy was telling the Army that three replacement squadrons were already in the process of transfer.[1] By year's end, between new transfers and repairs to damaged planes, the Navy's two patrol wings in Oahu had just under one hundred patrol bombers on station—more than they had three weeks earlier on the day of the attack.

Reinforcement by sea lift was another matter. The Army wanted to quickly reinforce and resupply its garrison on Oahu following the attack. The islands did not have adequate reserves of ammunition, aircraft, or other war readiness equipment, and of course some had either been expended or permanently lost—as in the case of pursuit aircraft. In its anxiety for reinforcement the Army was willing to take greater risks than the Navy in getting men and matériel to the islands. The Navy, on the other hand, was cognizant of the risks involved in transporting across the sea from California to Oahu. No one could be sure if the attack was a preamble for additional raids or perhaps even for a serious landing attempt. Enemy submarines were clearly deployed against seaborne traffic in this corridor in the weeks following the attack. At least one initial assessment had credited the Pearl Harbor attack to just three aircraft carriers, and no one was sure of just where other such groups or supporting surface vessels might be. The Navy insisted on the use of escorted convoys in all Pacific Coast ship movements following the attack.

At this time there was more than just a perceived threat in the waters between Hawaii and California. The Japanese deployed much of their submarine fleet as an integral part of the initial attack on the U.S. Pacific Fleet. The Sixth Fleet under Vice Admiral Mitsumi Shimizu at Kwajalein deployed no less than thirty large ocean-going *I*-boats for the war in eastern Pacific waters. Besides the five subs carrying the midget attack subs for the attack, three accompanied the carrier force as patrol and downed-crew recovery, four were in a patrol line extending north of Oahu, seven patrolled between Molokai and Oahu, nine were stationed on a line south of Oahu, three performed a reconnaissance of Lahaina Roads, and one each scouted the Aleutians and Fiji/Samoa prior to the attack. Basically the mission of this force was to provide pre-attack scouting, to track down and attack any vessel trying to escape Pearl Harbor, and to intercept any attempted counterattack. High hopes were placed on this mission—in fact, there was anticipation in some quarters that the subs might inflict as much damage on the Americans as the actual carrier air attack. In this respect the deployment was a dismal failure. There was no interception of fleet units.[2]

Patrolling Japanese subs did spot *Enterprise* in the days immediately following the air attack. While an unsuccessful pursuit was attempted, the effort only resulted in the first Japanese submarine loss of the war—*I-70* was caught by an SBD dive-bomber from *Enterprise* and sent to the bottom on December 10. Several merchantmen were, however, found by the patrolling subs. The first lost was the U.S. Army-chartered *Cynthia Olson.* The ship carried lumber and engineering supplies for the Army from Puget Sound to Oahu. She was found by *I-26*, which had performed the floatplane recon of the Aleutians on her way to Hawaii. The vessel was attacked within minutes of the Oahu air assault, and after a prolonged period of shelling she eventually went down. Distress calls were picked up, but nothing could be done. The ship was lost with all hands, a civilian crew of thirty-three and two Army soldiers—a radio operator and a medical technician. It was only after the war that the entire story of her loss could be reconstructed. Three days later the Panamanian *Donerail* was sunk by *I-10* two hundred miles southeast of Hawaii. All but sixteen of the crew of forty-three were lost when the Japanese machine-gunned the survivors in their lifeboats after they had abandoned the ship. The other immediate loss was SS *Lahaina*, carrying molasses and scrap iron to San Francisco; she was sunk by *I-9* about eight hundred miles northeast of Hawaii late on the eleventh.

After the initial deployment, nine submarines were ordered to continue operations against American targets along the West Coast, while another small group remained for a week in Hawaiian waters and a few others left for home. Despite this relatively large force and the obvious lack of preparedness on the part of the defenders, there were few successes. Only a couple of ships were accounted for off the California coast in the last half of December, though there were several more unsuccessful attacks and ships damaged. Another three American merchant ships were lost within two hundred miles of Hawaii between the fifteenth and nineteenth of December. The important point is that while the loss of eight merchant ships in total in these three weeks—none with a critical military cargo—was under the circumstances not a significant problem, this was obvious proof that a large and potentially dangerous enemy force was deployed across Hawaiian shipping lanes. Until it could get better organized and assess Japanese intentions, the American military in general, and the U.S. Navy in particular, were unwilling to ignore this threat.

By December 12 the Army had prepared the first two ships of its relief plan. Thanks to the arrangements already made to accelerate shipments to the Philippines, the vessels, troops, and for the most part matériel were already available in San Francisco. Two fast vessels, *Monterey* and *Matsonia*, were ordered to prepare for sailing by 11 PM on the thirteenth. They were to be loaded with machine-gun ammo, and all the infantry and fighters they could hold. Already in negotiations, the Army asked the Navy for permission to allow these vessels to proceed at high speed without escort, to be followed on about the seventeenth by another convoy of other essential men and supplies. Two U.S. Navy rear admirals, Ingersoll and Taffinder, maintained that the waters off San Francisco were still too dangerous, and that adequate escorts could not be provided until after December 15. Additionally the Navy wanted to include *Lurline* in the same convoy, but she needed to make a trip first to San Diego to pick up sailors. A few memos were exchanged with some pointed words, but eventually the Navy agreed to transport its sailors by expedited rail to San Francisco and have all three vessels prepared for escorted sailing late on the fifteenth.

This convoy—the first seaborne resupply to reach Oahu since the attack, finally slipped out of San Francisco late on December 16. Hard on its heels three additional convoys were organized and dispatched during the remaining days of December. These convoys and principal cargo were as follows:

Table 14. Reinforcement Convoys for Hawaii, December-January 1942[3]

Convoy/Ships/Speed/ Escort/Dates	**Units and Major Cargo Items**
Convoy No. 2005 USS *Lurline*, SS *Matsonia*, SS *Monterey* 19 knots Escort: USS *St. Louis*, *Smith*, *Preston* Depart SF 12/16/41 Arrive Hawaii 12/21/41	34th, 161st Infantry Regts, 101st Signal Bn, 2/138th Field Artillery Regt, 145th Field Artillery Regt (−1st Bn), 30 casuals and 30 pilots 6,195 Army officers and men 2,988 Navy, Marine Corps, contractor, foreign, civilian passengers 58 P-40Es, 8 P-39Ds, bombs, machine-gun ammunition, refrigerated foodstuffs, gas masks, camouflage netting, currency, Navy repair supplies and tools
Convoy No. 2004 USATS *President Garfield*, *Tasker H. Bliss*, USS *Harris*, USS *Aldebaran*, Tankers: USS *Platte*, *Sabine* 14 knots Escorts: USS *Phoenix*, *Cushing*, *Perkins* Depart SF 12/17/41 Arrive Hawaii 12/24/41	2nd Bn 57th Coast Artillery Regt Part 161st Infantry Regt 1,941 Army officers and men 250 Army fillers and Navy personnel 54 P-40Es, 2 C-53s, 28 155-mm guns, 33 105-mm howitzers, 9 37-mm anti-tank guns, machine guns, bombs, artillery shells, small-arms ammunition, naval supplies, fuel oil, gasoline
Convoy No. 2007 USAT *Etolin*, *President Johnson*, *President Taylor*, *Maui* 12 knots Escorts: USS *Detroit*, *Clark*, *Cummings* Depart SF 12/27/41 Arrive Hawaii 1/07/42	95th Coast Artillery (−1st Bn), 57th Coast Artillery (−2nd Bn), 2nd Bn 52nd Coast Artillery, 47th Engineer Regt, 193rd Tank Bn 5,005 Army officers and men 1 C-53, machine-gun ammunition, mortar ammunition, hand grenades, gas masks, vehicles, subsistence
Convoy No. 2006 USS *Henderson* Sixteen freighters 8 knots Escorts: USS *Detroit*, *Clark*, *Cummings* Depart SF 12/27/41 Arrive Hawaii 1/08/42	No Army units or personnel except 1,400 Navy transfer sailors and contractors on *Henderson* 2 C-53s, 4 37-mm guns, AA and artillery ammunition, bombs, 16,000 gallons drummed gasoline, construction supplies, lumber, burlap bags, cement, lubricating oil, storage tanks, aircraft parts, engineering vehicles, ordnance supplies, subsistence, civil and commercial cargo

The most urgent demand from the Hawaiian Department was for more fighter aircraft. A plan was even discussed to put seventy-five P-40s on an aircraft carrier in San Diego and take them directly to the island. This had been done successfully with the pursuit transfers earlier in the year, and certainly was technically feasible. The Army figured the loading could be accomplished within forty-eight to seventy-two hours of authorization. On December 16 the Army passed the suggestion on to the Navy. The Navy, however, was not keen on tying up one of its very few effective assets in a ferry role when the precise whereabouts of the Kidō Butai was unknown. By the next day the idea was scrapped, though the Navy promised to look for alternate ships available for large-scale transfers. Eventually this led to the availability of the seatrains, and probably also prompted the Navy to address the quick assignment and organization of convoy escorts for the Army shipments.

Between the first two convoys, 120 fighters (mostly P-40Es, but also the first P-39Ds deployed to the Pacific) were carried to Oahu. The first convoy alone made up for the forty-six Army fighters permanently lost to the Japanese attack. Each of the December convoys took out large quantities of aerial bombs and machine-gun ammunition earmarked for the air defense. The Army also did not neglect replacing and reinforcing its heavy bomber force in the islands. Of course, the advantage with B-17s was that they could be flown direct, as three previous flights had already proven. The onward transfer of the ten bombers of the 38th and 88th Reconnaissance Squadrons was suspended. Another squadron of the 7th Bomb Group—the 22nd Bombardment Squadron—had been checking out new B-17Es at Sacramento in preparation for a follow-on flight to Hawaii when war started. After flying patrols off the California coast for a couple of days, ten of these Flying Fortresses left Hamilton Field for Hickam on the sixteenth of December. They were the first Army Air reinforcements for Hawaii since the start of the war, and were warmly welcomed.[4]

A temporary victim of the attack was the shipment of ready military equipment to America's lend-lease partners. While certainly understanding the logic and principal of what was essentially a presidential initiative, the Army had been less than enthusiastic about seeing precious arms production go to allies all along. As most of the earliest supplied arms (there were plenty of key raw materials, too) were airplanes, guns, and tanks, the Army and its Air Force were particularly hard hit. Chief of Staff General Marshall was himself a loyal supporter of the administration's policies, but he chafed at the inherent conflict between helping those fighting Germany and his responsibilities to quickly prepare the United States for the war.[5] In June 1941, both the British and American administrations strongly endorsed helping the Russians. The Soviet demands were placed on top of the previous obligations to other allies, and they were huge. On June 30, just four days after the opening of the German offensive, the Soviets asked for three thousand each of fighters and light bombers. Marshall wrote that he was unalterably opposed to the release of any additional U.S. planes until after the Philippine defenses were re-equipped. At the end of July Roosevelt insisted that two hundred P-40s be sent. These were to be sourced from planes the British would release from their own lend-lease account (about forty) and from active U.S. Air Force units (the other 160). While this seems like a small number of planes, the actual number of modern fighters in American units was abysmally small. Only 149 P-40s were in U.S. service, though another 168 were sidelined awaiting replacement of defective parts. It would take virtually the entire inventory of operational U.S. planes to satisfy even this token transfer.[6]

It is important to remember that this quantity of matériel was simply not available in the United States. While the long-range industrial capacity of the country was immense, there was no large pool or inventory of modern equipment to pull from. In almost all cases, new production right off the manufacturing line had to be divided between lend-lease clients and the Army itself. In the case of aircraft, 68 percent of the total U.S. production through June 30, 1942 went to clients abroad. The increase in the pace of production was such that for 1943–1945 there was on the whole adequate production to satisfy both demands. But for 1941 and at least the first half of 1942 this was not the case. For these critical months the supply of airplanes for the Philippines, Hawaii, and Australia had to compete with the equally important demands of the British and Soviets.

However, the shock of the Pearl attack was such that a suspension of all foreign aid occurred for several weeks in mid-December 1941. The War and Navy Departments ordered a halt in any lend-lease shipments from American ports, though it allowed shipments already in progress. Needless to say the British were fearful of the effect this might have on the Soviets as well as concerned over their own supply. Specifically they were told that the services were making an evaluation to determine whether any lend-lease supplies should be diverted to the defense of the West Coast, Hawaii, or other places in the Far East.[7] Continuation of the aid commitments was an important part of the joint Washington conference that began even before 1941 ended. The suspension only lasted a few weeks, and was really only applied to certain finished war goods like airplanes and anti-aircraft artillery. By the first of the year the president publicly announced the full continuation of aid and a schedule to make up any delayed or postponed shipments by the first of April. Still, the short breather allowed most of the production of aircraft for the month of December to be immediately available for shipment to Hawaii and Australia. It made possible the replacement of Hawaiian losses from the December 7 attack and filled the handful of ships going to Brisbane in the first six weeks of the war.

The second major Hawaiian demand was for more ground troops—primarily infantry. Starting with the first fast convoy reinforcement, soldiers were dispatched. Most of these units were initially slated for deployment to the Philippines, and fortunately were in the San Francisco area or in transit. Most of the armament of the units was included in the same convoys, which had not occurred with the *Pensacola* convoy. There was reasonably good overlap between what was available and what it would take to complete the reorganization of the two Hawaiian infantry divisions. The "Hawaiian Division" had been split to form the 24th and 25th Infantry Divisions just a few months before the war began, but had not received units or fillers to allow them to expand to full strength. The two fully equipped infantry regiments in San Francisco would allow each division to quickly come to full strength.[8] Likewise the divisions were each short a light field artillery battalion, which also could easily be made up from the assets in San Francisco.

The Navy also started assembling men and matériel to help with repairs at Pearl Harbor right after the attack. On the eighth of December the chief of naval operations directed the Eleventh Naval District (San Diego) to prepare Advance Base Destroyer Units One and Two for movement to Pearl Harbor on twelve-hour notice. These repair units were directed to take with them all portable tools and equipment that could be spared or could be obtained locally. Newly available Navy transport *Lurline* was assigned as transport. The men of the San Diego Destroyer Base were ordered by telephone to take the train to San Francisco as per agreement with the Army to accelerate movement. They arrived in the city on the fifteenth and sailed away on *Lurline* on the sixteenth.[9] Other passengers on *Lurline* consisted of replacement naval and Coast Guard personnel, a few Marines, some Australian and New Zealand military men, several hundred civilian contractors, civil service mechanics, and even a few civilians, FBI agents, and members of the press. Altogether there were 2,988 passengers in the ship. Mail, $1.5 million worth of currency, medical stores, and naval ordnance fuses rounded out the manifest.

After their arrival early on December 22, the three liners returned with the same escort. On the voyage out there had been medical personnel on board *Lurline*, intended to care for the wounded evacuees of the attack. On the return she carried a full load of naval and civilian passengers, *Monterey* had 804 passengers made up of Army casualties and dependent families, and *Matsonia* had 836 civilians, including vacationers and businessmen trapped by the start of war.[10] Also, the ships had left San Francisco so urgently that all three were still unarmed, and that would have to be rectified on the West Coast before undertaking another transport mission. The three left Hawaii on the twenty-sixth, and arrived back in San Francisco on the last day of the year.

In the meantime, arrangements had to be made to get ships temporarily held in either Pearl Harbor or Honolulu on to their proper destinations. Japanese submarines still lurked in the waters off both the Hawaiian and California coasts, and the Navy rightfully insisted that all ships going both ways, to the mainland and back, be escorted whenever possible. The first two ships prepared for the return to California were Army transports *Hugh L. Scott* and *President Coolidge.* This was the *Louisville* convoy that had been at sea on the seventh, and had been diverted to Honolulu. The Army asked specifically for the earliest practical return of the ships in view of the urgent cargoes of ammunition and supplies waiting to be loaded in San Francisco.[11] Organized as Convoy No. 4024 they departed Oahu at 10:12 PM on the nineteenth. Escort was provided by old light cruiser *Detroit*, and two destroyers. Taking advantage of the escorts, two other merchant ships tagged along part of the way in order to get back home to Los Angeles—SS *Hualalai* and SS *Memphis City*. The main convoy made good time at the relatively high speed of fifteen to sixteen knots, arriving in San Francisco at 10:15 PM on Christmas Day.

One unforeseen source of reinforcement for the Hawaiian garrison was armament from sunk, damaged, or altered naval ships. Both high- and low-angle 5-inch guns removed from sunk or severely damaged ships from the Pearl Harbor attack were salvaged and reconditioned by the Navy's ordnance shop. Damaged battleship USS *California* contributed nine 5-inch/51-caliber low-angle surface guns and eight 5-inch/25-caliber anti-aircraft guns. USS *West Virginia* gave up ten of her broadside guns and eight anti-aircraft guns. Capsized USS *Oklahoma* and severely wrecked USS *Arizona* had no readily usable armament to yield up—the ten guns removed were mostly found too damaged. The three wrecked destroyers were tapped too: USS *Cassin*, *Downes*, and *Shaw* each yielded their five 5-inch/38-caliber dual-purpose guns.

In the days immediately following the attack both the Army and Navy moved to install additional temporary defensive batteries around the island. The Navy transferred a number of older 7-inch ex-battleship broadside guns and some 3-inch and 4-inch guns to the Army for new coastal batteries. The pool of guns recently removed from the battleships was used also. The Navy constructed four new four-gun, 5-inch anti-aircraft batteries. Built in the first weeks of 1942, they were soon turned over to the Army for operation. Of the 5-inch/51s, eleven ultimately were given to the Army, though several (maybe as many as eight) were provided to the Marines to augment the armament available for the defense battalions.

The second, follow-on Oahu-bound convoy carried more of the same type of cargo. Artillery pieces to modernize the Hawaiian field artillery were included—though the 105s had originally been scheduled for the Philippines. These guns were the first of this type to reach one of the American overseas departments. Navy freighters carried mostly equipment and supplies for the ongoing salvage efforts in Pearl Harbor. Two tankers brought fuel oil and aviation gasoline needed for continuing naval operations. Each of the six transports and oilers was given a special communication liaison unit by the San Francisco Port Director, composed of a naval officer and signal and radiomen. However, the really big effort to resupply Oahu was scheduled for December 27, twenty days after the attack. A total of twenty-one transports and freighters were involved. All of the civilian freight, cargo, and mail movement had also been suspended since December 7. A considerable portion of the goods carried on the big convoy was simple civilian goods and most importantly foodstuffs. The islands had gone four weeks with only stockpiles and no meaningful resupply. While agriculture was an important part of the islands' economy, it was heavily concentrated in pineapples and sugar. At the start of the war calculations found that roughly a thirty-seven-day food supply for the islands' population existed, and even that had serious shortages. To feed the civilian population would require about 32,000 tons of food a month. Of course, that quantity could only come on commercial shipping that was both scarce and at least temporarily suspended due to enemy activity and the requirements for escorts. Also, the Army wished to create a six-month emergency reserve of rations requiring another 48,000 tons of shipping.

Congress approved a special $35 million revolving fund to finance acquisition and shipment of food, and the convoy of December 27 represented the first of this effort.

In fact, another incident helps illustrate the concern over food supplies for the island's population. The modern MV *Roseville*, a Norwegian ship under British charter en route from the West Coast to the Philippines, had been diverted into Honolulu after the Pearl Harbor attack. She arrived in harbor at 3:30 PM on December 10. Much of her cargo appears to have been both canned and perishable foodstuffs. Lieutenant General Emmons asked the War Department for help in acquiring the vessel's cargo. Specifically he suggested the food be purchased and made available to the local population, but also the usual import duties be suspended to make the purchase reasonable. After endorsements about the critical need, Stimson asked Treasury Secretary Henry Morgenthau to request the president waive the duties as he was empowered under the applicable law.[12] In the flurry of requests that were exchanged, the War Department explained that the population of the Hawaiian Islands was 425,000, exclusive of military and dependents. Rationing was already under way. At this point the departments became entangled in bureaucracy: the Agriculture Department, deeply committed to its own solutions, did not endorse the War Department's request for waiving of duties. Eventually the cargo of MV *Roseville* was sold at public auction under direction of the military governor of Hawaii, though it's not clear whether the proscribed duties were paid or not.

Convoy No. 2007 with the four faster ships was composed of Army transports *Etolin*, *Maui*, *President Johnson*, and *President Taylor*. These ships carried all the complete Army units destined for the islands this go-around, along with as much of the personal and unit gear that could be accommodated. Units ordered for transfer on December 12 were now available for loading and shipment. This included the new engineer regiment and a National Guard tank battalion. A considerable number of Air Corps civilian employees, Army unit fillers, and even quite a few naval men were also included. Altogether the four transports took almost seven thousand officers and men to Oahu. The slow convoy was made up of one naval transport and sixteen commercial or Army-chartered freighters. Military cargo was mostly bulky construction material. Large quantities of general supplies and foodstuffs were carried for civilian accounts. It appears that USS *Henderson* carried the only meaningful count of personnel: she had 350 Navy contract employees, 750 enlisted men from San Diego troop centers, and 300 ship personnel from the receiver ship in San Francisco. The slow convoy arrived on January 10, splitting up at the last moment between Pearl Harbor and Honolulu.

A systematic schedule of convoys prevailed for the following months to keep Hawaii regularly supplied. As mentioned above, the islands were not self-sufficient in several key categories; much of the arranged cargo was foodstuffs, fuel, and consumer goods. Usually both services used the opportunity to also ship rotating personnel, construction material, and equipment. These were not really reinforcement efforts, but more like routine resupply efforts. Starting with the New Year, Convoy No. 2012, with three transports and a freighter escorted by three destroyers, departed San Francisco on January 11. Additional large convoys continued on January 15, 17, and 25. In the latter the convoy got much more than a token escort. Besides three destroyers and a submarine, opportunity was taken to use battleship USS *Mississippi* to accompany the convoy. This ship was the first to arrive of the three *Idaho*-class battleships being transferred back to the Pacific from the Atlantic as replacements for the ships lost at Pearl Harbor. The battleship came within five hundred miles of Oahu before it turned around and escorted another convoy back to San Francisco. Supply convoys continued like this throughout the war, usually two large and several smaller convoys going to and from Honolulu each month.

The three convoys of December that brought troop reinforcements had safely delivered over 15,000 soldiers to Oahu. This included both intact units specifically requested by the Hawaiian Department and general fillers required to bring the units already in the islands up to strength. Likewise, the most glaring equipment deficiencies had been made up. By a month after the attack—on January 7—the fighter squadrons in Hawaii had been extensively reconstituted. There were now three squadrons of P-40Es, one of P-40Ds, and one of P-39Ds totally replacing the old P-26s and P-36s of the pre-attack defenses. However, almost immediately after the arrival of the last troops of this wave on January 3, the reinforcement of Hawaii temporarily ceased. Army command simply couldn't justify more troops for Hawaii vs. using scarce prepared units and shipping space in favor of the communication line through the South Pacific. With the two divisions in the islands mostly up to strength, and the seacoast and anti-aircraft regiments reinforced, Washington was content, at least temporarily. In truth the force present, now almost 60,000 men, should have proved adequate to prevent all but a massive invasion. So for the rest of January and February Hawaii did not receive any significant troop reinforcements, and actually in some cases saw a slight decrease in strength. However, by early March a new initiative began.

Right after the attack, the services expressed a strong desire to extend the defenses beyond Oahu to the other Hawaiian islands. For several years a regiment of the Hawaiian National Guard had been posted to several of the other islands. A week before the attack one battalion each of the 299th Infantry Regiment was on Kauai, Maui, and Hawaii, and one company was on the island of Molokai. Small detachments of Air Corps service troops and platoons of signal corps specialists for radar stations were also spread among these other islands. On December 11, 1941, Stark wrote Marshall a succinct letter entitled "The Dangerous Situation in the Pacific Ocean."[13] Stark declared that the Japanese had their naval force free to operate again against Hawaii, and could capture Samoa, Canton, Christmas, Palmyra, or Johnston Islands. They had an ample number of seasoned troops to launch further attacks. While Oahu probably could not be immediately captured, it would be possible for the enemy to occupy other Hawaiian islands and use them as stepping-stones to isolate and eventually take Oahu. Stark wanted substantial reinforcements sent to the all of the larger Hawaiian islands. Marshall responded just a day later that while he concurred with the strategic importance, there was a higher priority to enhance both the continental and Panama Canal defenses. Also, while the troops were available, the equipment was not. So reinforcement was desired, but needed to be done as part of a deliberate and cohesive plan.

In late January the availability of the troops to implement a wider defense of the Hawaiian Islands coincided with the opportune availability of the additional shipping freed up by the decisions of the Atlantic Conference. The Army could not logistically maintain a new full division at each of the three outlying islands (two full divisions—the 24th and 25th—were still on Oahu). A single new division was assigned the role to provide outer island defense. The National Guard 27th Division was selected.[14]

A conference was held at the War Plans Division in Washington on December 24 to discuss these next reinforcements. Interestingly this movement was specifically behind the priority of both the Philippines and Australia. Authorized for movement to Oahu were another anti-aircraft regiment and multiple quartermaster port, maintenance, depot, and bakery companies, a medical supply depot, and three general and three station hospitals. Split to the other islands was to be the new division, along with part of yet another anti-aircraft regiment. Altogether the total movement would involve 31,146 men. All the troop equipment, impedimenta, and thirty days' supplies, with five units of fire for weapons, would accompany the shipments. Finally in late January the Army prepared to move the 27th Division to the islands. It was recognized that coordinating such a move would be difficult. The unloading facilities at these islands were far fewer than at Honolulu. It was possible that shipments might have to be phased over a period of time rather than being made in a single movement.

An advance party under command of the division's G-2 officer, Lt. Col. Alfred D. Reutershan, was dispatched to Hawaii on February 28 on board USS *Republic.* An officer from each major unit of the division and three security platoons made the first journey. The party arrived on March 10 at Hilo. Ultimately the movement of the 27th Division and the other units of this expedition were spread over four months—March to June of 1942. A sort of shuttle service bringing units out to the Hawaiian Islands started with the March 7 sailing of a convoy of six ships. The 27th quickly assumed its garrison duties, though it was moved back to Oahu later in 1942. From Hawaii the 27th Division eventually was used for the attack on the Marshall Islands in the fall of 1943 and served in other Pacific campaigns up to the end of the war.

While the command in Pearl Harbor was necessarily occupied immediately after the air attack, thoughts soon turned to defending the outlying outposts—particularly Midway and Wake. In fact, Kimmel had previously spent considerable effort on this topic, and the related idea of using either post as an opportunity to trap enemy forces into combat. At one point in April he wrote to Stark: "For the Japanese to reduce it would require extended operations of the naval force in an area where we might be able to get at them, thus offering us an opportunity to get at naval forces with naval forces."[15] While it had already been acknowledged that the outposts could be overcome with a determined enemy attack, there were several good reasons for attempting a reinforcement effort. First, these bases were judged to be tough nuts to crack, and a rather minimal reinforcement might make the difference in their defense. In fact, the repulse of the first attempted Japanese landing on Wake seemed to prove just that situation. Secondly, there was a morale issue: it would be very difficult to not make a genuine effort to assist these outposts when potential aid was as close as Hawaii. That's what made this issue so different from the Philippines, even after the attack of December 7. Finally, there was still hope that perhaps a portion of the enemy's forces could be engaged by the aircraft carriers and cruisers of the Pacific fleet.

Admiral Kimmel started trying to gather his carriers for a potential relief effort on December 9.[16] Staff work began on a plan for the relief of Wake and Midway the next day. Based on the premise that both Wake and Midway would receive early reinforcement, an analysis of ship and plane assets was undertaken. While *William Ward Burrows* was already en route to Wake on a voyage that started pre-attack, her load of contractor civilians (only thirty-two Marines were on board), subsistence, and construction supplies in a towed barge was not what the garrison needed just then. Plus, she was not escorted and only minimally armed. In any event *Burrows* was soon rerouted to Johnston and was not of immediate use for a relief attempt. The relief plan was endorsed by Navy secretary Knox on the twelfth.

Selected as a relief ship was the seaplane tender *Tangier.* Pending orders for this expedition, she began unloading unnecessary and potentially dangerous cargo on the twelfth. Off came dozens of torpedoes and her supply of aviation gasoline normally carried for her seaplane tender role. Obviously the men and items loaded were a combination of what was requested and thought necessary by the defenders and what was immediately available in Marine warehouses and units already at Pearl Harbor.

Besides the direct shipment of men and matériel on *Tangier* would be additional fighter aircraft for the Marine air contingent. *Saratoga* would be re-loaded with the F2A Brewster Buffaloes of Marine squadron VMF-221. These planes had just been on *Saratoga* for delivery to Midway, scheduled for the morning of the seventh, when that mission was cancelled and the ship recalled immediately to Pearl Harbor. The planes had flown off to Ewa

Table 15. Manifest of Wake Relief Ship *Tangier*[17]

Wake Relief Ship	Major Units and Cargo Items
USS *Tangier*	205 Marine Corps defense battalion officers and men 5 Navy medical corps members 12 .50-caliber anti-aircraft machine guns 2 height finders, 1 director for 3-in AA, 1 5-in rangefinder 3 radar sets (1 SCR-270B, 2 SCR-268) Spare parts as requisitioned Ammunition for guns, machine guns, small arms

Airfield upon approach to Oahu. Now just a few days later they again were to embark on the same carrier, but this time with a destination of Wake. The ground contingent of the squadron, along with spare parts, would be on *Tangier*. She was to deliver supplies and aircraft to Wake and also evacuate wounded and a portion of the civilian workers. On this date the number of wounded was estimated at between thirty and seventy, and it was thought that 650 of the roughly one thousand civilian workers should be removed. *Tangier* was already loaded with supplies and ammunition for Wake in anticipation of this mission, but still needed to load the equipment and some personnel of VMF-221.

Escorting *Tangier* was Rear Adm. F. J. Fletcher's Task Force 14, centered around carrier *Saratoga*. A key phrase of the operational order was the stated assumption: "That WAKE has not been captured by the Japanese prior to the arrival of *Task Force Fourteen*." This operation was not to attempt to repel, nor was equipped to land against, an enemy occupation. D-day for arrival and unloading was set at 10:30 AM on December 23. The Americans of course did not know it, but this was about nine hours after the other D-day time selected by the Japanese for their second landing attempt. Two other American carrier task forces would be deployed within supporting distance of the reinforcement elements. Vice Adm. Wilson Brown and his Task Force 11 with carrier *Lexington* was to attack Japanese installations on Jaluit in the Marshall Islands. Brown was authorized to make a single air attack, on the day immediately prior to the scheduled Wake relief, December 22, afterwards retiring directly to Pearl Harbor. The admiral was permitted by Kimmel to "change your objective to other installations and forces in Eastern Marshalls or to withdraw without attacking as your judgment and the circumstances dictate."[18] After cancellation of the diversionary attack on Jaluit, Brown was ordered northward to more directly and closely support Fletcher. The third carrier task force involved was Vice Adm. William Halsey's Task Force 8 with *Enterprise*. He was generally to operate at sea in support of both TF-11 and TF-14. The initial operational area was to be westward of Johnston Island and to the south of Midway.

After leaving Pearl Harbor on the seventeenth, TF-14 did not exactly hurry to Wake. Fletcher caught up with *Neches* and *Tangier* as planned, but then as the decision was made to refuel the accompanying destroyers, the presence of the old oiler constrained the combined task force to a maximum speed of just twelve knots. In addition a false report that the enemy's Fifth Carrier Division was present in the Japanese mandate islands caused the cancellation of the Jaluit raid and caused Fletcher to be more cautious.[19] Even as late as the twenty-second Fletcher was still concerned about the fuel levels of his escorting destroyers. Unfortunately the weather had turned bad and the seas were rough. On that day it took ten hours to refuel just four destroyers, forward progress being reduced to just seven knots. The admiral planned to take the twenty-third to refuel the rest of his destroyers prior to approaching Wake and encountering any possible action.

While Kimmel started his Wake Relief planning on the ninth, the Japanese by coincidence also began thinking on the same day about ways to exploit their Pearl Harbor victory. At 9 PM on the ninth Vice Admiral Nagumo received Combined Fleet Order No. 14, stating: "If the situation permits, the task force will launch an air raid upon Midway Island on its return trip and destroy it completely so as to make further use impossible."[20] Nagumo took the excuse that his ships were already seven hundred miles from Midway, and taking a severe beating from the harsh seas and weather they were enduring. It was not possible to comply, and the words "if the situation permits" were applied in the negative. For a couple of days it was considered that an alternate offensive plan might be undertaken. Finally a realistic look at the requirements of fuel, along with a lack of pre-planning, scuttled this option too. What emerged was a plan to actively assist the renewed attack on Wake Island.

In the meantime the Japanese Fourth Fleet renewed its attempt to take Wake, no doubt spurred on by the rather humiliating fate of the first assault. It was about the only place where the initial Japanese attack had been repulsed, and imperial pride began to show its face. On December 20 a new, reinforced assault team left Roi for Wake. While many of the original ships had to be repaired, it appears that only *Kongo Maru* was not able to rejoin the new expedition. Of course, the two sunken destroyers had to be replaced, and also joining the attack were Rear Admiral Aritomo Gotō and the 6th Cruiser Squadron. The most substantial addition to the attack was the assignment of two aircraft carriers returning home from the Kidō Butai under Rear Admiral Hiroaki Abe. This detachment included the fleet carriers *Hiryu* and *Soryu*, escorted by heavy cruisers *Chikuma* and *Tone* and destroyers *Tanikaze* and *Urakaze*. On account of fuel concerns, it was predicted that this extra force would not be available for long, perhaps just a single air raid (actually they conducted raids on three consecutive days). On the twenty-first, at 8:50 AM, the carrier bombers began their mission to soften up Wake. There the only flyable F4F was still on the ground, waiting for the usual noontime attack. It got to the air only as the raid ended. During the afternoon the G3M2 land-based bombers added their bombs to the attack. Though some were damaged from anti-aircraft fire, all the carrier and land-based bombers returned safely to their bases.

They struck again on the twenty-second; this time the thirty-nine carrier planes encountered the last two operational Marine F4Fs. Two enemy fighters were shot down, but the last of the Marine fighters were permanently put out of action. At midnight on the twenty-second the amphibious assault arrived off the island—just enough in advance of the American relief expedition to eliminate most of its options. The Japanese landing force itself had been increased: totally available were almost three times the troops than the first effort had brought to the island.[21] Learning from their earlier fiasco, the Japanese decided to forgo the shore bombardment and instead to rush troops ashore. Within just a few hours the Japanese were ashore in substantial numbers and overwhelmed many of the American positions. Devereaux called Cunningham about 7:30 AM to get permission to surrender. The fighting ended finally around 2 PM. Total U.S. casualties were reported as 120 killed and forty-nine wounded. The Japanese reported capturing 470 Marines, 1,300 construction workers, one airplane, eighteen guns, forty-six machine guns plus rifles, ammunition, and vehicles. There was no official Japanese account of their total losses during the campaign. The land forces of the second assault reported eight officers and 103 men killed, with another five officers and ninety-two men wounded.[22] Besides about five hundred Japanese sailors lost in the two destroyers sunk on the eleventh, a total of about 320 were killed and another three hundred wounded during the land assault and in aircraft shot down during the brief campaign.

Keeping in touch with the developments, Vice Adm. William S. Pye for a short period considered a quick run-in by *Tangier*, and did give the various task force commanders looser restrictions on operating areas. Then, with some reluctance, he issued orders to cancel the relief efforts at 9:11 AM on December 22. Of course this was the twenty-third on Wake, and actually a few hours prior to the news of the surrender reaching Pearl Harbor. While the command at Pearl Harbor did not yet know the precise details of the new attack, they did know that Japanese carrier attack aircraft had been used on Wake. Pye was understandably not willing to accept hazard to the surviving carriers of the Pacific Fleet. All three task forces at sea were given new orders. Brown took *Lexington* directly back to Pearl Harbor, but Halsey and *Enterprise* were ordered to cover *Saratoga* taking *Tangier* and their relief supplies and men to Midway in lieu of Wake. Fletcher and his TF-14 had been just 425 miles from Wake on the morning of December 23. The Japanese support forces quickly vacated the area. Apparently the Japanese had no knowledge of the American relief plans and never realized how close a potential encounter might have been.

Understandably the orders to abort the mission were sorely received by most of the tactical units deployed. From the lowest-ranking deck hands to the vice admirals, all involved were itching to "get back" at the Japanese following the disastrous and, to many, humiliating defeat on December 7. Of course, additionally the brave defenders of Wake, almost the only fighting force that seemed to have adequately performed under attack, were to be abandoned at the moment of need. Strategically probably the right decision was made. Wake was inherently indefensible at this moment of the war, and the risk of losing one or more precious fleet carriers was not justified. Still the men at sea at that moment remember this decision with dismay. Supposedly when Vice Admiral Halsey learned of the decision he swore vehemently for half an hour and had to be dissuaded from ignoring his orders and advancing on Wake independently.

Almost immediately following the Pearl Harbor attack emergency efforts were hatched to augment the defensive garrisons at the ferry bases. In fact, some forces were actually at sea in transit. Aircraft carrier *Lexington* had returned to Pearl Harbor from its aborted attempt to fly the Vindicators of VMSB-231 to Midway. The aircraft were transferred to Oahu's Ewa Airfield on December 10, while *Lexington* restored her regular air complement in anticipation of early action. Finally on December 17 the Marine planes flew nonstop from Oahu directly to Midway. This was a very long flight for a single-engine aircraft, in fact setting a Navy record for distance. Fortunately weather and navigation cooperated, and all of the aircraft successfully made the trip.

The three Marine-garrisoned bases in the central Pacific all were sent reinforcements immediately following the Pearl Harbor attack. Midway fortunately received two supply deliveries right before war started. *Regulus* had brought fresh supplies and the first three new 7-inch guns on December 4. USS *Wright* had also just been at Midway, dropping men and supplies for the scout bomber squadron on December 3, and picking up some rotating contractors for departure. The ship sailed into Pearl Harbor on December 8, picking its way carefully between the debris and flotsam of the attack. Eleven days later, on December 19, she left Pearl again for Midway with a hurriedly

Table 16. Reinforcements for the Outlying Naval Stations

Destination/Ships/Dates	Units and Major Cargo Items
Johnston Island USS *Burrows* (diverted from Wake) Arrive 12/15/1941	Small number of rotating Marines and contractors 1,800 tons construction supplies, lumber Refrigeration reefers, food, gasoline
Johnston Island USS *Lamson*, *Mahan*, *Navajo* Arrive 12/30/1941	247 Marines of the 4th Defense Battalion 2 5-in seacoast guns, 4 3-in anti-aircraft guns 2 SCR-270B radar sets Food, ammunition, supplies
Midway Island USS *Wright* Arrive 12/24/1941	137 Marines of 4th Defense Battalion 1 7-in gun, 2 sets 7-in fire-control equipment 4 3-in anti-aircraft guns 6 .50-cal and 6 .30-cal machine guns 2 24-in searchlights 1 SCR-270B radar set Spare parts, sand bags, camouflage equipment Food, ammunition, supplies
Midway Island USS *Tangier* (diverted from Wake) Arrive 12/26/1941	205 Marines from various defense battalions 5 Navy medical corps members 12 .50-caliber anti-aircraft machine guns 2 height finders, 1 director for 3-in AA, 1 5-in rangefinder 3 radar sets (1 SCR-270B, 2 SCR-268) Spare parts as requisitioned Ammunition for guns, machine guns, small arms Food, supplies
Palmyra Island USS *McFarland*, *Sumner*, *Thornton* Arrive 12/27/1941	323 Marines from 1st and 3rd Defense Battalions Food, ammunition, supplies

assembled group of reinforcements. As part of the attempt to reduce the civilian contractor population on the islands, *Wright* took away 205 men of the CPNAB organization. Another reinforcement arrived on December 26 when the men and supplies on *Tangier* were diverted to Midway from the aborted Wake relief attempt. The final reinforcement for Midway was also not originally intended. On board *Saratoga* as part of the Wake Island relief expedition was Marine fighter squadron VMF-221. These fourteen F2A Brewster Buffaloes had been dispatched for reinforcement of Wake's beleaguered VMF-211. When the relief expedition was cancelled, orders were placed to drop the planes at Midway instead. While certainly not the best pursuit plane in the American arsenal, these were the first and for quite a while the only defensive fighters this garrison would obtain. The flight of all fourteen aircraft landed on Christmas Day.

Similarly sized and timed reinforcements were quickly planned and executed for the garrisons at Johnston and Palmyra. In the rush to supply men to the outpost islands, it appears that little attempt was made to protect the organizational integrity of the individual defense battalions. At 7 AM on December 24 three ships departed Oahu carrying the planned reinforcements to Palmyra. Various reinforcement elements were collected from the 1st and 3rd Defense Battalions then resident at Pearl Harbor, totaling thirteen officers and 310 enlisted men.[23] Soon after the Pearl Harbor attack, recommendations came to remove the civilian workers on both Johnston and Palmyra Islands. Since the start of the emergency most of the contractor personnel had been employed on the improvement of defense structures, including splinter-proof shelters for all personnel. At Johnston the runway was rushed, so that by December 20 it was available, along with temporary stations for refueling and loading munitions. Four 25,000-gallon tanks for aviation fuel were placed in the ground and covered with earth for protection. A report of December 13 stated that the contractor morale was generally good, though many of the men wanted to be released to go home.[24]

Johnston's first resupply since the outbreak of war was also an unplanned delivery. Navy transport *Burrows* had been loaded with 1,800 tons of construction supplies, lumber, reefer containers, and gasoline, along with normal small contingents of rotating Marine, naval, and contractor personnel for Wake. *Burrows* was ordered to divert her supplies and barge *PAB-7* to Johnston for use there. Opportunity was taken upon her arrival to load seventy-eight contractors for the return to the Hawaiian Islands. That night she was fired on by a Japanese submarine, one shell coming within thirty yards of her fantail. Undamaged, she immediately departed. On the eighteenth two naval patrol bombers flew into Johnston to act as a locally based air arm. Just a couple of days after the Palmyra-bound group departed, three other small ships similarly left Pearl Harbor for Johnston Island. Two destroyers composed this little convoy. Included was a strong detachment of the 4th Battalion along with the long-requested additional 5-inch seacoast battery of two guns and a full 3-inch anti-aircraft battery of four guns. The expedition arrived on December 30 without incident.

Throughout January and February additional increments of Marines were sent to the two southern bases to bring them to optimal strength. For example, Palmyra Island was sent from Honolulu on January 17 USS *McFarland* and fifty-six men, on January 19 USS *Preston* with sixty-two men of two intact rifle platoons, on January 23 USS *Hulbert* with sixty-three more men, and on February 7 USS *Ballard* with fifty-two men. Later in the summer Palmyra even received a small detachment of nine Marine light tanks to supplement its mobile defense capabilities.

Reinforcing Samoa was much more complicated. Because of the distance involved and the quick exhausting of resources in Oahu, Samoa was to be directly reinforced from the West Coast. A large convoy with heavy escort was quickly organized by the Marines by year's end.

These reinforcements were organized on December 24 as the 2nd Brigade in San Diego where several key elements were stationed. The command was given to Col. Henry L. Larsen at Camp Elliott. At Samoa they would join the 7th Defense Battalion already stationed there and form a considerable defensive force.

Departing together were the large transports. As they had yet to be modified to military transport configuration and retained many of their peacetime amenities, in later years the Marines on board thought back fondly to the rooms with real beds (instead of bunks); stewards waited on tables in the dining halls and the lounges were still available. Even the portholes had not yet been sealed. Except for the usual encounters of men inexperienced with ocean sailing and seasickness, the trip to southern waters was uneventful. Landfall was made on January 19. The local garrison was nervous, having endured a Japanese submarine bombardment just a few days before, and welcomed the new arrivals. Providing distant support and protection was Task Force 17—aircraft carrier *Yorktown*, heavy cruiser *Louisville*, and four destroyers. After seeing their charges safely to Samoa, the covering *Yorktown* task force participated in a successful series of raids on the Marshall and Gilbert Islands on the first of February.

The unloading at Samoa proceeded smoothly. Immediately the 8th Marines assumed beach defense responsibilities from the 7th Defense Battal-

Table 17. Reinforcement Convoy to Samoa[25]

Convoy/Ships/Speed/Escort/Dates	Units and Major Cargo Items
Convoy No. 1005	2nd Marine Brigade:
	8th Regiment
USS *Lurline*	2nd Battalion 10th Regiment (Artillery)
SS *Matsonia*	2nd Defense Battalion
SS *Monterey*	Detachment of 2nd Division engineer battalion
USS *Jupiter*	
USS *Lassen*	Company B, 2nd Tank Battalion
USS *Kaskaskia*	Detachment of 2nd Division service battalion
Independent follow-on: USS *Procyon*	Detachment of 2nd Division medical battalion
14 knots	Total of 4,798 Marines
Escort: *St. Louis*, *Smith*, *Preston*	
Depart San Diego 1/06/42	Construction supplies, ammunition, food, general supplies, mining equipment, Higgins boats
Arrive Samoa 1/19/42	

ion. The 2nd Defense Battalion set up anti-aircraft guns around the harbor, and the 10th Marines put their field guns into temporary emplacements. A small unit of Marine amphibian airplanes assumed local scouting and anti-submarine patrols.[26] The engineers actively turned to the airfield work. It was pushed around the clock with the assistance of lights, and reported ready for aircraft in less than two months—on March 17. True to the plan, transports were turned around quickly and returned to the West Coast. The Marines played a valuable role in safeguarding what was then the front line with the Japanese. However, by fall the necessity of tying up an entire trained regiment in a rather remote section of the Pacific was no longer necessary. The Marine units of the 2nd Division left in October for service on another island—Guadalcanal.

CHAPTER NINETEEN

Further Adventures of the Artillery Battalions

On January 6, 1942 the transport *Willard A. Holbrook* arrived at Port Darwin with the men and much of the equipment of the 147th and 148th Field Artillery Regiments. The soldiers were disembarked gradually pending the construction of adequate camp facilities.[1] Of course, shore leave was arranged, but Port Darwin did not offer a lot of entertainment. In 1942 the full population would probably have been about 2,500, but most women and children had already been evacuated, reducing it to probably something more like two thousand. Perhaps one thousand Australian military personnel were also at hand. The town was really a frontier station, complete with dirt streets, just a single hotel, one Chinese-run general store, a couple of banks, a hospital, the Star Theatre and (importantly) several pubs.[2] Even the port itself had just one pier, capable of accommodating a total of two medium-sized ships. Recreational facilities really did not exist in any capacity. While a rail line left Darwin for the interior, it dead-ended about three hundred miles distant. Land transport to the rest of Australia had to be conducted subsequently by truck over very dusty dirt roads.

Darwin received some military attention by the Australians prior to the war. In the 1930s a modern fixed coast artillery battery was installed. In 1938 a new Royal Australian Air Force flying station and field was begun, and it was ready to start operations in July 1939. Lack of aircraft and the heavy demands for planes and crews to serve with the Australian Imperial Force (AIF) elsewhere meant that only No. 13 Squadron of a dozen Lockheed Hudson bombers was stationed here at the war's outbreak. In fact, that squadron moved to Ambon, and No. 2 Squadron passed through for Timor in early December according to a pre-war schedule. In mid-February 1942 Australia's combat forces were mostly limited to the army's 23rd Brigade. A very few Hudsons, Wirraways, and the usual miscellaneous collection of transports and trainers represented the Royal Australian Air Force. The naval base itself was more of an enlarged refueling station; there were only limited facilities for other ship services and not much of a shore establishment. A depot repair ship, two sloops, and a few minesweeping and escort craft were at the navy station.

While the troops on *Holbrook* were disembarked with efficiency, it can't be said to have been the same with the equipment and supplies. Already encountered at Brisbane, the problems with the Australian stevedoring system were quickly revisited. Australia had been in the war for over two years; the strain on the domestic labor situation was intense with most able-bodied men already in the military services. Understaffed, with many older workers comfortable with a union labor system that did not emphasize efficiency, the available labor could not get ships promptly unloaded. Called "wharfies" by the troops, it was apparent, at least with the Darwin contingent, that the stevedores considered the military traffic in port a bonanza to their earning capabilities that should be prolonged as long as possible.[3] When the U.S. Army tried to use its own personnel to accelerate unloading, it ran afoul of the union. The confrontation eventually was settled by agreeing to allow the stevedores to unload certain hatches at their pace, while the Army unloaded the more critical and larger part of the cargo with their own labor. For a considerable length of time the American artillery units were temporarily detailed as labor. This was far from the last time that this situation was encountered, and eventually it was bounced to very high levels before working solutions were found.

After arrival in Darwin late on January 5, *Bloemfontein* stayed in the roadstead with the soldiers of the 2/131st on board. A new convoy, consisting of *Bloemfontein* and Asiatic Fleet escort cruisers *Boise* and *Marblehead*, and destroyers *Barker*, *Bulmer*, *Parrott*, *Pope*, and *Stewart* departed on January 8. The relatively short trip of three days to Surabaya did hold some excitement. Japanese submarines were by this time deployed in some numbers around both ends of Java. During the voyage the ship picked up a report from a Norwegian freighter ahead of them being chased by a Japanese submarine. Also, USAT *Liberty* was lost to a Japanese submarine off Bali on the eleventh of January. Tensions were high and imaginations active; several passengers were convinced that the ship narrowly avoided one or more torpedoes fired at them.

While the convoy did not actually sight a sub, they did take course precautions before entering Surabaya Harbor.[4]

The little convoy carrying the 2/131st and 26th Field Artillery Brigade Headquarters arrived in Surabaya Harbor at 3 PM on January 11. Disembarkation of the men occurred relatively quickly; they were immediately moved by narrow-gauge railway to the hill country near the town of Malang over fifty miles south from Surabaya. The equipment on *Bloemfontein* took until at least the seventeenth to unload. From Malang they went to Singosari Airfield, which had been selected to be the home airfield for American heavy bombers. The brigade headquarters moved at first to Malang, but then received orders on the twenty-fourth to go to Bandoeng. This unit, probably amounting to something like 120 men at this point, was of little use in Java. With the battalion headquarters for the 2/131st there was no use for yet another higher echelon headquarters. In fact, there was no other Army combat unit in Java of any sort to command, only skimpy airfield maintenance outfits. It appears that the 26th headquarters mainly acted as clerical and administrative support to the small American Army command structure on Java. In any event it was evacuated back to Australia just six weeks after its arrival, though not before seventeen of its men joined the 131st.

At Singosari the artillery battalion quickly settled into camp. Additional 75-mm ammunition finally arrived in early February at Tjilatjap on *President Polk*. Starting in early February the airfield came under Japanese air attack. The artillery gunners placed some of their 75s into improvised elevated positions to fire back, and took over .50-caliber anti-aircraft guns salvaged from wrecked aircraft to provide some airfield defense. There is no record of success in this capacity, but the ability to return fire must have greatly improved their morale. Soon a far more valuable role emerged for these troops. The number of airfield service troops was severely limited. A few mechanics, ordnance men, and technicians left the Philippines riding in the riddled bombers of the 19th Bomb Group. A larger contingent of about two hundred arrived on January 28 from the 22nd Bomb Group on board *President Polk*. Still, there were not enough men to service these bombers between missions. The Texan National Guardsmen pitched in. They helped with labor-intensive tasks like camouflaging, building revetments, gassing aircraft, and particularly in towing them with their heavy prime mover trucks. Usually the battalion was asked to contribute sixty to seventy men and a dozen trucks a day to assist the overtaxed bomber ground crew. On a more permanent basis, twenty-three men transferred to the 19th Bombardment Group.

Other Allied forces were also coming to Java. While not particularly sanguine over the prospects of a successful defense, the British and Australians also realized that politically they needed to support the ABDA alliance, and that meant ground troops in addition to the contribution of air and naval forces. The British in particular were in an awkward situation: since they had gladly accepted Dutch fighter and bomber units for the fields in Malaya and Sumatra during the defense of Singapore, they could hardly ignore their ally's similar request now. The experienced Australian AIF corps that had fought Rommel in North Africa was now on its way back for the defense of the homeland, having departed in late January after the outbreak of war in the Pacific. A few of the lead elements of this movement—the advance echelon of the 7th Australian Division, AIF—were on transport *Orcades* and were ordered to land in Java (over the vocal dissent of the commander of 1 Australian Corps). Composed of a battalion each of machine gunners and pioneers with some other minor units, the ad-hoc force was organized as a brigade under the command of Brigadier Arthur S. Blackburn. This force was known as "Blackforce."

America's contribution to Blackforce was the bulk of the 2nd Battalion, 131st Field Artillery Regiment. The battalion headquarters and two of its three firing batteries left Singosari for new positions with the force in western Java. On the night of February 28, the Japanese landed on Java. On the morning of March 3 a detachment of the Japanese 16th Regiment proceeded along one of the few major roads eastward ten miles to Leuwiliang, where the road crossed a bridge on the Tjianten River. There they met Blackforce, the best-prepared Allied force on the island, and fought a brief but relatively intense action. The two American field artillery batteries were assigned to back up two major Australian units holding the bridge.

From their position behind the bridge, the gunners of Battery "D," under Maj. W. R. Rogers, opened fire on the Japanese at 2:30 PM on the fourth.[5] There are no specific documents surviving that detail the results of the barrage, but both Australian battalions in the defensive position report that the fire was accurate and punishing to the Japanese. This action at Leuwiliang bridge was just about the only stiff resistance encountered by the Japanese land forces on Java. Dutch army forces were exclusively native troops indifferently trained and equipped, commanded by just a few Western officers with their own preoccupation about their families still on the island. Despite elaborate plans and hopes, when confrontation happened, most of the Dutch colonial forces generally melted away rather than fight. No American casualties were sustained in this action.

On February 26 the American 26th Brigade headquarters received word to be at Tjilatjap later that evening for evacuation by boat from Java. With the exception of the inevitable man or two that got left behind or had been "drafted" into the 131st, the headquarters and its remaining one hundred men withdrew in good order to Australia. One incident of personal self-sacrifice during these movements stands out. Col. Albert C. Searle was commander of the 26th Brigade and senior American ground forces officer on Java. After seeing his unit safely into a transport bound for Australia, he personally refused to board and returned to the 2/131st. As a professional Army officer, he could not ethically witness the sacrifice of the National Guardsmen from Texas while the "regulars" managed to get away. Searle surrendered with his fellow artillerymen and went into prison camp with the National Guard troops he determined not to abandon.[6]

After its couple of days of retreat and separation, the inevitable end came for Blackforce. On March 8 British Major General H. D. W. Sitwell ordered the various Allied forces to surrender, and Blackforce itself complied with the surrender order on the ninth. Several weeks were spent by the prisoners shuttling between several camps. Eventually almost three thousand Allied prisoners were concentrated at what was called Bicycle Camp near Batavia by late April 1942. The continuing story of the prisoners, in common with most Allied military personnel taken in early 1942, was not pleasant. In October 1942 three large contingents of American prisoners were moved in stages to Singapore, and many went on to work on the famous Burma Railroad.

Apparently Battery "E" was to follow the rest of the battalion shortly after completing storage of the unit's luggage and non-essential stores, and after assisting the final servicing of B-17s at the airfield. Unfortunately events moved ahead too rapidly to ever allow this battery to rejoin its parent organization; delayed by tasks with the bombers, by the time it was ready to move the Japanese were already landing. The battery, with its four 75-mm guns, was hurriedly attached to the eastern Java defense forces.[7] Under the command of Capt. Thomas A. Dodson the battery moved from Malang to a plantation six miles from Surabaya late on the twenty-seventh. Then on March 5 they received orders to move even closer to the city, to help establish a defensive line. On March 7 a short but sharp action was held with advancing Japanese elements. The men of Battery "E" used both their artillery and rifles in repulsing a strong Japanese probing attack. However, resistance was crumbling, and later that same day the men disabled their guns by removing the breechblocks and firing pins and throwing them in the river.[8] With only ammunition for personal pistols left, the unit prepared itself for the inevitable. By the evening of the eighth the men of Battery "E," 2/131st, were in Japanese hands.

Meanwhile, in Australia the three artillery battalions belonging to the other two American artillery regiments were put under the tactical command of the Australian Seventh Military District. The combat forces in this northern theatre of Australia were under the command of Australian Major General D. V. J. Blake. It was not long before the Americans decided to contribute one of the regiments to the multi-national reinforcement of Timor Island.

Timor Island is located four hundred miles to the northwest of Darwin. ABDA commander General Wavell was personally convinced that the division of his limited forces between the various Dutch East Indies islands was unwise and an invitation to piecemeal defeat. Usually he vigorously refused requests to send token defense forces to locations beyond Java, but for Timor he made an exception. Understanding that the island was the essential ferry link to getting American short-ranged aircraft to Java, he authorized reinforcement of the garrison in late January 1942. Until this time the defensive forces were limited to an undersized Dutch battalion of about five hundred men and the Australian 2/40th Infantry Battalion. The situation in reality was more complicated than this, as the island was actually occupied by two colonial administrations—the Dutch with a neighboring Portuguese colony. Portugal was attempting to remain neutral in the war, but wished to plan at least some measures for opposing an attempted Japanese takeover. Local Portuguese forces amounted to about four hundred mostly native soldiers organized into a rifle company, and a cavalry platoon.

On January 26 the Portuguese commercial merchantman *João Belo* left Lorenço Marques in Mozambique with reinforcements for the Portuguese Timor garrison. On board was a battalion combat group consisting of two native rifle companies, a company of native pioneers, and a light artillery battery. Under command of Captain-Lieutenant Raúl Lima Ferreira de Carvalho, the force totaled about eight hundred men. The ship was escorted by the 2nd-class sloop *Gonçalves Zarco*. Sailing by way of Beira and Colombo, the small task force was due to arrive at the latter port about February 18. An Allied move into Portuguese territory on the seventeenth, followed by the Japanese conquest on the twentieth, found the ships still at sea. Attempts to acquire safe passage provisions from the Japanese failed even though the countries were still not at war. After some delay and anxiety about remaining fuel levels, the two ships returned with their passengers to Mozambique. The Portuguese had to live with the occupation of their colony for the rest of the war.

In any event additional Allied reinforcements for Timor were to come from two sources. From assets in Java a British AA unit was contributed.[9] It was more difficult to identify the requested infantry battalion needed. Finally on February 5 the Australian War Cabinet agreed to the transfer of the 2/4th Pioneer Battalion, which was part of the Darwin defenses, and a troop of anti-tank guns. The American command agreed to release one of the field artillery battalions at Darwin as artillery support. The 148th Field Artillery Regiment (still with just its first battalion and its twelve 75-mm guns) was chosen. As always at this stage of the war, shipping was not easy to arrange; sufficient vessels would not be available until February 15. Fortunately a small convoy of three ships had arrived on January 19 at Darwin—SS *Mauna Loa*, SS *Portmar*, and USAT *Meigs*. Transport for the Australian troops would be the American *Mauna Loa* and *Meigs*—the latter an original participant with the *Pensacola* convoy. Somewhat ironically she would now be transporting not the American units but Australians and their equipment.[10]

Two other transports were selected to carry the American contingent of the force. The American commercial freighter SS *Portmar* had arrived in Sydney in late December. After working her way to Darwin on February 8 via Brisbane, she was virtually shanghaied by the USAFIA command for further Army usage.[11] *Portmar* was ordered back to Darwin to load a contingent of the Timor expedition. On Valentine's Day of 1942 the 148th packed their gear and headed for the pier. Two batteries under the command of Maj. George A. Whitely boarded *Portmar*. MV *Tulagi* took on the other battery and the service battery under the immediate control of the battalion commander, Lt. Col. James C. Patterson.

The convoy of four vessels was escorted by Asiatic Fleet flagship *Houston*, American destroyer *Peary*, and the Australian sloops HMAS *Swan* and *Warrego*. *Houston* was damaged from the bombing she had received in the Flores Sea. While patched up and seaworthy (though her burned-out aft 8-inch turret was useless), the heavy cruiser was still of utility for escorting purposes. No fighters were available at Darwin for dedicated air cover, though arrangements were made to allow *Houston* Captain Albert H. Rooks to call for protection if needed. The convoy departed on the fifteenth. On the second day out it was spotted by a Japanese seaplane based at Kendari. A call back to Darwin brought out a lone P-40 flown by Lt. Robert J. Buel. (The lieutenant and his plane from the 3rd Pursuit Squadron had been left behind with minor mechanical problems when this squadron flew through Darwin to Timor earlier in the month.) Upon arrival Buel had difficulty locating the snooping seaplane, even when *Houston* fired at it in order to reveal its location. Eventually Buel did spot the shadower, and gave chase. The two planes disappeared over the horizon, and were soon replaced with a large flash. Neither plane returned to its squadron, but some of the Japanese aircrew were rescued by the Australians and told the story of the attack by the P-40 that resulted in the destruction of both craft.

Apparently the spotting report from the Japanese got through, as the next day a major air attack on the convoy developed. On the seventeenth the Japanese attacked with nine flying boats and a formation of thirty-five two-engine G3M bombers. Without any aerial cover, the convoy was left to the anti-aircraft defenses of its escort. Only *Houston* had heavy anti-aircraft batteries capable of reaching the approaching Japanese planes. During the previous Flores Sea bombing, the cruiser had been disappointed in the quality of its ammunition—something like 70 percent of the heavy 5-inch shells proving to be duds. Fortunately, before departing the theatre *Boise* had transferred five hundred good rounds to *Houston*, which were put to good effect in this encounter. In fact, *Houston* spent the attack racing through the convoy continuously firing at the Japanese formations. Observed by the captain of *Meigs*, the master was heard to repeatedly shout in reference to *Houston*'s performance, "Look at those bastards go!"[12] Most of the other ships in the convoy could not do much; *Portmar* and *Tulagi* carrying the American contingents were only armed with machine guns. At the end of the battle *Houston* sailed through the convoy to the rousing cheers of the assembled crew and passengers of the transports.

The attack started at eleven o'clock and lasted for about forty-five minutes, but for a change the Japanese seemed to lack the accuracy they had demonstrated in recent encounters. For all the bombs dropped, undisturbed by any Allied air cover, no direct hits were obtained. Numerous near-misses occurred, and one bomb late in the encounter landing near *Mauna Loa* killed one of the ship's crew and wounded two others. Within a few hours, orders were issued for the convoy to reverse course and return to Darwin. The convoy anchored back in Darwin on February 18. *Houston* and *Peary* were urgently needed back in Java, and left immediately after refueling. On the way out of harbor *Peary* pursued an enemy submarine contact, and expended so much oil that she returned again to Darwin to refuel.

As it turns out, while the Allies were juggling to get reinforcements to Timor, the Japanese onslaught continued and the next troops to be landed at Koepang were theirs. On February 17 nine transports escorted by a destroyer squadron left Ambon for Timor. By the twenty-fourth the important airfields and towns were all under Japanese control.

When the Timor reinforcement convoy returned to Darwin on the eighteenth, *Meigs* and *Mauna Loa* moved to the wharf and unloaded their Australian troops. Unfortunately the limited dock space did not allow for the debarking of the two ships carrying the Americans; that would have to wait until the next day. However, on that next day, the nineteenth, the Japanese neutralized any potential Allied reaction by delivering a devastating aerial attack on Darwin itself. A coordinated attack by carrier and land-based air caught the Allies by surprise.

The attack found the harbor fairly bursting with targets. An enemy aircraft reconnaissance on the tenth had revealed twenty-seven ships in harbor and an estimated thirty planes on the two airfields. Allied shipping in the harbor was heavily targeted. Among those receiving enemy attention were the ships just recently returned from the aborted Timor expedition. Only *Houston* was not present, having left for Java late the day before the attack. Destroyer *Peary* was not so lucky. She was hit and burned ferociously before sinking later in the day. Heavy casualties were sustained—eighty sailors were killed and thirteen wounded. Another Asiatic Fleet veteran was damaged—seaplane tender *William B. Preston.* Taking several direct hits and several near-misses, she managed to leave harbor and eventually make Broome, Fremantle, and Sydney. In the attack she lost eleven sailors.

SS *Mauna Loa* took two bombs in No. 5 hold, blowing holes in the hull. Fortunately she had already unloaded her Australian troops; her crew and master got away in boats, and the complement of thirty-four lost just one man. The ship herself was a total loss. USAT *Meigs* also took two bomb hits, with about the same results. One bomb hit amidships, the other went into a cargo hold, causing the ship's sinking. Of the crew of sixty-seven, one was lost—the third mate. *Portmar* was also holed, plus she suffered much damage to the deck and superstructure from strafing fire. With ninety-eight separate holes, she was beached in shallow water to prevent her from sinking. Still having the American artillerymen on board, she lost one seaman out of a crew of thirty-five, and one soldier was killed out of an estimated three hundred soldiers on board. Later in early April she was refloated and eventually repaired. MV *Tulagi* was also hit during the attack, and was beached to prevent sinking.

On board, three of the American artillerymen she was carrying were killed. The day was hard on the artillerymen—thirty-four Purple Hearts and five Silver Stars were earned.

While not part of the Timor convoy, another *Pensacola* convoy veteran was in port. SS *Admiral Halstead* was carrying a load of 14,000 barrels of gasoline. With such a flammable cargo on board, the captain and crew quickly evacuated the ship during the attack. Observing the ship intact, they returned and progressively unloaded her cargo over the next six days. Successful attempts were later made to obtain the vehicles and particularly the 75-mm guns on *Portmar* and *Tulagi*. The British ship was soon brought back to dock and its contents salvaged with relative ease. *Portmar* was more of a challenge. A barge and crane were needed to individually offload trucks and guns at low tide. Most of the work had to be done at night. Eventually all eight guns were brought out, taken apart, completely reconditioned, and put back into the unit's service.[13]

Serving locally for some time, the Americans began to become more Australian-like. They cut off their khaki pants to make shorts, and were equipped with Australian boots and Enfield rifles. Needless to say their appearance, especially since they also still wore their old-style, British-appearing helmets, was most confusing to later American arrivals. Finally at the end of April the 148th re-equipped with recently arrived 105-mm howitzers.

The 147th Field Artillery Regiment, still commanded by Colonel Jensen, had stayed behind in Darwin when the 148th departed on its ill-fated trip to Timor. Not until June 29, 1942 did the 147th leave Darwin, to eventually fight in New Guinea and, several years later than planned, the Philippines.

CHAPTER TWENTY

The New South Pacific and African Air Ferry Routes

Even before the inaugural flight of B-17s to the Philippines in September 1941 the Army began looking for a safer, alternate route. It was always recognized that the existing—sometimes referred to as the "northern" route—passed over the Japanese-controlled Marshall and Caroline Islands. Even if not crossing Japanese airspace, the bases and route from Wake to Rabaul and then Darwin were too exposed to potential attack in the event of hostilities. A less vulnerable route for transfer of landplanes appeared feasible among the relatively abundant island chains in the southern latitudes. On August 16, 1941 the chief of staff directed the joint Army-Navy planning committee to make a recommendation for consideration by the Joint Board. That study looked at options based on factors such as: distances to be traveled, adequacy of existing facilities, defensibility, difficulties in development, and weather. While a few of the potential sites were already established or under development as naval air bases, the infrastructure of a commercial route did not exist. Also, some of the sites had diplomatic complications that would have to be resolved. In any event, even with a high priority, it was recognized that more than a few months would be needed to properly acquire and develop such a route. Chief of Air Staff Brigadier General Spaatz qualified his endorsement with: "This matter is very urgent; it must be thought of in terms of weeks and not years; every possible expedient must be visualized and utilized in order to complete this project in the minimum time."[1]

Almost simultaneously with the Washington-based committee analysis, the Army command in Hawaii initiated the first steps. In early October the department was given approval and funds to expedite the airfield work immediately. On October 15 Lieutenant General Short ordered the construction of ten primary fields and five alternate airfields operable in ninety days. In addition to those in the Hawaiian Islands, the Army Department was responsible for fields at Christmas, Canton, Fiji, and Noumea. Plans and survey teams were dispatched and reported by the end of October. At Canton Island the Commercial Aviation Authority had already laid out an airfield. At this island work was assigned to contractors, while the projected Christmas Island facility was to be built by the Army's 804th Aviation Engineer Battalion. While both islands were selected as alternatives to the Navy's field on Palmyra, Canton was given a higher priority. Navy transport USS *Antares*, loaned for this trip only, arrived at Canton on November 14 with barges of supplies, a derrick, fifty initial garrison troops, and two hundred contract workers.

The committee reported to the Joint Board on November 28; even then the urgency of the project was so great that the Hawaiian Department was already authorized to start work. While acknowledging that it was working from incomplete information, the committee nonetheless reported that the best new route appeared to be: Hawaii–Palmyra–Canton–Samoa–Fiji–New Caledonia–Rockhampton (Australia)–Philippines. It was declared that Christmas Island had potential for development as a reasonable alternative. After collecting additional survey data the committee went on to describe each individual candidate site, some of which were already experiencing construction under the local initiative:[2]

PALMYRA: An American-owned coral atoll of about fifty islets. Already occupied by a Marine garrison with fixed defenses. Commandant 14th Naval District reports that it should have a usable runway by the middle of March to eventually measure five thousand by five hundred feet—expected to be completed about June 30, 1942.

CHRISTMAS: A very large coral atoll about thirty miles long and ten miles wide, land area about 250 square miles. Population currently about forty, including radio personnel. Sovereignty over island is claimed by both the United States and the United Kingdom. The 804th Engineer Battalion is already at work preparing the first of three 5,000-by-500 foot runways. The initial runway will be available for use by January 15, 1942.

CANTON: A small coral atoll about twelve miles long and three miles wide, includes central lagoon. No water available. Excellent seaplane facilities inside lagoon. Sovereignty is claimed by both the United States and the United Kingdom. The Civil Aeronautics Board has been requested to initiate the immediate establishment of an airport on Canton Island. Work is being pushed by Army engineers and it is expected that the first of three runways will be completed by January 1, 1942.

SAMOA: American-owned volcanic island chain, of which Tutuila is the largest island with an operational small open harbor and naval station at Pago Pago. Tutuila has fixed defenses and a garrison of Marine and native troops. Navy constructing a landing field at Tafuna; will have two runways. One runway will be usable by February 10, 1942; the other by February 20. By April 1, one runway will be paved to a width of two hundred feet. Surrounding mountains and forests constitute obstructions.

FIJI: Territory of United Kingdom, being defended by New Zealand. The airdrome now consists of four strips; two 3,000 feet long and two 2,400 feet long. It is expected that one runway, 4,500 feet or more in length, and suitable for heavy bombers, will be available by January 15, 1942. The New Zealand government, assisted by U.S. Army engineers, is expediting in every way possible the extension of runways on Suva.

NEW CALEDONIA: A French dependency. It is reported that three land bases will be available eventually on New Caledonia. Adequate runways will be available by approximately January 30, 1942, according to the State Department. Noumea has a seaplane landing and base facilities and some Marine unloading facilities.

ROCKHAMPTON: A mainland Australian town, definitely unpractical for use by heavy bombardment airplanes and recommended that Townsville be substituted. Efforts being made to improve Townsville, The runways are being extended by the Australian government to five thousand feet, but can be used now.

It is not quite true that this was an entirely new route. At least some of its length had been developed by Pan American as yet another seaplane route. Pan Am had wanted for several years to expand its Pacific service to the South Pacific, particularly Australia. It encountered the same commercial resistance as it had at Hong Kong, and licenses were not forthcoming. New Zealand proved more willing to cooperate, and in 1938 engineers were sent out to locate atolls with suitable lagoons to serve as intermediate stops for a new service between Hawaii and New Zealand. A routing was selected that had seaplane facilities at Canton Island and Isle Nou in the bay at Noumea. The first survey flight was made along this route in August 1939, and facilities consisting of quarters, power, water supplies, pier, and customer hotel were soon constructed—though not as elaborate as those on Wake, Midway, and Guam. Passenger and mail service began in July 1940, though just a few trips were made before the war ended the service. Of course, seaplane facilities were much simpler than what was required for a bomber landing strip, but the availability of some habitation and even the 137,000 gallons of gasoline stored at Canton proved highly useful when the Army began construction.[3]

Both Canton and Christmas were jointly claimed by the United States and the United Kingdom. Christmas Island is in the Line Islands, located relatively close to Palmyra, which is just 380 miles to the northwest. While discovered by British Captain James Cook in 1777, and occupied by a small commercial settlement off and on for many years, the island was still claimed by the United States. Canton Island is part of the Phoenix Group, was annexed by Great Britain, and had occasionally been used for its guano and copra. As an uninhabited island, conflicting claims were easier to resolve. In 1936 the United States and Great Britain agreed to jointly administer the island under a legal condominium, and in 1939 Canton was placed under shared British and American control for fifty years.[4] The incentive for this amiable resolution was Pan American's stated desire to build a seaplane station on the island, which was indeed established by the end of 1939. The U.S. administration preferred that the initial surveys and contract work be taken by the Civil Aviation Administration vs. one of the military branches.

In the early stages of development considerable juggling of priority was made between Canton, Christmas, and Palmyra. Ultimately the urgency of the program led to work being pushed on all three locations simultaneously. At the beginning of work it was thought possible that Noumea on New Caledonia would be found unsuitable for use. It was noted that when construction was completed at Palmyra, Samoa, and hopefully New Caledonia, shorter-ranged two-engine bombers could potentially be ferried by this route in addition to the heavy bombers. The report to the board stated that each location should be actively protected. The Marines were already present and responsible for Palmyra and Samoa. Townsville, Fiji, and New Caledonia defense would be undertaken by the Australian and New Zealand governments. The

U.S. Army and Navy were cooperating with organizing the defensive forces for Canton and Christmas Islands. At Canton the Navy was willing to provide a small detachment of weapons with Marine crews, while Army engineer troops on both islands were equipped with rifles and automatic weapons. Unlike the earlier route that used pre-existing naval bases, this new series of bases would be used only for the transient movement of Army land-based aircraft. Consequently the U.S. Army financed the bases, and provided construction crews and defensive garrisons for them.

In fact, the entire route represented a complicated set of administrative problems. The coordination—with the British on the sovereignty issue, with the Free French on usage of New Caledonia, and with the Australian and New Zealand governments for the defense of New Caledonia and Fiji respectively—was one thing. Then there were the interests of the U.S. Navy and its Marine Corps for the development, defense, and continued logistical support of the bases it was charged with (Samoa, Palmyra, Johnston). The U.S. Army and its semi-autonomous Air Force branch were responsible for Christmas and Canton. Even within the Army there were jurisdictional challenges—the Hawaiian Department was initially given logistical support responsibilities for the bases relatively close, but the farther bases like New Caledonia were managed directly by the War Department and its supply agent, in this case the San Francisco Port of Embarkation. There was lots of overlap of responsibility and surely a significant amount of friction and inefficiency, but somehow the job got done and the construction and supply of the bases accomplished. Later in the last half of 1942 administrative changes were made that significantly simplified the lines of responsibility.[5]

Christmas Island development got under way first. A party of thirty Army engineers landed from destroyer USS *Ellet* on October 29. To everyone's surprise they found a small New Zealand team on the island doing precisely the same thing—laying out plans for an airfield. Fortunately both teams realized the advantage of cooperation, and they quickly combined efforts. New Zealand resources were much more severely stretched than American, and that nation quickly deferred any serious effort at construction to their partners. The survey team was quickly followed up by a serious construction effort. As soon as November 18 the chartered interisland freighter *Haleakala* brought out part of the Army's 804th Engineer Battalion (Aviation). Six officers and 150 men of this unit were accompanied by seventy civilian contractors. The usual American abundance of heavy construction equipment was also included. Additional supplies came by barge, and the final load of supplies delivered pre-war was brought by USAT *Ludington* on December 1. It is interesting to note the variety of vessels used for an inter-service project like this. The first four deliveries were via Navy destroyer, chartered private freighter, naval store ship, and finally an Army-owned transport.

The War Department championed the early development of Christmas Island. Initially the Navy preferred ferry runways on Palmyra, particularly with questions concerning the eventual sovereignty; however, when it was admitted by the Fourteenth Naval District that Palmyra couldn't be ready until August 1942 (an estimate that turned out to be woefully pessimistic), emphasis shifted back to Christmas Island. The Navy was not initially prepared to defend Christmas, so the Army by default was left with this responsibility. The 804th Engineers had some training and the personnel possessed the unit's organic weapons, though nothing larger than machine guns. In late November the Hawaiian Department provided two excess Model 1917 75-mm guns and eight hundred rounds of ammunition, along with a field artillery sergeant to instruct and train gun crews from willing engineers. In mid-December Christmas obtained its heavier Army armament. As the Army did not normally have access to the Navy's supply of 5-inch and 7-inch guns, it typically used the 155-mm Model 1918 "GPF" long-range field gun in its coast defense role. In place on the island at year's end were four 155-mm guns, four 3-inch anti-aircraft guns, the two 75-mm field guns, and twelve machine guns.[6] Manpower stood at 125 engineer, medical, and signal personnel, 110 civilian contractors, and several hundred contractors recently evacuated from Canton Island—though these were scheduled to leave soon.

Even though they were not directly targeted, the Pearl Harbor attack had an immediate impact on the new bases of the southern ferry route. New urgency for the work was soon imparted with the loss of Wake in December and of Rabaul in January. Still, the attack interrupted the methodical shipment of supplies and construction equipment. The voyage of USAT *Ludington* to both Canton and Christmas was cut in half, and the cessation of all sea traffic in the days immediately following the attack cancelled several small shipments. This included the movement of 5-inch guns for Canton on *Haleakala*. Canton was thought so vulnerable that its contract personnel were ordered evacuated, though they ultimately were used to help the completion of an entirely different air ferry base.

Unlike on Canton, the contract personnel were not withdrawn from Christmas Island, though that does not mean that worker relations were what they should have been. The civilians (numbering 193 by the time of the attack) demanded of military commander Maj. John Shield their immediate return. As talk turned ugly, the major had to put the island and its civilian occupants under martial law. In response the workers demanded immediate release from their contracts. In truth, while there was certainly some concern for personal safety, many of the workers simply wanted to see to their families in those nervous days, and many others wanted to enlist or serve their country in ways that seemed more important than working on an airfield in an obscure place. Even with these labor problems, good progress was made on constructing the runway, it being reported completed on January 22, 1942. Total cost of this project was $5.3 million.

Soon after the first of the year plans were made to provide Christmas with its permanent garrison. By January 10 a garrison composed of two coast artillery batteries and an infantry battalion of the 102nd Regiment with detachments of medical and other service units was selected for transfer. Additional armament was added too. Col. Paul W. Rutledge of the Coast Artillery Corps (CAC) was appointed commander of these defense forces at Christmas Island, known and designated in the Army's code structure as "Birch." Additionally the 12th Pursuit Squadron was selected to provide dedicated air defense. However, it was not until February 10 that this unit, with its P-39 fighters, arrived at Christmas Island.[7]

Canton, while uninhabited, still demanded some circumspection in development. Even General Marshall thought it wise to call for the construction of a civil airport as it would be less objectionable to other parties.[8] In early December the Army did assume responsibility to provide guns and a defense detachment. Back on November 14 *Antares* had arrived towing a derrick and carrying the first substantial construction team. It was intended that two barges with supplies would also be delivered, but unfortunately on the journey from Honolulu both were lost in tow, and initial progress in construction lagged as a consequence. Commercial Matson liner *Mariposa* arrived with more civilians direct from the mainland on the twentieth of November. The next supply deposit should have been made by Army freighter *Ludington*, carrying 1,189 ship-tons of material (but no personnel) to both Christmas and Canton. The ship had arrived at the first named island on December 1, but after the attack on Pearl Harbor she returned to California and the cargo never made it to Canton.

As was the case elsewhere, development efforts at Canton increased dramatically right after the Pearl Harbor attack. While the Army for a short while suspended shipping additional detachments to the islands, acquisition of construction materials and physical work by the contractors moved ahead rapidly. Now that the United States and Great Britain were formally allies, the pretenses of civilian work disappeared. The Army moved ahead on rapid development and defense; the islands were to be made suitable for ferry support of the largest bombers, and seaplane facilities were also to be developed. However, unlike on Christmas Island, it seems that defensive arrangements lagged the start of construction work. By the end of December only sixty-five Army men were present, and just ten of these were artillerymen. The island's total defenses rested in two 75-mm field guns and just twelve machine guns, sent only after the start of war on December 12 on the ship also slated to pick up the contract employees. Also, a pursuit squadron and an air support detachment were requested in December. However, Lieutenant General Emmons advised against sending the squadron due to lack of space for dispersal and protection. This advice was taken and the planes were diverted elsewhere. Consequently Canton was significantly delayed in receiving a dedicated fighter defense of its own. Only in September 1942 did the specially activated 333rd Fighter Squadron with its eighteen P-39Ds move to the island.

The exposure of large numbers of civilian contractors to the dangers of war quickly became real after the start of hostilities. Over 1,100 such men had surrendered on Wake, and dozens were killed in the attacks on that island, the Philippines, and Guam. A judgment call was made that Christmas Island was far enough out of the way to justify continued work, but that the civilian force on Canton should be evacuated in favor of military construction workers. On December 18 the Army ordered the evacuation of the three hundred workers at Canton temporarily to Christmas Island. Plans were to eventually stage these workers to New Caledonia to continue airfield work there. Canton was not to be abandoned however. An attempt would be made to hold both Canton and Christmas with small garrisons. "Small," though, was thought bigger than just the sixty-five men present. Plans were made to augment these with a small reinforcement of men, radar, machine guns, and ammunition then on their way from Honolulu. Short did not believe Canton could be held against a serious attack, but at the same time the showing at Wake demonstrated what an alert defensive force could do to interrupt an enemy's plans. The construction men of Hawaiian Contractors, Inc. had quite an adventure. Two hundred men were taken by towed barge on December 14 to Christmas Island. Next they journeyed to Samoa, but because of an outbreak of anemic dysentery, were quarantined on their cramped, hot, unsanitary barge for several days. Eventually, after seventeen days afloat, *Haleakala* arrived to take them on to New Caledonia.[9]

By early January of 1942 the Army prepared plans for a full reinforcement and garrisoning of Canton and Christmas Islands. It seems the Army engineers that had been left on Canton were able to make remarkable progress even without the civilian contractors. The rapid completion of the runway permitted the first ferried aircraft to transit on January 5. It was now time to place an adequate defensive garrison in both locations. No longer was there any discussion of what service was responsible, though maybe with some reluctance, the Army moved ahead quickly to prepare the forces needed. At the end of January two large transports, one for each island base, were attached to a convoy going from San Francisco to Australia. *President Johnson* left San Francisco on January 31 with Convoy No. 2030. Arriving at Christmas Island about February 10, she unloaded and then returned unescorted to California. She carried mostly new units designed as the permanent garrison of the island. A total of 2,047 men and officers were scheduled for the trip, representing detachments of coast artillery, infantry, a medical hospital, a pursuit squadron, radar, and service personnel. *President Taylor* made a similar stop at Canton Island, with a very similar cargo. A slightly smaller garrison, but of the same type of units, was scheduled for this smaller island. Both island bases received two 155-mm guns, two 75-mm field guns, and eight more .50-caliber anti-aircraft machine guns in these deliveries.[10]

Unlike the journey of *President Johnson* to Christmas Island, *President Taylor*'s to Canton Island was not routine. This liner had only been in Army hands since late in 1941, and had made only a single Army voyage—round-trip to Hawaii on the fast convoy of December 27. Returning to San Francisco on January 24, she began loading for the trip to Canton. For protection she also joined as part of Convoy No. 2030, and arrived at Canton on February 13, 1942, under the escort of destroyer USS *Porter.* A submarine warning had been received on the previous day. Unloading was attempted, but heavy swells interfered with efficient use of the one large lighter available. Due to the submarine warning, task force commander Capt. H. E. Overesch on destroyer *Porter* ordered the transport to close to within two thousand yards of the island the night of the fourteenth, despite protests by *President Taylor*'s captain about maneuvering in shallow waters; the transport ran aground at 6:20 PM.

On the fifteenth all the passengers were unloaded successfully. Rain, heavy swells, wind, and tides delayed getting salvage ships and experts from Oahu to the site. Serious recovery efforts were prevented from starting until February 24. By then heavy damage had occurred to the ship's bottom and many compartments were flooded. In several batches the ship's crew was evacuated. A large portion left for Honolulu on March 14 in the recently arrived freighter MV *Japara*. Food and fuel was sent either ashore or to the little flotilla of salvage vessels that attended the liner. The last of the ship's crew left the island on April 3 on board the Matson Navigation Company's SS *Makua*. The War Shipping Administration, successor to the Maritime Commission and contractor for the ship's service from the President Lines, continued to try and salvage the vessel. Unfortunately she was by now hard aground. Further damaged by periodic bombings by Japanese seaplanes, she never left her spot on the shoals and was eventually scrapped postwar. Fortunately all the passengers, crew, and a significant portion of her cargo were removed before her total loss.[11]

Fiji's development and defense were assigned to New Zealand, but as in so many places where a high American priority encountered overstretched Allied resources, it soon received extensive American help. In January USAT *President Monroe* brought an American contingent to Fiji. On board were the 70th Pursuit Squadron (and its twenty-five P-39D fighters), a matériel squadron, a platoon of the 693rd Ordnance Company, the 8th Signal Platoon, and air warning and decontamination detachments.[12] New Zealand was very active in its ground defense assignment, early on sending a complete brigade group, and eventually formed the bulk of the country's second wartime division here. As an assistance to the Fiji defenders, on board *Monroe* was a considerably quantity of lend-lease material—3,900 Enfield-pattern rifles, 142 .30-caliber machine guns, one hundred Thompson submachine guns, six 37-mm anti-tank guns, an appropriate supply of ammunition for these weapons, and twenty-three radio sets.[13] In early March the Army repeated this mission, sending another freighter to Fiji in conjunction with an Australian convoy. On board were supplies and a refrigeration plant for the U.S. Air Force garrison already in Fiji, along with bombs, mines for the Navy, and additional lend-lease munitions. Later in the spring the Army sent a major force to Fiji both to aid in the garrison duties and also as a forward deployment for potential offensive use in the Pacific.

Very impressive progress was made on the fields of the new route in late December and early January. Even the optimistic estimate of completion by January 15 was exceeded. One of the immediate challenges of this early readiness was the supply of men, fuel, and other service items to the ferry bases. It was estimated that each base would need something like 250,000 gallons of aviation gasoline—the amount needed to refuel one hundred heavy bombers—in stock prior to operations starting. Major General Arnold issued terse instructions for fuel requirements simply as "take care of this at once."[14] The fuel was available; necessary shipping took a bit longer. Also, lubricating oil, hydraulic fluid, breathing oxygen, spare parts, and other essential items for the planes had to be stocked. In addition to defensive forces, communications, weather, and servicing personnel detachments were quickly needed. By December 28 only Christmas Island lacked a sufficiently advanced runway to begin the ferry operations.

The lack of Christmas Island's facility was mitigated by the Navy's rapid completion of the field at Palmyra. All along, Palmyra and Christmas were viewed somewhat as substitutes for each other. Bombers could fly to either base, refuel, and then continue with a comfortable margin to Canton. Three B-17s left Oahu on January 6 and made the inaugural transit. The planes were part of the 7th Bombardment Group, whose ground echelon was already in Australia. By January 21 minimum facilities were ready at Christmas, and on that date a flight of two LB-30s transited through. Also, the first planes used Noumea's Tontouta Field on New Caledonia, but by the end of January the new field at the Plaines des Gaiacs was ready. Thus by the first of February the fields along the entire intended ferry route were ready, if somewhat haphazardly equipped.

In the early days of the war in the Pacific, Allied reversals were coming so quickly that even the new ferry route, far away from the Japanese pre-war mandates, was not considered secure. Plans in late 1941 and early 1942 were cast for yet another, more circuitous route from the American West Coast to Australia. Projected to go from Hawaii to Penrhyn (in the northern Cook Islands) to Aitutaki (southern Cook Islands) then Tongatabu and thence westward, this new route was authorized in May 1942. Fortunately the war situation stabilized, and such a circuitous route was not needed. At several of these locations military bases were constructed later in 1942. Penrhyn (also known as Tongareva) was developed as a Navy air refueling post, and Tongatabu had both an Army and a large Navy presence as an advance operating base.

After the loss of Wake and then Rabaul, and before the new southern route to Canton or Christmas was ready for service, a totally different route was needed. Thanks to some work that was done pre-war to get lend-lease aircraft to the Allies in the Middle East, the essential pieces of an Atlantic–Africa–

India route were available. For a few weeks from mid-December 1941 to the end of January 1942 this "African" (also known as the South Atlantic) route would prove to be the only mechanism available to quickly get heavy bombers to the Far East. The attrition rate was heavy on planes and crews sent along this route, almost two-thirds the way around the globe. However, in retrospect it appears that without this link these planes may simply not have gotten to the war theatre at all, or at least only as disassembled parts that would have taken so long to ship and reassemble as to be unavailable prior to the end of the Dutch East Indies campaign.

Fortuitously the route was not entirely new or without the beginnings of preparation. The Americans had had an interest in the Brazilian fields for a considerable period prior to their nation's entry into the war, though primarily for hemisphere defense rather than ferry bases. Negotiations for access to and improvements of the fields in the northeastern hump of Brazil's Natal Province had been ongoing with the Brazilians prior to the start of war. Meanwhile the British had developed an air supply line from West Africa to the Middle East. Since September 1940 they had shipped aircraft to Takoradi in the Gold Coast and then onward to Sudan and Egypt via existing airfields. With the prospect of more aircraft becoming available with the passing of the Lend-Lease Act in March 1941, interest in the route increased. In June 1941 Pan American Airways was approached by the British to contractually manage an air supply route across Africa, essentially to shuttle not airplanes but supplies to Egypt or the Middle East as a more efficient alternative to maritime convoys making the journey all the way around the Cape of Good Hope.[15] The first aircraft transferred on this route by Pan Am were twenty lend-lease transports taken from Lagos, Nigeria, to Khartoum in Sudan in June. Then in the latter half of 1941 the route was used for lend-lease aircraft delivered to the Russians via Persia. By the fall of 1941 a fairly steady flow of airplanes used at least portions of the route to get aircraft to Cairo, India, and China for the British, and to Persia for the Russians.

The United States actively assisted this plan. When contracts were signed in August, it was in fact a three-way partnership. Britain gave access to fields and facilities in the Caribbean, Africa, and Asia, and secured the air passage rights from the involved governments. The United States paid for the construction work (mostly with a Pan Am subsidiary known as the Airport Development Program), obtained rights in Brazil, and supplied the aircraft fleet to Pan Am. Pan Am personnel oversaw the contracts for construction, manned the facilities, and flew the aircraft. Within a month the British also asked Pan Am for assistance in ferrying warplanes across the route, even in piloting the aircraft to Egypt. At the same time the Air Corps Ferrying Command, interested in the proposed route's availability for potential movement of U.S. aircraft, launched a major survey mission headed by Lt. Col. Caleb Haynes and Maj. Curtis E. LeMay. By contract the U.S. Air Force had free rights of access to the fields and all ground-based facilities funded on behalf of Pan Am.

Pan Am formed new subsidiaries to perform these assignments; one of the most important was Pan American Airways–Africa, created on July 15, 1941. Within a few months construction began on facilities at the selected African bases. Several ships carried men, construction equipment, and supplies to the African coast. While not extravagant, all the selected airfields needed control towers, radio facilities, refueling facilities and supplies, a certain amount of repair and maintenance capability (including spare parts if possible), and quarters and mess for resting crews as well as for the local personnel. Significant work really had just gotten under way in October and November, though much more had to be done. But without these preliminary steps, any use of this ferry route in December 1941 and January 1942 would have been impossible.[16]

The bases in Brazil were less primitive to begin with, but ultimately they too were improved with U.S. airport development funds and Pan Am assistance. The War Department had contracted with Pan Am for development of a site in Natal for both land and seaplane facilities. The Navy also expressed interest, particularly in the seaplane base. Even before the war, in November of 1941, naval patrol plane squadron VP-52 with PBY-5s was based at Natal. The Brazilian government, still a non-belligerent like the United States, proved most cooperative and creative in finding ways to facilitate the creation of these air bases. In their early forms many of these fields were little more than runways with few support facilities. Even a heavily used site such as Natal had just four officers and fifty-seven enlisted men in May of 1942.

One of the consistent problems of the early ferry days was the lack of spare parts for maintenance. Many planes had to be parked and await a separate transport bringing in key parts and mechanics to make repairs. Thus flights or batches of planes sent along the route quickly became spread out, and at the other end planes tended to arrive sporadically. In Asia proper, more reliance had to be placed on British efforts, as there was no previous American existence at the fields in Iraq and India.

The planes themselves were available. B-17s were now steadily coming off Boeing's assembly line near Seattle in useful quantities. Thanks to the temporary suspension of lend-lease shipments to England, other quantities of bombers were also available. In particular, one batch of fifteen B-24s prepared for supply to the British was taken over. Because they were of slightly modified design from the American types, they were given a new designation as "LB-30s." By the end of February a total of 165 bombers were scheduled for transfer. Crews were a little more difficult to come up with. There simply were not enough trained aircrew for the "new" planes, and nothing was gained by taking them from other existing squadrons. Many of the planes in the movement to Australia and the East Indies had to be flown by pilots, co-pilots, navigators, and other crewmen with only partial training, or trained only in smaller types of aircraft.

The scheme to take a number of new bombers to the Far East by the African route was dubbed Project X. It was the first overseas movement organized and facilitated by the new Ferrying Command within the Air Force. New Boeing B-17s first had to move from their manufacturing plant in Seattle to the Sacramento Air Depot for modifications and preparations for the long flights. From there both these bombers and those LB-30s taking this route congregated at MacDill Field in Tampa, Florida. Here they were assigned the crew that would take them forward—and eventually operate them. The route from here was Trinidad Island off the coast of Venezuela, Belém and then Natal in Brazil, Takoradi in the Gold Coast of Africa, Khartoum in Sudan, Cairo in Egypt, Habbaniya in Iraq, and then Karachi in western India, and finally Bangalore, India. From India instructions would be given as to the final destination—India, Australia, Java, or even China. For the reinforcement of Java, planes would go to Colombo in Ceylon, Palembang in Sumatra, and then Bandoeng on Java. It was hoped that planes could be dispatched in batches of three to six per day until the transfer goal was met.

Two significant flights or waves of aircraft were authorized for this route. Fifteen LB-30 bombers under Maj. Austin A. Straubel were issued travel orders on December 19 to take the African route. Events intervened to eventually send nine bombers by Pacific routes, but six bombers did accomplish the trip to Tampa and beyond. The aircrews found were those of the 7th Bomb Group otherwise delayed in transit on the West Coast, even though they had only had training in B-17s. In the case of both types of bombers, in addition to the combat crews, each ninth plane dispatched was supposed to carry a medical officer.

The second, larger group to go was sixty-five B-17s. These were to be brand-new airplanes from the production line, and consequently their availability was in batches. All also had to go through the Sacramento facility for installation of additional fuel tanks and other preparations. This group received its first transit orders four days after the first, on the twenty-third of December.[17] The original schedule for ferrying bombers to the Far East proved to be excessively optimistic. Originally three B-17s were to leave each on the fifteenth and twenty-fourth of December, with six planes per day thereafter. Eighty heavy bombers (the fifteen LB-30s and sixty-five B-17s) were to be on their way by January 6. In fact, by this day just twenty B-17s and six LB-30s were en route, using either the African or South Pacific ferry way.

At one point early in the program, worries were expressed about the security of the fields selected, particularly in view of Vichy French attitudes. It was thought that the West African airfields were just too close to unfriendly French fields that could potentially host German aircraft. So, just like in the Pacific, alternate plans were explored to move the entire route even farther south. A possible new route would go from Natal in Brazil to Ascension Island in the mid-Atlantic, through French Equatorial Africa, Belgian Congo, Tanganyika, Mombasa, Seychelles or other Indian Ocean islands, and then Australia. Fortunately the military situation never warranted this development. However, by the middle of 1942 Ascension Island in the mid-Atlantic was developed into a full station of the ferry route, primarily to reduce the range required for ferrying of two-engine transports and medium bombers.

Use of the full African route to take heavy bombers to the ABDA theatre was made only for a relatively short time. For about a five-week period (mid-January to mid-February) both Pacific and Atlantic routes were in simultaneous operation. On February 3 it was reported that twenty-six heavy bombers had arrived in the theatre—eighteen by the African route and eight from the Pacific route. Another fifteen bombers were between Tampa and Natal, eight between Natal and Cairo, and fifteen more between Cairo and Bangalore, India. Two weeks later, on February 17, forty-one heavy bombers had been delivered, the original eight from Hawaii and now a total of thirty-three from Natal and the African route. Twenty-three more were en route.[18]

The Japanese capture of Sumatra in early 1942 effectively cut the final ferry leg between India and Java or Australia. The route continued to be used to get planes to the newly developing air forces in India and China. A total of fifty-eight heavy bombers were dispatched east on the African route; eight others of this original contingent were able to go the Pacific route. Forty-four of the planes were delivered in time to serve with the air units fighting in the southwest Pacific. A couple of planes were delayed along the route and joined the 10th Air Force in India after combat in the Dutch East Indies ended. Five were lost along the way due to accidents, and several were delayed for parts or repairs for a considerable period of time. Four Navy PBYs were also ferried on the South Atlantic route to the Dutch in the East Indies in early 1942, and of course the route was in use and continued to be so for the "regular" ferrying of lend-lease aircraft to the Allies. The Pacific route also continued to be the main source of heavy and medium bombers sent to Australia and other bases in the Southwest Pacific Area. Much was learned in these early ferrying activities, and for a short while in early 1941 they served as the only readily available way to get fighting material to the front lines in Southeast Asia.

CHAPTER TWENTY-ONE

Shipping Challenges of Early 1942 and the Pacific Task Forces

After America's entry into the Second World War, the choice of where and how to apply its military strength was one of the key strategic issues that had to be confronted. The dramatic and mostly disastrous beginning of the Pacific conflict had not been as thoroughly planned out as had the eventual involvement in the European conflict. While the United States had unequivocally shared the British proposal of a "Germany-first" strategy, the reality of the situation in the western Pacific caused a painful readjustment. A practical strategic compromise developed—essentially agreeing to the Germany-first plan in the long-term, but only after the military and logistical situation in the Pacific stabilized. That meant that the buildup of the Australian bases and protection of the lines of communication would have priority for scarce shipping and resources of trained men and matériel before any offensive or even significant buildup occurred for Europe. This practical strategy clearly emerged during the first wartime Anglo-American meeting, the Washington Conference, in late December 1941 and January 1942.

British prime minister Winston Churchill was the driving force for this meeting. While there had been a previous meeting between the heads of state in Newfoundland the preceding August, Churchill moved to secure a meeting with the Americans as soon as December 8. The British had concerns about the impact of the Pearl Harbor attack on the previously approved strategic guidelines, as well as on the planned levels of armament supply under lend-lease. The two major Western allies needed to coordinate war plans, strategic and tactical, between them. Roosevelt and the military administration in the United States were less enthusiastic about the timing of the meeting. The immediate needs of bringing the United States to an at-war stance were tremendous, and none felt too comfortable about hosting a major conference with an important ally when other matters needed attending. Nonetheless Churchill was most persistent, and he departed on a British battleship on December 13 with a staff of thirty-eight, including the minister of supply, first sea lord, chief of air staff, and a qualified stand-in for the British army general staff. In appreciation of the American preoccupation, the conference would be held in Washington, D.C. The British contingent arrived on December 22, and departed on January 14 after three weeks of intensive joint planning.

Prior to the British arrival the Americans prepared their positions in advance of the anticipated meetings. Stimson led the American strategic effort, with help from Marshall, Arnold, and the two able staffers from the War Plans Division—Gerow and Eisenhower. On the twentieth the president was presented with a document describing the strategic recommendations. They ranked the southwest Pacific as the theatre of highest priority. For immediate action were three steps: to secure North Atlantic communications with the British, to protect the air and water route to both the Near East and Far East, and to build up as rapidly as possible air and sea communications with Australia. At least temporarily, the war against Japan was to assume priority over Germany.[1] Thus the stage was set for a significant conflict with the proposed British priorities. The actual situation in the Far East was rapidly deteriorating while positions were being formulated by both allies. For example, the British situation in Malaya, Hong Kong, and Burma looked much stronger on December 13 when the British contingent left England than it did three weeks later when some of the toughest priorities on shipping were discussed. On December 21 a presidential conference with the American team endorsed Secretary Stimson's memorandum.

For the next two weeks a variety of meetings were held, either between the two heads of state and selected advisers, or directly between the chiefs of services of the two countries in a sort of joint staff meeting. Topics ranged over issues such as armament supply, joint or separate operational command structures, and operational priorities. Early in the process of working together, much was learned about the operating style and even personalities of the individuals involved. Rarely was the process smooth, but the necessity of the task ahead usually held forth, and compromise or accommodation was usually found.[2] Everyone seemed to realize that the game was for keeps.

Early in the conference the prime minister began to actively push his scheme for a joint invasion of North Africa. Churchill saw this as a way to get the Americans quickly involved in a military theatre that had several advantages to the British—it was clearly part of the Europe-first priority, could substantially help the precarious British military position in Libya, and would enable the Americans to get "blooded" and committed to fighting. The operation was termed "Gymnast," and envisioned the landing of several British divisions (the estimate was 55,000 soldiers) in Algeria, and the Americans landing about 25,000 (soon to be reinforced by additional forces amounting to 125,000 men) farther west in Morocco. Initially the British positioned the American entry as one that would be invited, but the reality of that was less than firm. These were still Vichy-French controlled territories, and the diplomatic picture as to whether such an invasion would be resisted or actively assisted was not clear. Another key element would be that the British troop strength needed would be offset by American troops taking over the full defense of Iceland and at least part of Northern Ireland—known as Operation Magnet. It was thought that partially trained or equipped American forces in these latter two places could aid in their security and complete their preparation for action while at the same time releasing a like number of British soldiers for other campaigns.

The Americans had previously agreed to help garrison Iceland—a Marine brigade moved there during the summer of 1941—and agreed to the gradual movement of units to the British Isles prior to any proposed European operation. However, the timing for the North Africa move now proposed caught the Army staff off guard. Churchill tried to force the issue into a separate joint staff analysis. Meanwhile, Roosevelt was politely supportive of a North Africa move, but much more tentative about just when it could be undertaken. Marshall raised issues about American readiness and matériel limitations, plus everyone seemed to doubt British assertions that the occupation would be "invited" by French North African authorities. At least part of the British enthusiasm for an invasion was due to their favorable tactical position in Libya, where the German and Italian forces had been temporarily ejected from Cyrenaica. They thought the enemy forces might soon collapse and an opportunity existed for completely occupying all of North Africa. The new, and ultimately most dangerous, Axis counter-offensive in Africa would start later in January, but of course that was not known by anyone at the conference.

For a short period of time during the conference, the American staff worked under the impression that forces were required for virtually all of the high priorities—including more for Iceland, the Northern Ireland move, North Africa, and all of the many Pacific needs. Even harder than finding the trained, equipped forces was finding the necessary transport. The British were also shocked at finding that America, in their minds the wellspring of all matériel, was woefully lacking in appropriate shipping. General Marshall summarized the troop movement needs so far in the conference on December 26 as: four divisions to Ireland, one to Hawaii, three or four to Northwest Africa, and possibly another to Brazil.[3] The first move of American forces to Northern Ireland was to begin with a major convoy due to depart the East Coast on January 15. Both allies thought its successful journey would help buoy civil morale and demonstrate America's quick willingness to get involved in the war, even if this were for a non-combative assignment. The realization of the utter impossibility of completing all these plans soon dawned.

At an informal staff get-together on December 26 the shipping issue came to a head. The Americans reported that they now believed that limitations in shipping and naval escort made it impossible to carry out the North African plan, at the same time as the Ireland and Iceland movements. Then on January 4 the two leaders met with their military advisers, with the major topic being the North African plan. Stimson came out basically opposed to the scheme, fearing it would realistically call for much more in forces than the British anticipated, that the reaction of the Vichy French (and Spanish) was too problematical, and that even the German reaction was not clear. Now most of the combined staff observed that there simply wasn't the shipping for all the Atlantic/North African plans on the docket. Churchill began to back away from his pet project. At the War Plans Division Eisenhower was trying to juggle transport for the urgent Pacific transfers. He recorded: "We are trying to ship staff and personnel needed. But we have got to have ships!! And we need them now."[4]

Then on the two meetings of January 11–12, the study of available sealift capacity finally came into full discussion. The U.S. Navy (two admirals, Stark and King) suggested that troop transfer in the Atlantic be cut to allow the shipping to be used to shore up critical needs in the communications line between the United States and Australia. Marshall agreed on the part of the Army, suggesting that the North Atlantic transfer be limited to just ten thousand men. The British were reluctant at first to agree, but did also see a need to try and strengthen the line against the Japanese. Certainly in the three weeks they had been in Washington almost all of the news from Malaya and the Dutch East Indies had been bad. The chiefs could not agree on specifics, and turned for advice to the combined shipping experts. Heavily favoring the American desire to give priority to the urgently required Pacific shipments, the experts and subsequently the staff supported:

1. Cut Iceland (Indigo) near-term shipment from 8,000 men to 2,500.
2. Cut Northern Ireland (Magnet) near-term shipment from 16,000 to 4,000.
3. Shift Atlantic shipping to carry 21,800 men from New York to the South Pacific.
4. Reduce lend-lease shipments to Russia by 30 percent.

After additional discussion with the two heads of state the evening of the twelfth, the shipping experts thought they could find a way to avoid any cut in Russian aid. Also, Northern Ireland shipments were to begin with a month's delay. Though not directly stated, the North African expedition was delayed too. On the fourteenth it was agreed that the operation could not be started until May 25.[5] Events would ultimately delay the North African invasion until November.

On the twelfth a memorandum was circulated among the Americans proposing the opportunity to organize a division-sized force for Java. Ground forces of roughly 21,800 well-equipped men could be identified. Most came from the 26th Division (New York National Guard), plus coast artillery and engineers. A large quantity of newly produced aircraft, including 250 P-40s, eighty-six B-25s, fifty-seven A-20s, and almost five million gallons of aviation gasoline could be amassed to join the ground troops for shipment by January 20 from New York. Again, shipping was the rub. Several alternatives were considered, but recommended in this memo was taking the mostly Navy-allotted ships slated for the Irish and Icelandic movements. The Maritime Commission could provide the necessary freighters, but only by interfering with the promised lend-lease deliveries. Secretary of War Stimson personally approached President Roosevelt for his agreement to these painful tradeoffs.[6]

Thus by the fourteenth of January the pressure was effectively off for making substantial shipments of troops in the Atlantic. The credit must go to both General Marshall and Admiral Stark for consistently opposing the allocation of scarce trained and equipped units and the shipping needed to carry them to either garrison duties or to a premature and potentially disastrous combat introduction. With this relief, the planners turned to using the assets released to address the glaring deficiencies in the Pacific. Another important development was the rejection of Java as the destination of the Pacific expedition, and the ultimate substitution of New Caledonia. This new large contingent, the same 21,800 men mentioned above, was now pushed hard toward a January 20 departure date. It required seven troop transports on the East Coast directly reassigned from the cancelled Atlantic shipments. Approximately thirty freighters needed for the equipment and supplies of these units were to ship from San Francisco and come from the Pacific shipping pool.

The Navy had been a strong supporter of an aggressive Pacific policy all along. While the two admirals, Stark and King, both publicly supported the Germany-first position, they also felt that the Pacific danger had to be neutralized before the damage became too extensive. King in particular was concerned over the safety of a secure line of communication to Australia. During the conference at a session of the eleventh he emphasized the great importance of New Caledonia to the situation in the southeast Pacific. Its loss to the enemy would mean that all American reinforcements would have to further detour south of New Zealand to reach Australia and the ABDA theatre. He was of the opinion that the Japanese must be stopped prior to the Australian supply line, or else the entire southwest Pacific would be lost.[7] When an involved discussion with Roosevelt prompted the Army to consider reducing the garrison plans for New Caledonia, the Navy voiced a strong dissent.

The actual January 1942 departure dates for major U.S. troop movements overseas clearly demonstrates the priority given to reinforcing the Pacific line of communications.

New Caledonia had figured heavily as a destination of major forces since the very start of the war. It was an ideal spot for a final ferry base between the southern islands of Samoa or Fiji, and Australia. Not only was it well positioned geographically, it held valuable mineral deposits of nickel, chrome, and cobalt useful to either the Allied or Axis war effort. Its transition after the surrender of France in Europe to control by the Free French had not been easy; in 1941 there were still local elements sympathetic to the Vichy government. French military forces were negligible, amounting to about 1,400 poorly armed native troops. Nominally assigned to the Australians for defense, the latter were so hard-pressed for troops that only a single independent company of about 350 men was on the island when the Pacific war started.

The French Pacific High Commissioner Admiral Georges Thierry d'Argenlieu had concluded negotiations for the construction of military airfields with the Allies in October of 1941. The effort was fully supported by Charles de Gaulle and the Free French government. Their major concern was that both the Australians and Americans recognize all aspects of French sov-

Table 18. Major U.S. Overseas Troop Movements, January 1942

Departure Date	From	Destination	Contents
January 6	San Diego	Samoa	4,800 Marines
January 12	San Francisco	Australia Fiji	7,000 Army 700 Army
January 15	New York	Northern Ireland	3,900 Army
January 23	New York	Australia	3,600 Army
		New Caledonia	16,900 Army
January 27	Charleston	Bora Bora	4,300 Army & Navy
January 31	San Francisco	Australia	9,400 Army
January 31	San Francisco	Canton Island	1,100 Army
January 31	San Francisco	Christmas Island	2,000 Army

ereignty in their territories, regardless of temporary wartime jurisdictions or responsibilities. The Free French clearly wished that wartime occupation, even by allies, not be in conflict with their postwar reestablishment of sovereignty.

Airfield construction actually began with a small Australian civilian force, but soon it was overtaken by American efforts. It had been decided that the construction in New Caledonia be conducted by private contract using local labor. Eventually the civilian contractors removed from Canton Island reached New Caledonia to work on permanent runways on the Plaines de Gaiacs. The facility was ready by February 17, 1942. Intermediate runways were also built near Noumea, the major port of the island some distance to the south. Immediately after the start of the war the French National Committee took a strong position against the Japanese, and Allied cooperation with the French administration in New Caledonia was cordial and forthcoming.

A difficult diplomatic situation developed soon after the war started. The French administration in New Caledonia became concerned about the lack of defensive forces locally. They feared, probably with some justification, that as both sets of airfields neared completion, the Japanese would be tempted to invade and take them for themselves. Also the Vichy government in France had named their own rival high commissioner, and was anxious to re-assert control over the French Pacific possessions. While the Americans were planning to set a force onto New Caledonia, the specifics could not be shared with Admiral d'Argenlieu for fear of compromising security. Frustrated and fearing that he was just being put off by vague promises, the admiral issued an ultimatum to Lieutenant General Emmons in Hawaii that further work on the airfields would be halted unless the island was protected by substantial Allied forces. The issue was only resolved by sending Brig. Gen. Alexander M. Patch Jr., the commander of the task force, by airplane directly to the island to confer with the admiral and take him into his confidence.[8]

The assignment of a task force was very quickly accomplished during the first three weeks of January. There had been no pre-war plan for the defense of this island, and only after the loss of the inner ferry route—Wake and Rabaul—did the new route assume its critical importance. The core of the new task force was composed basically of those units identified in early January as available for dispatch to ABDA and potential service in Java. The troop transports themselves were not confirmed until the cancellation and rearrangement of other Atlantic priorities made during the Washington Conference just a week prior to the anticipated sailing date.

Most of the ships utilized were purposely diverted from service in either the North Atlantic troop movements to Europe or the South American trade. One ship in particular illustrates the extraordinary measures taken to obtain transports. The large Swedish cruise ship MV *Kungsholm* had been taken over by the United States in December 1941.[9] At first the State Department wished to use her for a special repatriation mission of Axis diplomatic personnel and dependents back to Europe, and then the Navy expressed interest in her conversion to an aircraft carrier. It took a major interdepartmental understanding to allow her allocation to the Army. In February she emerged as USAT *John Ericsson.* At the time, the relatively modern (1928), large (21,552-ton), fast (fifteen-knot) ship could carry over 4,500 troops and thus ranked as one of the few large transports available to the American military.

The unit selected was an ad-hoc assembly designated Task Force 6814. Of roughly division-size, its various units were chosen from a variety of unattached regiments and battalions apparently based on both what might be needed and on what was immediately available. It was described in one of the Army's official histories as an "odd conglomeration . . . [a] military stew of men and equipment."[10] Most of the key units were leftovers from the recent reduction in size performed when the National Guard 26th and 33rd Divisions were converted from square to triangular format. Assigned to command the task force was Brigadier General Patch. He had previously commanded an infantry training center in South Carolina. As task forces could organizationally hold any Army unit, a pursuit squadron and airfield service units for New Caledonia were included—something which would not have been possible with a conventional division organization. Command relationship was also unique: Patch had an independent command reporting directly to Washington, D.C., though his logistical support came from San Francisco's Port of Embarkation, and control of the airfields themselves was in Hawaii with Lieutenant General Emmons. To further confuse things, at this stage the airfield construction was still mostly being done by Australian contractors, and everything had to be coordinated with the French, who were very concerned with matters of present and future sovereignty.

As the situation in the Pacific was changing daily during early 1942, it was thought best that the convoy be scheduled to go direct to Australia first. There was reasonable doubt that New Caledonia might still be in Allied hands when the convoy arrived, or that further diplomatic arrangements needed to be made with the French prior to landing, or even that another final destination might be more endangered and thus a higher priority. Consequently the convoy was earmarked for Melbourne, that port selected partly because Sydney and Brisbane were otherwise very busy handling other American shipments. After unloading and re-loading, the convoy, including both transports and escorts, was to move on to Noumea. With this routing, the opportunity was taken to include some additional units required in Australia. These would disembark in Melbourne and go to duty stations locally. Two general service engineer regiments urgently needed for Australian construction projects, the ground echelon of a heavy bomber squadron, and other miscellaneous units composed the Australian-bound portion. Altogether these units bound for just Australia totaled 3,576 officers, men, and female nurses. Between the two destinations, Convoy No. BT-200 carried 20,463 military men and women.

The units and at least part of their equipment were ordered to the New York Port of Embarkation during the second week of January 1942. In fact, the movement was ordered even prior to the final selection of the destination. Some of the heaviest equipment and much of the consumable supplies went to San Francisco to be shipped out over the next few months by a stream of freighters. While some progress had been made in organizing shipments,

Table 19. Convoy of Task Force 6814 for New Caledonia[11]

Convoy/Ships/Speed/Escort/Dates	Units and Major Cargo Items
Convoy No. BT-200	**New Caledonia–bound portion** (TF-6814)
Depart New York 1/23/42	
Depart Panama 2/1/42	51st Infantry Brigade HQ
Join Convoy No. 2030 off Bora Bora 2/14/42	132nd Infantry Regiment
	180th,123rd Field Artillery Regiments
Arrive Melbourne 2/26/42	70th Coast Artillery Regiment
New Caledonia–bound portion depart Melbourne 3/06/42	244th Coast Artillery Regiment (part)
	22nd, 51st Ordnance Company
Arrive Noumea 3/12/42	101st Engineer Regiment
	101st Quartermaster Regiment
USAT *Argentina*	101st Medical Regiment
USAT *Thomas Barry*	9th, 10th, 109th Station Hospitals
USAT *Cristobol*	810th Engineer Battalion (Avn) (Colored)
USAT *John Ericsson* (ex–SS *Kungsholm)*	811th Engineer Battalion (Avn) (Colored)
USAT *J. W. McAndrew*	67th Pursuit Squadron
USAT *Santa Elena*	676th Ordnance Company (Pur)
USAT *Santa Rosa*	Other small units and detachments
Escorts:	Organic equipment, guns, tanks, 25 P-39 airplanes
From New York USS *Vincennes*, USS *Milwaukee*, and seven destroyers	
From Panama USS *Milwaukee,* USS *Trenton*	Total of 16,887 officers and men
From Bora Bora USS *Honolulu* and two destroyers	**Australia-bound portion**
From Melbourne USS *Honolulu* and two destroyers	43rd, 46th Engineer Regiments (General Service)
	4th General Hospital
	13th Reconnaissance Squadron (H)
	705th Quartermaster Company
	Other small units and detachments
	Total of 3,576 officers and men

many of the units were still badly split up between several ships, and unit equipment was often not on the same ship as the unit. As an example of one extreme case, it was thought that the heavy 155-mm howitzers had not been shipped with the field artillery battalions. In Australia the Army found itself borrowing guns from its ally before re-locating to New Caledonia. Only later was it found that the guns had indeed been in one of the ships of the convoy all along.

The voyage itself was made without major incident. Compared to the journeys just a couple of months previous, the Pacific was now beginning to show considerable traffic in American troop convoys. Two convoys—this one initially to Australia, and one just a couple of days behind to Bora Bora—were proceeding from the East Coast, through the Panama Canal, and across the South Pacific. Each convoy had its own cruiser escort. Then, west of Samoa, New Caledonia Convoy No. BT-200 met with Convoy No. 2030. The latter was one of the major Australian reinforcement convoys, and consisted of four ships escorted by light cruiser USS *Honolulu.* Through careful manipulation of schedules and communications these two otherwise unrelated convoys matched up and shared escort until they split up again in Australian waters. On February 18 the impatience in Washington for the garrisoning of New Caledonia showed through. Washington asked about the possibility of having the convoy sail directly to Noumea, bypassing the more distant and time-consuming stop in Australia. The brass was reminded that the force was not only thoroughly mixed with Australian-bound equipment and men, but that much of the heavy equipment was not even on the convoy, but shipping independently on freighters from the West Coast. The suggestion of a change was quickly dropped.

The seven large transports of Convoy No. BT-200 left New York on January 23, escorted by heavy cruiser *Vincennes* and several destroyers. The cruiser turned back in the vicinity of Key West. At the Canal Zone the convoy picked up as escort light cruiser USS *Trenton* of the Southeast Pacific Force to augment sister ship USS *Milwaukee* of the Atlantic Fleet. Both cruisers kept the convoy company until the vicinity of Bora Bora. The convoy joined Australia-bound Convoy No. 2030 on February 14. Escorts *Milwaukee* and *Trenton* stayed to cover arrival of the Bora Bora task force, and cruiser *Honolulu* and two destroyers provided escort onward to Melbourne and Brisbane.

Upon arrival in Melbourne on February 26, the transshipment of Task Force 6814 for New Caledonia began. This effort was easy to simply state in an order but, this early in the war, far harder to carry out. All troops were disembarked, and the 3,500 or so meant for Australian destinations departed after reclaiming their equipment, which was mixed in with the rest. The task force troops were temporarily quartered locally. To their credit, the Melbourne dockworkers performed admirably and reloading was accomplished by the departure date of March 6. The task force and its escort arrived at Noumea on the twelfth. Brigadier General Patch had already arrived to finish the arrangements with d'Argenlieu. For most of the colonial bases, local agreements had to be made in addition to the general consent of the owning or host government. Things like labor contracts, wages, access to piers and wharves, leasing of property, legal and dispute jurisdiction, and resolution processes had to be worked out with the local government.

While never intended as part of the air ferry system, another South Pacific site was additionally scheduled for major development. With the buildup in Australia and New Zealand, and the involvement of American port facilities on the gulf and East Coast, there arose a need for a naval refueling facility in the South Pacific. Convoys needed to refuel and pick up fresh water at a convenient stop along the Panama Canal–New Zealand route. Relatively early in the war the Free French–administered Society Islands were selected as the preferred location for such a facility. On New Year's Day 1942 Admiral King requested all necessary steps be taken to make Bora Bora, an island group in the leeward part of the Society Islands, an effective, defended fueling station.[12] It was thought that a tank farm facility to house 200,000 barrels of fuel oil and 37,500 barrels of gasoline would be required. Negotiations with the Free French were conducted to allow access, but a detailed agreement had to be left until actual arrival. The new U.S. naval station at Bora Bora was actually the site of the first new overseas naval base authorized during the war.

Meanwhile the Commandant of the Marine Corps acknowledged that he had no troops available for such a garrison, and suggested that the Army be called upon to furnish any defensive force. Of course, the Navy itself would provide the operation of the actual fueling and supply facility. At first it was estimated that a garrison of roughly battalion-size, similar to those provided for the air ferry bases, would suffice, but soon that number was increased to a much larger force of almost four thousand. Within a few days the Navy and Army worked out an agreement in concept that the Army would provide the protective force, its subsistence and anti-aircraft equipment, and exercise local command under CinCPac. The Navy would supply eight 7-inch guns, a construction company of 250 men, and all the required Quonset huts, boats, barges, harbor nets, water distillation units, refrigerators, a radio station, and the refueling depot itself. More importantly, in view of the critical shipping shortage, the Navy would provide all the transports, freighters, and the surface escorts to get the force to the Society Islands. The code name "Bobcat" was selected for the base, and thus "Bobcat Task Force" for the defensive unit. It was known during assembly and voyage as Task Force 5614.

A force was quickly organized for shipment from the Charleston, South Carolina, port of embarkation, and prepared to be able to depart about January 20. The Navy kept its part of the commitment by identifying and securing the two transports and four freighters necessary. The hurried, and sometimes changed, orders provided for the units involved was typical for both this and the New Caledonia shipment that left New York just days before. For example, the 198th Coast Artillery Regiment, then assigned in Boston, had received notification of an impending move on January 5. Their forwarding address was a New York APO address, usually indicative of an Atlantic or European destination. On the seventh the unit began medical screening of its men for overseas units and gave inoculations to all. However, on the eleventh the forwarding address was changed to San Francisco—the indicator of Pacific duty and a different medical screening protocol.

The Navy contributed an ad hoc construction detail for the expedition. Organized construction battalions (CBs or later known as "SeaBees") did not exist yet; in fact, the unit organized for this trip can probably be considered

Table 20. Convoy of Task Force 5614 for Bora Bora[13]

Convoy/Ships/Speed/Escort/Dates	Units and Major Cargo Items
Convoy No. BC-100 SS *Arthur Middleton* SS *Mercury* SS *President Tyler* USS *Alchiba* SS *Irenee Dupont* USS *Hamul* Escort: USS *Richmond* and Destroyers Depart Charleston, SC 1/27/42 Pass Panama Canal Arrive Bora Bora 2/17/42	Task Force 5614: 102nd Infantry Regiment (less 1st and 3rd Battalions) Battery A and C, 99th Field Artillery Battalion 198th Coast Artillery Regiment (AA), HQ and HQ Battery 3rd Battalion and Batteries F & H of 13th Coast Artillery 8th Station Hospital 2 sections Company C 94th Quartermaster Battalion 1 radio repair section of 179th Signal Company 695th Air Warning Company Detachments of quartermaster, medical, ordnance, and finance departments Naval fueling depot 8 7-in coast defense guns Ammunition, fuel, subsistence, military stores and supplies Total of 3,838 Army officers and men

the direct predecessor of the type eventually formed. The Navy sent 484 officers and men: 258 as a detachment of the 1st Construction Battalion, 139 for the fuel oil depot, and 87 for Scouting Squadron VS2D-14. The latter unit included its eight observation floatplanes. Fortunately a pre-war plan to stockpile base supplies for use in Great Britain to form American naval bases (known logically as the England Project) meant that materials were available at Quonset, Rhode Island. Materials from this accumulation were released for the Bora Bora project, though it meant that the Navy had to direct ships first to Quonset and then to Norfolk to pick up men and supplies prior to voyaging to Charleston to complete the Navy and Army loading. Needless to say, the logistics of the project were complicated, and in consequence problems at the other end would soon be evident.

Problems were encountered with the two transports. *President Tyler* was an older ship not in the best state of repair, and *Arthur Middleton* was not properly ballasted after being armed specifically before this voyage. In fact, the lack of balance at first was ignored; the ship had to be partially unloaded and then reloaded in Charleston to take care of a resulting list. All six ships had to be armed and assigned gun crews prior to the voyage. To augment the anti-aircraft capability, the 198th Coast Artillery was directed to place its 37-mm automatic anti-aircraft guns on deck with cleared fields of fire. Escort was provided all along the route, from Charleston with six destroyers and old light cruiser USS *Richmond.* While the cruiser was an older vessel, she should have been able to handle a stray raider, and still carried observation planes useful for scouting ahead.

It was planned for this convoy to rendezvous with the Australian-bound convoy departing New York and share escort until they had to break apart near Bora Bora. However, when time for departure drew close, some unplanned delays were encountered. Repairs to ships, including the ballast problem with *Arthur Middleton* mentioned above, and late-arriving additional freight dockside delayed departure until the early hours of January 28. Reluctantly the Army and Navy had to let the Australian-bound convoy proceed alone, such was the urgency to get a garrison to New Caledonia. In fact, as it turned out the Bora Bora convoy (BC-100) was just two to three days behind larger convoy BT-200 carrying Task Force 6814. On the way a scouting was made of Bora Bora by the lead convoy to make sure it was still in friendly hands and safe for the follow-up convoy. The actual voyage was uneventful from a military standpoint. The usual rumors of enemy ships and subs in the area abounded. One even included the preposterous theory that the German battleship *Tirpitz* was in the area! One disturbing fact received was true: the British surrender at Singapore on February 15. The seeming invincibility of the Japanese brought home the urgency of the task at hand and made some wonder if the relative distant isolation of Bora Bora was really far enough.

The convoy made landfall at the island group on February 17, but the unloading process did not go easily. According to plan, the local French authorities were only notified of the precise arrival date one day ahead of time. While the island had two large, good anchorages, port facilities were practically nonexistent. In fact, the Navy had brought along a new sort of disassembled barge to aid in unloading, but even this was not enough. The Americans had prepared the expedition on faulty information about the islands. The best maps available were French ones from the mid-nineteenth century. They did not portray the island's topography correctly. Also it was assumed that fresh water was readily available, when in fact it was not. Much of the initial construction work had to be directed to building a water supply, before work on the fueling depot could begin.

The unloading process was a nightmare. While it was known that the local piers and unloading facilities were limited, the task force was really not prepared for an orderly unloading. The initial haphazard loading of the cargo caused serious delays. Much of the heavy equipment and pontoon barges were buried furthest down in the freighters. Luckily several thirty-ton tank lighters were on deck and they were quickly employed, but they were insufficient for the task. Much of the freight was not labeled, and crates had to be broken into and searched for contents. The Maritime Commission freighters had no slings or cargo nets, and still carried just commercial rig suitable for unloading at a well-equipped established port, not an isolated small beach town. It took weeks to unload all the men and equipment. On February 28—eleven days after arrival—less than one-quarter of the cargo had been unloaded. On the same date the 198th Coast Artillery Regiment finally got their men off their transport. In the opinion of the naval commander, three to four weeks were lost. Luckily the unloading was not contested by enemy action. Actual work on the fuel tanks didn't start until late May, almost three months after the expedition arrived.[14] Still, even these problems had a silver lining. Important lessons were learned; voluminous reports and studies were published as a result of the Bora Bora experience and widely circulated within both services.

Within the time scope of this work, three major large movements were planned and at least partially executed by the Army. The first was the shipment of a long list of units and essential supplies to the Philippines scheduled for early December 1941. The Army secured most of its required transport space from its own and Maritime Commission ships. By using newly acquired or outfitted vessels and chartering certain commercial ships for single voyages the necessary tonnage was obtained. Of course, the outbreak of the war cancelled the movement of most of these ships, though a substantial amount of the shipping was used to move much of the men and some of the equipment to Hawaii and to a lesser extent Australia instead. The second campaign was for the movement of substantial task forces for New Caledonia, Bora Bora, and Australia in late January. The ships for this movement were found by using Atlantic transports released by the adjustments and delays agreed upon with the British at the Washington Conference.

Now in mid-February 1942 the Army attempted to locate shipping to allow the movement of an entire division to a Pacific outpost and to complete the transfer of units to New Caledonia in order to build the task force there into a division-strength unit. On February 14 Marshall and Somervell approached Vice Adm. Emory S. Land and Harry L. Hopkins (key to any adjustments to lend-lease shipments) for help in finding shipping to move 26,000 men immediately to Australia. Within its own resources the Army could find just one large liner on the West Coast to lift six thousand troops. Just a few days later the Army added its requirements for the 27th Division's movement to Hawaii's outlying islands. Altogether the planned movement for March/April involved two full divisions (one for Hawaii, one for Australia) and about 40 percent of another (for New Caledonia).

In late February the final plan envisioned the use of seven large Atlantic transports, the *President Monroe*, and a couple of British-loaned liners, including *Queen Elizabeth*. Freight would be supplied by twenty cargo vessels from the Maritime Commission. The movement at this point for the South Pacific consisted of 8,206 service personnel (requested engineer, quartermaster, signal, ordnance, and other services) for Australia, a division of 15,245 men, an 800-man tank destroyer battalion, and 1,331 field artillery soldiers for New Caledonia. In total 25,582 soldiers would be involved, the bulk departing from New York and the rest San Francisco. The major unit for Australia was the 41st Division.

After the usual delays, adjustments to the precise units involved, and substitution of ship transports, the big movement for March 1942 was ready. From Brooklyn on SS *Santa Paula* and *Uruguay* came the 162nd Regiment, the 641st Tank Destroyer Battalion, and the 41st Recon Troop. The ships left on March 3 and arrived at Melbourne on April 9. The troops had in fact been transported across country to Fort Dix prior to sailing, just in order to accommodate the presence of waiting transports on the East Coast. The next contingent to sail was the largest group. The 163rd Regiment, 167th Field Artillery Battalion, 41st Signal Battalion, 116th Engineer Battalion, and 41st Divisional Headquarters sailed on British-loaned *Queen Elizabeth* and American transports *President Coolidge* and *Mariposa*. The ships left San Francisco on March 19 and arrived April 6 in Melbourne and Sydney (*Queen Elizabeth* was too large for Melbourne's harbor). The final contingent of the 186th Regiment and three field artillery battalions with the divisional artillery headquarters sailed on *Argentina* and *Matsonia* from San Francisco and arrived in Melbourne on May 13.

Selected to complete the Americal Division on Noumea were the 164th Regiment, several artillery battalions, and an air warning company. These units shipped out with the same convoys taking the new division to Australia. By the end of May major American combat forces were forward-deployed along the communication line to Australia—and it would be these forces that first engaged the Japanese on the long road to Tokyo. A new phase of the war would soon start when the battles of Coral Sea and Midway transferred the offensive from the Japanese to the Americans.

The reinforcement efforts generally came to an end by the close of February 1942. The forces necessary to rationally defend the Hawaiian Islands, garrison the island ferry bases, and support the first phase of Air Force buildup in Australia were complete. Starting in March larger division-sized forces began to move to the Pacific. These forces were viewed initially as additional garrison forces, but soon—and more importantly—as offensive forces deployed to forward bases closer to the enemy. The first of these was the task force that ultimately became the nucleus of the Americal Division, which left the continental United States on January 23. On March 10 the first echelon of the 27th Division began its move to the Hawaiian Islands. On the nineteenth of the same month the 41st Division began moving to Australia. A second division for Australia, the 32nd, began transferring on April 22. Finally in this phase the 37th Division moved to Fiji starting on May 26.[15] Obviously the course of the war was not known at this time; all these divisional movements were planned well in advance of the serious Japanese defeat at Midway. Still, they should be properly viewed as the beginning of the offensive phase of the American war in the Pacific rather than the end of the defensive phase.

The original effort to build up Philippine defenses did not have enough time to truly be effective. Frankly, considering the geographical and military challenges of late 1941, probably no reasonable amount of reinforcement could have prevented a determined Japanese conquest. It should be said that the Fil-Am ground forces in Bataan and Corregidor certainly gave a good account of themselves, in stark comparison to some other Allied campaigns in this same phase of the war. The men, weapons, and supplies that had arrived before the start of the war allowed a better defense—one that delayed the Japanese schedule at a most critical time. Unfortunately most of the men and scarce fighting equipment went into the hands of captors, and the experience of American POWs in Asia was horrific. Likewise, the rather minimal efforts to reinforce Oahu in early 1941 with aircraft and some attempts to address manpower shortages later in the year ultimately had very little impact on either the Japanese decision to attack the naval base or on the military's ability to defend it. However, this is not to say that the late 1941 strategic effort to reinforce the Pacific military outposts was wasted.

The military's infrastructure for this shipping effort was invaluable in the early phases of the war. The Army's port and transportation network, ably assisted by the Navy's help in escorting and manning transports and the Maritime Commission's ability to make ocean-going ships available, was already working at capacity when the war began. The air ferry routes in both the Pacific and Atlantic were being aggressively developed. While initially being built to facilitate the transfer of bombers to the Philippines and lend-lease airplanes to the Allies, the same routes were just as important in getting fighting planes quickly to the new theatres of Southeast Asia. And finally, the accumulation of trained soldiers, already formed into units, and essential war matériel at the West Coast ports entirely facilitated the military's ability to shore up its defense of Hawaii, build the air ferry bases, and begin the buildup of forces necessary in Australia. The successful 1942 campaigns in New Guinea and Guadalcanal simply would not have been possible without the groundwork and assets started in the reinforcement attempt of 1941.

NOTES

Abbreviations used in Notes.

PHI: *Pearl Harbor Attack: Hearings before the Joint Committee on the Investigation of the Pearl Harbor Attack* (Washington, D.C.: Government Printing Office, 1946)

OCT: Army Office of the Chief of Transportation

Chapter 1. The Situation in the Philippines

1. Most overseas "areas" were designated Departments by the Army. These were designed to be sort of integrated commands, containing in addition to fighting troops the various support functions (like engineers, ordnance, medical, signal, etc.). One command structure and commander would manage all of the service's activities in the isolated geography and theoretically reduce inter-departmental confusion and conflict. It seemed to work relatively well in the 1920s and 1930s, though primarily viewed as defensive in nature. The Philippine Department as such had originally been organized in 1913.
2. RG-165, Entry 281, File 3251-55, August 14, 1941.
3. RG-165, Entry 284, File 325, April 30, 1941.
4. RG-165, Entry 284, File 325, June 16, 1941.
5. RG-165, Entry 281, File 3251-46, June 12, 1941.
6. RG-38, CinCPac Operation Order 4-41, February 13, 1941.
7. Adm. James O. Richardson (Ret.), *On the Treadmill to Pearl Harbor: The Memoirs of Admiral James O. Richardson, USN (Retired)*, interviewed by Vice Adm. George C. Dyer (Ret.), (Washington, D.C.: Naval Historical Division, Department of the Navy, 1973), 406.
8. Rear Adm. Edwin T. R. Layton (Ret.), with Capt. Roger Pineau (Ret.) and John Costello, *"And I Was There": Pearl Harbor and Midway—Breaking the Secrets* (New York: Quill William Morrow, 1985), 93.
9. RG-38, CinCPac Operation Order 7-41, March 37, 1941.

10. Daniel Ford, *Flying Tigers: Claire Chennault and the American Volunteer Group* (Washington, D.C.: Smithsonian Institution Press, 1991), 65–66.
11. RG-38, Operation Order 22-41.
12. *President Taft* had been acquired by the Army transportation service in June, but apparently was not renamed by them (as *Willard A. Holbrook*) until September.
13. RG-165, Entry 281, File 3633-17, August 15, 1941.
14. It should be noted that the term "radar" was not in widespread use at this time, at least in the U.S. Army. The correspondence on this subject invariably calls the sets "detection devices" or simply "detectors." In late 1941 the Army had three sets in limited production. Designated "SCR" for Signal Corps Radio, these were the SCR-268 used for short-ranged gun and searchlight direction, the mobile SCR-270 longer-ranged air-warning set, and the SCR-271, a fixed-station version of the same type.
15. RG-165, Entry 281, File 4359-1, April 26, 1941.
16. RG-165, Entry 281, File 4359-1, June 4, 1941.
17. AAFHS No. 111, 22.
18. Cordell Hull, *The Memoirs of Cordell Hull, Vol. 2* (New York: The Macmillan Company, 1948), 1012.
19. Japanese Monograph No. 147, 5.
20. John Costello, *Days of Infamy: MacArthur, Roosevelt, Churchill—The Shocking Truth Revealed* (New York: Pocket Books, 1994), 56.
21. Hull, *Memoirs, Vol. 2*, 1014.
22. Gordon W. Prange, *At Dawn We Slept: The Untold Story of Pearl Harbor* (New York: Penguin Books, 1982), 168.
23. Prior to this, missions had only been offered and operated in Central and South America.
24. Michael Schaller, *Douglas MacArthur: The Far Eastern General* (New York: Oxford University Press, 1989), 26–27.
25. Mark Goldberg, *The "Stately President" Liners: American Passenger Liners of the Interwar Years, Part I, The "502"s* (Kings Point, NY: American Merchant Marine Museum, 1996), 419.
26. RG-165, Entry 281, File 4389-23, September 24, 1941.
27. Marshall on several instances opposed lend-lease or aid allocations that seriously hampered the expansion or training of American forces.
28. James Walker, "The Decision to Reinforce the Philippines: A Desperate Gamble" (PhD diss., Temple University, 1996), 130–131 and 182.
29. RG-165, Entry 284, Joint Board minutes for September 19, 1941.
30. Theodore A. Wilson, *The First Summit: Roosevelt and Churchill at Placentia Bay, 1941* (Boston: Houghton Mifflin Company, 1969), 69.

Chapter 2. Pacific Fleet Basing and the Problem of Oahu Defense

1. *Pearl Harbor Attack: Hearings before the Joint Committee on the Investigation of the*

Pearl Harbor Attack (Washington, D.C.: Government Printing Office, 1946), hereafter PHI, Part 14, 993–999.

2. Larry Bland, Sharon Ritenour, and Clarence Wunderlin, eds., *The Papers of George Catlett Marshall*, vol. 2, *We Cannot Delay, July 1, 1939–December 6, 1941* (Baltimore: The Johns Hopkins University Press, 1986), 411–413.
3. Marshall states that the required planes were found by "robbing" existing squadrons, cutting them down to just three planes each to allow at least some level of training in these units to continue. See PHI, Part 3, 1059. Other sources state that the majority of the planes came from Hamilton, Moffett, and Selfridge Fields.
4. Allison Ind, *Bataan: The Judgment Seat* (New York: The Macmillan Company, 1944), 6.
5. PHI, Exhibit V of Joint Committee Report. It is interesting to compare these numbers to the report of Secretary Stimson to Secretary Knox on February 7. In ten months the number of 3-inch guns had increased by just four (from eighty-two to eighty-six), 37-mm guns by none (from twenty at sea to twenty present), and .50-caliber anti-aircraft machine guns decreased by two (from 109 to 107).
6. RG-407, Entry 360A, File 320.2, September 5, 1941.
7. Michael Gannon, *Pearl Harbor Betrayed: The True Story of a Man and a Nation under Attack* (New York: Henry Holt and Company, 2001), 23.
8. Erwin N. Thompson, *Pacific Ocean Engineers, 1905–1980* (Washington, D.C.: U.S. Army Corps of Engineers, 1985), 79.
9. Prange, *At Dawn We Slept*, 62–63.
10. RG-494, Box G-29, General Short–General Marshall correspondence, February 19, 1941.
11. Karl Dod, *The Corps of Engineers: The War against Japan*, United States Army in World War II (Washington, D.C.: Office of the Chief of Military History, United States Army, 1966), 42–44.
12. Husband E. Kimmel, *Admiral Kimmel's Story* (Chicago: Henry Regnery Company, 1955), 15. Planes for the Pearl Harbor naval district had been requested of the chief of naval operations on at least December 20, 1940, May 7, 1941, and October 17, 1941.
13. *William P. Biddle* also carried part of the 7th Defense Battalion that did not disembark in Hawaii, but continued in the transport to Samoa.
14. Charles L. Updegraph Jr., *Special Marine Corps Units of World War II* (Washington, D.C.: Historical Division, U.S. Marine Corps, 1972), 65. There were at Pearl Harbor on December 7, 1941 the following personnel from various defense battalions:
    1st Defense Battalion (20 officers + 241 enlisted men)
    3rd Defense Battalion (40 officers + 823 enlisted men)
    4th Defense Battalion (38 officers + 780 enlisted men)
    6th Defense Battalion (4 officers + 17 enlisted men)

15. Adm. Ernest J. King and Cdr. Walter Muir Whitehill, *Fleet Admiral King: A Naval Record* (New York: W. W. Norton & Company, Inc., 1952), 340.

Chapter 3. Initial Reinforcements—September 1941

1. RG-165, Entry 281, File 3251-55, August 14, 1941. The others were: a composite air wing, an infantry division, and approximately 2,300 additional harbor defense troops.
2. Frank Fujita, *Foo: A Japanese-American Prisoner of the Rising Sun* (Denton: University of North Texas Press, 1993), 31.
3. Dorothy Cave, *Beyond Courage: One Regiment against Japan, 1941–1945* (Las Cruces, NM: Yucca Tree Press, 1992), 35.
4. Cave, *Beyond Courage*, 37–38.
5. RG-336, Entry 5, File "Movement Philippines" and name file "Coolidge"; RG-165, Entry 234A, File G-4/33700; RG-496, Entry 540, File 569.4.
6. Maj. Gen. Bruce Jacobs (Ret.), "The Evolution of Tank Units in the Pre-WWII National Guard and the Defense of Bataan," *Military Collector & Historian* 38, no. 3 (1986): 126.
7. Col. E. B. Miller, *Bataan Uncensored* (Little Falls: Military Historical Society of Minnesota, 1991), 35–39.
8. During the Second World War the primary difference between the two types of cruisers was armament—light cruisers usually were armed with 6-inch guns while heavy cruisers had 8-inch guns. The larger light cruisers, such as the *Brooklyn*–class cruisers *Phoenix* and *St. Louis*, had all the size, endurance, and aircraft capabilities as their heavy cruiser counterparts.
9. Pat Jones, *The USS* Astoria *and the Men Who Sailed Her* (Hillsboro, OR: Premier Press, 1992), 22.
10. RG-165, Entry 281, File 4560, July 30, 1941.
11. RG-165, Entry 281, File 3602-17, June 22, 1939.
12. RG-165, Entry 281, File 3251-55, August 14, 1941.
13. D. Clayton James, *The Years of MacArthur, Vol. 1, 1880–1941* (Boston: Houghton Mifflin Company, 1970), 613.
14. Bland, Ritenour, and Wunderlin, *We Cannot Delay*, 599.
15. Warren F. Kimball, ed., *Churchill & Roosevelt: The Complete Correspondence, Vol. 1* (Princeton: Princeton University Press, 1984), 235–236.
16. RG-38, Op-38, Serial 077338 of September 26, 1941 for the original plan, and RG-38, Op-38 Serial 089938 of October 20, 1941 for the final, adopted plan.

Chapter 4. Philippine Reinforcements—October 1941

1. Samuel A. Goldblith, "The 803rd Engineers in the Philippine Defense," *The Military Engineer* (August 1946): 323.
2. Walter D. Edmonds, *They Fought With What They Had: The Story of the Army Air Forces in the Southwest Pacific, 1941–1942* (Washington, D.C.: Zenger Publishing Co., Inc, 1982), 35.

3. RG-165, Entry 281, File 2789; RG-336, Entry 5, File "Movement Philippines" and "Name File" *Coolidge, Liberty*; RG-165, Entry 234A, File G-4 /27573-18; RG-407, Entry 360A, File 370.5; RG-496, Entry 540, Files 569.4–569.5.
4. *Tasker H. Bliss* and *Willard A. Holbrook* carried 486 and 421 non-organizational soldiers respectively to Hawaii.
5. The 809th was still working on the Nichols Field facilities as of this date.
6. PHI, Part 12, 290–316.
7. Mark S. Watson, *Chief of Staff: Prewar Plans and Preparations*, United States Army in World War II (Washington, D.C.: Center of Military History, United States Army, 1991), 35.
8. USAT *Hunt* failed to actually make this pickup, apparently due to being overloaded with rubber previously, at Belawan and Batavia.
9. Col. Melvin H. Rosen (Ret.), *History of the Philippine Scouts Field Artillery* (privately printed, 2000), 5.
10. RG-407, Entry 360A, File 045.4.
11. RG-38, CinCPac file A16(CV)/(11), October 13, 1941.
12. 14-CL41, Exhibit 21 of Hart Inquiry, PHI.

Chapter 5. The Naval and Marine Reinforcements

1. Despite the nomenclature as being the *P*-class, the boats of this type had nautical creature names not necessarily beginning with the letter "P."
2. Roger J. Spiller, ed., *Dictionary of American Military Biography*, vol. 2, *H–P* (Westport, CT: Greenwood Press, 1984), 457.
3. Richardson, *On the Treadmill to Pearl Harbor*, 404.
4. RG-38, Op-12-CTB, February 7, 1941.
5. James Leutze, *A Different Kind of Victory: A Biography of Admiral Thomas C. Hart* (Annapolis: Naval Institute Press, 1981), 190.
6. Norman Friedman, *U.S. Small Combatants: An Illustrated Design History* (Annapolis: Naval Institute Press, 1987), 110–113. This book contains a rather detailed account of the Philippine torpedo-boats' design process and results.
7. Leutze, *A Different Kind of Victory*, 215–217.
8. PHI, Part 5, 2284.
9. J. Michael Miller, *From Shanghai to Corregidor: Marines in the Defense of the Philippines* (Washington, D.C.: Marine Corps Historical Center, 1997), 16–17.
10. Chester M. Biggs Jr., *The United States Marines in North China, 1894–1942* (Jefferson, NC: McFarland & Company Inc., 2003), 203–204. An American Marine was shot by a Japanese soldier in an incident on October 28, 1941.
11. Goldberg, *The "Stately President" Liners*, 418–419 and 626–627.

Chapter 6. Philippine Reinforcements—November 1941

1. RG-165, Entry 281, File 4559-3, September 13, 1941.
2. RG-336, Entry 5, File "Movement Philippines"; RG-165, Entry 234A, File G-4/33700; RG-496, Entry 540, File 569.4.

3. RG-407, Entry 360, File 320.2, November 5, 1941.
4. Frank Emile McGlothlin, *Barksdale to Bataan: History of the 48th Materiel Squadron, October 1940–April 1942* (privately published, 1948), 41.
5. Lt. Col. William E. Dyess, *The Dyess Story* (New York: G. P. Putnam's Sons, 1944), 23–25.
6. McGlothlin, *Barksdale to Bataan*, 27–31.
7. RG-165, Entry 281, File 3602-3, July 23, 1940.
8. RG-165, Entry 281, File 4389-28, November 1, 1941.
9. RG-24, *Boise* deck log.
10. Layton, *"And I Was There,"* 212.
11. RG-165, Entry 234A, File G-4/32113, May 29, 1941.
12. Henry Lewis Stimson, *The Henry Lewis Stimson Diaries in the Yale University Library* (New Haven, CT: Yale University Library Microfilm, 1973), diary entries for November 6 and November 24, 1941.
13. RG-165, Entry 281, File 4389-29, November 13, 1941.
14. See for example the *Chicago Tribune* for November 16, 1941. The size of the unit or its strength is not provided, but because the commander was a brigadier general, it was not a major intellectual jump to guess that the force would be about a brigade in size.
15. Forrest C. Pogue, *George C. Marshall: Ordeal and Hope, 1939–1942* (New York: Viking Press, 1966), 187.
16. William Manchester, *American Caesar: Douglas MacArthur, 1880–1964* (Boston: Little, Brown and Company, 1978), 196–197. Also see an account of this meeting from one of the attending reporters, Hanson Baldwin, *Great Mistakes of the War* (New York: Harper & Brothers Publishers, 1949), 64.
17. Leutze, *A Different Kind of Victory*, 212.
18. James, *The Years of MacArthur*, 615.
19. Gen. Jonathan M. Wainwright, *General Wainwright's Story* (Westport, CT: Greenwood Press, 1970), 12–13.
20. Bland, Ritenour, and Wunderlin, *We Cannot Delay*, 680, note 8.
21. James, *The Years of MacArthur*, 595–597.
22. RG-336, Entry 5, File "Movement Philippines."
23. RG-407, Entry 1053, Quartermaster Report of the U.S. Armed Forces in Luzon, 41.
24. RG-165, Entry 281, File 3602-3, July 23, 1940, and File 4389-28, October 31, 1941.
25. Ibid., 55.

Chapter 7. The Philippine Army

1. The U.S. Army did review its position on Philippine defense. It adopted a policy of continued presence, particularly with the harbor defenses of Manila Bay, but it would not make any permanent improvements that were not clear cost savings.

2. Ricardo Trota Jose, *The Philippine Army, 1935–1942* (Manila: Ateneo de Manila University Press, 1992), 57–60.
3. RG-165, Entry 281, File 3602-12, September 29, 1937. Note that the original design of the division envisioned only one of the two artillery battalions would be armed with artillery pieces, the other would have mortars. By 1941 it was revised so that both artillery battalions would be gun-armed. Thus the artillery component for the first ten reserve divisions "doubled" from 120 to 240 pieces (plus whatever was needed for reserves and training).
4. Jose, *Philippine Army*, 132. It should be noted that the Philippine Commonwealth did directly purchase some of its weapons. For example, in 1939 the budget included the purchase of twenty-four 81-mm mortars, fifteen machine guns, and forty sets of high-speed wheel adaptors for the 75-mm field guns it had recently secured.
5. The Enfield-pattern Model 1917 was a rather heavy rifle compared to others of the time, and that was a problem with the small-stature Filipinos. Worse, it had one technical flaw: the rifle's extractor, a device that withdrew the spent shell casing, was "weak" and tended to break. That in turn necessitated that a user had to occasionally eject the casing manually by inserting a rod down the barrel and forcing it out. This was not only a nuisance; it also meant a substantial reduction in rate of fire during a fast-paced engagement.
6. C. S. Ferris, *United States Rifle Model of 1917* (Export, PA: Scott A. Duff Publications, 2004), 142–143. Apparently only the initial 75,000 guns were actually sold; arrangements for the next 220,000 were as "loaned" weapons. Shipments began with the sailing of SS *President Taft* on April 9, 1936 and continued incrementally until September 1939.
7. RG-165, Entry 234A, File G-4/33861, March 22, 1942.
8. James, *The Years of MacArthur*, 600.
9. Jose, *Philippine Army*, Appendix 4, 228.
10. RG-165, Entry 281, File 4560-2, August 29, 1941.
11. By comparison the standard for an American triangular division was listed as over 1,300 vehicles.
12. RG-165, Entry 281, File 3602-21, September 5, 1941.
13. RG-165, Entry 234A, File G-4/27573/18, October 1, 1941.
14. RG-165, Entry 281, File 4559-2, November 2, 1941.
15. RG-165, Entry 281, File 3489-21, December 1, 1941.
16. Louis Morton, *The Fall of the Philippines*, United States Army in World War II (Washington, D.C.: Office of the Chief of Military History, United States Army, 1953), 28–29.
17. RG-165, Entry 281, File 3251-44, February 1, 1941.
18. The old (circa 1900) 2.95-inch mountain gun had been an American purchase and subsequent manufacture of a British Vickers-design gun. By this

time virtually all the remaining guns (about sixty) and the entire remaining stock of ammunition were concentrated in the Philippines. It was due for eventual replacement by the new 75-mm pack howitzer, but that had not yet been accomplished in 1941.

19. The memo does provide an interesting summary of what was present. On November 3 the Philippines had, in the hands of both the U.S. and Philippine armies: 6,536 M1s, 22,612 Model 1903 Springfields, and 238,725 Model 1917 Enfield-pattern rifles.

Chapter 8. B-17s and the First Air Ferry Route

1. Bland, Ritenour, and Wunderlin, *We Cannot Delay*, 74.
2. Robert L. Gandt, *China Clipper: The Age of the Great Flying Boats* (Annapolis: Naval Institute Press, 1991), 72–111.
3. Wesley Frank Craven and James Lea Cate, eds., *The Army Air Forces in World War II*, vol. 1, *Plans and Early Operations: January 1939 to August 1942* (Chicago: University of Chicago Press, 1948), 172.
4. RG-38, Entry 230A, Ship Movement Division.
5. Craven and Cate, *Plans and Early Operations*, 172.
6. James, *The Years of MacArthur*, 589.
7. Gen. H. H. Arnold, *Global Mission* (New York: Harper & Brothers Publishers, 1949), 208.
8. Schaller, *Douglas MacArthur*, 47; James, *The Years of MacArthur*, 589.
9. Pogue, *Ordeal and Hope*, 186.
10. Ibid.
11. John H. Mitchell, *On Wings We Conquer: The 19th and 7th Bomb Groups of the United States Air Force in the Southwest Pacific in the First Year of World War Two* (Springfield, MO: G. E. M. Publishers, 1990), 30.
12. RG-38, Entry 230A, Ship Movement Division.
13. RG-496, Entry 540, File 452.1. This contains a description of the journey by the 14th Squadron contained and Maj. E. O'Donnell's report.
14. PHI, Part 10, 5146. On the second flight the final report says this: "The equatorial front, an ever-present weather phenomenon between Wake and Port Moresby, offers a flight problem worthy of much consideration. This front was successfully penetrated by this Group at altitudes from 1,000 to 28,000 feet. Clouds in this front are characterized by severe turbulence at intermediate altitudes and are to be avoided. Moonlight aids in the perception and avoidance of these clouds."
15. RG-165, Entry 234A, File 29367-120, October 13, 1941.
16. OCT Historical Monographs, A. J. Bingham, "Reinforcement of the Philippines" (1947), 5.
17. MacArthur Archives—Microfilm Reels 4, USAFFE Radiograms.
18. RG-165, Entry 12, File 18136-25.
19. PHI, Part 10, 5142–5147. This contains a description of the journey by the 19th Group.

20. Ibid.
21. PHI, Part 10, 5143.
22. Ibid.
23. Leatrice R. Arakaki and John R. Kuborn, *7 December 1941: The Air Force Story* (Hickam AFB, HI: Pacific Air Forces Office of History, 1991), 72–75.
24. Ibid., 75.
25. RG-165, Entry 284, Joint Board minutes for November 26, 1941.
26. RG-165, Entry 281, File 4544-9, November 26, 1941.

Chapter 9. Marine Corps Base Defense

1. Admiral Hepburn had recently been commandant of San Francisco's Twelfth Naval District, and prior to that assignment the commander in chief of the Pacific division of the U.S. Fleet.
2. House Document No. 65, 76th Congress, 1st Session.
3. A very exhaustive history of the politics of Guam's defense is contained in Earl S. Pomeroy, *Pacific Outpost: American Strategy in Guam and Micronesia* (Stanford, CA: Stanford University Press, 1951).
4. David O. Woodbury, *Builders for Battle: How the Pacific Naval Air Bases Were Constructed* (New York: E. P. Dutton and Company, Inc., 1946), 41–54.
5. The three original members were Raymond Concrete Pile Company, Hawaiian Dredging Company, and Turner Construction Company.
6. In reality all of the island locations were actually atolls that had several islands and exposed reefs. Each island was named separately, but common usage of the time has left us with just a single entity to conveniently refer to each "collection" of islands.
7. Woodbury, *Builders for Battle*, 99.
8. Ibid., 149.
9. The two firms were Morrison Knudsen and J. H. Pomeroy.
10. The last three partners were Utah Construction Company, Byrne Organization, and W. A. Bechtel Company.
11. Updegraph, *Special Marine Corps Units*, 61. While this role may seem obvious, the Marines had numerous other duties (like forces on board ships, at embassies and foreign stations, and at training and administrative centers) pulling on limited manpower. The FMF were to be those units and forces immediately available for expeditionary use.
12. Updegraph, *Special Marine Corps Units*, 62–63.
13. RG-127, List 6, Letter from CNO to CinCUS, January 17, 1941.
14. RG-127, List 6, Letter Com14 to CNO, February 11, 1941.
15. For some reason a number of written reports mistakenly identify the second cruiser as *Nashville*; however, she had been serving in the Atlantic fleet since transferred in May 1941.
16. This contingent totaled thirty-four officers and 750 enlisted men.
17. RG-127, List 6, Excerpt from DPWO Conference Memo to War Plans Officer, February 6, 1941.

18. RG-165, Entry 281, File 4571-12. The machine-gun count for Palmyra on November 28, 1941 was twenty .50-caliber and twenty .30-caliber machine guns.
19. RG-127, List 6, Memorandum District Marine Officer to Com, Midway, December 4, 1941, and RG-24 *Regulus* deck log.
20. RG-38, Op-38, Op-30D1-EP, December 2, 1941.
21. PHI, Part 12, 3984.
22. While the strength of the Marine contingent is reported fairly consistently, the Guamanian forces are less definite. The numbers here are from Lt. Col. Frank O. Hough, Maj. Verle E. Ludwig, and Henry I. Shaw Jr., *History of U.S. Marine Corps Operations in World War II*, vol. 1, *Pearl Harbor to Guadalcanal* (Washington, D.C.: Historical Branch, U.S. Marine Corps). Also on Guam, though not armed, were 271 naval personnel and about 130 civilian contractors or Pan Am employees.
23. Pacific Fleet command requested that eighteen 1,000-pound, thirty-six 500-pound, and 150 100-pound bombs be sent and stored at Midway.
24. *Lexington* was organized as Task Force 12 and escorted by *Chicago*, *Astoria*, *Portland*, and Destroyer Squadron 5 less Destroyer Division 10.
25. Apparently there was confusion both on board and ashore as to which unit was to land at which island. At first it was assumed that the bomber squadron was to be landed at Wake, and much of its equipment had been offloaded before clarification from Pearl Harbor straightened out the assignments. Equipment had to be exchanged before *Wright* could proceed to Midway.
26. RG-407, Entry 360A, File 381, December 5, 1941.
27. An Army letter from this discussion admits twenty miles as the limit.

Chapter 10. *Pensacola* Convoy Begins

1. RG-165, Entry 281, File 2789, September 17, 1941.
2. RG-407, Entry 360A, File 370.5, October 15, 1941, and File 370.5, October 18, 1941.
3. Strictly speaking, after a state unit was called into federal service, it was no longer a National Guard unit. While it is probably more correct to continue to refer to these units as "ex–National Guard," the personnel at the time and the Washington Army staff continued to use the term National Guard for those units that had originated in that system.
4. As these complement numbers reflect the actual manpower on the date of the memo, they tended to differ over time, even for the same unit. Turnover of personnel continued, reinforcements and drafts occurred, and almost inevitably some personnel would not make a trip due to illness, personal situations, or even desertion. Thus numbers should be taken as close approximation, and certainly not static.
5. Jensen was a prominent politician from South Dakota, most recently serving as state governor from 1937 to 1939.

6. Clyde Fillmore, *Prisoner of War: History of the Lost Battalion* (Wichita Falls, TX: Nortex Press, 1984), 2.
7. Richard Cropp, "A History of the 147th Field Artillery Regiment, 1939–1942," *Report and Historical Collections (South Dakota Historical Society)* 309 (1960): 494.
8. RG-407, Entry 361A, File 472.12-821. Reported numbers for the various guns vary considerably between letters and reports. General King's post-war summary lists a total of 208 75-mm M1917 guns available.
9. RG-165, Entry 281, File 4559-2, November 12, 1941.
10. RG-407, Entry 361A, File 472.1, July 3, 1941.
11. Ibid., November 4, 1941.
12. Ibid., November 11, 1941.
13. Ibid., November 26, 1941. The report is a list of what was physically loaded on the transport, and also lists the quantity as forty-eight M1917A1 guns. All were placed on USAT *Meigs.*
14. Cropp, "A History of the 147th Field Artillery Regiment," 294, and Kyle Thompson, *A Thousand Cups of Rice: Surviving the Death Railway* (Austin, TX: Eakin Press, 1994), 16.
15. RG-165, Entry 281, File 4559-2, November 12, 1941.
16. The unit's responsibilities and capabilities can be found in Brook E. Kleber and Dale Birdsell, *The Chemical Warfare Service: Chemicals in Combat*, United States Army in World War II (Washington, D.C.: Center of Military History, United States Army, 1990), 280–282.
17. Peter Smith, *Douglas SBD Dauntless* (Ramsbury, UK: Crowood Press Ltd., 1997), 58–59.
18. Cropp, "A History of the 147th Field Artillery Regiment," 489.
19. RG-38, Entry 348, File Convoy No. 4002, USAFIA Report; RG-165, Entry 234A, File G-4/27573 and G-4/33700; RG-407, Entry 360A, File 565.2; RG-496, Entry 540, File 569.4.
20. Many of the accounts, and even archival records, differ on the status of *Republic.* A transport owned and operated by the Army since the 1930s, the vessel was one of several given over to the Navy in the summer of 1941 for manning and operations. Thus the vessel carried a naval crew and was commissioned as a naval vessel. However, the Army was still the official "owner" of the vessel and made the determination of cargo, destination, and other usage. Army records still often refer to the ship as an "USAT," and certainly many passengers—seeing the vessel tying up to the same piers in San Francisco, Honolulu, and Manila with the same name painted on the bow—continued to assume she was a full Army-operated transport. This account will use the naval commissioning as an indicator of vessel operator, with the appreciation of the unusual circumstances of the vessel's history.
21. Sometimes reports say fifty-five A-24s. There were several subsequent shipments totaling fifty-five fighter aircraft, so these reports might be con-

fusing. From assembly and usage reports in Australia it does appear to be pretty firm that the actual number was fifty-two as used here.

22. Stanley Weintraub, *Long Day's Journey into War* (New York: Truman Talley Books, 1991), 323.
23. Another source claims 245 vehicles were on board, but that figure probably includes trailers.
24. RG-38, Entry 348, File: Convoy No. 4002.
25. Prange, *At Dawn We Slept*, 402–413.
26. Fujita, *Foo*, 36.
27. No sailing date from San Francisco has been located for *Coast Farmer.*
28. It is interesting how both official and personal accounts vary on the actual date of the equator crossing. Some accounts even vary as to whether it occurred before or after the Pearl Harbor attack announcement. Logs and the Army diaries in USAFIA all record December 6 as the date of crossing.
29. Stimson, *Diaries*, December 6, 1941.

Chapter 11. *Pensacola* Convoy after December 7

1. Fujita, *Foo*, 47.
2. MacArthur radioed Marshall on December 8 that he had concluded a conference with Admiral Hart about the possibility of the convoy making it through.
3. RG-38, Entry 348, File: Convoy No. 4002.
4. Stimson, *Diaries*, December 10, 1941.
5. Manchester, *American Caesar*, 213.
6. Pogue, *Ordeal and Hope*, 265–266.
7. Manchester, *American Caesar*, 243.
8. The times of the course changes are as recorded in the deck log of USS *Pensacola*. There are slight variations of time (up to an hour) for several of the other ships in the convoy.
9. Center for Military History, Washington, D.C., "Report of Organization and Activities United States Army Forces in Australia (USAFIA) from December 7, 1941 to June 30, 1942, with Enclosures and Appendices," 144.
10. Army Officer Biographical Files, U.S. Army Heritage and Education Center, Carlisle Barracks, PA.
11. USAFIA Report, 5.
12. Cropp, "A History of the 147th Field Artillery Regiment," 490.
13. Fillmore, *Prisoner of War*, 4.
14. Cropp, "A History of the 147th Field Artillery Regiment," 495.
15. It is somewhat surprising that on this and many other voyages there did not seem to be a complete manifest available to the convoy or troop commander. The troops of *Pensacola* convoy really did not know the numbers and types of vehicles, weapons, and ammunition that were actually loaded on the various ships in their task group.

16. USAFIA Report, 153.
17. USAFIA Report, 158.
18. Hollis G. Allen, *The Lost Battalion* (Jacksboro, TX: Leigh McGee, 1963), 20.
19. Thompson, *A Thousand Cups of Rice*, 23.
20. USAFIA Report, 159.
21. Cropp, "A History of the 147th Field Artillery Regiment," 511.
22. Stimson, *Diaries*, December 8, 1941.
23. Larry L. Bland and Sharon R. Stevens, eds., *The Papers of George Catlett Marshall*, vol. 3, *The Right Man for the Job, December 7, 1941–May 31, 1943* (Baltimore: The Johns Hopkins University Press, 1991), 15–16.
24. Merle Miller, *Ike the Soldier: As They Knew Him* (New York: G. P. Putnam's Sons, 1987), 334.
25. Alfred D. Chandler Jr. et al., eds., *The Papers of Dwight David Eisenhower* (Baltimore: The Johns Hopkins University Press, 1970), 1:8, 17, 21, 35, 40.
26. Allen, *The Lost Battalion*, 23.
27. USAFIA Report, Quartermaster appendix, 9.
28. USAFIA Report, 172.
29. Bland and Stevens, *The Right Man for the Job*, 37.
30. Ray S. Cline, *Washington Command Post: The Operations Division, United States Army in World War II* (Washington, D.C.: Office of the Chief of Military History, United States Army, 1951), 379. On April 18, 1942, Barnes (then a major general) once more replaced Lieutenant General Brett.
31. This was SS *President Polk* dispatched from San Francisco unescorted on December 18.
32. RG-407, Entry 360A, File 565.2, December 12, 1941.

Chapter 12. Caught at Sea

1. PHI, Part IV, 1680.
2. Dates vary for this sailing of *Ludington.* Some original sources place it as November 19, but that may also be the date for leaving Honolulu and not San Francisco.
3. RG-165, Entry 281, File 4630; RG-336, Entry 5, File "Movement Philippines"; RG-165, Entry 234A, File G-4/27573 and G-4/33700; RG-407, Entry 360A, Files 320.2 and 370.5; RG-496, Entry 540, Files 541.2, 569.1–569.5.
4. At least she appears on an Army chart of vessel positions as at Samoa on December 13, 1941.
5. There is much confusion about the identity of this ship in the secondary records of the War Department. There were three Lykes Bros. ships being used for military shipments in the Pacific in December 1941. *John Lykes* was a member of the *Boise* convoy and had arrived in the Philippines just a few days prior to the start of war. *Joseph Lykes* was based out of New Orleans, and was carrying military cargo as part of a charter and

was in the southeast Pacific at the start of war. She was diverted back to San Francisco. *James Lykes* departed San Francisco in early December, but turned around and returned to that port after the start of the war. She was released to complete her voyage at the middle of the month. Official Army correspondence and later historical accounts based on these often substitute one name for the other—in particular *James* and *Joseph* are mixed up in these letters and even in some naval war diaries. The accounting of the ship voyages here is the best the author can make from the fragmentary records remaining. There is a possibility that *Joseph Lykes* is the ship that completed the Australian voyage, and *James Lykes* remained in San Francisco–Hawaiian waters at this time.

6. Both of the days on either side of the twenty-sixth (the twenty-fifth and twenty-seventh) are also in documents for the initial sailing date of *Portmar*.
7. Documents vary as to whether this port of entry was Sydney or Brisbane—although *Portmar* soon transited to Brisbane even if Sydney was the initial port. At this point of time Brisbane was clearly the center of the American presence, but it had limited port facilities and in some cases Sydney was used as an alternate or even "overflow" cargo harbor.
8. Existing documents do not specifically designate the role of the soldiers. Possibilities include cargo guards, or technical specialists assigned to the classified radar in the cargo. *Malama* was a freighter, with normally no provision for general passengers.
9. RG-165, Entry 234A, File G-4/33700.
10. According to the Fourteenth Naval District War Diary these were SS *Prusa* for Panama, SS *Permanente* and SS *Pat Doheney* for California, SS *Admiral Chase* for Sydney, and SS *Manini* and SS *Malama* for Wellington, New Zealand.
11. Rear Adm. Edwin T. Layton (Ret.), "24 Sentai—Japan's Commerce Raiders," U.S. Naval Institute *Proceedings* (June 1976): 57, and Capt. Arthur Moore, *A Careless Word . . . A Needless Sinking* (Kings Point, NY: American Merchant Marine Museum, 1993), 285.
12. RG-407, Philippine Archives, Report of the Cebu Advanced Quartermaster Depot, 3.
13. Moore, *A Careless Word*, 550.
14. There is in Army records a clear photograph showing *Liberty* with at least a small forward gun on a bandstand-type mounting. The photo also shows Manila piers in the background, indicating the ship must have been armed pre-war. As *Liberty* was in Manila during the immediate pre-war period in mid-summer 1941 and for the short visit to unload in early November, the arming had to have occurred either in Manila prior to the photography in one of these visits or more likely back stateside earlier. Whether there was a specific reason for the arming or she just happened to be the first USAT to be armed (which the Army had hoped to do, pending funding for most

of the year) is unknown. There is no evidence that she was supplied with a dedicated gun crew to serve the weapons.

15. RG-336, Entry 2, File: "Name File," *Liberty*, contains a thorough report by master Earl S. Evey.
16. MV *Roamer* had been the Danish MV *African Reefer*, built in 1935. A relatively small ship (1,771 tons), she was equipped with refrigeration equipment to serve the fruit trade. The ship was taken over by the Maritime Commission in American waters after the capitulation of Denmark in 1940. She was allocated to the Army for six months, and then in mid-1942 allocated to the U.S. Navy (as USS *Roamer*) through the end of the war.
17. RG-407, Entry 360A, File 370.5, November 14, 1941.
18. RG-165, Entry 284, File No. 325, Secret, November 12, 1934.
19. The exact quantity and type of material present has been elusive to find in the historical record. It does appear that at least *some* amount of gas—most likely mustard gas—was in inventory during the 1941–1942 campaign and was probably destroyed by the Filipino-American forces prior to capitulation.
20. RG-165, Entry 280, File 3602-8, May 16, 1939.
21. RG-165, Entry 281, File 3602-8, July 8, 1941.
22. RG-407, Entry 360A, File 370.5, November 14, 1941.
23. RG-165, Entry 281, File 4630-44, March 27, 1942.

Chapter 13. Aborted Convoys from San Francisco

1. OCT Historical Monographs, E. H. Cates, "Shipping Situation at San Francisco Port of Embarkation Following Pearl Harbor," 1944. At this date there were approximately 19,000 American Army personnel (8,000 belonging to the Air Force) in the islands, 12,000 American Philippine Scouts, and 100,000 troops in the Philippine Army.
2. The principal, long-standing Philippine Scout units were: the 45th and 57th Infantry Regiments, the 14th Engineer Regiment, the 23rd and 24th Field Artillery Regiments (these five units being part of the Philippine Division), and the separate 88th Field Artillery Regiment, 26th Cavalry Regiment, and 91st and 92nd Coast Artillery Regiments.
3. RG-165, Entry 12; RG-165, Entry 281, Files 2789-17 and 4561-6; RG-407, Entry 360A, Files 320.2 and 370.5.
4. Christopher Gabel, *The U.S. Army GHQ Maneuvers of 1941* (Washington, D.C.: Center of Military History, United States Army, 1992), 9–12.
5. Lt. Col. John W. Whitman (Ret.), *Bataan, Our Last Ditch* (New York: Hippocrene Books, 1990), 22–23.
6. RG-177, Entry 8B, File 676-15A, November 13, 1941.
7. Elson Matson, *Golden Gate in Forty-Eight: History of the 161st Infantry*, vol. 1 (privately published, 1944), 12.
8. Ibid., 12–13.
9. RG-165, Entry 234A, File G-4/27573-18, October 31, 1941.

10. RG-336, Entry 5, File "Movement Philippines."
11. RG-407, Entry 360A, File 370.5, November 14, 1941.
12. RG-165, Entry 281, File 2789-17, November 10, 1941.
13. RG-336, Entry 2, File "San Francisco Port of Embarkation," November 21, 1941.
14. RG-336, Entry 2, File "Pacific Area"; RG-165, Entry 234A, Files G-4/27573 and G-4/33700; RG-407, Entry 360A, File 320.2; RG-496, Entry 540, File 569.4; Cates, "Shipping Situation."
15. RG-165, Entry 234A, File G-4/27573-18, December 5, 1941.
16. Cates, "Shipping Situation."
17. RG-407, Entry 360A, File 370.5, January 3, 1942.
18. Capt. James W. Hamilton and 1st Lt. William J. Bolce Jr., *Gateway to Victory: The Wartime Story of the San Francisco Army Port of Embarkation* (Stanford, CA: Stanford University Press, 1946), 4.

Chapter 14. War Commences

1. Capt. Robert J. Bulkley (Ret.), *At Close Quarters: PT Boats in the United States Navy* (Washington, D.C.: Naval History Division, U.S. Navy, 1962), 3.
2. Walter Lord, *Day of Infamy* (New York: Henry Holt and Company, 1957), 106.
3. *Antares* activities from "Pearl Harbor Attack: USS *Antares* (AKS-3) Action Report," dated December 10, 1941, Naval Historical Center, www.history.navy.mil/docs/wwii/pearl/ph20.htm.
4. Sources do not uniformly agree on the total PBY availability on this date. The action report of PatWing 2 states that eighty-one PBYs were on the ledger—thirty-three at Kaneohe Bay, twenty-eight at Ford Island, eleven at Midway (VP-21), and nine under repair. A table in the Pearl Harbor Investigation (Part 12, 352) lists twelve PBYs each with the three squadrons at Kaneohe Bay (thirty-three available, three under repair). At Ford Island were two full squadrons (VP-22 and VP-23), one squadron at half-strength (VP-24 with just six planes), and three miscellaneous planes (one belonging to Midway's VP-21 and two older PBY-1s of VJ-2). This table thus totals seventy-one—sixty-three available planes and another eight under repair.
5. Andrew Hendrie, *Flying Cats: The Catalina Aircraft in World War II* (Annapolis: Naval Institute Press, 1988), 113.
6. Samuel Eliot Morison, *History of the United States Naval Operations in World War II*, vol. 3, *The Rising Sun in the Pacific, 1931–April 1942* (Boston: Little, Brown and Company, 1961), 122–123.
7. AAFHS No. 34, 11–12.
8. PHI, Part 4, 2019.
9. Some earlier Marine Corps historical monographs mistakenly identify the second destroyer as *Akebono* rather than *Sazanami*. *Akebono* had been originally scheduled to be included in this mission, but mechanical problems forced her to stay behind in Japan.

10. Lt. Col. R. D. Heinl Jr., *The Defense of Wake* (Washington, D.C.: Historical Section, Division of Public information, Headquarters, U.S. Marine Corps, 1947), 11–15.
11. This is not the only example where, during the initial Japanese offensive, a gross mismatching of forces occurred. For all the supposed intelligence the Japanese had gathered on their opponent's military dispositions, frequent mistakes were made in sizing attack forces. In several cases (like Guam and several Dutch East Indies assaults) too much force was allocated, and in others (Wake, the proposed Midway landing force, and the first attack on the Marines on Guadalcanal) far too little was applied.
12. Much is made of the extent of Japanese knowledge of American bases pre-war, particularly places like Guam that had a native Japanese population and frequent opportunity for air and naval observation. Obviously as in this case some of that information was incomplete or incorrect. If nothing else this event illustrates that even the best prepared armies occasionally encounter the unpredictable or unanticipated.
13. Apparently the Japanese used mostly 50-kilogram (112-pound) bombs, which would have given them thorough ground coverage. The use of the G3Ms for strafing is less easily understood. These would not have been particularly good aircraft for this usage. The plane mounted one 20-mm gun in a dorsal turret that would not have had much ground capability except in a difficult orientation. Other armament was usually one light 7.7-mm machine gun on each side in a waist gun position and another in a second dorsal position. The plane had no downward-bearing guns. Also this plane did not have self-sealing fuel tanks or any crew armor, and would have been highly vulnerable to return fire at low altitude. Nonetheless, all accounts agree to the extensive (and effective) strafing of these planes on this occasion.
14. Some accounts list ten Pan Am Airways casualties in this attack.
15. RG-127, List 6. Contains a report of the defense dated December 20, 1941 from CO Wake (Cunningham) to CO Fourteenth Naval District.
16. Paul S. Dull, *A Battle History of the Imperial Japanese Navy (1941–1945)* (Annapolis: Naval Institute Press, 1978), 23.
17. RG-127, List 6, "Report of Wake Action, 7 December 1941 to 24 December 1941," 3.
18. Ibid., 5.
19. Hough, Ludwig, and Shaw, *Pearl Harbor to Guadalcanal*, 125; Robert J. Cressman, *A Magnificent Fight: The Battle for Wake Island* (Annapolis: Naval Institute Press, 1995), 163.
20. The dates reported by the Americans and Japanese often don't agree and some significant variations occur. In some cases this has led to the interpretation of more attacks than actually took place.
21. Japanese Monograph No. 139, 2.
22. Whitman, *Bataan, Our Last Ditch*, 100.

23. Cave, *Beyond Courage*, 75.
24. For a good report of PatWing 10's activities, see Dwight R. Messimer, *In the Hands of Fate: The Story of Patrol Wing Ten, 8 December 1941–11 May 1942* (Annapolis: Naval Institute Press, 1985).
25. Clay Blair Jr., *Silent Victory: The U.S. Submarine War against Japan, Vol. 1* (New York: J. B. Lippincott Company, 1975), 60. This had not been the case during a similar scare in the spring of 1941. At that time Hart moved all his forces, including subs, to the southern Philippines when he thought an attack on Manila was imminent. They returned when nothing happened. Perhaps in December he had a stronger confidence in the ability of the Army Air Forces to defend Luzon than he had earlier.
26. Capt. W. G. Winslow (Ret.), *The Fleet the Gods Forgot* (Annapolis: Naval Institute Press, 1982), 25.
27. Col. C. P. Stacey, *The Official History of the Canadian Army in the Second World War*, vol. 1, *Six Years of War* (Ottawa: Queen's Printer and Controller of Stationery, 1966), 445–448.
28. Sources vary on this date; some record its arrival pre-war on December 6.
29. Stacey, *Six Years of War*, 445; RG-165, Entry 281, File 4525, December 18, 1941.
30. The Philippines, as a populous island archipelago, had a well-developed system of inter-island maritime transport. A fleet of relatively large, modern motor vessels of about 1,200 tons each served with firms like Compania Maritima. They continued to be of critical importance in the supply picture of the first 1941–1942 campaign in the islands.
31. Morison, *The Rising Sun*, 178.
32. Gene Eric Salecker, *Fortress against the Sun: The B-17 Flying Fortress in the Pacific* (Conshohocken, PA: Combined Publishing, 2001), 82.
33. Blair, *Silent Victory*, 124–126.
34. After the war there was some disagreement in the written accounts of General Weaver and Colonel Miller about the number of tanks lost in this incident. Weaver contended that fifteen tanks were reported lost to him at the time, while Miller implies in his postwar memoirs (Miller, *Bataan Uncensored*, 108–110) that just two of the company's three platoons were lost, thus making it about ten tanks abandoned on the north side of the Agno River.
35. William H. Bartsch, *Doomed at the Start: American Pursuit Pilots in the Philippines, 1941–1942* (College Station: Texas A&M University Press, 1992), 428.
36. The Infantry School manuscript, 1st Lt. Sheldon H. Mendelson, "Operations of the Provisional Air Corps Regiment in the Defense of the Bataan Peninsula, P. I., 8 January–19 April 1942," 10.
37. Mendelson, "Operations of the Provisional Air Corps Regiment"; Whitman, *Bataan*, 454–455.
38. Morison, *The Rising Sun*, 200.

39. For a good account of this unit's brief history, see Lt. Col. William F. Prickett, "Naval Battalion at Mariveles," *Marine Corps Gazette* 34, no. 6 (June 1950): 41–43.

Chapter 15. Running the Blockade

1. RG-496, Entry 540, File 452.1, December 14, 1941.
2. CMH, Elizabeth Bingham and Richard Leighton, "Development of the United States Supply Base in Australia: The Period of Defense and Build-up," 109.
3. James H. Belote and William M. Belote, *Corregidor: The Saga of a Fortress* (New York: Harper and Row, 1967), 47.
4. RG-165, Entry 234A, File G4/27573-16, December 16, 1941.
5. RG-165, Entry 281, File 4639-3, January 3, 1942.
6. Richard M. Leighton and Robert W. Coakley, *Global Logistics and Strategy, 1940–1943*, United States Army in World War II (Washington, D.C.: Office of the Chief of Military History, Department of the Army, 1955), 169–170.
7. *President Polk*, *Hawaiian Planter*, and USS *Pecos*.
8. Robert L. Underbrink, *Destination Corregidor* (Annapolis: Naval Institute Press, 1971), 33.
9. Table data from Robert M. Browning Jr., *U.S. Merchant Vessel War Casualties of World War II* (Annapolis: Naval Institute Press, 1996); Charles Dana Gibson and E. Kay Gibson, *Over Seas: U.S. Army Maritime Operations, 1898 through the Fall of the Philippines* (Camden, ME: Ensign Press, 2002); David H. Grover, *U.S. Army Ships and Watercraft of World War II* (Annapolis: Naval Institute Press, 1987); Underbrink, *Destination Corregidor*.
10. Gibson and Gibson, *Over Seas*, 246–248.
11. Donald J. Young, *The Battle of Bataan* (Jefferson, NC: McFarland & Company, Inc., 1992), 201.
12. Actually the port for Batavia was known as Tandjong Priok (or Tanjong Priok), but often correspondence of the time simply refers to the larger community of Batavia.
13. Underbrink, *Destination Corregidor*, 76.
14. Underbrink, *Destination Corregidor*, 88–89. A different account is in Whitman, *Bataan, Our Last Ditch*, 405. According to the latter version, *Florence D.*'s crew forced the abandonment of the mission after spotting enemy aircraft, and the ship was actually returning to Darwin when spotted and sunk by the Japanese aircraft of the carrier attack wave.
15. OCT, James Masterson, "U.S. Army Transportation in the Southwest Pacific Area, 1941–1947" has an arrival date of March 10.
16. OCT, James Masterson, "U.S. Army Transportation in the Southwest Pacific Area, 1941–1947" has an arrival date of March 20.
17. RG-165, Entry 234A, File G-4/27573-16, February 11, 1942.
18. RG-407, Entry 360A, File 400, February 14, 1942.

19. Sheila Carlisle, ed., *U.S. Naval Cryptographic Activities in the Philippines Prior to World War II* (Laguna Hills, CA: Aegean Park Press, 1982), 57.
20. Blair, *Silent Victory*, 172.
21. RG-165, Entry 281, File 4630-36, February 22, 1942 (MacArthur radiogram No. 344).
22. RG-165, Entry 234A, File G-4/33817, February 22, 1942.
23. RG-165, Entry 234A, File G-4/33817, March 4, 1942. However, the Australian command was also coming to the same conclusion. On March 4 General Hurley wrote to General MacArthur that routes to the Philippines from Australia and vicinity were becoming increasingly hazardous, and risking ships and cargoes that could not be spared no longer appeared justified. In fact, the routes through safer waters were as long as those direct from Hawaii to the Philippines. They (Brett, Hurley, and Robenson) recommended that the Philippines be henceforth supplied from the United States via Hawaii.
24. Underbrink, *Destination Corregidor*, 171–174.
25. Col. Sid Huff, USA, and Joe Alex Morris, *My Fifteen Years with General MacArthur* (New York: Paperback Library, Inc., 1964), 42.
26. Manchester, *American Caesar*, 245.
27. Huff, *My Fifteen Years*, 47. While Huff's account seems to reflect an eyewitness perspective, other accounts—like Paul R. Rogers, *The Good Years: MacArthur and Sutherland* (New York: Praeger Publishers, 1990), 137—are more tentative about whether the story can be confirmed.
28. Belote and Belote, *Corregidor*, 78.
29. Bartsch, *Doomed at the Start*, 357–360.
30. RG-407, Entry 1053, Quartermaster Report of the U.S. Armed Forces in Luzon, 247; AAFHS No. 34, 76–77.
31. Underbrink, *Destination Corregidor*, 174–176.
32. Morton, *The Fall of the Philippines*, 400.
33. CMH, Bingham and Leighton, "Development of the United States Supply Base in Australia," 108.
34. Underbrink, *Destination Corregidor*, 178–180.

Chapter 16. Airplanes for ABDA

1. Douglas Gillison, *Royal Australian Air Force, 1939–1942* (Canberra: Australian War Memorial, 1962), 296–297.
2. Edmonds, *They Fought*, 279.
3. USAFIA Report, 18.
4. Arnold, *Global Mission*, 290.
5. Edmonds, *They Fought*, 281–283.
6. Ibid., 281–290.
7. This airplane destroyed on January 24 appears to be the first aircraft combat loss of those planes delivered by *Pensacola* convoy.
8. B-18s were thought to be of such insufficient combat capability that they

wound up being used as transports. There is not a single example of this aircraft actually ever being used on a bombing mission in the campaign.

9. USAFIA Report, 19.
10. USAFIA Report, 15.
11. RG-336, Entry 2, File "Pacific Area."
12. RG 165, Entry 234A, File G-4/27573-16. On the fifteenth the most critical items specified for the cargo were munitions released from the Western Defense Command and urgently needed in the Philippines:
    442,000 rounds .50-caliber AP & tracer
    20 million rounds .30-caliber ball
    30,000 rounds 3-inch anti-aircraft
    5,000 rounds 75-mm HE shell
    15,500 rounds 81-mm mortar M43 HE
    2,060 300-pound bombs
13. RG-165, Entry 281, File 4622, December 16, 1941; RG-336, Entry 5, File "Aircraft Movement."
14. Edmonds, *They Fought*, 380–382.
15. Detailed account taken from the report of Ens. G. M. Letteau, Armed Guard Commander, SS *Mormacsun* in RG-38, CinCUS WWII Action Report.
16. Some documents mistakenly name the ship "*James M. Gregg*."
17. Edmonds, *They Fought*, 274.
18. It should be noted that the accounts of these provisional squadrons (in fact, virtually all of the air units involved in the early war campaign in the Philippines and East Indies) vary as to the accounting of aircraft numbers. Frequently the official accounts, early historical narratives, and first-person accounts are plus or minus one or two planes from each other. It is virtually impossible today to be absolutely precise in these counts, though the magnitude of the challenge and losses these pilots faced remain clear.
19. Edmonds, *They Fought*, 324.
20. Edmonds, *They Fought*, 324; Craven and Cate, *Plans and Early Operations*, 387. Note that some accounts spell the commander's name as Mahoney.
21. AAFHS No. 34, 56–57; Smith, *Douglas SBD Dauntless*, 60–62.
22. USAFIA Report, 19.
23. AAFHS No. 34, 60.
24. Salecker, *Fortress against the Sun*, 144.
25. Numbers vary slightly between reports; for B-17s, documents and authors have stated thirty-seven, thirty-eight, and thirty-nine as the number arriving in Java via the air ferry routes.
26. Winslow, *The Fleet*, 33.
27. Gillison, *Royal Australian Air Force*, 465–467.

Chapter 17. Building the Australian Base

1. RG-38, Entry 348, Convoys No. 2013, 2030, and 2033; RG-336, Entry

5, Ship Movement Cards; RG-165, Entry 234A, Files G-4/27573 and G-4/33700.

2. RG-336, Entry 2, File "Navy," December 26, 1942. Actually on December 23 the Navy received information that the Army was gathering over ninety aircraft in San Francisco for shipment to Australia. Admiral Turner communicated to the War Plans Division that the Army could have whichever seatrain arrived first on the West Coast, and that could be used for the Australian run.
3. These were a group of sixteen senior staff officers meant to take key administrative positions in the staff of the U.S. Army Forces in Australia command. The senior officer was Lt. Col. Harry Baird. The functions represented included medical, ordnance, quartermaster, signal, judge advocate general, inspector general, finance, engineer, chemical, postal, and adjutant general.
4. Craven and Cate, *Plans and Early Operations*, 396–397; RG-24 deck log for USS *Phoenix*; RG-336, Entry 5, File "Movement X."
5. AAFHS No. 12, 8–9.
6. RG-165, Entry 234A, File G-4/33861, February 2, 1942.
7. AAFHS No. 9, 40.
8. The term used at the time was "colored." Units composed of black soldiers, usually with white officers, were designated in the usual Army terminology, followed by the word "colored" in parentheses. For example, the first such unit sent to Australia was designated the 394th Port Battalion (Colored).
9. RG-165, Entry 281, File 4628-18, February 5, 1942.
10. The manifest showed she had the ground echelon of 43rd Bombardment Group (Heavy) with its 64th and 65th Bomb Squadrons. Supporting this group was the 11th Matériel Squadron, 441st and 73rd Ordnance Companies, 8th Air Base Group, 40th Coast Artillery Brigade (AA), 94th Coast Artillery Regiment (AA) (Semi-mobile), 101st Coast Artillery Battalion (AA), several other minor units, and a number of Air Force replacement personnel. American troop strength was 330 officers and 7,812 enlisted men. *Queen Mary* also carried seventy-seven returning Australians.
11. Peter Plowman, *Across the Sea to War: Australia and New Zealand Troop Carriers from 1865 through two World Wars to Korea and Vietnam* (Dural, AU: Rosenberg Publishing, 2003), 254.

Chapter 18. Frantic Efforts to Reinforce Hawaii and Its Outposts

1. RG-165, Entry 284, Joint Board minutes for December 8, 1941.
2. Dorr Carpenter and Norman Polmar, *Submarines of the Imperial Japanese Navy* (Annapolis: Naval Institute Press, 1986), 11–17.
3. RG-38, Entry 348, Convoys No. 2006 and 2007; RG-165, Entry 281, File 4622; RG-336, Entry 5, File names "Aircraft Movement" and "Coolidge"; RG-165, Entry 234A, File G-4/33700.

4. Martin Bowman, *B-17 Flying Fortress Units of the Pacific War* (Oxford: Osprey Publishing, 2003), 13.
5. Marshall was not the only military man who was concerned that aircraft aid to America's allies, particularly the Soviets, was seriously interfering with domestic rearmament. Both Secretary of War Stimson and Air Force Chief of Staff Arnold were also very vocal about their concerns.
6. Bland and Stevens, *The Right Man for the Job*, 581.
7. Edward R. Stettinus Jr., *Lend-Lease: Weapon for Victory* (New York: The Macmillan Company, 1944), 155.
8. The Hawaiian Division had been split to form the 24th and 25th Infantry Divisions on October 1, 1941. The 24th subsequently had the 299th Infantry Regiment assigned as its third regiment, the 25th got the 298th. After shipments to the islands, eventually the 24th incorporated the 34th regiment as its third unit, the 25th received the 161st. The two Hawaiian National Guard regiments continued for a while to be attached to their parent divisions, but before the war ended both were deactivated.
9. U.S. Navy, *Administrative History, Twelfth Naval District 1939–1945, Vol. 4* (Washington, D.C.: Office of Naval History, 1946).
10. Numbers of passengers from *Ships in Gray* (San Francisco: Matson Navigation Company, 1946), 15, 18, and 31.
11. RG-38, Entry 348, File: Convoy No. 6002.
12. RG-165, Entry 281, File 4449-4, letters of January 13, 14, 22, 1942.
13. RG-165, Entry 422, Box 40, letter of December 11, 1941.
14. RG-165, Entry 281, File 4571-33, January 30, 1942.
15. Bill Sloan, *Given up for Dead: America's Heroic Stand at Wake Island* (New York: Bantam Books, 2003), 33–34.
16. Stephen D. Regan, *In Bitter Tempest: The Biography of Admiral Frank Jack Fletcher* (Ames: Iowa State University Press, 1994), 73.
17. RG-127, List 6, Memorandum from Commander Marine Corps, Fourteenth Naval District to CoS Fourteenth Naval District, December 15, 1941.
18. RG-38, CinCPac Operation Order 40-41, December 13, 1941.
19. John Prados, *Combined Fleet Decoded: The Secret History of American Intelligence and the Japanese Navy in World War II* (New York: Random House, Inc., 1995), 233.
20. Prange, *At Dawn We Slept*, 574.
21. The specific size of the force finally available to the Japanese is difficult to assess. There were probably about one thousand men in the special landing force, and perhaps an additional six hundred armed sailors supplementing them.
22. Cressman, *A Magnificent Fight*, 240.
23. Also included as equipment in this shipment were 138 rounds 5-inch, 1,730 rounds 3-inch anti-aircraft, 134,000 rounds .50-caliber, 564,500 rounds .30-caliber, four 3-inch anti-aircraft guns, four searchlights, sixteen

.50-caliber guns, thirty .30-caliber guns, two sets 5-inch fire-control apparatus, and sixty-four tons of dry food supplies.

24. RG-127, List 6, Letter from Johnston Island resident work officer to CPNAB Office, December 13, 1941.
25. Hough, Ludwig, and Shaw, *Pearl Harbor to Guadalcanal*, 88; RG-38, Entry 348, Convoy No. 1005.
26. This was squadron VS1D-14.

Chapter 19. Further Adventures of the Artillery Battalions

1. Bill Heath, *The 148th Field Artillery Story, World War II* (Boise: Idaho Military Historical Society, 2005), 4–5; Cropp, "A History of the 147th Field Artillery Regiment," 517. Based on first-person accounts, it appears that the 1,300 men of the 148th disembarked starting on January 7 for a new camp about twenty miles from Port Darwin at Noonamah. The seven hundred men of the 147th departing from the ship were delayed, at least some of the troops not leaving until a week later on the fourteenth. They went to a camp at Howard Springs.
2. Heath, *148th Field Artillery*, 10.
3. Alan Powell, *The Shadow's Edge: Australia's Northern War* (Melbourne: Melbourne University Press, 1988), 66. To be truthful, there were other factors also impacting the unloading problems in Darwin. Recent weather problems had delayed unloading, and the single pier was poorly organized and simply not equipped for optimal performance.
4. Allen, *The Lost Battalion*, 26–27.
5. As is the case in many instances in this campaign, sources vary as to the date of this action. Several other accounts say the American artillery support fired on the third, but I have used the Australian battalion histories for the date of the fourth.
6. Gibson and Gibson, *Over Seas*, 277n32.
7. Col. Blucher Tharp, "Diary 1941–1942," manuscript at Texas Military Forces Museum, Camp Mabry, Austin.
8. Fujita, *Foo*, 77 and 82.
9. These were two troops—with eight 40-mm guns—of the British 79th Light Anti-Aircraft Battery. They were sent on February 9.
10. For some reason published histories often get the assignment of the U.S. artillery unit and the ships utilized for the movement incorrect. However, archival documents make it clear that just the 148th Field Artillery was shipped on this convoy, and that all the American troops and equipment were on *Portmar* and *Tulagi*.
11. Gibson and Gibson, *Over Seas,* 243n10. Apparently the Army never formally contracted for the services of *Portmar*; she was contracted under a time charter by the Maritime Commission but operated by the Army in the Southwest Pacific Area.

12. Capt. W. G. Winslow (Ret.), *The Ghost That Died at Sunda Strait* (Annapolis: Naval Institute Press, 1984), 104.
13. Heath, *148th Field Artillery*, 23.

Chapter 20. The New South Pacific and African Air Ferry Routes

1. RG-165, Entry 281, File 4571.
2. RG-165, Entry 281, File 4571-12, November 28, 1941.
3. Jon E. Krupnick, *Pan American's Pacific Pioneers: The Rest of the Story* (Missoula, MT: Pictorial Histories Publishing Co., Inc., 2000), 344–352.
4. U.S. Army, "History of Canton Island" (circa 1945), U.S. Army Heritage and Education Center, Carlisle Barracks, PA.
5. Leighton and Coakley, *Global Logistics*, 186–187.
6. RG-165, Entry 281, File 4571-23, December 31, 1941.
7. RG-165, Entry 4571-22, January 12, 1942.
8. RG-165, Entry 281, File 4571-2, November 5, 1941.
9. Thompson, *Pacific Ocean Engineers*, 86–88.
10. RG-165, Entry 281, File 4571-22, January 14, 1942.
11. Goldberg, *The "Stately President" Liners*, 475–479.
12. RG-165, Entry 234A, File G-4/33700, January 6, 1942.
13. RG-336, Entry 5, File "Movement X."
14. AAFHS No. 45, 69.
15. Lockheed Company also participated by loaning aircrew through Atlantic Airways Ltd.
16. Tom Culbert and Andy Dawson, *PanAfrica: Across the Sahara in 1941 with Pan Am* (McLean, VA: Paladwr Press, 1999), 3–25. While not describing the Army Air Force's ferrying efforts in detail, this is a good treatment of Pan Am's involvement in the African route.
17. Craven and Cate, *Plans and Early Operations*, 332.
18. RG-165, Entry 281, File 4630-59, February 3, 1942, and February 17, 1942.

Chapter 21. Shipping Challenges of Early 1942 and the Pacific Task Forces

1. David J. Bercuson and Holger H. Herwig, *One Christmas in Washington: The Secret Meeting Between Roosevelt and Churchill that Changed the World* (Woodstock, NY: The Overlook Press, 2005), 119.
2. For a good general description of the entire conference, see Bercuson and Herwig, *One Christmas in Washington*.
3. Bland and Stevens, *The Right Man for the Job*, 39.
4. Chandler et al., *Papers of Dwight Eisenhower*, 1:39.
5. Bland and Stevens, *The Right Man for the Job*, 51.
6. RG-165, Entry 234A, File G-4/29717-115, January 12, 1942.
7. King and Whitehill, *Fleet Admiral King*, 364.
8. Louis Morton, *Strategy and Command: The First Two Years*, United States

Army in World War II (Washington, D.C.: Office of the Chief of Military History, Department of the Army, 1962), 208–209.

9. The vessel was soon purchased, that is to say her owner, the Swedish-American Line, was compensated for her forced acquisition.
10. Morton, *Strategy and Command*, 209.
11. RG-38, Entry 348, Convoy No. BT-200; RG-165, Entry 281, File 4630-51.
12. RG-165, Entry 281, File 4571. The island's name was spelled in a variety of ways in this time period. The most frequent, and the treatment used here, is Bora Bora, as two separate, capitalized words.
13. RG-38, Entry 348, Convoy No. BC-100; RG-336, Entry 5, Ship Movement Cards; Evan F. Kushner, *Bogged Down in Bora Bora: A History of the 198th Coast Artillery Regiment (Antiaircraft) on Bora Bora Island, 1942–1943* (Patterson, NJ: self-published, 1984), 194.
14. Duncan S. Ballantine, *U.S. Naval Logistics in the Second World War* (Princeton: Princeton University Press, 1947), 67–69.
15. Actually an even earlier movement should be mentioned. The dispatch of the 2nd Marine Brigade to Samoa on January 6 was also begun as an enhancement to the local defense of that island, but eventually this brigade was built back into the 2nd Marine Division and left the island for offensive service during the war.

BIBLIOGRAPHY

PRIMARY SOURCES

Center of Military History, Washington, D.C.:

Bingham, Elizabeth and Richard Leighton. "Development of the United States Supply Bases in Australia: The Period of Defense and Build-up," 1944.

Report of Organization and Activities, United States Army Forces in Australia from Dec 7, 1941 to June 30, 1942 with Enclosures and Appendices (generally known as the "USAFIA Report").

The Infantry School, Fort Benning, GA,
Advanced Officer's Course 1946–1947:

Operations of the Provisional Air Corps Regiment in the Defense of Bataan Peninsula, P.I., 8 January–10 April 1942, 1st Lt. Sheldon H. Mendelson.

MacArthur Archives, Norfolk, VA:

RG-2, Microfilm Reels 4–7, USAFFE Radiograms

National Archives and Records Service, College Park, MD, Textual Archives:

RG-18, Entry 293, Air Force Chief of Staff confidential correspondence file

RG-24, Entry 118L, Ship deck logs

RG-38, Entry 230A, Ship Movement Division

Entry 348, Convoys and Routings

Entry 348, Naval Transportation Service

Entry UD-351, World War II Action Reports and War Diaries

Plans, Orders, and Related Documents

RG-127, List 6, Marine Corps Garrison Forces

RG-165, Entry 281, War Plans Division

Entry 234A, Supply section of Army Chief of Staff

Entry 284, Records of the Joint Army Navy Board
RG-178, Maritime Commission vessel movement cards and ship "901" files
RG-319, Records from the Army's Center for Military History
RG-336, Entry 2, Historical Records of the Office of Chief of Transportation
Entry 5, Confidential Correspondence, Office of Chief of Transportation
RG-407, Entry 360 and 360A, Correspondence Files, Adjutant General's Office
RG-407, Entry 1053, Philippine Archives Division
RG-407, Entry 1113, Philippine Archives Division, Unit History of USAFFE/USFIP 1941–1942, Boxes 1485–1489 (generally known as the "Wainwright Papers"), Philippine Archives Division, Claims, Boxes 1564–1568
RG-496, Entry 540, USAFFE Records

Official Monographs:

Army Office of the Chief of Transportation (OCT)
Historical Monographs:
Bingham, A. J. "Blockade Running to the Philippines," 1947.
———. "Reinforcement of the Philippines," draft, 1947.
Cates, E. H. "Shipping Situation at San Francisco Port of Embarkation Following Pearl Harbor," 1944.
Larson, Harold. "The Army's Cargo Fleet in World War II," 1945.
———. "Handling Army Cargo in the Second World War," 1945.
———. "Troop Transports in World War II," 1945.
———. "Water Transportation for the United States Army, 1939–1942," 1944.
Masterson, James. "U.S. Army Transportation in the Southwest Pacific Area, 1941–1947."

Army Air Forces Historical Studies:
AAFHS No. 9, The AAF in Australia to the Summer of 1942.
AAFHS No. 12, The Tenth Air Force, 1942.
AAFHS No. 34, The Army Air Forces in the War Against Japan 1941–1942.
AAFHS No. 45, Development of the South Pacific Air Route.
AAFHS No. 111, Army Air Action in the Philippines and Netherlands East Indies, 1941–1942.

Japanese Studies in World War II. Monographs
compiled by the HQ Army Forces:
Far East, Military History Section, Japan Research Division:
No. 1 Philippines Operations Record, Phase I, 6 November 1941–June 1942.
No. 25 French Indo-China Area Operations Record, 1940–1945.
No. 66 The Invasion of the Netherlands East Indies (November 1941–March 1942).

No. 139 Outline of Operations of the Navy's South Seas Force (December 1941–March 1942).

No. 147 (Japanese) Political Strategy Prior to the Outbreak of War.

U.S. Army Heritage and Education Center, Carlisle Barracks, PA:

Army Officer Biographical Files

"History of Canton Island" (circa 1945)

SECONDARY SOURCES: BOOKS, ARTICLES, DISSERTATIONS, AND PAPERS

Aitken, E. F. *The Story of the 2/2nd Australian Pioneer Battalion*. Melbourne: 2/2nd Pioneer Battalion Association, 1953.

Allen, Hollis G. *The Lost Battalion*. Jacksboro, TX: Leigh McGee, 1963.

Arakaki, Leatrice R., and John R. Kuborn. *7 December 1941: The Air Force Story*. Hickam AFB, HI: Pacific Air Forces Office of History, 1991.

Arnold, Gen. H. H. *Global Mission*. New York: Harper & Brothers Publishers, 1949.

Avery, N. L. *B-25 Mitchell: The Magnificent Medium*. St. Paul, MN: Phalanx Publishing, 1992.

Baldwin, Hanson W. *Great Mistakes of the War*. New York: Harper & Brothers Publishers, 1949.

Ballantine, Duncan S. *U.S. Naval Logistics in the Second World War*. Princeton: Princeton University Press, 1947.

Bartsch, William H. *December 8, 1941: MacArthur's Pearl Harbor*. College Station: Texas A&M University Press, 2003.

———. *Doomed at the Start: American Pursuit Pilots in the Philippines, 1941–1942*. College Station: Texas A&M University Press, 1992.

Bellair, John. *From Snow to Jungle: A History of the 2/3rd Australian Machine Gun Battalion*. Sydney: Allen & Unwin, 1987.

Belote, James H., and William M. Belote. *Corregidor: The Saga of a Fortress*. New York: Harper and Row, 1967.

Bercuson, David J., and Holger H. Herwig. *One Christmas in Washington: The Secret Meeting Between Roosevelt and Churchill that Changed the World*. Woodstock, NY: The Overlook Press, 2005.

Biggs, Chester M., Jr. *The United States Marines in North China, 1894–1942*. Jefferson, NC: McFarland & Company Inc., 2003.

Blair, Clay, Jr. *Silent Victory: The U.S. Submarine War against Japan, Vol. 1*. New York: J. B. Lippincott Company, 1975.

Bland, Larry L., Sharon R. Ritenour, and Clarence E. Wunderlin Jr., eds. *The Papers of George Catlett Marshall*. Vol. 2, *We Cannot Delay, July 1, 1939–December 6, 1941*. Baltimore: The Johns Hopkins University Press, 1986.

Bland, Larry L., and Sharon R. Stevens, eds. *The Papers of George Catlett Marshall*. Vol. 3, *The Right Man for the Job, December 7, 1941–May 31, 1943*. Baltimore: The Johns Hopkins University Press, 1991.

Bowman, Martin. *B-17 Flying Fortress Units of the Pacific War*. Oxford: Osprey Publishing, 2003.

Boyd, Carl, and Akihiko Yoshida. *The Japanese Submarine Force and World War II*. Annapolis: Naval Institute Press, 1995.

Brereton, Lt. Gen. Lewis H. *The Brereton Diaries*. New York: William Morrow, 1946.

Browning, Robert M., Jr. *U.S. Merchant Vessel War Casualties of World War II*. Annapolis: Naval Institute Press, 1996.

Bulkley, Capt. Robert J., Jr. (Ret.). *At Close Quarters: PT Boats in the United States Navy*. Washington, D.C.: Naval History Division, U.S. Navy, 1962.

Carlisle, Sheila, ed. *U.S. Naval Cryptographic Activities in the Philippines Prior to World War II*. Laguna Hills, CA: Aegean Park Press, 1982.

Carpenter, Dorr, and Norman Polmar. *Submarines of the Imperial Japanese Navy*. Annapolis: Naval Institute Press, 1986.

Casey, Maj. Gen. Hugh J. *Engineers of the Southwest Pacific, 1941–1945*. Vol. 1, *Engineers in Theater Operations*. Tokyo: Office of the Chief Engineer, Army Forces, Pacific, 1947.

Cave, Dorothy. *Beyond Courage: One Regiment against Japan, 1941–1945*. Las Cruces, NM: Yucca Tree Press, 1992.

Chandler, Alfred D., Jr., et al., eds. *The Papers of Dwight David Eisenhower, Vol. 1*. Baltimore: The Johns Hopkins University Press, 1970.

Charles, Roland. *Troopships of World War II*. Washington, D.C.: The Army Transportation Association, 1947.

Cline, Ray S. *Washington Command Post: The Operations Division, United States Army in World War II*. Washington, D.C.: Office of the Chief of Military History, United States Army, 1951.

Coletta, Paolo E., ed. *United States Navy and Marine Corps Bases, Overseas*. Westport, CT: Greenwood Press, 1985.

Conn, Stetson, Rose C. Engelman, and Byron Fairchild. *Guarding the United States and Its Outposts*. United States Army in World War II. Washington, D.C.: Office of the Chief of Military History, Department of the Army, 1964.

Costello, John. *Days of Infamy: MacArthur, Roosevelt, Churchill—The Shocking Truth Revealed*. New York: Pocket Books, 1994.

Craven, Wesley Frank, and James Lea Cate, eds. *The Army Air Forces in World War II*. Vol. 1, *Plans and Early Operations: January 1939 to August 1942*. Chicago: University of Chicago Press, 1948.

———. *The Army Air Forces in World War II*. Vol. 7, *Services Around the World*. Chicago: University of Chicago Press, 1958.

Cressman, Robert J. *A Magnificent Fight: The Battle for Wake Island*. Annapolis: Naval Institute Press, 1995.

Cropp, Richard. "A History of the 147th Field Artillery Regiment, 1939–

1942." *Report and Historical Collections (South Dakota Historical Society)* 309 (1960).

Culbert, Tom, and Andy Dawson. *PanAfrica: Across the Sahara in 1941 with Pan Am*. McLean, VA: Paladwr Press, 1998.

Dod, Karl C. *The Corps of Engineers: The War against Japan*. United States Army in World War II. Washington, D.C.: Office of the Chief of Military History, United States Army, 1966.

Dull, Paul S. *A Battle History of the Imperial Japanese Navy (1941–1945)*. Annapolis: Naval Institute Press, 1978.

Dyess, Lt. Col. William E. *The Dyess Story*. New York: G. P. Putnam's Sons, 1944.

Edmonds, Walter D. *They Fought With What They Had: The Story of the Army Air Forces in the Southwest Pacific, 1941–1942*. Washington, D.C.: Zenger Publishing Co., 1982.

Ferris, C. S. *United States Rifle Model of 1917*. Export, PA: Scott A. Duff Publications, 2004.

Feuer, A. B. "Pawn of Fate: The Pensacola Convoy." *Sea Classics* 23, no. 12 (1990): 12–17.

Fillmore, Clyde. *Prisoner of War: History of the Lost Battalion*. Wichita Falls, TX: Nortex Press, 1984.

Ford, Daniel. *Flying Tigers: Claire Chennault and the American Volunteer Group*. Washington, D.C.: Smithsonian Institution Press, 1991.

Friedman, Norman. *U.S. Small Combatants: An Illustrated Design History*. Annapolis: Naval Institute Press, 1987.

Fujita, Frank. *Foo: A Japanese-American Prisoner of the Rising Sun*. Denton: University of North Texas Press, 1993.

Gabel, Christopher R. *The U.S. Army GHQ Maneuvers of 1941*. Washington, D.C.: Center of Military History, United States Army, 1992.

Gandt, Robert L. *China Clipper: The Age of the Great Flying Boats*. Annapolis: Naval Institute Press, 1991.

Gannon, Michael. *Pearl Harbor Betrayed: The True Story of a Man and a Nation under Attack*. New York: Henry Holt, 2001.

Generous, William Thomas, Jr. *Sweet Pea at War: A History of USS* Portland. Lexington: The University Press of Kentucky, 2003.

Gibson, Charles Dana, and E. Kay Gibson. *Over Seas: U.S. Army Maritime Operations, 1898 through the Fall of the Philippines*. Camden, ME: Ensign Press, 2002.

Gill, G. Hermon. *Royal Australian Navy, 1939–1942*. Sydney: Williams Collins, 1985.

Gillison, Douglas. *Royal Australian Air Force, 1939–1942*. Canberrra: Australian War Memorial, 1962.

Goldberg, Mark H. *"Caviar & Cargo": The C3 Passenger Ships*. Kings Point, NY: American Merchant Marine Museum, 1992.

———. *"Going Bananas": 100 Years of American Fruit Ships in the Caribbean*. Kings Point, NY: American Merchant Marine Museum, 1993.

———. *The "Stately President" Liners: American Passenger Liners of the Interwar Years, Part I, The "502"s.* Kings Point, NY: American Merchant Marine Museum, 1996.

Goldblith, Samuel A. "The 803d Engineers in the Philippine Defense." *The Military Engineer* (August 1946): 323–325.

Grover, David H. *U.S. Army Ships and Watercraft of World War II*. Annapolis: Naval Institute Press, 1987.

Grover, David H., and Gretchen G. Grover. *Captives of Shanghai: The Story of the* President Harrison. Napa, CA: Western Maritime Press, 1989.

Hamilton, Capt. James W., and 1st Lt. William J. Bolce Jr. *Gateway to Victory: The Wartime Story of the San Francisco Army Port of Embarkation.* Stanford, CA: Stanford University Press, 1946.

Heath, Bill. *The 148th Field Artillery Story, World War II*. Boise: Idaho Military Historical Society, 2005.

Heinl, Lt. Col. R. D., Jr. *The Defense of Wake.* Washington, D.C.: Historical Section, Division of Public Information, Headquarters, U.S. Marine Corps, 1947.

Hendrie, Andrew. *Flying Cats: The Catalina Aircraft in World War II.* Annapolis: Naval Institute Press, 1988.

Hough, Lt. Col. Frank O., Maj. Verle E. Ludwig, and Henry I. Shaw Jr. *History of U.S. Marine Corps Operations in World War II*. Vol. 1, *Pearl Harbor to Guadalcanal*. Washington, D.C.: Historical Branch, G-3 Division, Headquarters, U.S. Marine Corps.

Huff, Col. Sid, USA, and Joe Alex Morris. *My Fifteen Years with General MacArthur*. New York: Paperback Library Inc., 1964.

Hull, Cordell. *The Memoirs of Cordell Hull, Vol. 2*. New York: The Macmillan Company, 1948.

Ind, Allison. *Bataan: The Judgment Seat*. New York: The Macmillan Company, 1944.

Jacobs, Maj. Gen. Bruce (Ret.). "The Evolution of Tank Units in the Pre-WWII National Guard and the Defense of Bataan." *Military Collector & Historian* 38, no. 3 (1986): 125–133.

James, D. Clayton. *The Years of MacArthur. Vol. 1, 1880–1941*. Boston: Houghton Mifflin Company, 1970.

Jones, Pat. *The USS* Astoria *and the Men Who Sailed Her*. Hillsboro, OR: Premier Press, 1992.

Jordan, Roger. *The World's Merchant Fleets, 1939*. Annapolis: Naval Institute Press, 1999.

Jose, Ricardo Trota. *The Philippine Army, 1935–1942*. Manila: Ateneo de Manila University Press, 1992.

Kimball, Warren F., ed. *Churchill & Roosevelt: The Complete Correspondence*. Vol. 1, *Alliance Emerging: October 1933–November 1942*. Princeton: Princeton University Press, 1984.

Kimmel, Husband E. *Admiral Kimmel's Story*. Chicago: Henry Regnery Company, 1955.

King, Adm. Ernest J., and Cdr. Walter Muir Whitehill. *Fleet Admiral King: A Naval Record*. New York: W. W. Norton & Company, Inc., 1952.

Kleber, Brook E., and Dale Birdsell. *The Chemical Warfare Service: Chemicals in Combat*. United States Army in World War II. Washington, D.C.: Center of Military History, United States Army, 1990.

Klimow, Mathew S. "Lying to the Troops: American Leaders and the Defense of Bataan." *Parameters: U.S. Army War College Quarterly* 20, no. 4 (December 1990): 48–60.

Krupnick, Jon E. *Pan American's Pacific Pioneers: The Rest of the Story*. Missoula, MT: Pictorial Histories Publishing Co., Inc., 2000.

Kushner, Evan F. *Bogged Down in Bora Bora: A History of the 198th Coast Artillery Regiment (Antiaircraft) on Bora Bora Island, 1942–1943*. Patterson, NJ: self-published, 1984.

Layton, Rear Adm. Edwin T. R. (Ret.), with Capt. Roger Pineau (Ret.) and John Costello. *"And I Was There": Pearl Harbor and Midway—Breaking the Secrets.* New York: Quill William Morrow, 1985.

———. "24 Sentai—Japan's Commerce Raiders." U.S. Naval Institute *Proceedings* (June 1976): 53–61.

Leighton, Richard M., and Robert W. Coakley. *Global Logistics and Strategy, 1940–1943*. United States Army in World War II. Washington, D.C.: Office of the Chief of Military History, Department of the Army, 1955.

Leutze, James. *A Different Kind of Victory: A Biography of Admiral Thomas C. Hart.* Annapolis: Naval Institute Press, 1981.

Lloyd's War Losses, The Second World War. Vol. 1, *British, Allied, and Neutral Merchant Vessels Sunk or Destroyed by War Causes*. London: Lloyd's of London Press, 1989.

Lord, Walter. *Day of Infamy*. New York: Henry Holt, 1957.

Mallonée, Richard C., II, ed. *The Naked Flagpole: Battle for Bataan*. San Rafael, CA: Presidio Press, 1980.

Manchester, William. *American Caesar: Douglas MacArthur, 1880–1964.* Boston: Little, Brown and Company, 1978.

Matson, Elson. *Golden Gate in Forty-Eight: History of the 161st Infantry, Volume 1.* Privately published, 1944.

Mayo, Lido. *The Ordnance Department: On Beachhead and Battlefront*. United States Army in World War II. Washington, D.C.: Office of the Chief of Military History, United States Army, 1968.

McGlothlin, Frank Emile. *Barksdale to Bataan: History of the 48th Materiel Squadron, October 1940–April 1942.* Privately published, 1948.

Mellnik, Gen. Steven (Ret.). *Philippine Diary, 1939–1945*. New York: Van Nostrand Reinhold Company, 1969.

Messimer, Dwight R. *In the Hands of Fate: The Story of Patrol Wing Ten, 8 December 1941–11 May 1942*. Annapolis: Naval Institute Press, 1985.

Miller, Col. E. B. *Bataan Uncensored*. Little Falls: Military Historical Society of Minnesota, 1991.

Miller, Edward S. *War Plan Orange: The U.S. Strategy to Defeat Japan, 1897–1945*. Annapolis: Naval Institute Press, 1991.

Miller, J. Michael. *From Shanghai to Corregidor: Marines in the Defense of the Philippines*. Washington, D.C.: Marine Corps Historical Center, 1997.

Miller, Merle. *Ike the Soldier: As They Knew Him*. New York: G. P. Putnam's Sons, 1987.

Mitchell, John H. *On Wings We Conquer: The 19th and 7th Bomb Groups of the United States Air Force in the Southwest Pacific in the First Year of World War Two*. Springfield, MO: G. E. M. Publishers, 1990.

Moore, Capt. Arthur R. *A Careless Word . . . A Needless Sinking*. Kings Point, NY: American Merchant Marine Museum, 1993.

Morison, Samuel Eliot. *History of the United States Naval Operations in World War II*. Vol. 3, *The Rising Sun in the Pacific 1931–April 1942*. Boston: Little, Brown and Company, 1961.

Morton, Louis. *The Fall of the Philippines*. United States Army in World War II. Washington, D.C.: Office of the Chief of Military History, United States Army, 1953.

———. *Strategy and Command: The First Two Years*. United States Army in World War II. Washington, D.C.: Office of the Chief of Military History, Department of the Army, 1962.

Pearl Harbor Attack: Hearings before the Joint Committee on the Investigation of the *Pearl Harbor Attack*. Washington, D.C.: Government Printing Office, 1946.

"Pearl Harbor Attack: USS *Antares* (AKS-3) Action Report," dated December 10, 1941. Naval Historical Center, www.history.navy.mil/docs/wwii/pearl/ph20.htm (accessed May 2010).

Plowman, Peter. *Across the Sea to War: Australia and New Zealand Troop Convoys from 1865 through two World Wars to Korea and Vietnam*. Dural, Australia: Rosenberg Publishing, 2003.

Pogue, Forrest C. *George C. Marshall: Ordeal and Hope, 1939–1942*. New York: Viking Press, 1966.

Pomeroy, Earl S. *Pacific Outpost: American Strategy in Guam and Micronesia*. Stanford, CA: Stanford University Press, 1951.

Powell, Alan. *The Shadow's Edge: Australia's Northern War*. Melbourne: Melbourne University Press, 1988.

Prados, John. *Combined Fleet Decoded: The Secret History of American Intelligence and the Japanese Navy in World War II*. New York: Random House Inc., 1995.

Prange, Gordon W. *At Dawn We Slept: The Untold Story of Pearl Harbor.* New York: Penguin Books, 1982.

Prickett, Lt. Col. William F. "Naval Battalion at Mariveles." *Marine Corps Gazette* 34, no. 6 (June 1950): 41–43.

Regan, Stephen D. *In Bitter Tempest: The Biography of Admiral Frank Jack Fletcher.* Ames: Iowa State University Press, 1994.

Richardson, Adm. James O. (Ret.). *On the Treadmill to Pearl Harbor: The Memoirs of Admiral James O. Richardson, USN (Retired).* Interviewed by Vice Adm. George C. Dyer (Ret.). Washington, D.C.: Naval Historical Division, Department of the Navy, 1973.

Rogers, Paul R. *The Good Years: MacArthur and Sutherland.* New York: Praeger Publishers, 1990.

Rosen, Col. Melvin H. (Ret.). *History of the Philippine Scouts Field Artillery.* Privately printed, 2000.

Salecker, Gene Eric. *Fortress against the Sun: The B-17 Flying Fortress in the Pacific.* Conshohocken, PA: Combined Publishing, 2001.

Schaller, Michael. *Douglas MacArthur: The Far Eastern General.* New York: Oxford University Press, 1989.

Sherwood, Robert E. *Roosevelt and Hopkins: An Intimate History.* New York: Harper & Brothers, 1948.

Ships in Gray. San Francisco: Matson Navigation Company, 1946.

Simpson, B. Mitchell, III. *Admiral Harold R. Stark: Architect of Victory, 1939–1945.* Columbia: University of South Carolina Press, 1989.

Sloan, Bill. *Given up for Dead: America's Heroic Stand at Wake Island.* New York: Bantam Books, 2003.

Slone, Reuben. *The Light behind the Cloud.* Waco, TX: Texian Press, 1992.

Smith, Peter C. *Douglas SBD Dauntless.* Ramsbury, UK: Crowood Press Ltd., 1997.

Spiller, Roger J., ed. *Dictionary of American Military Biography.* Vol. 2, *H–P.* Westport, CT: Greenwood Press, 1984.

Stacey, Col. C. P. *The Official History of the Canadian Army in the Second World War.* Vol. 1, *Six Years of War.* Ottawa: Queen's Printer and Controller of Stationery, 1966.

Stettinus, Edward R., Jr. *Lend-Lease: Weapon for Victory.* New York: The Macmillan Company, 1944.

Stimson, Henry Lewis. *The Henry Lewis Stimson Diaries in the Yale University Library.* New Haven, CT: Yale University Library Microfilm, 1973.

Stindt, Fred A. *Matson's Century of Ships.* Modesto, CA: Privately published, 1982.

Tharp, Col. Blucher. "Diary 1941–1942." Manuscript at Texas Military Forces Museum, Camp Mabry, Austin.

Thompson, Erwin N. *Pacific Ocean Engineers, 1905–1980.* Washington, D.C.: U.S. Army Corps of Engineers, 1985.

Thompson, Kyle. *A Thousand Cups of Rice: Surviving the Death Railway*. Austin, TX: Eakin Press, 1994.

Underbrink, Robert L. *Destination Corregidor*. Annapolis: Naval Institute Press, 1971.

Updegraph, Charles L., Jr. *Special Marine Corps Units of World War II*. Washington, D.C.: Historical Division, U.S. Marine Corps, 1972.

———. *Administrative History, Twelfth Naval District 1939–1945, Vol. 4*. Washington, D.C.: Office of Naval History, 1946.

U.S. Navy. *Building the Navy's Bases in World War II: History of the Bureau of Yards and Docks and the Civil Engineer Corps, 1940–1946, Vol. 2*. Washington, D.C.: Government Printing Office, 1947.

Wainwright, Gen. Jonathan M. *General Wainwright's Story*. Westport, CT: Greenwood Press, 1970.

Walker, James A. "The Decision to Reinforce the Philippines: A Desperate Gamble." PhD diss., Temple University, 1996.

Watson, Mark S. *Chief of Staff: Prewar Plans and Preparations*. United States Army in World War II. Washington, D.C.: Center of Military History, United States Army, 1991.

Webber, Bert. *Silent Siege—III*. Medford, OR: Webb Research Group, 1992.

Weintraub, Stanley. *Long Day's Journey into War*. New York: Truman Talley Books, 1991.

———. *Bataan, Our Last Ditch*. New York: Hippocrene Books, 1990.

Whitman, Lt. Col. John W. (Ret.). "Decision that Starved an Army." *Army Logistician* (March–April 1995): 36–39.

Wilson, Theodore A. *The First Summit: Roosevelt and Churchill at Placentia Bay, 1941*. Boston: Houghton Mifflin Company, 1969.

Winslow, Capt. W. G. (Ret.). *The Fleet the Gods Forgot: The U.S. Asiatic Fleet in World War II*. Annapolis: Naval Institute Press, 1982.

———. *The Ghost that Died at Sunda Strait*. Annapolis: Naval Institute Press, 1984.

Woodbury, David O. *Builders for Battle: How the Pacific Naval Air Bases Were Constructed*. New York: E. P. Dutton and Company, Inc., 1946.

Woodward, Sir Llewellyn. *British Foreign Policy in the Second World War, Vol. 2*. London: Her Majesty's Stationery Office, 1971.

Wukovits, John. *Pacific Alamo: The Battle for Wake Island*. New York: New American Library, 2003.

Young, Donald J. *The Battle of Bataan*. Jefferson, NC: McFarland & Company Inc., 1992.

INDEX

ABOUT the AUTHOR

GLEN M. WILLIFORD is a native of San Diego, CA. However, his interest in military history started as a result of being a military dependent. His father was career Air Force; as a result Williford grew up in places like Phoenix, Anchorage, Lincoln, Great Falls, Guam, and Germany. He returned from high school in Germany to attend and graduate from the University of California. His 1970 B.S. degree is in Soil Science from U.C.-Davis.

In 1970 Williford started a thirty-year career with the agricultural business of the Dow Chemical Co. Starting in sales, he held a variety of positions in sales, marketing, and business management, culminating in director of business development. He was president of an industry-wide coalition for electronic commerce from 1996–1998. He retired in 2000 to pursue his lifetime interest in military history.

One of his earliest military interests is in the American experience with coast artillery. He has spent many years both visiting existing fortification sites and researching the technology of that service. In 1974 he became a co-founder of the Coast Defense Study Group, which is still the only American historical society dedicated to this service branch. For over thirty years he has volunteered for this organization and contributed many studies and articles to its journal and at annual meetings. His expertise in American forts has also facilitated contract-writing projects for the National Park Service, and he became a tour organizer and leader for both historical groups and private military history tour agencies.

His other historical interests are in the logistical aspects of the early World War II Pacific campaign and in the military-industry technology interface of the late nineteenth century.

Glen has been happily married to his wife, Rosina, for thirty-nine years. They have raised two sons and currently reside near Indianapolis, IN.

The Naval Institute Press is the book-publishing arm of the U.S. Naval Institute, a private, nonprofit, membership society for sea service professionals and others who share an interest in naval and maritime affairs. Established in 1873 at the U.S. Naval Academy in Annapolis, Maryland, where its offices remain today, the Naval Institute has members worldwide.

Members of the Naval Institute support the education programs of the society and receive the influential monthly magazine *Proceedings* or the colorful bimonthly magazine *Naval History* and discounts on fine nautical prints and on ship and aircraft photos. They also have access to the transcripts of the Institute's Oral History Program and get discounted admission to any of the Institute-sponsored seminars offered around the country.

The Naval Institute's book-publishing program, begun in 1898 with basic guides to naval practices, has broadened its scope to include books of more general interest. Now the Naval Institute Press publishes about seventy titles each year, ranging from how-to books on boating and navigation to battle histories, biographies, ship and aircraft guides, and novels. Institute members receive significant discounts on the more than eight hundred Press books in print.

Full-time students are eligible for special half-price membership rates. Life memberships are also available.

For a free catalog describing Naval Institute Press books currently available, and for further information about joining the U.S. Naval Institute, please write to:

Member Services
U.S. NAVAL INSTITUTE
291 Wood Road
Annapolis, MD 21402-5034
Telephone: (800) 233-8764
Fax: (410) 571-1703
Web address: www.usni.org